Dear John,
I hope this is somewhat
useful.
All best,
Paul

Contemporary Materialism

Contemporary Materialism brings together the best recent work on materialism by many leading contemporary philosophers. This is the first comprehensive reader on the subject.

The majority of philosophers and scientists today hold that all phenomena are physical; materialism, or "physicalism", is now the dominant ontology in a wide range of fields. Until now, no single book reflected the comprehensive impact that materialism has had on contemporary metaphysics, philosophy of mind, the theory of meaning, and the theory of value.

The contemporary classics in this collection chart the current problems, positions, and themes on the topic of materialism. At the invitation of the editors, many contributors have provided follow-up pieces which assess the significance of the original paper and trace developments since its first appearance.

The book's selections are largely non-technical and accessible to advanced undergraduates. The editors have provided a topical bibliography as well as a substantial introduction designed to guide the reader through the dominant themes in materialism. *Contemporary Materialism* will be vital reading for anyone interested in the impact of materialism on contemporary philosophy, from metaphysics and meaning to mind and ethics.

Editors:
Paul K. Moser is Professor of Philosophy and **J. D. Trout** is Associate Professor of Philosophy and Adjunct at the Parmly Hearing Institute, Loyola University of Chicago.

Contributors:

David M. Armstrong
Richard N. Boyd
Tim Crane
Daniel C. Dennett
Michael Friedman
Jaegwon Kim
Hilary Putnam
J. J. C. Smart

Simon Blackburn
Paul M. Churchland
Donald Davidson
Jerry A. Fodor
Frank Jackson
D. H. Mellor
W. V. O. Quine
Bernard Williams

Contemporary Materialism

A Reader

Paul K. Moser and J. D. Trout

London and New York

First published 1995
by Routledge
11 New Fetter Lane, London EC4P 4EE

Simultaneously published in the USA and Canada
by Routledge
29 West 35th Street, New York, NY 10001

Typeset in Baskerville by
Solidus (Bristol) Limited
Printed and bound in Great Britain by
Biddles Ltd, Guildford and King's Lynn

British Library Cataloguing in Publication Data
A catalogue record for this book is available from the British Library

Library of Congress Cataloguing in Publication Data
Contemporary materialism : a reader / Paul K. Moser and J.D. Trout.
     p.   cm.
   Includes bibliographical references and index.
    ISBN 0–415–10863–2 : $59.95. – ISBN 0–415–10864–0 (pbk.) : $18.95
    1. Materialism.   2. Philosophy, Contemporary–20th century.
  I. Moser, Paul K., 1957– . II. Trout, J.D.
  B825.C64   1994   94–32686
  146'.3–dc20   CIP

ISBN 0–415–10863–2
ISBN 0–415–10864–0 (pbk)

Contents

Part III Materialism and Meaning

Part IV: Materialism and Value

Contributors

David M. Armstrong is Professor of Philosophy Emeritus at the University of Sydney.

Simon Blackburn is Professor of Philosophy at the University of North Carolina, Chapel Hill.

Richard Boyd is Professor of Philosophy at Cornell University.

Paul M. Churchland is Professor of Philosophy at the University of California, San Diego.

Tim Crane is Lecturer in Philosophy at University College, University of London.

Donald Davidson is Professor of Philosophy at the University of California, Berkeley.

Daniel Dennett is Professor of Philosophy at Tufts University.

Jerry A. Fodor is Professor of Philosophy at Rutgers University.

Michael Friedman is Professor of Philosophy at Indiana University.

Frank Jackson is Professor of Philosophy at Australian National University.

Jaegwon Kim is Professor of Philosophy at Brown University.

D.H. Mellor is Professor of Philosophy at University of Cambridge.

Hilary Putnam is Professor of Philosophy at Harvard University.

W.V.O. Quine is Professor of Philosophy Emeritus at Harvard University.

J.J.C. Smart is Professor of Philosophy Emeritus at Australian National University.

Bernard Williams is Fellow at Corpus Christi College, University of Oxford.

Preface

Materialism, put broadly, affirms that all phenomena are physical. Questions about materialism, or "physicalism," currently guide work in various areas of philosophy: for example, metaphysics, philosophy of mind, philosophy of language, and theory of value. Materialism is now the dominant systematic ontology among philosophers and scientists, and there are currently no established alternative ontological views competing with it. As a result, typical theoretical work in philosophy and the sciences is constrained, implicitly or explicitly, by various conceptions of what materialism entails. Reductive and eliminative versions of materialism now compete with nonreductive species for the best rendition of materialism as a systematic ontology.

This anthology represents some of the best recent work on materialism, in connection with metaphysics, philosophy of mind, philosophy of language, and theory of value. The anthology charts the major contemporary problems, positions, and themes on the topic of materialism. Arguments for a materialist interpretation of a particular subject matter are now typically complex. Materialist arguments about the nature of the mind, for example, characteristically depend on associated claims about psychological explanation and causation, and the latter claims draw on lessons from the philosophy of science. Similarly, an ethical theory compatible with materialism may depend on a parity of methods in scientific and ethical inquiry, and on more remote issues, such as whether we can give an acceptable semantics for moral terms. Since assessment of a broad philosophical position ordinarily rests on a judgment of overall philosophical plausibility, only a wide-ranging collection of readings on materialism can effectively serve the purposes of philosophical assessment. To further enhance the purpose of philosophical assessment, we have included brief invited follow-up pieces by some of the contributors.

This book contains major papers in four areas of philosophy where the doctrine of materialism has had an especially potent impact:

Part I Materialism and Naturalism This section surveys the most general thematic features of physicalism as they relate to the emergence of scientific, naturalistic accounts of mind, meaning, and value. Accordingly, the papers assess the apparent significance of the tendency in the development of scientific theories to provide evidence for materialism, especially in light of the "generality of physics": in particular, the demise of dualist accounts of psychological processes and of vitalistic accounts of biological function.

Part II Materialism and Mind The papers in this section cover the developments resulting from advances, both philosophical and psychological, in theories of the mind. In particular, they discuss such issues as the material basis of mentality, the irreducibility of functional states, and the problem of qualia.

Part III Materialism and Meaning If all phenomena in the universe are physical, it is unclear in virtue of what facts language has intentional content or meaning. The papers in this section represent some prominent physicalist approaches to meaning that explain intentional word–world relations and thought–world relations in terms of physical relations.

Part IV Materialism and Value Is there room for value in a world where all phenomena are physical? This section addresses whether materialism can accommodate issues of value, as well as questions about mechanisms of reference to normative phenomena. Recruiting lessons from the preceding section, the papers in Part IV raise special semantic issues about bivalence and evaluative realism.

The book's selections are largely nontechnical and uniformly accessible to advanced undergraduates. For purposes of teaching and research, a nontechnical general introduction and a topical bibliography on contemporary materialism are included. In designing this book for advanced undergraduates, graduate students, and scholars, we have benefited from comments from many people, including the following: Adrian Driscoll (Philosophy Editor at Routledge), Michael Happold and Chris Meyers (our research assistants at Loyola University of Chicago), Phil Gasper, John Heil, Rob Wilson, David Yandell, and several anonymous referees. Finally, we thank Dwayne Mulder for help with the index, and Aaron Bunch and Matthew Edgar for help with the proofs.

P.K.M. and J.D.T.
Chicago, Illinois

Copyright Information

General Introduction: Contemporary Materialism

Paul K. Moser and J. D. Trout

Materialism, of the kind accepted by many philosophers and scientists, is a general view about what actually exists. Put bluntly, the view is just this: Everything that actually exists is material, or physical. This general view originated with western philosophy itself, among the pre-Socratic philosophers in ancient Greece. Many philosophers and scientists now use the terms "material" and "physical" interchangeably; we shall follow suit. (Likewise, we shall use "materialism" and "physicalism" interchangeably.) Understood as a general position about what exists, materialism is an *ontological*, or a *metaphysical*, view. Characterized thus, it is not just an epistemological view about how we know, or just a semantic view about the meaning of terms. What, however, is the exact meaning of "material," or "physical"? In the absence of an answer to this question, materialism will be an obscure ontological view. It will then be difficult, if not impossible, to confirm or to disconfirm materialism.

1 MATERIALISM VERSUS DUALISM

Two prominent construals of "material" are noteworthy. First, according to many philosophers, something is material if and only if it is spatial, extended in space. One might thus propose that what it means to say that something is material is that it is extended in space. This construal of "material" is inspired by Descartes's influential characterization of material bodies, in *Meditation* II. Given this construal, materialism is just the view that everything that exists is extended in space, that nothing non-spatial exists. This portrayal of materialism is attractively simple, but may be unilluminating.

The problem is that the relevant notion of spatial extension may depend on the very notion of material in need of elucidation. If there is such dependence, conceptual circularity hampers the proposed characterization of materialism. The main worry here is that the notion of spatial extension is actually the notion of something's being extended in *physical* space, or the notion of something's being *physically* extended. It seems conceivable that something (perhaps a purely spiritual being) has *temporal* extension, in virtue of extending over time, even though that thing lacks extension in physical space. It does not seem self-contradictory, in other words, to hold that something is temporal (or, temporally extended) but is not a body. If this is so, the proposed characterization of materialism should be qualified to talk of *physical* space or *physical* extension. In that case, however, the threat of conceptual circularity is transparent. Even if there is no strict circularity here, the pertinent notion of spatial extension may be too closely related to the notion of material to offer genuine clarification. At a minimum, we need a precise explanation of spatial extension, if talk of such extension aims to elucidate talk of what is material. Perhaps a notion of spatial extension is crucial to an elucidation of materialism, but further explanation, without conceptual circularity, will then be needed (cf. Chomsky 1988).

The second prominent construal of "material" looks to the vocabulary of the natural sciences. The rough idea is that the language of the best natural sciences determines what it is to be material, or physical. A predicate (such as "is an electron," or "has spin") signifies a physical item, on this view, if and only if the natural sciences, individually or collectively, rely on that predicate in the formulation of their explanatory theories. This position faces two problems.

First, the natural sciences do not have an exhaustive list of truths about the physical world; they are, in this respect, incomplete. Such incompleteness evidently allows for there being predicates that the natural sciences do not rely on, but that nonetheless pick out something in the physical world. It is thus unclear that the natural sciences have a monopoly on predicates that signify physical items. Perhaps use of a predicate by the natural sciences is a sufficient (but not a necessary) condition for that predicate's signifying something physical. Even so, we would still need an account of what it means to say that something is material.

Second, the appeal to "the natural sciences" raises the problem of specifying exactly when something is a natural science. It would be unacceptable now to portray a natural science as a discipline that investigates (in a certain way) only the material, or physical, world. We now seek an elucidation of what it is to be material, or physical; therefore, we cannot rely on a notion of the physical world. Is clinical psychology, for example, a natural science? Or, at least, are the methods of clinical psychology continuous with those of the natural sciences? If so, in virtue of what? Clinical psychologists sometimes use mentalistic vocabulary (for example, talk of beliefs, desires, intentions, and emotions) that does not obviously signify material things. At least, we need an explanation of the sense in which clinical psychology is materialist, if it is a natural science. Materialists would do well, then, to offer a precise characterization of a natural science that does not rely on talk of what is material, or physical. (For other difficulties in giving an informative characterization of materialism, see Chapter 3, this volume; for follow-up discussion, see Pettit 1993 and Crane 1993. See also Charles 1992.)

Materialists oppose ontological dualism, the view that there are two irreducible kinds of things that actually exist. The most famous (or, at least, most infamous) kind of ontological dualism comes from Descartes. Cartesian dualism affirms that there are psychological substances (in particular, thinking individuals) as well as physical substances (in particular, material bodies), and that psychological substances do not depend onto-logically on physical things. Proponents of Cartesian dualism must specify exactly how, or in what sense, psychological substances are ontologically independent of physical things. Talk of ontological independence is less than clear on its own. Cartesians allow for relations of causal dependence between the psychological and the material, but they deny that psycho-logical things are part of the material realm. Being a psychological thing, according to Cartesians, is different in kind from being a material thing. Still, the relevant notion of ontological independence needs clarification. Since Cartesians allow for relations of causal dependence between psy-chological and physical phenomena, they must explain how ontological independence relates to causal independence.

Descartes himself held that it is coherently conceivable that psycho-logical, or mental, things exist without physical things. Coherent conceiva-bility, we may assume, is just conceivability without self-contradiction. Since it is coherently conceivable that thinking things exist without a body, according to Descartes, thinking things are ontologically independent of a material body. One might put the point in terms of concepts: The concept of a thinking thing does not depend for its meaning on the concept of a material body. Descartes drew questionable metaphysical lessons from conceptual points of that sort. In his *Discourse on Method* (Part IV), for example, Descartes offers an argument from considerations about coher-ent conceivability for his ontological dualism.

If there is indeed a coherently conceivable distinction between minds and material bodies, we must reject the view that materialism, understood as entailing mind–body identity, is conceptually, or analytically, true – that is, true just in virtue of the meanings of "mind" and "body." Given such a coherently conceivable distinction, we can also challenge any version of materialism implying that psychological concepts (for example, the con-cepts of belief and sensory pain) are defined in terms of the ordinary physical causes of belief states and pain states. (Such materialism has been proposed by D. M. Armstrong 1977, and David Lewis 1966.) If "pain" is defined in terms of the ordinary bodily causes of pain, then it will not be coherently conceivable that there is pain without bodies. The concept of pain will then depend for its semantic significance on the concept of a bodily cause.

Many philosophers oppose any argument from a coherently conceivable distinction between mind and material body to an actual ontological distinction between the two. An actual ontological distinction between minds and material bodies entails that minds are not material bodies. This is different from a distinction just between concepts or definitions; it is a difference between things. Even if it is not (conceptually) necessarily true that minds and material bodies are identical, it may nonetheless be contingently true that minds are material bodies. An identity relation between minds and material bodies may obtain as an actual matter of fact, even if it does not obtain as a matter of meaning, definition, or necessity. The contingency of an identity relation between minds and bodies does not threaten its actuality, according to many materialists. These materialists will thus be unmoved by any appeal to the coherent conceivability of a distinction between minds and material bodies. They can consistently acknowledge Descartes's point about the existence of such a coherently conceivable distinction. The coherent conceivability of the falsity of a position does not call into question the actual truth of the position. Contingent truth is truth enough for most materialists, with respect to their materialism. A demand for the *necessary* truth of materialism improperly exaggerates the position adopted by contemporary materialists.

Materialists uniformly reject Descartes's ontological dualism, in particular, its implication that a human mind is composed of an immaterial substance different in kind from material bodies. They also reject Descartes's view that some psychological properties are actually exemplified by certain immaterial things, things not spatially extended. Materialists are uniformly monistic in their view that all actually existing individuals are material, and in their view that only material things exemplify psychological properties. These two fundamental materialist views, according to most contemporary materialists, are justifiable empirically, not *a priori*. That is, the evidence for these views must come from considerations dependent on experience; neither reason nor definition alone can justify such views. This view seems fitting if materialism is indeed a logically contingent position.

Although materialism is ontologically monistic, not all ontological monists have been materialists. Idealism is a monistic immaterialist view claiming that the world is a collection of ideas. Being monistic, it holds that only one kind of substance exists – mental substances. George Berkeley offered semantic and epistemological versions of idealism as an alternative to the "bare substance" views of some medievals. Bare substance, the ontological basis of instantiated properties, was undetectable by the senses and so warranted ontological skepticism, according to Berkeley. Many philosophers, including Berkeley, have been led to idealism for epistemological, mainly antiskeptical, reasons. If our knowledge is to be well-founded, according to these idealists, it must derive from a basis over which we have epistemic authority. A presumed relation of resemblance between world and idea must itself be justified, and idealists have held that, lacking independent access to a mind-independent world, we must ground our knowledge in our own ideas to meet a skeptic's challenge. Ultimately, this form of idealism offered unacceptably complex explanations of our perceptual experience, at least in the eyes of many philosophers. Rather than simply postulating a mind-independent chair as the cause of my chair ideas (or appearances), for example, Berkeleyan idealists must offer different explanations for each person's chair-related appearances. When the doctrine was not rejected on the grounds that it led to phenomenalism or solipsism, it was often rejected because it lacked unifying explanatory power.

One prominent historical materialist reaction to idealism, especially the German idealism of Hegel, Fichte, and Schelling, comes from the German philosopher and economist Karl Marx. This materialist reaction had both a positive and a negative program. On the negative side – that of critique – the program raised doubts about the role of ideas in history, which were typically given primary force in idealist discussions. On the positive side, historical materialists claimed that history was moved by social forces and relations that were mysterious and likely ideological (in the pejorative sense) apart from a materialist analysis. Understood thus, historical materialism is part of a long materialist tradition of ontological unification. Higher-level, social and psychological phenomena, along with other apparently diverse phenomena, are all material. This doctrine has spawned research in current philosophy of the social sciences concerning methodological individualism and reductionism.

In rejecting idealistic monism, materialists must explain what exactly justifies the view that all actually existing individuals are material. They must specify the kind of evidence that supports this view. Do the natural sciences offer any evidence for the materialist view in question? Perhaps they do not actually offer evidence for materialism, but rather *presuppose* materialism as a groundrule for sound scientific explanation. Materialism regarding what exists, on this view, is a desideratum for explanation in the natural sciences; it is not an independent hypothesis confirmed by the natural sciences. Materialism might be, however, both a desideratum for the natural sciences and a view confirmed by the natural sciences. One option need not exclude the other. It is, however, an empirical issue whether materialism constrains the natural sciences, past or present. One must examine whether the natural sciences actually allow for explanations that depart from materialism. This task will require antecedent clarification of what exactly a departure from materialism involves; it thus harks back to our opening question. Many contemporary materialists, in any case, regard the natural sciences as supporting materialism. A prominent view is that considerations about best explanation of the data and procedures of the natural sciences confirm materialism (section 3 of this General Introduction returns to this theme).

Materialists do not share a uniform view about the nature of psychological properties, such as the properties of being a belief, being a desire, and being a sensory experience. In particular, they do not all hold that every psychological property is equivalent or identical to a conjunction of physical properties. Only proponents of *reductive* materialism hold the latter view, and they are a small minority among contemporary materialists. Proponents of *nonreductive* materialism reject the latter view, and affirm that psychological properties can be exemplified even in an immaterial world. Such nonreductive materialists include functionalists about the mind, who hold that psychological properties differ from material properties in virtue of the special causal or functional roles of the former. Functionalists differ from behaviorists in acknowledging the psychological relevance of causal relations among not only stimuli and behavior but internal states as well. A third prominent version of materialism, *eliminative* materialism, recommends that we eliminate most, if not all, everyday psychological discourse, on the ground that it rests on seriously misguided assumptions about human psychology – assumptions that will disappear with the advance of science.

According to many functionalists, the causal roles that determine psychological properties are specified by the taxonomies, or systems of classification, found in the best contemporary psychology. These causal roles can depend on relational considerations that are independent of considerations about the composition of what exemplifies psychological properties. Functionalism allows that psychological properties can be "multiply realizable," realizable in compositionally different systems. Both carbon-based and silicon-based physical systems (and even nonphysical systems), for example, might support such a psychological process as thinking. Thinking, according to functionalism, does not require a specific physical composition for thinkers. Physical composition can vary as long as the appropriate causal relational features obtain.

Some critics of functionalism about human psychology have objected that the view neglects some distinctive features of our psychology: for example, qualitative sensory states and meaning-laden interpretive, or intentional, states. John Searle, in particular, is well known for his "Chinese-room argument" against the view that thinking is just the manipulation of formal, uninterpreted symbols. Searle's argument relies on the possibility of a computational system that gives a perfect simulation of a certain cognitive capacity, understanding Chinese, even though that system fails to understand Chinese. Searle explains:

> Simply imagine that someone who understands no Chinese is locked in a room with a lot of Chinese symbols and a computer program for answering questions in Chinese. The input to the system consists in Chinese symbols in the form of questions; the output of the system consists in Chinese symbols in answer to the questions. We might suppose that the program is so good that the answers to the questions are indistinguishable from those of a native Chinese speaker. But all the same, neither the person inside nor any other part of the system literally understands Chinese .... Because the [computer] program is purely formal or syntactical and because minds have mental or semantic contents, any attempt to produce a mind purely with computer programs leaves out the essential features of the mind.
>
> (Searle 1992: 45; cf. Searle 1980)

Searle's argument bears not only on certain assumptions of artificial intelligence in cognitive science, but also on functionalist materialist models of the mind. Functionalists have found Searle's argument unconvincing, and have offered a variety of criticisms. (See Pylyshyn 1980, and Fodor 1980, for representative criticisms of Searle's Chinese-room argument. For a different antimaterialist argument arising from the nature of intentionality, see Bealer 1993.) Let us turn to a closer examination of the general motivation for nonreductive materialism.

2 NONREDUCTIVE MATERIALISM

Nonreductive materialists generally follow functionalists in emphasizing the importance of multiple realizability. Before we can appreciate the evidence for multiple realizability, we need an appropriate vocabulary. A *type* of state, property, process, object, or event (hereafter, simply "object"), is a class or kind of object that admits of instances. An egg, for example, is a type of single-celled organism. There are many concrete instances of eggs: for instance, in humans, in hatcheries, and in many refrigerators. These individual eggs are *tokens*. We understand an object as a type or a token relative to a taxonomy, a means of classification – although it does not follow that the existence of all tokens depends on language. A particular mastiff may be a token of the type *mastiff*, but it is also a token of the type *dog, mammal, animal, domesticated animal*, and *slobbering thing*. Types may be scientifically taxonomic, but are not so automatically; whether they are such depends on their role in a scientific theory. With these concepts in hand, let us turn to the issue of type–type, or "smooth," reduction.

The smooth reduction of one theoretical description to another preserves causal/explanatory role. This preservation of causal/explanatory role is reflected in at least one of two ways: (a) the laws in the reduced and reducing theories are similar (this concerns whether they isolate the same covariations in the world) and (b) theoretical–predicate pairs across the reduced and reducing theories isolate, or pick out, the same objects. (Cf. Churchland 1989, chs 1, 3, and Hooker 1981.) Traditional accounts of reduction imply that theories, laws, and terms can be objects of reduction. One law, for instance, is reducible to another if the law targeted for reduction is logically derivable from the corresponding law in the reducing domain. Reduction, construed ontologically, is a relation between two theoretically characterized domains of entities, whether postulated objects, properties, processes, states, events, or laws. (A postulated entity need not, of course, be an actual entity.)

A primary goal of reduction is ontological unification, at least unification regarding ontological postulates. A reduction will be successful if the reducing theory can replace – without loss of explanatory power – all the *explanations* of the reduced theory, including its ontological postulates. Even so, how can we assess similarity of ontology, explanation, and meaning? A common measure is causal, treating ontology, explanation, and meaning as having been successfully reduced when the postulated objects of the higher-level domain have been replaced with lower-level objects of similar causal role. Alchemy, for example, postulated personal, projective mechanisms of alchemical bonding that were eliminated by modern accounts, but alchemy nevertheless endorsed practices and vocabulary that sometimes isolated elements recognized by modern taxonomy, such as lead. When a theory's ontological postulates have been reduced or eliminated, its laws are not long to follow.

The type–type identity theory has the disadvantage that, as a formulation of materialism, there is inadequate evidence for it. For example, there is no evidence that it is generally the case that, for every type of *psychological* process (relative to the best psychological taxonomy), there is a corresponding type of *neural* process (relative to the best neuroscientific theory). Many materialists hold that there is evidence instead for a weaker, token–token identity theory, according to which any individual or token – a particular dog, a particular NaCl molecule, a particular cultural ritual – is entirely composed of physical phenomena. We might assure ourselves of this fact by a strategy of decomposition: Analyze all the constituents of the token, and determine whether any nonphysical phenomena are present. There is, of course, an epistemological question about how we might detect (and thus interact with) nonphysical phenomena. Awaiting evidence for nonphysical phenomena, materialists can perhaps be excused for withholding assent to such phenomena.

A multiple realizability argument from functionalists, involving mind–body dependence, may acknowledge token–token identity, but it challenges type–type reduction. Relative to dualism, acknowledgment of mind–body token identity may itself seem reductive because it rejects dependence of minds on nonphysical substances. Nonetheless, acknowledgment of just token identity is, as materialist doctrines go, a nonreductive formulation of materialism. Another nonreductive version of materialism, *compositional* materialism, casts even token-identity theories as too demanding.

Compositional materialism implies that physical (and thus, for the physicalist, psychological) events are not typically identical to their smaller constituent features. There is, according to compositional materialism, plasticity (or, multiple realizability) even within a single physical token, just as there is within a type susceptible to instantiation by different physical tokens. An example from some influential work on compositional materialism states that an individual car remains the same car even if its generator is replaced, at least on our ordinary criteria of car identity (Boyd 1980: 100). A difference in molecular constituents of the car in two possible worlds does not preclude, on this view, sameness of car. (For an assessment of compositional materialism and some other versions of nonreductive materialism relying on so-called supervenience relations, see Moser and Trout 1995; cf. Moser 1993, ch. 5.)

Citing empirical evidence from such sciences as biology, psychology, sociology, and anthropology, nonreductive materialists argue that, for many types of states appropriate for explanation in those sciences, each of those types can be physically realized in diverse ways. The empirical evidence for multiple realizability seems clear in organizationally complex systems, such as societies or biological organisms, where some properties seem realizable in a variety of compositions. Developmental biology offers an array of relevant examples. In developmental embryology, for example, there is a type of process called neural crest development. The process by which sections of the neural crest get differentiated normally occurs endogenously. In cases of injury to the neural crest, however, the same process of differentiation can be exogenously guided. The type of process called neural crest development is thus multiply realizable.

We can find actual cases of multiple realizability in anthropology and psychology. In anthropology, the study of cultures has revealed various properties of highly organized, integrated systems. Stable cultures tend, under normal stresses, to produce effects that reinforce the stability of those cultures. Many different specific effects (for example, different rituals and social activities) can serve this stabilizing function. The function that serves social stability is thus multiply realizable. In psychology, the process of producing sentences with a particular structural description can take place by normal means in Broca's area of the brain or by abnormal means, in the case of clinical damage, in the higher cortex. As biologically interesting as these distinct realizations are, what matters to psychological explanation (at least from the perspective of psycholinguistic accounts of syntactic processing) is the process of parsing sentences, not the specific biological description of this process.

Many nonreductive materialists regard multiple realizability as supportable not (just) by pretheoretical philosophical ideals, but by explanatory demands in our best sciences. Typically, nonreductive materialists claim that two theoretical reasons lead us to appeal to the higher-level, multiply-realizable character of many taxonomic states in the sciences. First, explanations in terms of a system's microstates often misrepresent the sensitivity of the system to changes both inside and outside that system, and thus those explanations are, to that extent, unacceptable. Second, when reductive analyses do not yield bad explanations, they often miss important generalizations about the system's behavior. For example, were we to identify a cohesion-producing social event with one of its realizations, such as a rain dance, explanations of the resulting social cohesion would mention essentially the occurrence of the rain dance, even if social cohesion would have resulted by some other actual means. The result would be omission of an important generalization about social cohesion, owing to a misplaced focus. Contemporary materialists are typically nonreductive materialists, given their widespread acceptance of the aforementioned lessons about multiple realizability.

3 MATERIALISM, NATURALISM, AND EXPLANATION

Philosophical naturalism has various expressions. Put generally, philosophical naturalism affirms that philosophy is continuous with the natural sciences. This broad characterization does not specify the intended understanding of continuity, which might be ontological, epistemological, semantic, or methodological. Contemporary motivation for naturalism (as opposed to traditional motivations found in Aristotle and others) derives largely from recent science. Many recent philosophers, in particular, have been impressed with the powerful lessons emerging from the natural sciences. These philosophers have noted that the natural sciences have been remarkably successful in representing their proprietary phenomena as uniformly physical. In opposition, many critics of materialism emphasize the apparent difficulty of assimilating or reducing the (intentional) phenomena of the "human" sciences (for example, psychology and sociology) to the phenomena of the natural sciences. According to these critics, the natural sciences illustrate, in a way that the social and behavioral sciences do not, that the effects of natural (particularly, nonintentional) kinds can be accounted for by their physical constituents. Because this accounting is so indebted to the unifying role that explanation plays in contemporary defenses of materialism, several concepts associated with explanation promise to illuminate the connection that philosophers have seen between materialism and naturalism.

The traditional twentieth-century account of explanation, called the covering-law or nomic-subsumption model, stems from a single idea: An event, property, state, or process is explained by its subsumption under a law. The covering-law model of explanation, the most influential variant of which is Carl Hempel's Deductive–Nomological Model, casts explanations as arguments, and it makes laws essential to causation (see Hempel and Oppenheim 1948). The basis for this view is the empiricist – specifically instrumentalist – model of theory testing that had dominated since the 1930s. The job of scientific theories, according to twentieth-century logical empiricists, is to generate and test predictions. How do we arrive at these predictions? Roughly, we deduce observational predictions from a set of general laws and specific background conditions. For example, we deduce the pressure values we may expect to observe from specific conditions involving a heated container of gas and from general laws about the way in which this type of gas reacts to heating.

Explanations need not be causal. Mathematical explanations, for instance, do not cite causes. One might explain why $2+5 = 7$ in terms of the addition relation and the nature of integers, without suggesting that the addition relation and the integers "2" and "5" *cause* the sum "7," or *cause* it to be the case that $2+5 = 7$. Perhaps the causal account of explanation is not complete, but it is not therefore mistaken. Scientific explanations, according to many philosophers, are at least typically causal. (For support for the opposing view that "in an advanced science the explanations and laws will not employ causal concepts," see Davidson 1990.) A controversial issue concerns the way in which causal notions are crucial to explanation but not to prediction. In fact, the asymmetry of explanation and prediction prompts one to face just this issue. (We shall return to this asymmetry presently, in connection with an example about a flagpole.)

As a model of theory testing, the covering-law account faces some difficulties from its harboring an instrumentalist account of theories. On the covering-law model, scientists characteristically deduce observational predictions from general laws. There apparently are, however, scientific theories (for example, historical geology and evolutionary theory) that do not characteristically make predictions. There is, moreover, a significant tendency in science toward unification or theoretical integration, a tendency difficult to explain if scientists are concerned mainly with the predictions their theories generate, and not with the comprehensive truth of their explanations.

The covering-law model of explanation faces two standard problems, both of which raise nomological and causal themes central to current debates about the proper formulation of materialism. The first problem is that there exist explanations arrived at without recourse to the type of derivation required by the covering-law model. The second problem, more widely discussed than the first, concerns cases in which an event is not explained, even though the "explanation" statement is derived from general laws and background conditions.

Regarding the first problem, there are explanations of phenomena (such as the performance of a certain kind of cultural ritual, the appearance of a certain type of predator, or the presence of a certain structural feature of the economy or of an institution) that do not appear to be linked to general laws. In these cases, one might argue, the event is explained if the theoretically plausible causal mechanism described is sufficient under the circumstances to bring about the effect. In some cultures, for example, the need for social cohesion occasions particular rituals, even though there are no (known) *laws* about such occasions, and so no derivations from laws. Another difficulty arises from events that are causally overdetermined: Events that would have occurred even if the specific conditions that in fact brought about those events had not obtained. Regarding such events, it is unclear *which* law is the one from which the explanation derives.

With respect to the second aforementioned problem, the most famous examples involve so-called asymmetries of explanation. In a famous example, the length of a shadow cast by a flagpole can be derived and thereby explained by facts about the height of the flagpole and the position of the sun. Given the same information about the position of the sun and the length of the pole's shadow, one could derive the height of the flagpole. The two cases are parallel, but the following problem exists for the covering-law model: We would suppose that the height of the flagpole explains the length of the shadow, but we would not suppose that the length of the shadow explains the height of the flagpole. What explains the height of the flagpole, it seems, are architectural intentions.

Logical empiricists gave explanation a role subsidiary to prediction. A theory's ability to explain, according to these empiricists, is not a reason for endorsing its truth, but is only a reason for holding the theory to be consistent, coherent, or unified. Such pragmatic features of explanation, according to many philosophers, are too modest to account for the work explanation must do in theory evaluation and the unification and integration of theories. Many philosophers hold, in addition, that causal considerations, understood relative to a broad theory, determine the goodness of explanations. In the tradition of logical empiricism, the covering-law account of explanation attempted to model explanation on logical relations of derivability. This approach to explanation as derivation aimed to serve empiricist purposes in reinterpreting causal relations in terms of empirical regularities among observable phenomena.

Historically, many materialists have held that causes in question must be deterministic. A system is deterministic, roughly speaking, if its state at any time is a necessary consequence of its states at an earlier time conjoined with the laws of nature. The view of causes as deterministic followed from a prominent conception of nomic subsumption implying that laws admit no exceptions. This view prompted questions about the material status of statistical phenomena. The final states of some systems, so-called indeterministic systems, are not completely determined by an initial state, but only with a certain degree of probability. How are we to understand this probability? Two interpretations of probability, physical and epistemic, are prominent, and will crop up either centrally or peripherally in discussions of materialism. Physical probability is a propensity, or a tendency, of a physical system to have a class of different effects, or different final states. Epistemic probability is the probability we assign to some phenomenon on the basis of relevant sampling information. If causes can be statistical (or "stochastic"), and laws are just counterfactual supporting generalizations that implicate causes, then causal laws can be indeterministic as well. On this basis, some philosophers have offered a statistical model of explanation designed to accommodate philosophical naturalism. (For a survey of relevant approaches to explanation, see Salmon 1989.)

Many philosophers now claim to be naturalistic, and their focus on explanation, causation, lawfulness, determinism and probability, is part of a widely shared effort to be properly naturalistic. But current philosophical literature represents different conceptions of naturalism, many of which are controversial. Conceptions of naturalism often place questionable, or otherwise problematic, requirements on a subject matter, such as reductionist or eliminativist requirements. Some versions of naturalism, for example, require that social and psychological phenomena fall under (strict) laws, sometimes with the rider that such laws be replaceable by physical laws.

The following two general views of the relation between naturalism and materialism are noteworthy:

(a) Naturalism is ontologically neutral regarding materialism, and thus is logically compatible with ontological dualism.
(b) Naturalism presupposes materialism, and thus is incompatible with dualism.

If (a) is correct, the defense of materialism on the basis of naturalism must appeal to additional supporting evidence, presumably empirical evidence. What kind of evidence, in particular, would lead one to suppose that higher-level (typically intentional) phenomena should be entirely composed of physical phenomena? Evolutionary theory is one source of this supposition. As evidence for human evolution has mounted, it has become more plausible for many to regard humans as part of the natural order. Evolutionary theory indicates that human cognitive, perceptual, and physiological behavior results from unmysterious physical interaction, of some sort, between our material bodies and our material environments.

If option (b) is correct, an appeal to naturalism in defense of materialism would be questionbegging, because materialism would then be part of the doctrine of naturalism. We suspect that most contemporary naturalists would prefer (a) to (b). It seems that W. V. O. Quine, for example, resists (b) with his following remarks:

> nowadays the overwhelming purposes of the science game are technology and understanding .... The science game is not committed to the physical, whatever that means .... Even telepathy and clairvoyance are scientific options, however moribund. It would take some extraordinary evidence to enliven them, but, if that were to happen, then empiricism itself – the crowning norm ... of naturalized epistemology – would go by

the board. For remember that that norm, and naturalized epistemology itself, are integral to science, and science is fallible and corrigible.

(Quine 1990: 20–1)

Quine seems to be endorsing the common view that naturalism, stressing continuity with the sciences, is not automatically committed to materialism.

One might defend materialism with the observation that the apparent irreducibility of social and psychological kinds presents a problem for materialism only if the version of materialism in dispute is reductionist; and, according to many philosophers, it need not be reductionist. Another suggestion in favor of materialism is that a materialist explanation of the remarkable success of the methods of the natural sciences is *simpler* – theoretically more economical – than dualist explanations or other alternatives. Explanations can, however, be simple or complex along various dimensions, and it is unclear that an explanation postulating the smallest number of basic ontological types is automatically simple in other theoretically important respects. Judgments of simplicity are theory-dependent and so, without some specification of the particular *respects* of simplicity and of how those respects are theoretically relevant, simplicity may not be a decisive consideration in favor of materialism.

Considerations about theoretical simplicity often stem from considerations about theoretical unification. On one view of theoretical unification, a good theory isolates a small number of explanatory patterns to explain a set of apparently diverse phenomena. (On this approach to explanation, see Kitcher 1981, 1989.) Though what counts as diverse will be determined by background theories, the desirability of limiting the number of irreducible facts is conceded by many theorists (scientists included) independently of the specific theory they hold. To the extent that it is reasonable to infer the approximate truth of a doctrine from its greater comparative explanatory power, the evidence, according to many philosophers, favors materialism over its rivals. This book's selections will enable one to assess the merits and demerits of contemporary materialism, the dominant ontological position among current philosophers and scientists.

4 THE SELECTIONS

Materialism and naturalism

Section 3 of this General Introduction noted some relations between materialism and naturalism. This subsection will identify some of the main points made in the essays by Armstrong, Fodor, and Crane and Mellor.

If one adopts a reductive version of materialism, implying either that all phenomena are describable in a vocabulary of physics or that the laws of higher-level disciplines are reducible to the laws of physics, then evidence concerning physics will determine the fate of reductive materialism. Because neuroscience, psychology, and the other higher-level disciplines have not been reduced to physics, their success is unavailable as a source of evidence for materialism. Indeed, the success of the higher-level sciences in their *unreduced* form is part of the motivation for nonreductive materialism in the first place.

Another motivation (seen at the close of section 3) for nonreductive materialism, or at least a materialism that is more modestly reductive, derives from the value that scientists place on explanatory unification. In light of the diversity of attitudes toward explanation, one might distinguish between philosophical and scientific explanation. Such a distinction would, however, thwart any desire for intellectual unification of disparate disciplines, at least according to some materialists. After all, materialism leads one to expect a trend toward the integration of explanatory practices and toward ontological unification too. Given that explanations normally reflect ontological commitments, the monistic materialist ontology constituting the objects of scientific and everyday explanation should lead one to expect similarly unified explanatory standards, not separate standards for philosophy and science.

In Chapter 1, David Armstrong introduces various issues central to a clear formulation of naturalism: Issues concerning ontology, universals, space-time, causation, purpose, Cartesian accounts of the mind, and theological conceptions of the soul. Armstrong conceives of naturalism as the comprehensive doctrine "that reality consists of nothing but a single all-embracing spatio-temporal system." Materialism, or physicalism, is a part of that doctrine.

Scientific realists, Armstrong holds, properly respect the success resulting from the postulation of theoretical entities in science. But not every theoretical postulate merits realistic interpretation. It does not follow, for example, that one must acknowledge the existence of abstract classes to account for the success of mathematics. Abstract classes serve only a semantic function; they "do not *bring about* anything physical in the way that genes and electrons do." Platonic realism, therefore, does not find a comfortable home in any plausible version of naturalism.

One consequence of Armstrong's conception of philosophical method is a view he calls *a posteriori* realism. According to this view, "Realism, Naturalism and Materialism are seen to rest upon a common intellectual basis. That basis is the view that the best guide we have to the nature of reality is provided by natural science." If we treat naturalism and materialism as "*specifications* of *a posteriori* Realism" (that is, as particular doctrines concerning "the general nature of those properties and relations that particulars actually have"), then we can hope to use science to resolve some of the most persistent philosophical problems surrounding the nature of causation and laws. This leaves us without a traditional First Philosophy, but many *a posteriori* realists hold that the foundations of natural science constitute all the First Philosophy needed.

"Special Sciences" (Chapter 2) presents Jerry Fodor's critique of classical reductionism. Underlying reductionism is a specific interpretation of a principle Fodor calls *the generality of physics*, "the view that all events which fall under the laws of any science are physical events and hence fall under the laws of physics." Fodor notes the peculiarity that, if reductionism were true, then "the more the special sciences succeed, the more they ought to disappear," precisely because special science events are thought to be subsumed by laws of physics. This reductive trend is, however, conspicuously absent from science. If anything, there has been a proliferation of special science research programs and journals; this would seem to indicate the separate integrity of the special science and their indifference to the much-advertised threat of classical reduction.

Fodor argues that justice to physicalism requires only the claim that, for any token state described by a higher-level theory, there is a token physical state. This is the strongest version of physicalism desirable, according to Fodor, and it captures the idea that all phenomena are physical. At the same time, it avoids the methodological excesses of reductionism. According to Fodor, the reductions in question are not forthcoming, because natural-kind predicates in psychology and other higher-level disciplines are, from the perspective of physics, hopelessly disjunctive. Think of all the actual physical realizations of, for example, money as it is implicated in economic generalizations: Copper, shells, gold, paper, etc. Generalizations indicating the specific physical compositions of instantiations of money are not just cumbersome, but are likely to be both theoretically unilluminating and deceptive: Unilluminating, because they cause you to miss the shared higher-level property that makes them instances of the same kind, and deceptive, because they present the misleading picture that their specific physical composition is essential to their type-identity. (For assessment of Fodor's views on reduction and the unity of science, see Papineau 1992, and Smith 1992.)

In Chapter 3, Tim Crane and D. H. Mellor raise a series of difficulties concerning contemporary versions of physicalism. They begin with problems associated with formulating an adequate characterization of physicalism. The claim that everything is physical is open to a variety of interpretations. Crane and Mellor argue that the only interpretation on which physicalism turns out to be true is vacuous.

The most familiar generic version of materialism states that all phenomena are physical. As traditionally understood, this kind of materialism sets *a priori* limits on the subject matter of physics. Distinguishing traditional materialism from contemporary physicalism, Crane and Mellor argue that, if physicalism is to be a substantial, nonvacuous doctrine, there have to be at least some disciplines to which physicalism does not apply. This is why Crane and Mellor examine physicalism characterized more narrowly, as the view that "mental entities, properties, relations and facts are all really physical." Neither reducibility to physics, causal considerations, nor the existence of intentionality provides the necessary sort of isolation of psychology from physics to make physicalism an informative doctrine. For example, the failure of extensionality induced by contexts of mental causation and intentionality might be thought to mark off the psychological from the physical but, Crane and Mellor argue, physics is dogged by the same difficulties of non-extensionality marking psychology. They argue, against Donald Davidson's anomalous monism, that the existence of psychophysical laws undermines the pertinent notion of the separability of the mental from the physical. Turning to a supervenience thesis offered by some nonreductive materialists, Crane and Mellor contend that modern physics itself implies the falsity of this supervenience thesis.

Crane and Mellor conclude that "no defensible definition of physicalism will deprive psychology of the ontological status of the nonmental sciences. In no nonvacuous sense is physicalism true." Because Crane and Mellor conceive physicalism as a doctrine "specifically about minds," this book's section on materialism and mind will put readers in a position to assess their claims as well as the implications of physicalism for psychology generally.

Materialism and mind

Materialists have always had the difficult task of explaining how their materialism can account for such psychological phenomena as thoughts, beliefs, desires, intentions, and sensory experiences – or at least for familiar *talk* of such phenomena. A materialist's options, put roughly, are these:

(a) Explain how ordinary talk of psychological phenomena ("folk psycho-logy," for short) can, at least for the most part, be reduced to language that does not commit one to any kind of ontological dualism.
(b) Explain how folk psychology is misguided to such an extent that it will disappear altogether with the advance of science.
(c) Explain how folk psychology is perfectly compatible with materialism even if the kind of reduction sought by (a) is unavailable – in particular, explain either (1) how psychological phenomena actually depend on physical phenomena, owing to nonreductive "supervenience" relations of some sort, or at least (2) how psychological phenomena are just special relational (for example, causal/functional) features of wholly physically composed systems.

Option (a) entails reductive materialism, for which J. J. C. Smart's "Sensa-tions and Brain Processes" (Chapter 4) is well known. Option (b) entails eliminative materialism, represented by Paul Churchland (Chapter 8), Richard Rorty (1965), and Stephen Stich (1983), among others. Option (c) entails nonreductive materialism. Alternative (1) of (c) receives support from supervenience materialism of the sort proposed by Donald Davidson (Chapter 5) and criticized by Jaegwon Kim (Chapter 7). Alternative (2) of (c) is represented by Hilary Putnam (Chapter 6), among many other functionalist writings, including Fodor (1981) and Pylyshyn (1984). Critics of functionalist materialism now include Putnam (1988) and Searle (1992). Similarly, the general antimaterialist argument by Frank Jackson (Chapter 9) challenges standard versions of functionalist materialism.

In Chapter 4, J. J. C. Smart claims that "science is increasingly giving us a viewpoint whereby organisms are able to be seen as physicochemical mechanisms." Smart's materialism, outlined in his paper "Materialism" (Smart 1963), affirms that there is nothing in the world over and above the entities postulated by physics and the relations between those entities described by such sciences as chemistry and biology. Such materialism entails that there are no nonphysical things and thus no causal interaction between physical and irreducibly mental phenomena. Smart recommends his materialism on the ground that it is unexplainable how irreducible nonphysical phenomena could arise in the course of animal evolution. He claims that we can vastly simplify our view of the world if we endorse a version of materialism that reduces sensations, and states of consciousness in general, to brain processes.

According to Smart's chapter, a person "is a vast arrangement of physical particles, but there are not, over and above this, sensations or states of consciousness." Smart resists the view that states of consciousness are simply "correlated" with brain states, on the ground that such talk of correlation implies that a state of consciousness is something over and above a brain state. In addition, Smart opposes the view that reports of sensations mean the same thing as, or can be translated into, reports about brain states. He holds, instead, that "in so far as 'after image' or 'ache' is a report of a process, it is a report of a process that *happens to be* a brain process." Sensations, according to Smart, are just brain processes, but this is contingently true; it is not a truth of logic or an analytic truth arising just from the meanings of "sensation" and "brain process." Smart's reductive materialism thus acknowledges that there are contingently true identity-statements involving psychological and physical phenomena.

Smart grants that people can fail to recognize that their sensations are identical to brain states. In particular, sensations, being identical to brain states, can have various neurological properties of which one is altogether ignorant. This kind of materialism is not behaviorism, as it acknowledges a crucial explanatory role for brain states over and above behavioral states. Smart holds that methodological principles of parsimony and simplicity decisively recommend his materialist identity theory over dualism.

In Chapter 5, Donald Davidson explains how although mental events interact causally with physical events, mental events do not fall under – and cannot be predicted or explained by – strict deterministic laws. Davidson offers a version of nonreductive materialism, committed only to token identity, that explains how mental events can have the aforementioned character. His nonreductive materialism affirms that mental events are physical events, but denies that there are strict psychophysical laws relating mental and physical events. Davidson thus opposes the assumption that the ground for accepting an identity theory of the mind comes from evidence for the existence of psychophysical laws. He also rejects the kind of reductive materialism defended by Smart. Davidson proposes that mental phenomena are dependent, or "supervenient," on physical phenomena. He adds that "such supervenience might be taken to mean that there cannot be two events alike in all physical respects but differing in some mental respect, or that an object cannot alter in some mental respect without altering in some physical respect." This kind of supervenience does not require that mental events be reducible to physical events by definition or even by causal law. The rejection of strict psychophysical laws and the endorsement of an identity relation between mental and physical events entail what Davidson calls "anomalous monism."

Davidson has a straightforward explanation of the irreducibility of psychological events and explanations to physical events and explanations.

He holds that "events are mental only as described," and that "the explanations of mental events in which we are typically interested relate them to other mental events and conditions," which do not constitute a closed system and thus fail of prediction and explanation by strict, exceptionless laws. Davidson claims that a scientific theory of physical events, in contrast, seeks a closed comprehensive system that subsumes physical events under strict laws.

Davidson emphasizes the role of normative considerations in the ascription of such psychological states as beliefs and intentions. He claims that "the content" of an intentional attitude, such as a belief, derives from that attitude's place in a pattern involving other intentional attitudes, and that such a holistic consideration blocks massive irrationality. He adds, in Chapter 5:

> There is no assigning beliefs to a person one by one on the basis of his verbal behaviour, his choices, or other local signs no matter how plain and evident, for we make sense of particular beliefs only as they cohere with other beliefs, with preferences, with intentions, hopes, fears, expectations, and the rest .... Crediting people with a large degree of consistency cannot be accounted mere charity: it is unavoidable if we are to be in a position to accuse them meaningfully of error and some degree of irrationality .... To the extent that we fail to discover a coherent and plausible pattern in the attitudes and actions of others we simply forego the chance of treating them as [rational] persons.

Davidson regards this holistic normative constraint on psychological explanation as absent from physical explanation. On this basis, he concludes that psychological explanation is normative in a way that physical explanation is not. Even if natural science lacks strict causal laws, as Davidson is now prepared to concede (Davidson 1985), it differs from psychological explanation regarding the role of holistic normative constraints.

Davidson holds that the holistic normative constraint on psychological explanation (but not on physical explanation) accounts for the absence of (a) strict laws in psychological explanation and (b) strict psychophysical laws linking the mental and the physical. Strict laws linking intentional actions and their reasons would require what Davidson (1974) calls "a quantitative calculus that brings all relevant beliefs and desires into the picture." Davidson denies that the sorts of reasons appropriate to the psychological explanation of intentional actions admit of such a calculus. Variability in background beliefs, desires, and intentions offers little hope for strict laws bridging reasons and actions. The pertinence of such background intentional states, on Davidson's view, comes from the afore-mentioned holistic normative constraint on psychological explanation; and it supports the irreducibility of psychology to physical science. Davidson thus recommends nonreductive materialism as an alternative to Smart's reductive materialism. (For recent commentary on Davidson's anomalous monism, see, for example, Davidson 1993, Kim 1993, and Sosa 1993.)

In Chapter 6, Hilary Putnam argues that "mentality is a real and autonomous feature of our world." Using analogies between minds and computer programs, Putnam contends that a psychological description of a person differs significantly from a physical–chemical description of that person. In particular, Putnam holds that a mental state is not identical with its actual physical realization because any mental state, like any computer program, could be realized in different physical constitutions. On the opposite view rejected by Putnam, "it is as if we met Martians and discovered that they were in all functional respects isomorphic to us, but we refused to admit that they could feel pain because their *C* fibers were different." Putnam thus argues for functionalist nonreductionism on the basis of the multiple realizability of psychological properties.

Putnam holds that psychological explanations of human behavior identify certain structural, functional features of humans that are omitted by physical explanations (he uses the example of a peg board to illustrate the key distinction between higher-level and lower-level explanations). Psychology offers higher-level explanations that are irreducible to explanations at the level of physics and chemistry. As Putnam notes, "whatever our mental functioning may be, there seems to be no serious reason to believe that it is *explainable* by our physics and chemistry." Psychology identifies a kind of "functional organization" that can be illustrated by the functioning of computing machines, but that cannot be captured by the lower-level explanations of physics and chemistry. Putnam contends, in addition, that the role of functional organization in human psychology does not require that we think of ourselves as "soul-stuff" or "ghostly agents." Materialists, as long as they are nonreductionists and regard their materialism as a contingent thesis, can endorse Putnam's functionalism; at least, many contemporary philosophers assume this.

In Chapter 7, Jaegwon Kim argues that nonreductive materialism is not a genuine option for materialists, that materialists must choose between reductive materialism and a kind of eliminative materialism that excludes psychological phenomena from the domain of reality. Kim directs his criticisms against nonreductive materialists who accept "the claim that all that exists in space-time is physical, but, at the same time, accept 'property dualism', a dualism about psychological and physical attributes, insisting that psychological concepts or properties form an irreducible, autonomous domain." These nonreductive materialists include proponents of Davidson-style anomalous monism and proponents of functionalist materialism relying on considerations about the multiple realizability of psychological properties.

Kim argues that anomalous monism does not permit a causal role for mental properties, on the ground that, given such monism, events are causes only in virtue of instantiating physical laws. Kim adds: "What does no causal work does no explanatory work either; it may as well not be there – it's difficult to see how we could miss it if it weren't there at all." Kim concludes that Davidson's anomalous monism "is essentially a form of eliminativism." Even if anomalous monism acknowledges the existence of mental events, it does not make room for such events in the causal structure of the world.

Regarding multiple-realizability arguments for nonreductive materialism, Kim contends that "where there is multiple realization, there must be psychophysical laws, each specifying a physical state as nomologically sufficient for the given mental state." The idea of a physical realization of a psychological state, according to Kim, involves the idea of a physical-structure type that generates certain psychophysical laws connecting physical and psychological phenomena. The availability of such laws lends support to reductive materialism, involving species-specific reductions (reductions relative to what Kim calls "physical–biological structure-types"), and challenges nonreductive materialism.

Kim explores the contribution of the idea of supervenience to nonreductive materialism. He argues that a prominent kind of supervenience, so-called global supervenience, does not serve the purposes of materialism, on the ground that such supervenience does not preserve the kind of mental–physical dependency relation crucial to materialism. If one offers support for global supervenience on the basis of specific psychophysical dependencies, those dependencies will raise the threat of psychophysical laws and reduction. The prospects for nonreductive materialism, Kim concludes, are dim indeed. (For another argument against nonreductive materialism, see A. D. Smith 1993.) Kim's sketch of an alternative position paves the way for a kind of materialism permitting species-specific reductions of psychological to physical phenomena. The latter reductions are local rather than global, being relative to a specific physical base that is typically narrower than a biological species.

In Chapter 8, Paul Churchland characterizes eliminative materialism as the view that "our common-sense conception of psychological phenomena constitutes a radically false theory, a theory so fundamentally defective that both the principles and the ontology of that theory will eventually be displaced, rather than smoothly reduced, by completed neuroscience." Given such eliminativism, we should not expect our ordinary talk of such psychological states as beliefs and desires to be translated into, or otherwise reduced to, nonpsychological language congenial to materialism. Instead, we should expect ordinary talk of beliefs and desires to disappear – to be left behind as misguided – with the advance of our physical sciences. Eliminative materialists often propose, accordingly, that beliefs and desires will be to future science what demons are to contemporary science: nonexistent entities that were falsely assumed to exist at an earlier time, but that play no role in our best scientific theories.

Churchland portrays common-sense psychology as an empirical theory that plays a role in the explanation and prediction of human behavior. He calls this theory "folk psychology," adding that "the structural features of folk psychology parallel perfectly those of mathematical physics; the only difference lies in the respective domain of abstract entities they exploit – numbers in the case of physics, and propositions in the case of psychology." Churchland asks how the ontology, or existence claims, of folk psychology relate to the ontology of completed neuroscience. A reductive materialist holds that the ontology of folk psychology is smoothly reducible to the ontology of neuroscience. Dualists and nonreductive materialists (including functionalist materialists) deny such reducibility. Dualists acknowledge a domain of immaterial entities, whereas functionalist materialists acknowledge a domain of states characterized in terms of functional organization. Eliminative materialists, in contrast, hold that folk psychology is not only irreducible to neuroscience, but also too defective to serve *any* legitimate theoretical purpose.

Churchland faults folk psychology for failing to explain a wide range of important psychological phenomena: The nature of mental illness, learning, memory, creative imagination, sleep, and so on. Such explanatory deficiencies of folk psychology, according to Churchland, "show decisively that folk psychology is *at best* a highly superficial theory, a partial and unpenetrating gloss on a deeper and more complex reality." In addition, Churchland finds that folk psychology is "a stagnant or degenerating research program, and has been for millennia." The physical sciences, according to Churchland, clearly outperform folk psychology on the score of explanatory development, even in areas supposedly covered by folk psychology. The physical sciences, unlike folk psychology, seem to be an integral part of a growing explanatory synthesis.

Churchland opposes standard defenses of folk psychology by functionalists. He argues that common functionalist considerations favoring folk psychology can be used to support alchemy. Churchland concludes, accordingly, that "it is at least possible for the constellation of moves, claims, and defenses characteristic of functionalism to constitute an outrage against reason and truth, and to do so with a plausibility that is frightening."

Churchland sketches what the elimination of folk psychology might actually involve. Minimally, it involves the elimination of reference to such propositional attitudes as beliefs and desires. Ordinary talk of such attitudes would give way to the language of our best neuroscience; even first-person introspective reports would use the latter scientific language. As Churchland says, "it is not inconceivable that some segment of the population, or all of it, should become intimately familiar with the vocabulary required to characterize our kinematical states, learn the laws governing their interactions and behavioral projections, acquire a facility in their first-person ascription, and displace the use of folk psychology altogether, even in the marketplace." Common objections noting that eliminative materialists must *believe* their eliminativism leave Churchland unmoved. He claims that they simply beg the question, regarding the existence of beliefs, against eliminative materialism. For an alternative challenge to eliminativism, see Trout 1991.)

In Chapter 9, Frank Jackson sketches an argument against physicalism (the view that the actual world is entirely physical), and defends the argument against some objections from Paul Churchland. The argument relies on the case of Mary, who comes to know everything there is to know about the physical nature of the world, while she is confined to a black-and-white environment. Mary acquires exhaustive knowledge of physics and the other physical sciences. The issue is whether Mary actually knows *all* there is to know.

It seems, according to Jackson, that when Mary is released from her black-and-white environment, she will learn what it is like to see something red, for instance. She will thus come to learn something she did not know before. In her black-and-white environment, Mary did not know what the relevant experience of red is like. Mary's exhaustive knowledge of physics and other physical sciences thus omitted something. If this is so, Jackson contends, physicalism is false. Jackson holds that his knowledge argument against materialism shifts a serious burden of explanation to materialists. (For additional support for Jackson's argument against materialism, see Jackson 1982, and Robinson 1993; for criticisms, see Churchland 1989, chs 3, 4.)

Materialism and meaning

The previous section identified some troubling questions raised by materialist treatments of the mind. These questions are not necessarily handled better by immaterialist accounts of the mind, and some of the materialist approaches sketched might seem promising after all. Even so, materialists need to provide at least an initial account of the manner in which mental phenomena are physical, or at least are dependent on what is physical, if materialism in this area is to be anything but programmatic.

One way to articulate materialism and to display its strength is to provide a materialist account of a class of phenomena essentially related to mentality. Linguistic phenomena seem well-suited to this illustrative role. One general view about the relation between language and mind, associated as much with common sense as with the work of H. P. Grice, claims that the semantic features of *language* are inherited from the semantic properties of *mental states*: What a sentence means, on this view, depends in part on the user's intentions, what the user has in mind, including the thought expressed by the linguistic item. In their attempt to accommodate this widely held idea, the two theories of meaning that have dominated contemporary philosophy of language – verificationist and truth-conditional theories – offer distinctive ways of treating the question of the material basis of meaning.

Verificationist theories of meaning identify meanings with verification conditions, such as possible stimuli or verifiable states of affairs. Philosophers dispute the conditions required for verifiability. However, when concerned with the contribution of psychological factors to meaning, there is pressure for those of general verificationist inclination to offer behavioral criteria of meaning, and thus to offer an account of meaning that is behaviorist in spirit. A behaviorist theory of meaning identifies the meaning of a term or sentence with a person's dispositions to assent or dissent in verbal behavior. This behaviorist position is developed by W. V. O. Quine Chapter 10. Quine himself has opposed the nonholism of traditional verificationism in "Two Dogmas of Empiricism" (1951). In the present chapter Quine focuses on an issue about reference, about how our words are related to objects. The archetypal referring terms, for Quine, are individuative: "table," "chair," "dog," etc. We shall not review all the philosophical machinery – much of it empiricist in spirit – that Quine has used to defend his behaviorist account of language, but two such theses merit attention: The underdetermination of theory by evidence and the indeterminacy of translation.

The underdetermination of theory by evidence states that the choice of a theory is not uniquely determined by the class of observation statements relevant to the theory. On the basis of the same observational evidence alone, according to this thesis, it will always be possible to arrive at two theories that are inconsistent with each other. In accordance with his behaviorism, Quine holds that the primary psychological relation of reference is that of conditioned response. As part of his ontological program, Quine defines a "liberalized notion of a physical object as the material content of any place-time, any portion of space-time", and describes the conditions under which this conception provides a basis for ontological commitment, commitment that can be as economical or uneconomical as one likes. Together with the behaviorist account of reference, this liberalized notion of physical object makes possible endless reinterpretation of our scientific objects, through the use of a rule (or "proxy function", as Quine says) that translates one term into another on the basis of the same observations. The term "dog," for instance, might be recast as "space-time of a dog" or "place-time of a dog." Because all of these interpretations are compatible with all the observations (that is, no empirical evidence distinguishes the interpretations), reference, Quine says, is inscrutable. After all, "structure is what matters to a theory, and not the choice of its objects." In prime behaviorist fashion, Quine claims that "the scientific system, ontology and all, is a conceptual bridge of our own making, linking sensory stimulation to sensory stimulation."

Quine's treatment of reference is behaviorist, but in what sense is Quine's account of the relation of reference naturalistic? It is naturalistic in its treatment of the relation of reference as part of the subject matter of science. This naturalism seeks to allow us to lay claim to knowledge and at the same time acknowledge that principles of epistemic evaluation are to be found within science itself. The science here is behaviorist psychology. Ultimately, Quine's position concerning reference is as tenable, or untenable, as the behaviorism grounding it.

In Chapter 11, Michael Friedman argues that Quine's indeterminacy of translation thesis is neither expressed nor defended uniformly. Friedman distinguishes between an epistemological and an ontological form of the indeterminacy of translation thesis. Citing passages from Quine, Friedman articulates the epistemological thesis, that our data and methods do not determine a unique choice of a translation manual (a set of guidelines for converting an alien language into a familiar language), because there are incompatible translation manuals (or theories) equally well supported by all the observational evidence. The ontological construal, in contrast, states that a unique translation manual (or theory) is not even determined by the totality of facts, or by the totality of truths about nature. The ontological interpretation finds its support in Quine's famous remark that there is "no fact of the matter" about what is the correct translation theory. Since, for Quine, the totality of truths of nature is given by statements of physics, the ontological construal implies that no translation theory is uniquely determined by the truths of physics.

Friedman argues that the reason that physical facts do not determine translational facts is that translational and other semantic considerations are part of a higher-level discipline (psychology). As a higher-level discipline, psychology is no different from biology; the physical facts alone would not determine biological facts. The conclusion of (physicalist) ontological indeterminacy would be rejected by many physicalists, but Friedman argues that Quine is driven to it because he links the indeterminacy of translation to behaviorism.

In formulating a semantic theory, a focus on individuative words has distinct limitations, particularly if sentences as well are treated as significant units of meaning, and even more so if one's favored semantic view is truth-conditional. For example, individuative words do not have truth conditions; only statements have truth conditions. Words can have satisfaction conditions, and the sensory stimulation discussed by Quine is associated with particular words as well as occasion sentences. To that extent, the issue of truth-conditional semantics is somewhat orthogonal to the behaviorist account of meaning and translation considered here. Some theories of meaning, however, do not use purely behavioral criteria of meaning, and are not tied to the requirement that we know the conditions under which a statement would be empirically verified in order for the statement to have meaning. Truth-conditional theories of meaning, for example, assert that the meaning of a statement is determined by the conditions that make it true.

Some prominent truth-conditional theories of meaning, affirming that meaning consists in truth conditions, draw from Alfred Tarski's so-called semantic theory of truth. (See, for example, Davidson 1967; for discussion, see Soames 1992, 1994.) Tarski (1944) introduced the following principle not as a definition of "truth" but as an adequacy condition that must be met by any acceptable definition of "truth": S is true if and only if P (where "P" stands for a declarative sentence, and "S" stands for the name of that sentence.) Given Tarski's condition, the sentence "All college students are studious" is true if and only if all college students are studious. Because what follows "if and only if" in Tarski's adequacy condition connotes an actual situation to which the relevant true sentence is appropriately related, various philosophers have regarded Tarski's condition as specifying a correspondence requirement on truth. Philosophers still disagree, however, over whether Tarski actually offers a correspondence approach to truth. In any case, some theorists hold that a truth-conditional theory of meaning need not "break out of the circle of language," or otherwise invoke extralinguistic – say, causal – relations between language and the world. A notion of truth is a semantic notion, but it is, according to many philosophers, clearer than a notion of meaning.

Some semantic theorists have wanted a full explication of the notion of truth on which meaning depends. We might, for example, want a theory of meaning that *explains* truth conditions, and for this we will arguably need a notion of reference. If we consider the form of the two (dated, but graphic) claims,

Reagan is tough.
Thatcher is tough.

it seems that what the terms "Reagan" and "Thatcher" *refer to* figure in an explanation of the truth conditions those claims have. In terms of syntactic role and order, these sentences are syntactically indistinguishable. What, then, makes it the case that "Reagan is tough" is true if and only if Reagan is tough and *undetermined* by the conditions that make "Thatcher is tough" true? To explain this fact, we need to consider the relation of reference. "Reagan" refers to a particular President of the US, and "Thatcher" refers to a particular British Prime Minister. (Hartry Field (1972) has argued that Tarski's theory must be supplemented with a theory of reference, in particular, a notion of *primitive denotation*; and Michael Devitt (1991) has emphasized the consequences of this view in connection with a defense of scientific realism.)

An important problem confronts any truth-conditional theory that makes use of a causal theory of reference: Some claims that apparently differ in meaning seem to have the same truth-conditions. Consider "The Evening Star is Venus" and "The Morning Star is Venus." These claims apparently have the same truth-conditions, and they both tell us more than the vacuous claim that Venus is Venus. In addition, these claims differ in meaning, as someone might believe one without believing the other; accordingly, they may place different inferential roles in a person's thought. A truth-conditional semantics, therefore, may have to offer a theory of sense as well as a theory of reference. (For discussion of the sense–reference distinction, see the essays in Moore 1993.)

The meaning of a term, on a traditional view, is a concept or set of concepts, sometimes called the term's *intension*. This view suggests that, as concepts, meanings are something mental – a view called psychologism. By contrast, a term's *extension* is the class of objects to which the term applies. The extension of the term "bird" is the class of all birds. The intension of the term "bird" is given by the set of concepts associated with being feathered, having a beak, etc. If "intension" means something psychological, Frege (1892) would not identify sense with intension. Arguing against psychologism, Frege was impressed with the fact that different people could "grasp" *the same* meaning, and inferred that sense could not be a mental entity. Sense is, according to Frege, an abstract entity, in the way that a mathematical set is abstract. This notion of sense is bothersome to many physicalists, because it is not clear how a relation to an abstract entity is explainable in terms appropriate to physicalism.

A traditional theory of meaning incorporates the following assumptions:

1   Knowing the meaning of a term is just being in a certain psychological state, and "grasping" meaning is an individual psychological act or state.
2   We can distinguish the meanings of coextensive expressions, such as "creature with a heart" and "creature with a kidney".
3   It is impossible that terms with the same intension can have different extensions; that is, intension determines extension.

A theory of reference formulated by Saul Kripke and Hilary Putnam raises doubts about these assumptions. On Putnam's causal theory of natural-kind terms, the meaning of a term is fixed by its extension. A scientist discovers the essence of some natural kind such as gold, and in so doing, she in effect "dubs" the sample "gold" and establishes a causal relation between the term and the actual extension of the term "gold." Her use of the term then filters down to the average speaker and regulates his use. Actual essential features of gold, rather than its nominal (or phenomenal) features, regulate the scientist's use of the term; and the relations between extension, term, and speaker (expert and average) are causal, according to Putnam's theory.

Having defended a causal theory of reference in earlier works, Putnam argues, in Chapter 12, that a causal theory of reference cannot do the work asked of it in contemporary versions of materialist metaphysical realism. Metaphysical realism implies that our thoughts are about mind-independent objects, and that some of these thoughts correspond to a mind-independent reality. This correspondence relation, according to some realists, is *causal*. These realists hold, with regard to correspondence relations for language, that a causal theory of linguistic reference accounts for the relevant relation between word and world.

Putnam argues that there is a conflict between metaphysical materialism and the denial of "intrinsic" properties. It is now a received part of the philosophical culture, according to Putnam, that it makes no sense to say that some property is intrinsic or essential to an object irrespective of a *description* of that thing. To the extent that a causal theory of reference involves a certain kind of essentialism, Putnam contends, it is at odds with this received doctrine.

According to a causal theory of reference, a referring term must stand in an appropriate causal relation to some aspect of the world. If Putnam's critique of intrinsic properties is correct, then "no relation *C* is metaphysically singled out as *the* relation between thoughts and things; reference becomes an 'occult' phenomenon," on a causal theory of reference. A causal theory of reference implies that the world must supply the favored relation, and that implication, Putnam claims, is indefensible. Even if we accept a metaphysical realist's notion of correspondence, according to Putnam, "there are still infinitely many ways of *specifying* such a correspondence." The motivation for Putnam's opposition to reliance on correspondence relations is expressed in this question: "How can we pick out any *one* correspondence between our words (or thoughts) and the supposed mind-independent things if we have no direct access to the mind-independent things?" Putnam argues that an act of will or intention will not do the job. In the end, Putnam rejects essentialism, and endorses a version of pragmatism (so-called internal realism) that does without a correspondence notion of truth. Putnam's view implies that truth is whatever it is ideally rational to believe.

Some objects, most notably objects like computers and books, display apparently meaningful features, such as outputs and sentences, features that are semantically evaluable. In such cases, many philosophers have placed much weight on the notions of *derived* vs. *intrinsic* (or *original*) intentionality, arguing (for example) that humans but not computers have the latter. In Chapter 13, Daniel Dennett uses evolutionary themes to undermine the traditional distinction between intrinsic and derived intentionality. According to the traditional distinction, intrinsic intentionality is possessed by minds, typically human minds, and derived intentionality is had by artifacts, such as texts and computers. Dennett develops a test case for distinguishing those who hold that the question of whether a system has intrinsic intentionality is legitimate from those who do not. The test case concerns a vending machine – the two-bitser – designed to be a detector of US quarters. When a US quarter is inserted, the two-bitser goes into state *O*. As impressive as this vending machine is, it is fallible; sometimes non-US quarters kick it into state *O*, and sometimes genuine US quarters fail to cause state *O*. If "slugs" (or what Dennett refers to as objects of kind *K*) that can trick the two-bitser occur more frequently in the environment, then designers face a problem concerning the cost-effectiveness of the system. Should they make the machine more sensitive to counterfeits if doing so will also make it more expensive? Dennett claims that "the only thing that makes the device a quarter-detector rather than a slug-detector or a quarter-*or*-slug detector is the shared intention of the device's designers, builders, owners, users." He adds that "it is only relative to that context of intentions that we could justify calling the device a two-bitser in the first place." According to proponents of the traditional distinction between intrinsic and derived intentionality, in contrast, the two-bitser's ability is a paradigm case of derived intentionality.

Dennett defends his view on the basis of the following scenario. Suppose that the vending machine is transported to another environment, this time Panama, where the system makes "errors" (or at least they would have been so regarded prior to the machine's transport) by accepting Panamanian quarter-balboas. In this environment, US quarters count as slugs, and US quarter induced *O*-states count as misrepresentations. And since the two-bitser "has no intrinsic, original intentionality, . . . there is no 'deeper' fact of the matter we might try to uncover. This is just a pragmatic matter of how best to talk, when talking metaphorically and anthropomorphically about the states of the device." If we imagine Mother Nature or evolutionary forces, rather than engineers, as the designers of the relevant system, then, Dennett concludes, there is no more a "fact of the matter" about whether humans (or minds) have intrinsic intentionality than there is about whether the two-bitser does. Along the way to this conclusion, Dennett surveys a range of opposing positions developed by some of his critics.

The relation between materialism and meaning surfaces, often in muted ways, in other sections of this book. The semantics of moral terms and their material basis, for example, is a prominent topic in the section on materialism and value, to which we now turn.

Materialism and value

Materialism, understood as a comprehensive account of the world, must explain how moral phenomena fit into an altogether physical world. Moral phenomena include rightness, wrongness, goodness, badness, praiseworthiness, and blameworthiness. Many people regard such phenomena as different from what is *factual,* or at least different from what is *objective.* Many of these same people regard what is physical as factual, and thus they contrast physical phenomena and moral phenomena, sometimes in terms of a fact–value distinction. Many people regard the fact–value distinction as contrasting what is descriptive and what is normative.

Materialists do not share a unified account of how moral phenomena fit into the physical world. Some materialists are moral realists, endorsing the factuality of moral phenomena. Others are moral antirealists, denying the factuality of moral phenomena. Still others resist choosing between moral realism and moral antirealism, on the ground that the terms posing the choice are semantically ill-formed. The essays in the section on materialism and value include arguments for moral realism and moral antirealism from naturalistic perspectives.

In Chapter 14, Bernard Williams examines the ordinary distinction between science and ethics. He proposes that

> in a scientific enquiry there should ideally be convergence on an answer, where the best explanation of the convergence involves the idea that the answer represents how things are, whereas in the area of the ethical, at least at a high level of generality . . . there is no such coherent hope.

Williams claims that even if convergence sometimes results from ethical inquiry, such convergence will not have been guided by "how things actually are." In this connection, Williams relies on an "absolute conception" of the world, involving a representation of the world that is maximally independent of the peculiarities of our perspective. The absolute conception of the world signifies the world as it is independently of human experience.

Williams considers whether there is available a theory of knowledge for the convergence of ethical inquiry on a kind of objective ethical reality, on how things really are ethically. The issue is whether ethics enjoys, with regard to objectivity, an epistemological status analogous to scientific inquiry as ordinarily understood. Williams doubts that ethics has such a status. In particular, he doubts that ethical inquiry can be given an objective grounding in considerations about human nature. Williams concludes, therefore, that "there is a radical difference between ethics and science." If Williams is right, materialists will be hard put to explain how ethical phenomena fit neatly into the material world of natural sciences.

In Chapter 15, Richard Boyd characterizes moral realism as, roughly, the view that moral statements are true or false largely independently of our moral opinions, and ordinary standards of moral reasoning are largely reliable for obtaining moral knowledge. Given Boyd's moral realism,

> such moral terms as "good", "fair", "just", "obligatory" usually correspond to real properties or relations and . . . our ordinary standards for

moral reasoning ... constitute a fairly reliable way of finding out which events, persons, policies, social arrangements, etc. have these properties and enter into these relations.

Boyd thus defends the view that moral beliefs and methods are significantly similar to scientific beliefs and methods as ordinarily understood. On this matter, Boyd and Williams take opposing positions.

Boyd explains how certain recent work in naturalized epistemology, and philosophy of science, and the philosophy of language lends support to his moral realism. In particular, he sketches an account of moral properties in accordance with an account of natural definitions. Boyd's homeostatic property-cluster account of definition is especially suited to structurally complex functional phenomena in biological, psychological, and social systems. According to this account, the terms employed in explanations and inductions concerning causal structures ("natural kind terms") have at least two important features:

1 The possession of some cluster of properties may be sufficient for falling within the extension of the term;
2 the extension may be logically indeterminate; it need not have logically necessary and sufficient conditions for its application.

In the case of (1), the strength of the correlation among properties in the cluster may be *elucidated* statistically, but the co-occurrence of those properties is not *merely* statistical; one property may favor the presence of another. "Healthy" is one term that illustrates this phenomenon; its extension contains properties that are nonindependent. In the case of (2), a healthy individual may possess only some of the properties of the cluster pertinent to health enjoyed by another healthy individual. The terms in question have natural definitions, and no more precision is desirable than is allowed by nature. Linguistic precision purchased by stipulation, therefore, carries with it the price of misleading exactness and artificiality. Some longstanding philosophical theses, such as that natural-kind terms have necessary and sufficient conditions, are tacitly dictated by a mistaken semantic theory, according to Boyd's view.

Boyd proposes that the role played by observation in natural science has an analogous role played by observation in ethics. He holds that "goodness is an ordinary natural property, and it would be odd indeed if observations didn't play the same role in the study of this property that they play in the study of all the others." More specifically, Boyd offers an account of goodness implying that moral inquiry about goodness is, like psychology, history, and social science, a form of empirical inquiry about people. Boyd recommends his naturalistic moral realism on the ground that it promotes a unified view of science and ethics.

In Chapter 16, Simon Blackburn argues that naturalism favors an antirealist projective theory about ethics. He seeks to characterize ethical commitments in a way that contrasts with beliefs, and to give an evolutionary account of why the states that are ethical commitments actually exist. An ethical commitment, according to Blackburn, is a "standing stance," whereby one is "set to react in some way when an occasion arises." Some standing stances have evolutionary success; others do not. Blackburn notes that "evolutionary success may attend the animal that helps those that have helped it, but it would not attend an allegedly possible animal that thinks it ought to help but does not." In this respect, evolution favors action and tendencies to act. Nonetheless, Blackburn does not offer any kind of reduction of an ethical commitment to something else. He offers only an evolutionary explanation of the existence of ethical commitments.

Blackburn's projectivism is antirealist because it does not rely on a commitment to moral properties or moral facts. Its explanations of moral phenomena seek to explain ethical activity "from the inside out – from the naturally explicable attitudes to the forms of speech that communicate them, challenge them, refine them, and abandon them." Blackburn finds support for his naturalistic projectivism about ethics in the writings of Hume and Wittgenstein. His projectivism seeks to avoid difficult problems arising from the need for an ontology of morals.

ACKNOWLEDGMENT

We thank David Yandell and referees for comments on this introduction.

REFERENCES

Armstrong, D. M. (1977) "The causal theory of the mind," *Neue Heft für Philosophie* 11, 82–95. Reprinted in Armstrong (1980) *The Nature of Mind*, 16–31. St Lucia, Queensland: University of Queensland Press.

Bealer, George (1993) "Materialism and the logical structure of intentionality," in Howard Robinson (ed.) *Objections to Physicalism*, 101–26. Oxford: Clarendon Press.

Boyd, Richard (1980) "Materialism without reductionism: what physicalism does not entail," in Ned Block (ed.) *Readings in Philosophy of Psychology, Volume 1*, 67–106. Cambridge, Mass.: Harvard University Press.

Charles, David (1992) "Supervenience, composition, and physicalism," in David Charles and Kathleen Lennon (eds) *Reduction, Explanation, and Realism*, 265–96. Oxford: Clarendon Press.

Chomsky, Noam (1988) *Language and Problems of Knowledge*, Cambridge, Mass.: MIT Press.

Churchland, Paul (1989) *A Neurocomputational Perspective: The Nature of Mind and the Structure of Science*, Cambridge, Mass.: MIT Press.

Crane, Tim (1993) "Reply to Pettit," *Analysis* 53, 224–7.

Davidson, Donald (1967) "Truth and meaning," in Davidson, *Inquiries into Truth and Interpretation*, 17–36. Oxford: Clarendon Press.

—— (1974) "Psychology as philosophy," in Davidson (1980) *Essays on Actions and Events*, 229–39. Oxford: Clarendon Press.

—— (1985) "Reply to Patrick Suppes," in Bruce Vermazen and M. B. Hintikka (eds) *Essays on Davidson: Actions and Events*, 247–52. Oxford: Clarendon Press.

—— (1990) "Representation and interpretation," in K. A. Mohyeldin Said, W. H. Newton-Smith, R. Viale, and K. V. Wilkes (eds) *Modelling the Mind*, 13–26. Oxford: Clarendon Press.

—— (1993) "Thinking causes," in John Heil and Alfred Mele (eds) *Mental Causation*, 3–17. Oxford: Clarendon Press.

Devitt, Michael (1991) *Realism and Truth*, 2nd edn, Oxford: Blackwell.

Field, Hartry (1972) "Tarski's theory of truth," *The Journal of Philosophy* 69, 347–75.

Fodor, Jerry (1980) "Searle on what only brains can do," *The Behavioral and Brain Sciences* 3, 431–2.

—— (1981) "The mind–body problem," *Scientific American* 244, 114–23. Reprinted in P. K. Moser (ed.) (1990) *Reality in Focus*, 240–52. Englewood Cliffs, NJ: Prentice-Hall.

Frege, Gottlob (1892) "On sense and reference," in A. W. Moore (ed.) (1993) *Meaning and Reference*, 23–42. Oxford: Oxford University Press.

Hempel, Carl and Oppenheim, Paul (1948) "Studies in the logic of explanation," *Philosophy of Science* 15, 135–75. Reprinted in Hempel (1965) *Aspects of Scientific Explanation*, New York: The Free Press.

Hooker, C. A. (1981) "Towards a general theory of reduction," *Dialogue* 20, 38–59, 201–36, 496–529.

Jackson, Frank (1982) "Epiphenomenal qualia," *The Philosophical Quarterly* 32, 127–36.

Kim, Jaegwon (1993) "Can supervenience and 'non-strict laws' save anomalous monism?" in John Heil and Alfred Mele (eds) *Mental Causation*, 19–26. Oxford: Clarendon Press.

Kitcher, Philip (1981) "Explanatory unification," *Philosophy of Science* 48, 507–31.

—— (1989) "Explanatory unification and the causal structure of the world," in Philip Kitcher and Wesley Salmon (eds) *Minnesota Studies in the Philosophy of Science, Volume 13: Scientific Explanation*, 410–505. Minneapolis: University of Minnesota Press.

Lewis, David (1966) "An argument for the identity theory," *The Journal of Philosophy* 63, 17–25. Reprinted in David Rosenthal (ed.) (1971) *Materialism and the Mind–Body Problem*, 162–71. Englewood Cliffs, NJ: Prentice-Hall.

Moore, A. W. (ed.) (1993) *Meaning and Reference*, Oxford: Oxford University Press.

Moser, Paul K. (1993) *Philosophy After Objectivity*, New York: Oxford University Press.

Moser, Paul K. and Trout, J. D. (1995) "Physicalism, supervenience, and dependence," in Ü. D. Yalçin and E. E. Savellos (eds) *Supervenience: New Essays*, Cambridge: Cambridge University Press.

Papineau, David (1992) "Irreducibility and teleology," in David Charles and Kathleen Lennon (eds) *Reduction, Explanation, and Realism*, 45–68. Oxford: Clarendon Press.

Pettit, Philip (1993) "A definition of physicalism," *Analysis* 53, 213–23.

Putnam, Hilary (1988) *Representation and Reality*, Cambridge, Mass.: MIT Press.

Pylyshyn, Zenon (1980) "The 'causal power' of machines," *The Behavioral and Brain Sciences* 3, 442–3.

—— (1984) *Computation and Cognition*, Cambridge, Mass.: MIT Press.

Quine, W. V. O. (1990) *Pursuit of Truth*, Cambridge, Mass.: Harvard University Press.

Robinson, Howard (1993) "The anti-materialist strategy and the 'knowledge argument'," in Howard Robinson (ed.) *Objections to Physicalism*, 159–83. Oxford: Clarendon Press.

Rorty, Richard (1965) "Mind–body identity, privacy, and categories," *The Review of Metaphysics* 19, 24–54.

Salmon, Wesley (1989) *Four Decades of Scientific Explanation*, Minneapolis: University of Minnesota Press.

Searle, John (1980) "Minds, brains, and programs," *The Behavioral and Brain Sciences* 3, 417–24.

Searle, John (1992) *The Rediscovery of the Mind*, Cambridge, Mass.: MIT Press.

Smart, J. J. C. (1963) "Materialism," *The Journal of Philosophy* 60, 651–62.

Smith, A. D. (1993) "Non-reductive physicalism?" in Howard Robinson (ed.) *Objections to Physicalism*, 225–50. Oxford: Clarendon Press.

Smith, Peter (1992) "Modest reductions and the unity of science," in David Charles and Kathleen Lennon (eds) *Reduction, Explanation, and Realism*, 19–43. Oxford: Clarendon Press.

Soames, Scott (1992) "Truth, meaning, and understanding," *Philosophical Studies* 65, 17–35.

—— (1994) "Introduction," in R. M. Harnish (ed.) *Basic Topics in the Philosophy of Language*, 493–516. Englewood Cliffs, NJ: Prentice Hall.

Sosa, Ernest (1993) "Davidson's thinking causes," in John Heil and Alfred Mele (eds) *Mental Causation*, 41–50. Oxford: Clarendon Press.

Stich, S. P. (1983) *From Folk Psychology to Cognitive Science: The Case Against Belief*, Cambridge, Mass.: MIT Press.

Tarski, Alfred (1944) "The semantic conception of truth and the foundations of semantics," *Philosophy and Phenomenological Research* 4, 341–75. Reprinted in R. M. Harnish (ed.) (1994) *Basic Topics in the Philosophy of Language*, 536–70. Englewood Cliffs, NJ: Prentice-Hall.

Trout, J. D. (1991) "Belief-attribution in science: Folk psychology under theoretical stress," *Synthese* 87, 379–400.

Part I

Materialism and Naturalism

1   Naturalism, Materialism, and First Philosophy

David M. Armstrong

In the first section of this paper, I define and defend a spatio-temporal account of the general nature of reality. I call this doctrine "Naturalism". In the second section, I define and defend the somewhat more specific, although still very general, doctrine of Materialism or Physicalism. (I take it to be a sub-species of Naturalism.) However, if we define ontology or "first philosophy" as the most abstract or general theory of reality, then it seems that neither Materialism nor even Naturalism is an ontology. In the third section, I sketch very briefly the ontology I favour. Unlike that adopted by many Naturalists and Materialists, it admits both particulars and universals. It is Realistic, not Nominalistic. I maintain, in particular, that only by adopting a Realistic (but not Platonistic) account of universals can the Naturalist and the Materialist solve the pressing problems of the nature of causation and of law-like connection.

NATURALISM

Naturalism I define as the doctrine that reality consists of nothing but a single all-embracing spatio-temporal system. It is convenient here to distinguish this proposition from the weaker claim that reality at least contains as a part a spatio-temporal system. I will say something in defence of the weaker claim first, and then defend the view that reality is nothing but this spatio-temporal system.

It is difficult to deny that a spatio-temporal system *appears* to exist. But, of course, many philosophers have denied that this appearance is a reality. Leibniz is an example. He held that reality consists of the monads and that space and time are illusions, even if illusions that have some systematic link with reality. Leibniz was at least a pluralist. But for Parmenides, for Hegel and for Bradley, reality is not a plurality but is simply one. The spatio-temporal system is an appearance that completely or almost completely misrepresents the one.

I will not spend any time considering such views, despite their importance. The arguments used to establish them are all *a priori*. I believe that they can all be answered. But in any case, as an Empiricist, I reject the whole conception of establishing such results by *a priori* argumentation.

But the Naturalist may seem to face a challenge to the view that there is a spatio-temporal system from a source that he must take more seriously:

from natural science itself. It is the impression of an outsider like myself that *some* speculations in fundamental physics lead to the conclusion that, at deep levels of explanation, space and time dissolve and require to be replaced by other, more fundamental, principles.

However, I suggest that such speculations need not perturb the Naturalist. I believe that he should draw the familiar distinction between denying that a certain entity exists and giving an account of that entity in terms of other entities. It is a very extreme view to deny that the world has spatio-temporal features. I find it hard to believe that even the most far-fetched speculations in fundamental physics require such a denial. But it involves no such denial to assert that the spatio-temporal features of things can be ultimately analysed in terms that do not involve any appeal to spatio-temporal notions. The Naturalist, as I have defined Naturalism, is committed to the assertion that there is a spatio-temporal system. But why is he committed to asserting that spatio-temporality cannot be analysed in terms of non-spatio-temporal principles? What is not ultimate may yet be real. I suppose that if the principles involved were completely different from the current principles of physics, in particular if they involve appeal to mental entities, such as purposes, we might then count the analysis as a falsification of Naturalism. But the Naturalist need make no more concession than this.

Consider, as a parallel example, the attitude of Materialists towards *purposes*. There are some Materialists who deny that men and other organisms have purposes. This seems to me to be a quite foolish position to adopt. Materialism may be true – my hypothesis is that it is true – but it is a speculative doctrine. The existence of purposes, on the other hand, is a plain matter of fact. The prudent Materialist therefore will argue in the following way. There is no reason to believe that what it is for an organism to have a purpose involves anything more than the operation of purely physical processes in the organism. (These mechanisms are, perhaps, very sophisticated cybernetic processes.) In this way, an account of purposes is proposed in terms of processes that do not themselves involve purpose. No doubt this is a somewhat deflationary view of what a purpose is. But it is a view of the nature of purposes, not a denial of them.

Spatio-temporality may be analysed, just as the Materialist claims that purpose can be analysed. However, in default of some quite extraordinary analysis of spatio-temporality – say, in terms of spiritual principles – Naturalism is not thereby falsified. But, just as it is an incredible view that purposes can be analysed *away*, so, I think, it is an incredible view that spatio-temporality could be analysed *away*. A priori reasoning should not convince us of the unreality of space and time. Nor, I have just argued, is it at all plausible that *a posteriori* reasoning will ever drive us to the same conclusion.

So much by way of brief defence of the positive content of Naturalism. I turn now to its negative contention: that the world is nothing *more* than a spatio-temporal system. Here we find that philosophers and others have postulated a bewildering variety of additional entities. Most doctrines of God place him beyond space and time. Then there are transcendent universals, the realm of numbers, transcendent standards of value, timeless

propositions, non-existent objects such as the golden mountain, possibilities over and above actualities ("possible worlds"), and "abstract" classes,
including that most dilute of all entities: the null-class. Dualist theories of
mind are interesting intermediate cases, because they place the mind in
time but not in space. The same holds for some theories of God and also,
apparently, for Karl Popper's recently proposed "third world" of theories,
which interacts with the "second" world of mind (Popper, 1973: chs. 3–4).

Despite the incredible diversity of these postulations, it seems that the
Naturalist can advance a single, very powerful, line of argument that is a
difficulty for them all. The argument takes the form of a dilemma. Are these
entities, or are they not, capable of action upon the spatio-temporal system?
Do these entities, or do they not, act in nature?

In the case of many of these entities, they were at least originally
conceived of as acting in nature. God acted in the world. The Forms in
Plato's *Phaedo* are causes, and the Forms were apparently transcendent
universals, as well as being transcendent numbers and transcendent
standards of value. Descartes' spiritual substances interact with matter, and
Popper's "third world" interacts with the "second world" of mind, which in
turn interacts with material things.

Nevertheless, there are very great difficulties involved in holding that any
of these transcendent entities act upon the spatio-temporal system.

First, there are logical or conceptual difficulties. A great many of these
entities are not thought of as capable of change. This holds for transcendent
universals, the realm of numbers and values, propositions, non-existent
objects, possible worlds and abstract classes. In many theological systems,
God is taken not to change. Now in typical cases of causation, one *change*
brings about another. It follows that, if these entities work causally in the
world, they do not work in this typical way. How, then, do they work? Could
they be conceived of as *sustaining* certain features of the natural world, or as
exerting some sort of steady, unchanging, *pressure* upon it that, when certain
circumstances arise in nature, gives rise to certain effects? Such a notion is
perhaps barely possible, but the actual *identification* of such alleged causal
operation is a major difficulty. For instance, where sustaining causes are
postulated *in nature*, hypotheses about such causes can be tested by observing
situations where the alleged sustaining cause is absent. If the alleged effect is
also absent, the hypothesis is supported. But no such verification is possible,
even in principle, in the case of unchanging entities.

In the *Parmenides* (133*b*–134*e*), Plato goes so far as to raise logical
difficulties for the conception of *any relation at all* (and so, *a fortiori*, a causal
one) between the Forms and spatio-temporal particulars.

Even in the relatively straightforward case of the interaction of spiritual
substance with material body, conceptual difficulties have been raised. For
instance, the impossibility of specifying any mechanism or other explanation of how the spirit acts upon its body has been thought to be a problem.
Descartes himself, as evidenced in particular by his correspondence with
Princess Elizabeth, thought that the action of spirit on matter involved
some conceptual difficulty.

In the case of many of the postulated transcendent entities, there never was any thought of crediting them with causal power in the natural world. Possible worlds, for instance, are not thought to act upon the actual world. But even in the case of entities originally credited with power in the natural world, considerations of the sort just sketched have been an important pressure towards denying that they had such power.

I confess, however, that it is not upon these conceptual difficulties that I, as a Naturalist, would place the most weight. Instead, I would appeal to natural science. It seems to me that the development of the natural sciences very strongly suggests that Nature, the spatio-temporal system, is a *causally self-enclosed system*. We have rather good scientific reasons to believe that, whatever occurs in this system, if it has a cause at all, is caused solely by other events (processes etc.) in the spatio-temporal system. Of course, this proposition is not susceptible of strict proof. But in the present state of scientific knowledge, it looks a promising bet.

In the past, religious thinkers thought of God as intervening freely in the spatio-temporal world. He might give victory to the righteous or answer prayers for rain *in defiance of the way that matters would have shaped if the spatio-temporal system had been left to its own devices*. But even those who still believe in a transcendent God are increasingly reluctant to believe that he acts upon Nature in this way. They hold that he created it, and created it for a purpose which is working itself out. But does he ever intervene?

Consider, again, the Dualist theory of the mind. Descartes saw clearly that, if Dualist Interactionism was to be made plausible, then he must postulate places in the human brain where physical events occurred, the immediate causes of which were, in part at least, spiritual happenings. He guessed that this happened in the pineal gland, but we now know that the pineal gland can play no such role. Where, then, do spiritual happenings have their immediate physical effects? Nobody has come up with a plausible suggestion. Most neurophysiologists would be astounded to hear that what happens to the brain has any other cause except earlier states of the brain and its physical environment.

Yet the cases of God and the soul are the two most plausible cases of things outside the spatio-temporal system acting upon it. (It is noteworthy that they are the two examples that *non-philosophers* would be most likely to give of things outside Nature acting upon Nature.) If the anti-Naturalist case is weak here, it is far more unpromising in the other cases. Suppose, for instance, that there is a transcendent realm of numbers. How scientifically implausible to think that this realm, or members of this realm, can act on brains!

So let us now explore the other horn of the dilemma. Let us assume that no transcendent entity acts in nature. I maintain that this remedy is worse than the disease. The anti-Naturalist goes from a hot frying-pan into a blazing fire.

The argument is simply this. The spatio-temporal system certainly exists. Whether anything else exists is controversial. If any entities outside the system are postulated, but have no effect on the system, there is no compelling reason to postulate them. Occam's razor then enjoins us not to postulate them.

Natural science has made spectacular advances as a result of the postulation of unobservable entities. Consider microbes, genes, atoms, molecules, electrons, quarks and black holes. The value of such postulations is a standing reproach to any positivistic conception of natural science. Now, contemporary analytic philosophers are deeply affected by the justified reaction against positivism. As a result, the fashionable defence of transcendent entities is to compare them with the theoretical entities of natural science of the sort just mentioned. For instance, "abstract" classes (classes over and above the aggregates of their members) are postulated on the ground that, by their means, we can explain what mathematics is about, mathematics which in turn is required for the truth of physics, which explains the workings of Nature. The justification for the introduction of abstract classes is thus no different from the justification for the introduction of electrons.

In fact, however, the resemblance is superficial only. There is this vital difference. Abstract classes, to continue with these as our example, provide objects the existence of which, perhaps, can serve as the *truth-conditions* for the propositions of mathematics. But this *semantic* function is the only function that they perform. They do not *bring about* anything physical in the way that genes and electrons do. In what way, then, can they help to explain the behaviour of physical things? Physics requires mathematics. That is not in dispute. But must it not be possible to give an explanation of the truth-conditions of mathematical statements purely in terms of the physical phenomena that they apply to?

Consider, as a parallel, the dispute in the philosophy of perception between upholders of the Representative theory and the Phenomenalists. The former theory postulates physical objects behind the immediately perceived sense-data, the latter gives an account of physical reality in terms of sense-data alone. Although I reject both theories, I have no doubt that the former is by far the more satisfactory. Suppose, however, that we were to knock away the central prop of the Representative theory and deny that physical objects had any power to *cause* sense-data. The Representative theory would then be a worthless one. It would be a bad joke to support it by pointing out that the postulated objects at least provide truth-conditions for physical-object statements. If, furthermore, the only possible alternative theory was Phenomenalism, then we would be under intellectual necessity to accept some Phenomenalist account of physical-object statements. Equally, I suggest, if the anti-Naturalist fails to endow his transcendent possibilities, numbers, classes, etc. with any this-worldly powers, then they explain nothing. We must insist, against him, that statements about possibilities, numbers, classes, etc. be given a this-worldly interpretation.

What these interpretations are to be is, of course, a very difficult matter. In the case of the statements of mathematics, for instance, I do not know that we have a currently satisfactory this-worldly account of them. But there surely must be such an account. The incredible usefulness of mathematics in reasoning about nature seems to guarantee this. It then must be correct to prefer such an account to one that postulates powerless entities outside that world.

In Plato's *Sophist*, the Eleatic Stranger suggests that power is the mark of being (274D–E). I think he is at least this far correct: if a thing lacks any power, if it has no possible effects, then, although it may exist, we can never have any *good reason* to believe that it exists. Like all contemporary analytic philosophers, I reject the Verification principle. But perhaps the Verification principle does grope for a truth: the Eleatic Stranger's principle weakened in the way that I have suggested. And if it is only spatio-temporal things that have power, the principle bids us postulate no other realities.

It seems, then, that the anti-Naturalist who nevertheless admits the existence of a spatio-temporal reality must try to endow his extra entities with power to affect that reality, on pain of making his postulation otiose. Yet, in the present state of scientific knowledge, it seems implausible to endow these entities with such power. I conclude that we have rather good reasons for accepting Naturalism.

MATERIALISM

It seems best to take Materialism as a sub-species of Naturalism. Contemporary Materialism can, of course, claim to be no more than the descendent of the Materialism of Leucippus, Lucretius and Hobbes. I follow J. J. C. Smart (1963) and identify contemporary Materialism (or Physicalism) with the view that the world contains nothing but the entities recognized by physics. Contemporary Materialism takes a Realistic view of the theoretical entities of physics – molecule, atom, fundamental particle, and so on – and then asserts that everything there is is wholly constituted by such entities, their connections and arrangements.

The Naturalist, we saw, has first to defend himself against the objection that, so far from being the sole reality, the spatio-temporal system is not real at all. In the same way, even after Naturalism has been accepted, the Materialist must defend himself against the objection that, so far from the theoretical entities of physics being the sole realities, all that is real are ordinary macroscopic objects. Such a view is held by those who take an Instrumentalist or Operationalist view of physics. They do not deny the truth of the propositions of physics, but they deny that the truth-conditions of these propositions require the existence of any of the *entities* that the propositions appear to name. The propositions of physics do nothing but tell us how macroscopic objects behave.

The credit of such doctrines is now deservedly low, as low as the credit of Phenomenalism about ordinary macroscopic objects. One striking argument, which I first heard put forward by C. B. Martin, is drawn from physics itself. According to physical theory, macroscopic objects consist of fundamental particles associated with each other in complex ways. But physical theory also allows that these particles may exist not so associated with each other, and it is theoretically possible that none of them should be so associated. In such a theoretically possible state of affairs there would be no macroscopic objects, although there would be fundamental particles. But, if Instrumentalism or Operationalism is correct, this state of affairs should be logically impossible.

I believe, therefore, that we should take a Realistic view of the entities of physics. We saw in discussing Naturalism that to accept the reality of the spatio-temporal system does not preclude the view that a deeper analysis of that system may yet be given in terms that do not involve spatio-temporal notions. In the same way, of course, to take a Realistic view of physics does not rule out the possibility of reaching a deeper level of analysis in terms of which a reductive account is given of the entities and principles currently treated as fundamental.

The main difficulties proposed for contemporary Materialism, at any rate by contemporary philosophers, are those of the apparent *irreducible intentionality* of mental processes, and the apparent *irreducible simplicity* of the secondary qualities. A word about each.

First, intentionality. Given what I take to be the utter implausibility of Behaviourism, then it seems that a Materialist must follow Hobbes and identify mental processes with some subset of processes in the central nervous system. But now consider such paradigm examples of mental processes as purposes and beliefs. They have the characteristic of *intentionality*: they point to a possible reality – the thing purposed or believed – which may or may not exist. Brentano held that intentionality was a defining characteristic of mental processes; and, more to the current point, that it was an irreducible characteristic. If intentionality is irreducible, then Materialism is false. (Irreducible intentionality may be compatible with *Naturalism*.) For such an irreducible characteristic has no place in physics as we now conceive physics. The Materialist therefore is committed to giving some *reductive* account of the intentionality of mental processes. Such an account is not all that easy to give.

A second objection to Materialism is provided by the alleged irreducibility of the secondary qualities, or, as Herbert Feigl calls them, the "raw feels". (His phrase is somewhat tendentious because it begs the question in favour of a *subjectivist* account of these qualities.) If they are irreducible, they fall outside the scope of physics. They are, in Feigl's famous phrase, "nomological danglers". They can only be linked to physical states of affairs by arbitrary bridge-laws (Feigl, 1967). (Once again, irreducible secondary qualities seem to be compatible with mere *Naturalism*.)

I believe, however, that the contemporary Materialist can argue against irreducible intentionality and irreducible secondary qualities in much the same way that, as we have seen, the Naturalist can argue against transcendent entities. The argument involves posing a dilemma parallel to the dilemma posed for Naturalism. "Does intentionality, and do the secondary qualities, bestow any causal power?"

Suppose first that they do bestow causal power. If they do, and if this power is to be detectable, then whatever entities have these properties, will, in suitable circumstances, act according to different laws from objects that lack these properties. Entities lacking these properties simply will obey the laws of physics. But particulars that have these extra or emergent properties also will obey extra or emergent laws.

I argued in the previous section that the anti-Naturalist does best to bestow causal powers on his transcendent entities. In the same way, I think that the Naturalist anti-Materialist who believes in irreducible intentionality and irreducible secondary qualities does best to treat these extra characteristics as bestowing extra powers. Nevertheless, as I now proceed to argue, to take this line is to embrace a scientifically implausible view.

It is, of course, being assumed at this point that a Realist view is taken of the theoretical entities of physics. Physical objects will be arrangements of, say, fundamental particles and will obey the laws of physics. Given certain very complex arrangements of fundamental particles, however, certain further properties of the complexes emerge – the property of intentionality and the secondary qualities. Complexes that have these further properties are supposed to obey further laws besides the laws of physics. Now there seems no conceptual difficulty in this supposition, but, in the light of present knowledge, it seems scientifically implausible. I do not claim that it is as scientifically implausible as the view that the spatio-temporal system is not causally self-contained. But the Materialist seems to be placing a good scientific bet if he bets against these emergent laws. There is little evidence, for instance, that the brain obeys any different laws from any other physical object. Yet it is the brain, if anywhere, where emergent laws might be expected.

At any rate, just as in the case of anti-Naturalism, many anti-Materialists are unwilling to credit their extra properties with bestowing any extra power. Intentionality and the secondary qualities, they conclude, are epiphenomenal, getting a free ride upon certain configurations of matter but doing no work themselves. In this way, anti-Materialists seek to compromise with Materialism. I think, however, that the result is only to compromise their anti-Materialism.

The argument against this second horn of the dilemma is the same as that against the anti-Naturalist. If these characteristics fail to endow the particulars that they characterize with causal powers, then, with regard to the rest of the world, it is as if they did not exist. The world goes on exactly as if they are not there – and note that "the world's going on" includes everything that anybody *says* or *thinks*. We can have no more reason to postulate such causally idle properties than causally idle objects. For instance, since the causes of the anti-Materialist's beliefs, on this hypothesis, are something other than these alleged properties, there seems no reason to hold the anti-Materialist beliefs.

Instead, I suggest, we do better to argue in this way:

1 The cause of all human (and animal) movements lies solely in physical processes working solely according to the laws of physics.
2 Purposes and beliefs, in their character of purposes and beliefs, cause human (and animal) movements.
∴ 3 Purposes and beliefs are nothing but physical processes working solely according to the laws of physics.

Again,

1 The cause of the expansion of mercury in a thermometer is always a purely physical one.

2 Something's being hot can cause the expansion of mercury in a thermometer.

∴ 3 Something's being hot is a purely physical state of affairs.[1]

In the case of Naturalism, we saw that the arguments for it require to be supplemented by giving a this-worldly account of statements that make ostensible reference to transcendent entities. That task is not easy, nor did I attempt it in this paper. In the case of Materialism, similarly, we require some positive account, at least compatible with Materialism, of the nature of intentional mental processes and of the secondary qualities. This task is not easy either, although I am hopeful that it can be accomplished.[2]

FIRST PHILOSOPHY

But if we mean by an ontology, or first philosophy, the theory of the most general categories of all – such notions as particularity, universality, number, substance and causality – then Materialism is not a first philosophy, nor even is Naturalism. What is more, Naturalism and Materialism seem to be *prima facie* compatible with various different first philosophies.

Historically, however, there is a link between Naturalism and Materialism, on the one hand, and *Nominalism*, interpreted as the doctrine that nothing exists except particulars, on the other. Naturalists and Materialists are regularly found denying the reality of universals.

What these three doctrines appear to have in common is their commitment to Empiricism, to the method of observation and experiment, the method of the natural sciences, as opposed to the attempt to gain knowledge by *a priori* reasoning. The central methodological postulate of natural science is that knowledge is not to be gained *a priori*. As Popper has insisted, scientific *hypotheses* need not be suggested by experience. But the testing and verification of hypotheses demands experience, observation and a submission to the facts as found. Since contemporary if not past Materialism claims to spring out of scientific results and plausible speculations, it is committed to Empiricism.

It is true that Materialism has sometimes seemed to be an anti-Empiricist doctrine. Both older and contemporary Materialism are doctrines that in some degree make rape of the senses, and hold that immediate observations give but a first and imperfect clue to the nature of reality. However, Materialism is only anti-Empiricist if we identify Empiricism with such doctrines as Phenomenalism, Positivism, Instrumentalism and Operationalism. These doctrines make immediate observation not merely the first, but the last, word about the nature of reality. They are excesses of Empiricism.

So the ontologies of Naturalism and Materialism have a natural link with the epistemology of Empiricism. Nominalism, it is often felt, has also a natural link with Empiricism. Realism about universals, on the other hand, is often linked with *a priori* reasoning (in particular, with the *a priori* science of mathematics).

In my view, there need be no such links. Naturalism and Materialism cannot, of course, have any truck with transcendent or Platonic Realism. But why cannot Naturalists and Materialists accept the more moderate doctrine of *universalia in rebus*? (And, for relations, *universalia inter res*?) Why should they not accept the view that particulars have objective properties and relations, properties and relations that are universals? Naturalism and Materialism then could be interpreted as very general theories about *what properties and relations particulars have.*

I cannot take the time here to discuss the difficulties facing Nominalism, but I am convinced that they are overwhelming. No version of Nominalism can ever explain the *unity* of the classes of particulars said to have the same property, nor give any coherent account of relations. Still more difficult is the attempt to combine Nominalism with Naturalism and Materialism, for then there is no question of calling in new entities, such as abstract classes or merely possible particulars, to make up for the missing properties and relations. It seems to me, indeed, that, despite tradition, it is intellectually most plausible to combine Naturalism and Materialism with moderate Realism. (Although the great American philosopher C. S. Peirce was not a Materialist, he was a Naturalist and a moderate Realist, and I think that he would have accepted the general stand I take here.)

Why have Naturalists and Materialists been attracted to Nominalism? Is it simply the agreeably hard-headed sound of the doctrine that nothing exists except particulars? Not altogether, perhaps. There is one line of argument for Realism about universals that appears to me to have had the effect of discrediting Realism, at least among Empiricists. It is the argument from the meaning of general terms. This is the argument that general words are meaningful, meaning is a dyadic relation, hence there must be entities for such words to mean, these somethings cannot be particulars, hence they are universals. This argument is very weak, depending as it does upon the untenable assumption that meaning is a *relation* between an expression and the thing it means. But far worse than this, it has served to destroy the credit of Realism with Empiricists. For if it is legitimate to move from the meaning of general terms or predicates to universals in this automatic way, it is established *a priori* that for each general term with a distinct meaning there is a distinct universal to be that meaning. It is this, I suggest, that Empiricists were unable to swallow. It offended against their central epistemological principle that knowledge of the existence of entities is to be gained *a posteriori*. Unfortunately, however, as often happens in such matters, Empiricists mostly drew what I think was the wrong moral. They should have concluded that the Argument from Meaning is unsound, and rested the case for universals, as it is easy to rest it, upon other considerations. (In particular, upon Plato's "One over Many" argument.) Instead they rejected Realism altogether.

I wish to combine Naturalism and Materialism with what may be called *a posteriori* Realism. Things (particulars) have objective properties and relations, and these properties and relations are universals, monadic and polyadic universals. But what properties and what relations there are is not to be read off from discourse. Universals are not meanings. It cannot be assumed that because a general predicate exists, that a universal exists in virtue of which this predicate applies. Normally it doesn't. Instead we should look to total science to tell us what properties and what relations there are. It is the properties and relations of particulars that determine the causal powers of the particulars.

In this way, *a posteriori* Realism, Naturalism and Materialism are seen to rest upon a common intellectual basis. That basis is the view that the best guide we have to the nature of reality is provided by natural science. Naturalism and Materialism, although of course still very general theories, then emerge as *specifications of a posteriori* Realism: they are views about the general nature of those properties and relations that particulars actually have.

Much remains to be said in defence of, and in elaboration of, *a posteriori* Realism, but little of that much can be said here.[3] I will indicate only, very briefly, how I think that such a Realism gives promise of solving the problem, which, if it *is* not, at least *ought to be*, the central problem that faces a Naturalist and a Materialist philosophy. This is the problem of the nature of causation and law-like connection.

That there is a deep problem here is very generally, if sometimes grudgingly, admitted by all Empiricists. It is difficult, I believe impossible, to make sense of causal connection apart from law-like connection, or of law-like connection apart from some sort of universal connection: "constant conjunction" in Hume's terms. Causation involves law, law involves regularity. So much seems to be indisputable. But then the question arises whether causation and law-like connection involve anything *more* than regularity. Here the difficulty has been to see what more could be involved. At the same time, it is a profoundly sceptical doctrine that nothing more is involved. The universe is surely more of a unity than Hume thought. Furthermore, it is a scepticism that seems unable to solve certain technical problems, in particular the way that statements of law-like connection appear to sustain contrary-to-fact conditional statements while statements of mere regularity do not. Yet the Empiricist who is also a Nominalist is locked, or, perhaps better, humed into this sceptical position with all its difficulties.

It has long been recognized, however – it appears that Plato and Aristotle realized – that the acceptance of a Realistic doctrine of universals is at least the first step to a solution of the problem. I would try to develop the solution further in the following way.

I distinguish first between *first-order* universals, which are properties and relations of ordinary, first-order particulars, and *second-order* universals. The latter are the properties and the relations of the first-order universals. Since the argument to universals from meanings has been rejected, the mere applicability of various one-place and many-place predicates to first-order universals does not automatically ensure that they themselves have properties and relations. But, although I make no attempt to argue the matter here, I think it can be successfully maintained that they do have certain properties and relations. However, these second-order properties and relations are all of the purely formal or topic-neutral sort.

With regard to the properties of universals, there will be such things as complexity (including, perhaps, infinite complexity) and other structural features. Whether certain universals are or are not, for instance, complex, is a matter to be determined *a posteriori*. As for the *relations* of universals, besides those of inclusion and overlap (partial identity), one universal may necessitate, probability in some degree, or exclude another universal.

Let us concentrate upon the relation of necessitation that one particular universal may bear to another. It is not logical necessitation. The relation would not obtain "in every possible world". Following in the footsteps of many other philosophers, we may call it *natural* necessitation. It is to be discovered *a posteriori*, by the experiential and experimental methods of natural science. But if such a relation exists between certain universals, then it entails a "constant conjunction" between the particulars falling under these universals. A particular fact about the connection of certain universals logically necessitates a general fact about the connection of (first-order) particulars. Take an artificially simple example, and suppose that the universal *being F* necessitates *being G*. This non-logical necessitation entails that, for all x, if x is F, then x is G. But the reverse entailment does not hold. It might be the case that, for all x, if x is F, then x is G, but fail to be the case that *being F* necessitates *being G*. In the latter case, there would be no more than an "accidental" universal conjunction of the two properties in the particulars.

Nomic or law-like necessity I take to be such a relation between universals. Causal connection I take to be a particular (and very complex) case of law-like necessity, and so to involve relations between universals.

I hope that this mere lightning sketch of a line of thought indicates some of the attractions that a moderate and *a posteriori* Realism has for an Empiricist like myself. It seems to me to be the natural first philosophy to combine with Naturalism and Materialism. But, more than that, *a posteriori* Realism, especially when linked with a doctrine of natural necessitation, furnishes a natural and fruitful perspective from which to view the whole dispute about the truth or falsity of these two very general cosmological hypotheses.

NOTES

1   For the first of these arguments, see Medlin, 1967: sect. 2.
2   My own suggestions for accomplishing it may be found in my *A Materialist Theory of the Mind* (1968) and *Belief, Truth and Knowledge* (1973).
3   I have tried to sketch an *a posteriori* Realism about universals in my "Towards a theory of properties: Work in progress on the problems of universals" (1975). The position is developed in my book *Universals and Scientific Realism* (1978).

REFERENCES

Armstrong, D. M. (1968) *A Materialist Theory of the Mind*, London: Routledge & Kegan Paul.
——— (1973) *Belief, Truth and Knowledge*, Cambridge: Cambridge University Press.
——— (1975) "Towards a theory of properties: Work in progress on the problems of universals", *Philosophy* 50, 145–55.

―――― (1978) *Universals and Scientific Realism*, 2 vols, Cambridge: Cambridge University Press.

Feigl, H. (1967) *The "Mental" and the "Physical"*, Minneapolis: Minnesota University Press.

Medlin, B. (1967) "Ryle and the mechanical hypothesis", in C. F. Presley (ed.) *The Identity Theory of Mind*, 94–150. St Lucia: Queensland University Press.

Popper, K. R. (1973) *Objective Knowledge*, Oxford: Oxford University Press.

Smart, J. J. C. (1963) *Philosophy and Scientific Realism*, London: Routledge & Kegan Paul.

POSTSCRIPT: "NATURALISM, MATERIALISM, AND FIRST PHILOSOPHY" RECONSIDERED

1 NATURALISM

In the first section of my paper I defended Naturalism, defined ontologically rather than epistemically as "a spatio-temporal account of the general nature of reality". I don't find much to disagree with in what I said there.

It has for long seemed to me that, before Darwin, the view that the organic part of nature, at least, had a transcendent designer had a lot to be said for it. As William Paley argued in his *Natural Theology* (fp 1802, 1964), just as a watch bespeaks a human designer, a functioning human eye is plausibly taken as bespeaking an indefinitely more powerful designer. Plausibly taken, that is, until we have the theory of natural selection over extremely long periods of time, backed up by contemporary genetic theory that sketches a mechanism for the details of such selection. No threat to Naturalism from biological fact then, I would suppose, nor even a threat to Materialism.

But a new challenge to Naturalism has emerged in recent years, coming not from biology but from physics. All that at present we know or can plausibly hypothesize about the world is that it begins with a "big bang" – which may create time and space – and which after 15 billion years or so of events that can more or less be traced, gives us our present situation and lets us go on to an uncertain future. There may be more to the space-time world than this, but we have no real evidence that there is anything more.

In this situation, there is a good deal of evidence that the creation of stars with planets, and so, presumably, the emergence of life and then mind, all as a result of the big bang, depends critically on certain values falling within a very narrow range in the governing physical equations. Furthermore, that these values fall within these ranges appears to be thoroughly contingent, in the sense that there seems to be no further theoretical reason why these values rather than others should be instantiated. *A priori*, it seems a surprise that the universe has life and mind within it. It is a prior improbability. This could be mere lucky accident. But the improbability would be explained if some larger mind had set these values. (See, for instance, John Leslie, 1989.)

There are hypotheses that would evade this conclusion. There is even a general metaphysical scheme that would so serve. This is the view of David Lewis (1986), that our actual world is but one of innumerable possible worlds, each one of which is actual relative to itself and merely possible relative to each of the other worlds. On this view, and given the contingency of the laws of nature, it is only some of these possible worlds in which stars, planets, life and mind emerge. It can be no surprise, and it requires no explanation, that we exist in such a world.

Not many would accept Lewis' theory of possible worlds. But hypotheses about our actual world are not wanting that are deflationary in the same way. A number of cosmologists hold to the view that present observable space is but a small and local part of reality. The settings of critical values in the equations that govern local space are, because of differences in initial conditions, likely to be different in the indefinitely numerous other localities. A world of stars, planets, life and minds is the winner of a lottery.

There is, then, an alternative cosmological explanation for the special and improbable features of our world. As a result, the argument does not appear to have the strength of the Argument from Design absent the theory of natural selection. But in the scientific and philosophical spirit of considering carefully the best current arguments against one's own most favoured view, a Naturalist such as myself should keep a weather eye on the suggestion, now coming from physics rather than biology, that the emergence of mind is an improbable affair.

2 MATERIALISM

The second section of my paper suggested that the main difficulties facing contemporary Materialism (Physicalism) are posed by the apparent irreducibility of intentionality (how can a mere physical brain have such properties?) and the apparent irreducibility and simplicity of the secondary qualities (how can such entities plausibly be fitted into physics?). The argument was the same in both cases. These phenomena are not epiphenomenal, they should be credited with causal power. But if they are not epiphenomenal, if they do some work in the world, then it is scientifically plausible to think that their causal action is governed by the laws of physics. But if so, they cannot be irreducible. They must be *complex* physical phenomena.

This argument does not, of course, tell us what positive account should be given of intentionality and the secondary qualities. But those of us that think that Physicalism is a plausible hypothesis will be encouraged by the causal argument to think that the phenomenology of the situation – the apparent simplicity or relative simplicity of intentionality and the secondary qualities – is mere appearance. Perhaps I should have mentioned *consciousness* also. It is easy to think of it as an unanalysable light that lights up a dark world. But if under the influence of the causal argument we deny that consciousness is epiphenomenal, then we will be inclined to think of it as some very complex physical process that occurs in the central nervous system. I think that it must be an information-acquiring process where the central nervous system acquires information (or misinformation) about (some) of its own current workings. See "What is consciousness?" in Armstrong (1981).

In giving a positive account of intentionality, the beginning of wisdom appears to be to note the formal resemblances between the intentional objects of mental entities and the *manifestations* of dispositions. The intentional object need not exist, the manifestation need not occur. This already points towards a naturalization of intentionality, since dispositions, whatever our metaphysical account of them (a tricky matter), have no special link with mentality. See C. B. Martin and K. Pfeifer (1986) and U. T. Place (1988: 210). This suggests that intentionality is to be analysed in terms of very complex dispositions and powers of the mind, dispositions and powers of the central nervous system.

The secondary qualities pose difficult problems. I hold what might be called an information-flow account of perception. According to me sense-impressions (and I think that bodily perceptions are a species of sense-impression) have *a purely intentional content*. My view is very close to an important and somewhat neglected paper of Brian Farrell's, "Experience", written as far back as 1950, and a somewhat later and more attended to paper by Elizabeth Anscombe (1965). This content may be thought of as propositional, informational, although not of course having anything to do with language. Sensory illusion is false information (which, however, the perceiver may discount): in such a case no real state of affairs corresponds to the intentional content. The content of the content, if I may so put it, is always some physical state of affairs, characteristically involving either some current environmental state of affairs, together with the relation of the objects or events involved to the perceiver's own body, or, more simply, a state of affairs that involves no more than the perceiver's body.

Given this approach, being a red surface, for instance, cannot be analysed as the sort of surface that characteristically produces red sensations in normal perceivers, with the sensations then identified with certain sorts of brain processes. For the red sensation is an impression that *something physical is red*. To preserve Physicalism, therefore, I identify colours with physical-respectable properties of physical surfaces, etc. Wishing not to meddle in matters beyond my competence, I refrain from much speculation about the details of the identifications. It does seem likely, however, that colours, in particular, will turn out to be highly disjunctive physical properties, and thus, in my view, second-rate properties. For some details see Armstrong (1987).

3 FIRST PHILOSOPHY

To be a Naturalist or a Materialist is to hold a metaphysical view, but it is not to take a stand on the most abstract and basic of metaphysical issues. In my paper I argued that it was possible and desirable to reject the orthodox package-deal of Naturalism, Materialism and Nominalism, meaning by the last of these the rejection of universals. While not resiling from this position, I should now like to emphasize the importance of upholding the objective reality of *properties* and *relations*. There is a sense in which any predicate that truly applies to an *n*-tuple of objects may be said to pick out a property or a relation. But the properties and relations I wish to uphold are relatively few in number and are the real joints of the world. They are to be discovered, so far as they can be discovered, *a posteriori*, on the basis of our best science. A contemporary Materialist will turn to our best physics, in particular, to say just what they are. When an object acts, it acts in virtue of these properties and relations, and the laws which govern such actions are linkages involving these entities.

It is a further question whether these properties and relations are universals, strictly identical in their different instantiations, or whether they are as particular as the objects that have them, having at best exact resemblance that is not grounded in identity. Since exact resemblance is symmetrical, transitive and reflexive, equivalence classes can be formed of these particularized properties and relations, classes which are interesting substitutes for universals, though in my view not fully satisfactory substitutes. I have discussed this in a book on universals (Armstrong, 1989).

Many philosophers think that it is not possible to combine Naturalism with a doctrine of universals. What is needed for the combination is an "Aristotelian" rather than a "Platonic" theory. The only universals admitted should be ones that are instantiated (at some time). It will be too crude to "bring universals down to space-time", as if putting them in a big pot. The best way forward, I think, is to develop a theory of facts or, as I prefer to call them, states of affairs. These will *be* instantiations of property and relation universals. Space-time, all that there is if Naturalism is upheld, will be analysed as, identified with, a vast interconnected assemblage of states of affairs. See my book, *A World of States of Affairs*, forthcoming.

REFERENCES

Anscombe, G. E. M. (1965) "The Intentionality of Sensation". In R. J. Butler (ed.) *Analytical Philosophy.* Oxford: Oxford University Press.

Armstrong, D. M. (1981) *The Nature of Mind and Other Essays*, Ithaca, New York: Cornell University Press.

—— (1987) "Smart and the secondary qualities", in Philip Pettit, Richard Sylvan and Jean Norman (eds) *Metaphysics and Morality: Essays in Honour of J. J. C. Smart*, 1–15. Oxford: Blackwell.

—— (1989) *Universals: An Opinionated Introduction*, Boulder, Colorado: Westview Press.

—— (forthcoming) *A World of States of Affairs*.

Farrell, B. (1950) "Experience", *Mind* LIX, 170–98.

Leslie, John (1989) *Universes*, London and New York: Routledge.

Lewis, David (1986) *On the Plurality of Worlds*, Oxford: Blackwell.

Martin, C. B. and Pfeifer, K. (1986) "Intentionality and the non-psychological", *Philosophy and Phenomenological Research* 46, 531–54.

Paley, William, [1802] (1972) *Natural Theology*, Houston: St Thomas Press.

Place, U. T. (1988) "Thirty years on – is consciousness still a brain-process?", *Australasian Journal of Philosophy* 66, 208–19.

2 Special Sciences

Jerry A. Fodor

A typical thesis of positivistic philosophy of science is that all true theories in the special sciences should reduce to physical theories in the long run. This is intended to be an empirical thesis, and part of the evidence which supports it is provided by such scientific successes as the molecular theory of heat and the physical explanation of the chemical bond. But the philosophical popularity of the reductivist program cannot be explained by reference to these achievements alone. The development of science has witnessed the proliferation of specialized disciplines at least as often as it has witnessed their reduction to physics, so the widespread enthusiasm for reduction can hardly be a mere induction over its past successes.

I think that many philosophers who accept reductivism do so primarily because they wish to endorse the generality of physics *vis à vis* the special sciences: roughly, the view that all events which fall under the laws of any science are physical events and hence fall under the laws of physics.[1] For such philosophers, saying that physics is basic science and saying that theories in the special sciences must reduce to physical theories have seemed to be two ways of saying the same thing, so that the latter doctrine has come to be a standard construal of the former.

In what follows, I shall argue that this is a considerable confusion. What has traditionally been called "the unity of science" is a much stronger, and much less plausible, thesis than the generality of physics. If this is true it is important. Though reductionism is an empirical doctrine, it is intended to play a regulative role in scientific practice. Reducibility to physics is taken to be a *constraint* upon the acceptability of theories in the special sciences, with the curious consequence that the more the special sciences succeed, the more they ought to disappear. Methodological problems about psychology, in particular, arise in just this way: the assumption that the subject-matter of psychology is part of the subject-matter of physics is taken to imply that psychological theories must reduce to physical theories, and it is this latter principle that makes the trouble. I want to avoid the trouble by challenging the inference.

I

Reductivism is the view that all the special sciences reduce to physics. The sense of "reduce to" is, however, proprietary. It can be characterized as follows.[2]

Let

(1) $S_1x \rightarrow S_2x$

be a law of the special science S. ((1) is intended to be read as something like "all S_1 situations bring about S_2 situations". I assume that a science is individuated largely by reference to its typical predicates, hence that if S is a special science "S_1" and "S_2" are not predicates of basic physics. I also assume that the "all" which quantifies laws of the special sciences needs to be taken with a grain of salt; such laws are typically *not* exceptionless. This is a point to which I shall return at length.) A necessary and sufficient condition of the reduction of (1) to a law of physics is that the formulae (2) and (3) be laws, and a necessary and sufficient condition of the reduction of S to physics is that all its laws be so reducible.[3]

(2a) $S_1x \leftrightarrows P_1x$
(2b) $S_2x \leftrightarrows P_2x$
(3) $P_1x \rightarrow P_2x$.

"P_1" and "P_2" are supposed to be predicates of physics, and (3) is supposed to be a physical law. Formulae like (2) are often called "bridge" laws. Their characteristic feature is that they contain predicates of both the reduced and the reducing science. Bridge laws like (2) are thus contrasted with "proper" laws like (1) and (3). The upshot of the remarks so far is that the reduction of a science requires that any formula which appears as the antecedent or consequent of one of its proper laws must appear as the reduced formula in some bridge law or other.[4]

Several points about the connective "$\rightarrow$" are in order. First, whatever other properties that connective may have, it is universally agreed that it must be transitive. This is important because it is usually assumed that the reduction of some of the special sciences proceeds via bridge laws which connect their predicates with those of intermediate reducing theories. Thus, psychology is presumed to reduce to physics via, say, neurology, biochemistry, and other local stops. The present point is that this makes no difference to the logic of the situation so long as the transitivity of "$\rightarrow$" is assumed. Bridge laws which connect the predicates of S to those of S^* will satisfy the constraints upon the reduction of S to physics so long as there are other bridge laws which, directly or indirectly, connect the predicates of S^* to physical predicates.

There are, however, quite serious open questions about the inter-pretations of "$\rightarrow$" in bridge laws. What turns on these questions is the respect in which reductivism is taken to be a physicalist thesis.

To begin with, if we read "$\rightarrow$" as "brings about" or "causes" in proper laws, we will have to have some other connective for bridge laws, since bringing about and causing are presumably *a*symmetric, while bridge laws express symmetric relations. Moreover, if "$\rightarrow$" in bridge laws is interpreted as any relation other than identity, the truth of reductivism will only guarantee the truth of a weak version of physicalism, and this would fail to express the underlying ontological bias of the reductivist program.

If bridge laws are not identity statements, then formulae like (2) claim at most that, by law, x's satisfaction of a P predicate and x's satisfaction of an S predicate are causally correlated. It follows from this that it is nomologically necessary that S and P predicates apply to the same things (i.e., that S predicates apply to a subset of the things that P predicates apply to). But, of course, this is compatible with a non-physicalist ontology since it is compatible with the possibility that x's satisfying S should not itself *be* a physical event. On this interpretation, the truth of reductivism does *not* guarantee the generality of physics *vis à vis* the special sciences since there are some events (satisfactions of S predicates) which fall in the domains of a special science (S) but not in the domain of physics. (One could imagine, for example, a doctrine according to which physical and psychological predicates are both held to apply to organisms, but where it is denied that the event which consists of an organism's satisfying a psychological predicate is, in any sense, a physical event. The up-shot would be a kind of psychophysical dualism of a non-Cartesian variety; a dualism of events and/ or properties rather than substances.)

Given these sorts of considerations, many philosophers have held that bridge laws like (2) ought to be taken to express contingent event identities, so that one would read (2a) in some such fashion as "every event which consists of x's satisfying S_1 is identical to some event which consists of x's satisfying P_1 and vice versa". On this reading, the truth of reductivism would entail that every event that falls under any scientific law is a physical event, thereby simultaneously expressing the ontological bias of reductivism and guaranteeing the generality of physics *vis à vis* the special sciences.

If the bridge laws express event identities, and if every event that falls under the proper laws of a special science falls under a bridge law, we get the truth of a doctrine that I shall call "token physicalism". Token physicalism is simply the claim that all the events that the sciences talk about are physical events. There are three things to notice about token physicalism.

First, it is weaker than what is usually called "materialism". Materialism claims *both* that token physicalism is true *and* that every event falls under the laws of some science or other. One could therefore be a token physicalist without being a materialist, though I don't see why anyone would bother.

Second, token physicalism is weaker than what might be called "type physicalism", the doctrine, roughly, that every *property* mentioned in the laws of any science is a physical property. Token physicalism does not entail type physicalism because the contingent identity of a pair of events presumably does not guarantee the identity of the properties whose instantiation constitutes the events; not even where the event identity is nomologically necessary. On the other hand, if every event is the instantiation of a property, then type physicalism does entail token physicalism: two events will be identical when they consist of the instantiation of the same property by the same individual at the same time.

Third, token physicalism is weaker than reductivism. Since this point is, in a certain sense, the burden of the argument to follow, I shan't labour it here. But, as a first approximation, reductivism is the conjunction of token physicalism with the assumption that there are natural kind predicates in an ideally completed physics which correspond to each natural kind predicate in any ideally completed special science. It will be one of my morals that the truth of reductivism cannot be inferred from the assumption that token physicalism is true. Reductivism is a sufficient, but not a necessary, condition for token physicalism.

In what follows, I shall assume a reading of reductivism which entails token physicalism. Bridge laws thus state nomologically necessary contingent event identities, and a reduction of psychology to neurology would entail that any event which consists of the instantiation of a psychological property is identical with some event which consists of the instantiation of some neurological property.

Where we have got to is this: reductivism entails the generality of physics in at least the sense that any event which falls within the universe of discourse of a special science will also fall within the universe of discourse of physics. Moreover, any prediction which follows from the laws of a special science and a statement of initial conditions will also follow from a theory which consists of physics and the bridge laws, together with the statement of initial conditions. Finally, since "reduces to" is supposed to be an asymmetric relation, it will also turn out that physics is *the* basic science; that is, if reductivism is true, physics is the only science that is general in the sense just specified. I now want to argue that reductivism is too strong a constraint upon the unity of science, but that the relevantly weaker doctrine will preserve the desired consequences of reductivism: token physicalism, the generality of physics, and its basic position among the sciences.

II

Every science implies a taxonomy of the events in its universe of discourse. In particular, every science employs a descriptive vocabulary of theoretical and observation predicates such that events fall under the laws of the science by virtue of satisfying those predicates. Patently, not every true description of an event is a description in such a vocabulary. For example, there are a large number of events which consist of things having been transported to a distance of less than three miles from the Eiffel Tower. I take it, however, that there is no science which contains "is transported to a distance of less than three miles from the Eiffel Tower" as part of its descriptive vocabulary. Equivalently, I take it that there is no natural law which applies to events in virtue of their being instantiations of the property *is transported to a distance of less than three miles from the Eiffel Tower* (though I suppose it is conceivable that there is some law that applies to events in virtue of their being instantiations of some distinct but co-extensive property). By way of abbreviating these facts, I shall say that the property *is transported* . . . does not determine a *natural kind,* and that predicates which express that property are not natural kind predicates.

If I knew what a law is, and if I believed that scientific theories consist just of bodies of laws, then I could say that P is a natural kind predicate relative to S iff S contains proper laws of the form $P_x \rightarrow \alpha_x$ or $\alpha_x \rightarrow P_x$; roughly, the natural kind predicates of a science are the ones whose terms are the bound variables in its proper laws. I am inclined to say this even in my present state of ignorance, accepting the consequence that it makes the murky notion of a natural kind viciously dependent on the equally murky notions *law* and *theory*. There is no firm footing here. If we disagree about what is a natural kind, we will probably also disagree about what is a law, and for the same reasons. I don't know how to break out of this circle, but I think that there are interesting things to say about which circle we are in.

For example, we can now characterize the respect in which reductivism is too strong a construal of the doctrine of the unity of science. If reductivism is true, then *every* natural kind is, or is co-extensive with, a physical natural kind. (Every natural kind *is* a physical natural kind if bridge laws express property identities, and every natural kind is co-extensive with a physical natural kind if bridge laws express event identities.) This follows immediately from the reductivist premise that every predicate which appears as the antecedent or consequent of a law of the special sciences must appear as one of the reduced predicates in some bridge, together with the assumption that the natural kind predicates are the ones whose terms are the bound variables in proper laws. If, in short, some physical law is related to each law of a special science in the way that (3) is related to (1), then every natural kind predicate of a special science is related to a natural kind predicate of physics in the way that (2) relates "S_1" and "S_2" to "P_1" and "P_2".

I now want to suggest some reasons for believing that this consequence of reductivism is intolerable. These are not supposed to be knock-down reasons; they couldn't be, given that the question whether reductivism is too strong is finally an *empirical* question. (The world could turn out to be such that every natural kind corresponds to a physical natural kind, just as it could turn out to be such that the property *is transported to a distance of less than three miles from the Eiffel Tower* determines a natural kind in, say, hydrodynamics. It's just that, as things stand, it seems very unlikely that the world *will* turn out to be either of these ways.)

The reason it is unlikely that every natural kind corresponds to a physical natural kind is just that (a) interesting generalizaions (e.g., counter-factual supporting generalizations) can often be made about events whose physical descriptions have nothing in common, (b) it is often the case that *whether* the physical descriptions of the events subsumed by these generalizations have anything in common is, in an obvious sense, entirely irrelevant to the truth of the generalizations, or to their interestingness, or to their degree of confirmation or, indeed, to any of their epistemologically important properties, and (c) the special sciences are very much in the business of making generalizations of this kind.

I take it that these remarks are obvious to the point of self-certification; they leap to the eye as soon as one makes the (apparently radical) move of taking the special sciences at all seriously. Suppose, for example, that Gresham's "law" really is true. (If one doesn't like Gresham's law, then any true generalization of any conceivable future economics will probably do as well.) Gresham's law says something about what will happen in monetary exchanges under certain conditions. I am willing to believe that physics is general *in the sense that it implies that any event which consists of a monetary exchange* (hence any event which falls under Gresham's law) *has a true description in the vocabulary of physics and in virtue of which it falls under the laws of physics*. But banal considerations suggest that a description which covers all such events must be wildly disjunctive. Some monetary exchanges involve strings of wampum. Some involve dollar bills. And some involve signing one's name to a check. What are the chances that a disjunction of physical predicates which covers all these events (i.e., a disjunctive predicate which can form the right hand side of a bridge law of the form "*x* is a monetary exchange $\leftrightarrows$ ...") expresses a physical natural kind? In particular, what are the chances that such a predicate forms the antecedent or consequent of some proper law of physics? The point is that monetary exchanges have interesting things in common; Gresham's law, if true, says what one of these interesting things is. But what is interesting about monetary exchanges is surely not their commonalities under *physical* description. A natural kind like a monetary exchange *could* turn out to be co-extensive with a physical natural kind; but if it did, that would be an accident on a cosmic scale.

In fact, the situation for reductivism is still worse than the discussion thus far suggests. For, reductivism claims not only that all natural kinds are co-extensive with physical natural kinds, but that the co-extensions are nomologically necessary: bridge laws are *laws*. So, if Gresham's law is true, it follows that there is a (bridge) law of nature such that "*x* is a monetary exchange $\rightleftarrows$ *x* is *P*", where *P* is a term for a physical natural kind. But, surely, there is no such law. If there were, then *P* would have to cover not only all the systems of monetary exchange that there *are*, but also all the systems of monetary exchange that there *could be*; a law must succeed with the counterfactuals. What physical predicate is a candidate for "*P*" in "*x* is a nomologically possible monetary exchange iff P_x"?

To summarize: an immortal econophysicist might, when the whole show is over, find a predicate in physics that was, in brute fact, co-extensive with "is a monetary exchange". If physics is general – if the ontological biases of reductivism are true – then there must *be* such a predicate. But (a) to paraphrase a remark Donald Davidson made in a slightly different context, nothing but brute enumeration could convince us of this brute co-extensivity, and (b) there would seem to be no chance at all that the physical predicate employed in stating the co-extensivity is a natural kind term, and (c) there is still less chance that the co-extension would be lawful (i.e., that it would hold not only for the nomologically possible world that turned out to be real, but for any nomologically possible world at all).

I take it that the preceding discussion strongly suggests that economics is not reducible to physics in the proprietary sense of reduction involved in claims for the unity of science. There is, I suspect, nothing special about economics in this respect; the reasons why economics is unlikely to reduce to physics are paralleled by those which suggest that psychology is unlikely to reduce to neurology.

If psychology is reducible to neurology, then for every psychological natural kind predicate there is a co-extensive neurological natural kind predicate, and the generalization which states this co-extension is a law. Clearly, many psychologists believe something of the sort. There are departments of "psycho-biology" or "psychology and brain science" in universities throughout the world whose very existence is an institution-alized gamble that such lawful co-extensions can be found. Yet, as has been frequently remarked in recent discussions of materialism, there are good grounds for hedging these bets. There are no firm data for any but the grossest correspondence between types of psychological states and types of neurological states, and it is entirely possible that the nervous system of higher organisms characteristically achieves a given psychological end by a wide variety of neurological means. If so, then the attempt to pair neurological structures with psychological functions is foredoomed. Physio-logical psychologists of the stature of Karl Lashley have held precisely this view.

The present point is that the reductivist program in psychology is, in any event, *not* to be defended on ontological grounds. Even if (token) psychological events are (token) neurological events, it does not follow that the natural kind predicates of psychology are co-extensive with the natural kind predicates of any other discipline (including physics). That is, the assumption that every psychological event is a physical event does not guarantee that physics (or, *a fortiori*, any other discipline more general than psychology) can provide an appropriate vocabulary for psychological theories. I emphasize this point because I am convinced that the make-or-break commitment of many physiological psychologists to the reductivist program stems precisely from having confused that program with (token) physicalism.

What I have been doubting is that there are neurological natural kinds co-extensive with psychological natural kinds. What seems increasingly clear is that, even if there is such a co-extension, it cannot be lawlike. For, it seems increasingly likely that there are nomologically possible systems other than organisms (namely, automata) which satisfy natural kind predicates in psychology, and which satisfy no neurological predicates at all. Now, as Putnam has emphasized, if there are any such systems, then there are probably vast numbers, since equivalent automata can be made out of practically anything. If this observation is correct, then there can be no serious hope that the class of automata whose psychology is effectively identical to that of some organism can be described by *physical* natural kind predicates (though, of course, if token physicalism is true, that class can be picked out by some physical predicate or other). The upshot is that the classical formulation of the unity of science is at the mercy of progress in the field of computer simulation. This is, of course, simply to say that that formulation was too strong. The unity of science was intended to be an empirical hypothesis, defeasible by possible scientific findings. But no one had it in mind that it should be defeated by Newell, Shaw and Simon.

I have thus far argued that psychological reductivism (the doctrine that every psychological natural kind is, or is co-extensive with, a neurological natural kind) is not equivalent to, and cannot be inferred from, token physicalism (the doctrine that every psychological event is a neurological event). It may, however, be argued that one might as well take the doctrines to be equivalent since the only possible *evidence* one could have for token physicalism would also be evidence for reductivism: namely, the discovery of type-to-type psychophysical correlations.

A moment's consideration shows, however, that this argument is not well taken. If type-to-type psychophysical correlations would be evidence for token physicalism, so would correlations of other specifiable kinds.

We have type-to-type correlations where, for every n-tuple of events that are of the same psychological kind, there is a correlated n-tuple of events that are of the same neurological kind. Imagine a world in which such correlations are *not* forthcoming. What is found, instead, is that for every n-tuple of type identical psychological events, there is a spatio-temporally correlated n-tuple of type *distinct* neurological events. That is, every psychological event is paired with some neurological event or other, but psychological events of the same kind may be paired with neurological events of different kinds. My present point is that such pairings would provide as much support for token physicalism as type-to-type pairings do *so long as we are able to show that the type distinct neurological events paired with a given kind of psychological event are identical in respect of whatever properties are relevant to type-identification in psychology.* Suppose, for purposes of explication, that psychological events are type identified by reference to their behavioral consequences.[5] Then what is required of all the neurological events paired with a class of type homogeneous psychological events is only that they be identical in respect of their behavioral consequences. To put it briefly, type identical events do not, of course, have *all* their properties in common, and type distinct events must nevertheless be identical in *some* of their properties. The empirical confirmation of token physicalism does not depend on showing that the neurological counterparts of type identical psychological events are themselves type identical. What needs to be shown is only that they are identical in respect of those properties which determine which kind of *psychological* event a given event is.

Could we have evidence that an otherwise heterogeneous set of neurological events have these kinds of properties in common? Of course we could. The neurological theory might itself explain why an n-tuple of neurologically type distinct events are identical in their behavioral consequences, or, indeed, in respect of any of indefinitely many other such relational properties. And, if the neurological theory failed to do so, some science more basic than neurology might succeed.

My point in all this is, once again, not that correlations between type homogeneous psychological states and type heterogeneous neurological states would prove that token physicalism is true. It is only that such correlations might give us as much reason to be token physicalists as type-to-type corelations would. If this is correct, then the epistemological arguments from token physicalism to reductivism must be wrong.

It seems to me (to put the point quite generally) that the classical construal of the unity of science has really misconstrued the *goal* of scientific reduction. The point of reduction is *not* primarily to find some natural kind predicate of physics co-extensive with each natural kind predicate of a reduced science. It is, rather, to explicate the physical mechanisms whereby events conform to the laws of the special sciences. I have been arguing that there is no logical or epistemological reason why success in the second of these projects should require success in the first, and that the two are likely to come apart *in fact* wherever the physical mechanisms whereby events conform to a law of the special sciences are heterogeneous.

III

I take it that the discussion thus far shows that reductivism is probably too strong a construal of the unity of science; on the one hand, it is incompatible with probable results in the special sciences, and, on the other, it is more than we need to assume if what we primarily want is just to be good token physicalists. In what follows, I shall try to sketch a liberalization of reductivism which seems to me to be just strong enough in these respects. I shall then give a couple of independent reasons for supposing that the revised doctrine may be the right one.

The problem all along has been that there is an open empirical possibility that what corresponds to the natural kind predicates of a reduced science may be a heterogeneous and unsystematic disjunction of predicates in the reducing science, and we do not want the unity of science to be prejudiced by this possibility. Suppose, then, that we allow that bridge statements may be of the form

(4) $\quad S_x \rightleftarrows P_1 x \vee P_2 x \vee \ldots \vee P_n x,$

where "$P_1 \vee P_2 \vee \ldots \vee P_n$" is *not* a natural kind predicate in the reducing science. I take it that this is tantamount to allowing that at least some "bridge laws" may, in fact, not turn out to be laws, since I take it that a necessary condition on a universal generalization being lawlike is that the predicates which constitute its antecedent and consequent should pick out natural kinds. I am thus supposing that it is enough, for purposes of the unity of science, that every law of the special sciences should be reducible to physics by bridge statements which express true empirical generalizations. Bearing in mind that bridge statements are to be construed as a species of identity statements, (4) will be read as something like "every event which consists of x's satisfying S is identical with some event which consists of x's satisfying some or other predicate belonging to the disjunction '$P_1 \vee P_2 \vee \ldots \vee P_n$.'"

Now, in cases of reduction where what corresponds to (2) is not a law, what corresponds to (3) will not be either, and for the same reason. Namely, the predicates appearing in the antecedent or consequent will, by hypothesis, not be natural kind predicates. Rather, what we will have is something that looks like (5).

(5)   Law of special science X: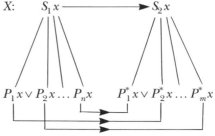

That is, the antecedent and consequent of the reduced law will each be connected with a disjunction of predicates in the reducing science, and, if the reduced law is exceptionless, there will be laws of the reducing science which connect the satisfaction of each member of the disjunction associated with the antecedent to the satisfaction of some member of the disjunction associated with the consequent. That is, if $S_1 x \rightarrow S_2 x$ is exceptionless, then there must be some proper law of the reducing science which either states or entails that $P_1 x \rightarrow P^*$ for some P^*, and similarly for $P_2 x$ through $P_n x$. Since there must be such laws, it follows that each disjunct of "$P_1 \vee P_2 \vee ... \vee P_n$" is a natural kind predicate, as is each disjunct of "$P_1^* \vee P_2^* \vee ... \vee P_n^*$".

This, however, is where push comes to shove. For, it might be argued that if each disjunct of the P disjunction is lawfully connected to some disjunct of the P^* disjunction, it follows that (6) is itself a law.

(6) $P_1 x \vee P_2 x \vee ... \vee P_n x \rightarrow P_1^* x \vee P_2^* x \vee ... \vee P_n^* x.$

The point would be that (5) gives us $P_1 x \rightarrow P_1^* x$, $P_2 x \rightarrow P_m^* x$, etc., and the argument from a premise of the form $(P \supset R)$ and $(Q \supset S)$ to a conclusion of the form $(P \vee Q) \supset (R \vee S)$ is valid.

What I am inclined to say about this is that it just shows that "it's a law that ———" defines a non-truth functional context (or, equivalently for these purposes, that not all truth functions of natural kind predicates are themselves natural kind predicates). In particular, that one may not argue from "it's a law that P brings about R" and "it's a law that Q brings about S" to "it's a law that P or Q brings about R or S". (Though, of course, the argument from those premises to "P or Q brings about R or S" *simpliciter* is fine.) I think, for example, that it is a law that the irradiation of green plants by sunlight causes carbohydrate synthesis, and I think that it is a law that friction causes heat, but I do not think that it is a law that (either the irradiation of green plants by sunlight or friction) causes (either carbohydrate synthesis or heat). Correspondingly, I doubt that "is either carbohydrate synthesis or heat" is plausibly taken to be a natural kind predicate.

It is not strictly mandatory that one should agree with all this, but one denies it at a price. In particular, if one allows the full range of truth functional arguments inside the context "it's a law that ———", then one gives up the possibility of identifying the natural kind predicates of a science with those predicates which appear as the antecedents or the consequents of its proper laws. (Thus (6) would be a proper law of physics which fails to satisfy that condition.) One thus inherits the need for an alternative construal of the notion of a natural kind, and I don't know what that alternative might be like.

The upshot seems to be this. If we do not require that bridge statements must be laws, then either some of the generalizations to which the laws of special sciences reduce are not themselves lawlike, or some laws are not formulable in terms of natural kinds. Whichever way one takes (5), the important point is that it is weaker than standard reductivism: it does not require correspondences between the natural kinds of the reduced and the reducing science. Yet it is physicalistic on the same assumption that makes standard reductivism physicalistic (namely, that the bridge statements express true token identities). But these are precisely the properties that we wanted a revised account of the unity of science to exhibit.

I now want to give two reasons for thinking that this construal of the unity of science is right. First, it allows us to see how the laws of the special sciences could reasonably have exceptions, and, second, it allows us to see why there are special sciences at all. These points in turn.

Consider, again, the model of reduction implicit in (2) and (3). I assume that the laws of basic science are strictly exceptionless, and I assume that it is common knowledge that the laws of the special sciences are not. But now we have a painful dilemma. Since "$\rightarrow$" expresses a relation (or relations) which must be transitive, (1) can have exceptions only if the bridge laws do. But if the bridge laws have exceptions, reductivism looses its ontological bite, since we can no longer say that every event which consists of the instantiation of an S predicate is identical with some event which consists of the instantiation of a P predicate. In short, given the reductionist model, we cannot consistently assume that the bridge laws and the basic laws are exceptionless while assuming that the special laws are not. But we cannot accept the violation of the bridge laws unless we are willing to vitiate the ontological claim that is the main point of the reductivist program.

We can get out of this (*salve* the model) in one of two ways. We can give up the claim that the special laws have exceptions or we can give up the claim that the basic laws are exceptionless. I suggest that both alternatives are undesirable. The first because it flies in the face of fact. There is just no chance at all that the true, counter-factual supporting generalizations of, say, psychology, will turn out to hold in strictly each and every condition where their antecedents are satisfied. Even where the spirit is willing, the flesh is often weak. There are always going to be behavioral leaps which are physiologically explicable but which are uninteresting from the point of view of psychological theory. The second alternative is only slightly better. It may, after all, turn out that the laws of basic science have exceptions. But the question arises whether one wants the unity of science to depend upon the assumption that they do.

On the account summarized in (5), however, everything works out satisfactorily. A nomologically sufficient condition for an exception to $S_1 x \rightarrow S_2 x$ is that the bridge statements should identify some occurrence of the satisfaction of S_1 with an occurrence of the satisfaction of a P predicate which is not itself lawfully connected to the satisfaction of any P^* predicate. (I.e., suppose S_1 is connected to a P' such that there is no law which connects P' to any predicate which bridge statements associate with S_2. Then any instantiation of S_1 which is contingently identical to an instanti-ation of P' will be an event which constitutes an exception to $S_1 x \rightarrow S_2 x$.) Notice that, in this case, we need assume no exceptions to the laws of the *reducing* science since, by hypothesis, (6) *is not a law.*

In fact, strictly speaking, (6) has no status in the reduction at all. It is simply what one gets when one universally quantifies a formula whose antecedent is the physical disjunction corresponding to S_1 and whose consequent is the physical disjunction corresponding to S_2. As such, it will be true when $S_1 \rightarrow S_2$ is exceptionless and false otherwise. What does the work of expressing the physical mechanisms whereby n-tuples of events conform, or fail to conform, to $S_1 \rightarrow S_2$ is not (6) but the laws which severally relate elements of the disjunction $P_1 \vee P_2 \vee \ldots \vee P_n$ to elements of the disjunction $P_1^* \vee P_2^* \vee \ldots \vee P_n^*$. When there *is* a law which relates an event that satisfies one of the P disjuncts to an event which satisfies one of the P^* disjuncts, the pair of events so related conforms to $S_1 \rightarrow S_2$. When an event which satisfies a P predicate is *not* related by law to an event which satisfies a P^* predicate, that event will constitute an exception to $S_1 \rightarrow S_2$. The point is that none of the laws which effect these several connections need themselves have exceptions in order that $S_1 \rightarrow S_2$ should do so.

To put this discussion less technically: we could, if we liked, *require* the taxonomies of the special sciences to correspond to the taxonomy of physics by insisting upon distinctions between the natural kinds postulated by the former wherever they turn out to correspond to distinct natural kinds in the latter. This would *make* the laws of the special sciences exceptionless if the laws of basic science are. But it would also lose us precisely the generalizations which we want the special sciences to express. (If economics were to posit as many *kinds* of monetary systems as there are kinds of physical realizations of monetary systems, then the generalizations of economics *would* be exceptionless. But, presumably, only vacuously so, since there would be no generalizations left to state. Gresham's law, for example, would have to be formulated as a vast, open disjunction about what happens in monetary system$_1$ or monetary system$_n$ under conditions which would themselves defy uniform characterization. We would not be able to say what happens in monetary systems *tout court* since, by hypothesis, "is a monetary system" corresponds to no natural kind predicate of physics.)

In fact, what we do is precisely the reverse. We allow the generalizations of the special sciences to *have* exceptions, thus preserving the natural kinds to which the generalizations apply. But since we know that the *physical* descriptions of the natural kinds may be quite heterogeneous, and since we know that the physical mechanisms which connect the satisfaction of the antecedents of such generalizations to the satisfaction of their consequents may be equally diverse, we expect both that there will be exceptions to the generalizations and that these exceptions will be "explained away" at the level of the reducing science. This is one of the respects in which physics really is assumed to be bedrock science; exceptions to *its* generalizations (if there are any) had better be random, because there is nowhere "further down" to go in explaining the mechanism whereby the exceptions occur.

This brings us to why there are special sciences at all. Reductivism as we remarked at the outset, flies in the face of the facts about the scientific institution: the existence of a vast and interleaved conglomerate of special scientific disciplines which often appear to proceed with only the most token acknowledgement of the constraint that their theories must turn out to be physics "in the long run". I mean that the acceptance of this constraint, *in practice*, often plays little or no role in the validation of theories. Why is this so? Presumably, the reductivist answer must be *entirely* epistemological. If only physical particles weren't so small (if only brains were on the *out*side, where one can get a look at them), *then* we would do physics instead of palentology (neurology instead of psychology; psychology instead of economics; and so on down). There is an epistemological reply; namely, that even if brains were out where they can be looked *at*, as things now stand, we wouldn't know what to look *for*: we lack the appropriate theoretical apparatus for the psychological taxonomy of neurological events.

If it turns out that the functional decomposition of the nervous system corresponds to its neurological (anatomical, biochemical, physical) decomposition, then there are only epistemological reasons for studying the former instead of the latter. But suppose there is no such correspondence. Suppose the functional organization of the nervous system cross-cuts its neurological organization (so that quite different neurological structures can subserve identical psychological functions across times or across organisms). Then the existence of psychology depends not on the fact that neurons are so sadly small, but rather on the fact that neurology does not posit the natural kinds that psychology requires.

I am suggesting, roughly, that there are special sciences not because of the nature of our epistemic relation to the world, but because of the way the world is put together: not all natural kinds (not all the classes of things and events about which there are important, counterfactual supporting generalizations to make) are, or correspond to, physical natural kinds. A way of stating the classical reductionist view is that things which belong to different physical kinds *ipso facto* can have no projectible descriptions in common; that if x and y differ in those descriptions by virtue of which they fall under the proper laws of physics, they must differ in those descriptions by virtue of which they fall under any laws at all. But why should we believe that this is so? Any pair of entities, however different their physical structure, must nevertheless converge in indefinitely many of their properties. Why should there not be, among those convergent properties, some whose lawful inter-relations support the generalizations of the special sciences? Why, in short should not the natural kind predicates of the special sciences *cross-classify* the physical natural kinds?[6]

Physics develops the taxonomy of its subject-matter which best suits its purposes: the formulation of exceptionless laws which are basic in the several senses discussed above. But this is not the only taxonomy which may be required if the purposes of science in general are to be served: e.g., if we are to state such true, counterfactual supporting generalizations as there are to state. So, there are special sciences, with their specialized taxonomies, in the business of stating some of these generalizations. If science is to be unified, then all such taxonomies must apply *to the same things*. If physics is to be basic science, then each of these things had better be a physical thing. But it is not further required that the taxonomies which the special sciences employ must themselves reduce to the taxonomy of physics. It is not required, and it is probably not true.

NOTES

I wish to express my gratitude to Ned Block for having read a version of this paper and for the very useful comments he made.
1   I shall usually assume that sciences are about events, in at least the sense that it is the occurrence of events that makes the laws of a science true. But I shall be pretty free with the relation between events, states, things and properties. I shall even permit myself some latitude in construing the relation between properties and predicates. I realize that all these relations are problems, but they aren't my problem in this paper. Explanation has to *start* somewhere, too.
2   The version of reductionism I shall be concerned with is a stronger one than many philosophers of science hold; a point worth emphasizing since my argument will be precisely that it is too strong to get away with. Still, I think that what I shall be attacking is what many people have in mind when they refer to the unity of science, and I suspect (though I shan't try to prove it) that many of the liberalized versions suffer from the same basic defect as what I take to be the classical form of the doctrine.
3   There is an implicit assumption that a science simply *is* a formulation of a set of laws. I think this assumption is implausible, but it is usually made when the unity of science is discussed, and it is neutral so far as the main argument of this paper is concerned.
4   I shall sometimes refer to "the predicate which constitutes the antecedent or consequent of a law". This is shorthand for "the predicate such that the antecedent or consequent of a law consists of that predicate, together with its bound variables and the quantifiers which bind them". (Truth functions of elementary predicates are, of course, themselves predicates in this usage.)
5   I don't think there is any chance at all that this is true. What is more likely is that type-identification for psychological states can be carried out in terms of the "total states" of an abstract automaton which models the organism. For discussion, see Block and Fodor (1972).
6   As, by the way, the predicates of natural languages quite certainly do. For discussion, see Chomsky (1965).

REFERENCES

Block, N. and Fodor, J. (1972) "What psychological states are not", *Philosophical Review* 81, 159–81.
Chomsky, N. (1965) *Aspects of the Theory of Syntax*, Cambridge, Mass.: MIT Press.

3   There is no Question of Physicalism

Tim Crane and D. H. Mellor

1 WHAT IS PHYSICALISM?

Many philosophers are impressed by the progress achieved by physical sciences. This has had an especially deep effect on their ontological views: it has made many of them physicalists. Physicalists believe that everything is physical: more precisely, that all entities, properties, relations, and facts are those which are studied by physics or other physical sciences. They may not all agree with the spirit of Rutherford's quoted remark that "there is physics; and there is stamp-collecting",[1] but they all grant physical science a unique ontological authority: the authority to tell us what there is.

Physicalism is now almost orthodox in much philosophy, notably in much recent philosophy of mind. But although often invoked, it is rarely explicitly defined. It should be. The claim that everything is physical is not as clear as it seems. In this paper, we examine a number of proposed definitions of physicalism and reasons for being a physicalist. We will argue both that physicalism lacks a clear and credible definition, and that in no non-vacuous interpretation is it true.

We are concerned here only with physicalism as a doctrine about the *empirical* world. In particular, it should not be confused with nominalism, the doctrine that there are no universals.[2] Nominalism and physicalism are quite independent doctrines. Believers in universals may as consistently assert as deny that the only properties and relations are those studied by physical science. And nominalists may with equal consistency assert or deny that physical science could provide enough predicates to describe the world. That is the question which concerns physicalists, not whether physical predicates name real universals. (We will for brevity write as if they do, but we do not need that assumption.)

As we will understand it, then, physicalism is not a doctrine about universals or other abstract objects, but about the empirical world, and specifically about minds. It says that mental entities, properties, relations and facts are all really physical. The mental is physicalism's chief target; but one we think it does not hit.

Physicalism is a kind of monism, opposing the dualist's distinction between two kinds of substance: matter and mind. As such, it is descended from *materialism*: the view that everything is matter – for instance, the view that nothing exists but collections of atoms in the void – as opposed say to Cartesian dualism, which held that as well as matter (extended substance) there is also mind (thinking substance). Many physicalists take their doctrine to be a modern version of materialism: defending the hegemony of modern matter against the mysteries of mental substance and of mind/matter interaction.

But physicalism differs significantly from its materialist ancestors. In its seventeenth-century form of mechanism, for instance, materialism was a metaphysical doctrine: it attempted to limit physics a priori by requiring matter to be solid, inert, impenetrable and conserved, and to interact deterministically and only on contact. But as it has subsequently developed, physics has shown this conception of matter to be wrong in almost every respect: the "matter" of modern physics is not all solid, or inert, or impenetrable, or conserved; and it interacts indeterministically and arguably sometimes at a distance. Faced with these discoveries, materialism's modern descendants have – understandably – lost their metaphysical nerve. No longer trying to limit the matter of physics a priori, they now take a more subservient attitude: the empirical world, they claim, contains just what a true complete physical science would say it contains.

But this raises two questions. What is physical science: that is, what sciences does it comprise? And what gives it this ontological authority? In other words, what entitles certain sciences to tell us *in their own terms* what the world contains – thereby entitling them to the physicalist's honorific title "physical"?

"Physical science" so construed certainly includes physics proper. Physics is the paradigm (hence "physical"). And chemistry, molecular biology and neurophysiology are also indisputably physical sciences. But not psychology, sociology and economics. One may debate the exact boundary of physical science: but unless some human sciences, of which psychology will be our exemplar, lie beyond its pale, physicalism, as a doctrine about the mind, will be vacuous.

What puts psychology beyond the pale of the physical? Not the a priori metaphysics of seventeenth-century materialism, since that has been refuted by physics itself. Nor the materialist's denial of mental substance. Psychology can – and mostly does – deny that too: but it still does not count as a physical science. The question of whether there is "mental substance" as well as "physical substance" is an irrelevant one. For that contrast of substances is really a contrast between their characteristic properties: between thinking, say, and being extended. A merely thinking substance is not a physically respectable entity because thinking is not a physically respectable property. But why not? What, if not the metaphysics of materialsim, prevents the empirical psychology of thought, and of other mental phenomena, adding in its own terms, as physics does, to our inventory of what there is?

It is often said that the human sciences have produced fewer results than the admittedly physical sciences. Their laws are said to be few and ill established, and their theories to proliferate, and to predict far less than those of gravity, say, or of molecular biology. Perhaps this paucity of results provides an epistemic basis for denying that psychology and the rest are physical – that is, entitled to tell us what there is. Perhaps they are just not good enough.

But that cannot be why psychology lacks the ontological authority of physics, chemistry and the rest. There are, as we shall see, many well-established psychological laws. And anyway, this epistemic argument is the wrong way round. Those who think psychology is epistemically suspect do so *because* its subject matter is not physical, and not vice versa. In other words, they have some other basis for taking physical science to exclude psychology, a basis from which psychology's epistemic inferiority is supposed to follow. And it is really quite obvious that this basis is not epistemic. For accepting the results of psychology does not entail accepting them as *physical*: on the contrary, the more such results physicalists accept, the more they reckon they have to explain (or explain away) in non-psychological terms.

The bounds of the physical are in fact set from the outside. Something about the mental is supposed to deprive psychology of the ontological authority of physics and chemistry. But what? What prevents psychology from telling us in its own terms what kinds of mental things and events there are? There are a number of answers to that question: but none, we shall argue, justifies the prima facie exclusion of psychology from the realm of the physical which is needed to make physicalism a non-vacuous doctrine about the mind.

2 REDUCTION TO PHYSICS

To assess physicalists' reasons for dismissing psychology as non-physical, and thus ontologically inconsequential, we must ask what makes them classify their favoured sciences as physical. What makes them count as physical not only the many diverse branches of physics itself (mechanics, electromagnetism, thermodynamics, gravity, and particle physics), but also sciences like chemistry and molecular biology?

One common answer is that these other sciences are physical because they *reduce* to physics, which for present purposes we may take to mean that a physics enhanced with suitable bridge principles (to link its vocabulary to theirs) would entail credible approximations of all their established laws.[3]

Some theories in other physical sciences have indeed been reduced to physics in this sense,[4] but by no means all. But those for whom reduction to physics is the touchstone of the physical do not propose to do it in practice. They simply insist that it can be done "in principle". But what is the principle? It cannot be physicalism. These sciences cannot be reducible in principle *because* they are physical if reducibility in principle (RIP) is supposed to tell us where the bounds of the physical lie. So what other principle will tell us which sciences could "in principle" be reduced to physics?

To answer this, we must first ask to *what* physics the RIP principle is supposed to be applied: to present physics, or to some hypothetical future physics? This question poses a dilemma. For applying the principle to present physics entails that any future extensions of it would not be physical: that physics, the paradigm physical science, is already complete. But no one believes this. And if we apply the principle to an otherwise unspecified future physics, we shall not be able to say which sciences are physical until we know which of them *that* physics must cover – which is just what the principle was supposed to tell us. To use RIP to future physics to say what that physics must cover if it is to cover everything physical is obviously viciously circular. So the physical cannot be defined as what is reducible in principle to physics, either present or future.

We think the RIP principle's specious appeal actually rests on two other prejudices. One is the old dream of the "unity of science", of being able to derive all scientific laws from one "ever more adequate grand scheme".[5] But we see no reason either to believe in or to aim for such a scheme. The world even of the admittedly physical sciences contains a vast number of very different kinds of entities, properties and facts. That is why so many different sciences, using widely different methods, are needed to study them. No one could think astrophysics and genetics unified even in their methods, except under the most abstract descriptions of scientific method-ology. And in their contents, they display no more unity than that of a conjunction. Nothing wrong with that: but then why cannot psychology supply another conjunct?

But even if some "unity of science" thesis were credible, it would not enable the RIP principle to define the physical. For even physics proper is not unified. Maybe it will be some day; but even if it is not, physicalists will still accept gravity, quantum and electromagnetic phenomena as physical, to be identified and described in their own terms by independent physical sciences. Similarly for the sciences of chemical, biological and neurophysio-logical phenomena. So why not for psychology, the science of mental phenomena?

The other source of the RIP principle's appeal is the idea that there is really no more to things than the smallest particles they are made up of. Let us call this thesis "microreduction", or "MR" for short.[6] The idea is very persistent. Take Eddington's two tables: his commonplace one, with extension, colour and permanence, versus his "scientific" one, nothing but myriad minute particles in empty space: the table which "modern physics has by delicate test and remorseless logic assured me ... is the only one which is really there".[7] Or more recently, McGinn's claim that science tells us that the way things are is very different from the way they look. The table that looks and feels so solid is, he thinks physics tells us, really full of holes.[8]

Now the study of the smallest entities is indeed traditionally called "physics": departments of physics have by long-established custom cornered that particular market. And this makes MR say that the empirical world is physical, since it consists only of its smallest particles. We are back with the doctrine of atoms in the void – or at least, in the field – which count as physical simply because they are microscopic.

The fact that physics by mere convention includes the study of the very small does indeed trivially entail that everything extended in space either is physical or has some physical parts; and for some, this trivial truth is all that physicalism means.[9] But for physicalism so defined to be non-vacuous, one must also take these smallest things to be all there is. But what reason is there to think this? Why should we suppose the existence of sub-atomic particles to require the non-existence of atoms, molecules, tables, trees, or tennis rackets, figs or fast food restaurants – or animals or people with minds?

Proponents of MR can of course distinguish our non-existence from that of, say, unicorns. There are undoubted facts which at least appear to be about us, whereas there are no such facts apparently about unicorns. And of course, since physics itself also studies very large things – galaxies, quasars, etc. – MR is also obliged to say why facts about even these admittedly physical things are different from facts about unicorns on the one hand and facts about sub-atomic particles on the other. What MR actually does say is that all these facts – about galaxies, minds and the rest – *reduce* to facts about their sub-atomic parts. So those parts are all there is, perhaps because we need not quantify over anything else in order to state all the facts – and we think with Quine that we should not multiply entities beyond quantificational necessity.[10]

But this appeal to reduction shows that MR itself needs a strong form of the very RIP principle it is supposed to support. And it cannot have it. For unless the sciences of the relatively large, including psychology, reduce to microphysics, we shall still need to quantify over entities described in those sciences' terms. But in fact, as we shall now show, even the *physics* of the relatively large does not reduce to microphysics. So even if all sciences were reducible in principle to physics, this would not entail that the smallest particles are all there is: MR would be false, even if the RIP principle were true. So the RIP principle cannot be used to support MR.

What *is* true is that facts about parts often explain facts about wholes. As a thesis about explanation, MR is often a good working hypothesis. But it is not always verified, even in microphysics. If for example we take the quantum mechanical description of a quantum ensemble to be complete (as orthodox interpretations do), the superposition principle entails that its properties will not be a function only of those of its isolated constituents plus relations between them. Orthodox quantum physics is not micro-reductive. And some physics is positively *macro*reductive: Mach's principle, for example, which makes the inertial mass even of microparticles depend on how matter is distributed throughout the universe. We realize of course that Mach's principle and orthodox quantum theory are controversial, and that a future physics might well abandon them. But they cannot be abandoned because they conflict with an MR entailed by modern micro-physics: since, as they show, it entails no such thing.

And even in the most ordinary physics, MR does not always hold. It is indeed usually true that where the parts of something go, the whole thing must go too: that a gas sample must go where its molecules go. But equally, its molecules must go where it goes: since any that do not will thereby cease to be *its* molecules. And that is not the only way in which a gas's molecules are as much governed by it as it is by them. Suppose for instance that our sample's volume is suddenly halved at a constant temperature. If the gas is ideal, Boyle's law entails that when its pressure settles down again it will be twice what it was. That law does not dictate all the interim behaviour of the sample's molecules – except that it must be such as will eventually double the sample's pressure. That much of their behaviour is determined – and thereby explained – *macro*reductively by a law governing the sample as a whole.

So even as a principle of explanation, MR does not always hold, even in physics. Its explanatory value cannot therefore support it as an ontological thesis. A fortiori, it cannot support physicalism. But it could not even do that if it were true. For no true reading of MR could entail that macroscopic entities, and their properties and relations, are *impugned* by being linked by laws to properties and relations of their smaller parts. They cannot be. For if they were, there would have to be some smallest entities, without parts: that is, a limit to the small-scale structure of matter. But there clearly need be no such limit. So the existence of the currently smallest known particles could not be refuted by the discovery of even smaller ones inside them. But then atoms too must be able to co-exist with their sub-atomic parts, molecules with their atoms, and so on, up to tables, trees – and us. The existence of animals and people, with their psychological and social properties and relations, cannot be denied just by crediting them with parts small enough to matter to microphysics.

The fact that physics takes in the very small has fostered the myth that it is a universal science in a sense in which others – like psychology – are not universal but merely "special sciences".[11] It has fostered this myth because it makes everything bigger than a point have (or have parts small enough to have) properties that are physical by mere definition. In a similar way, everything that moves has physical properties, such as inertial mass, just because physics by definition includes the science of mechanics. But that does not make these sciences *universal*, in the sense of encompassing all the properties and relations of things; nor *basic*, in the sense that other sciences must reduce to them. In any sense that would support a non-vacuous definition of the physical, which is what physicalism needs, mechanics and microphysics are no more universal or basic than psychology is. They are merely the special sciences of motion and of the very small.

In short, if the phenomena of psychology are less ontologically acceptable than those of physics and chemistry, it cannot be because psychology is irreducible to present or future physics. Reducibility to physics, or to microphysics, is a hopeless test of the ontological authority of a science: a test which not even a physicalist can apply consistently. For as we have seen, reducibility in practice is neither feasible nor to the point; while those who claim reducibility "in principle" either beg the question or appeal to principles, of the unity of science or of microreduction, which modern physics itself denies.

3 MENTAL CAUSATION AND INTENTIONALITY

How else might physical (that is, ontologically authoritative) science be defined so as to exclude psychology? Perhaps by causation, which many think is essentially physical. Perhaps the physical just is the causal, and what physicalism really means is that the empirical world comprises all and only those entities, properties, relations and facts which have causes or effects.

This definition clearly underlies one familiar formulation of the mind–body problem: how can mental states have effects in a physical world? This question would not pose such a problem if it were not assumed that causation is essentially non-mental.

But why should we assume this? It is surely obvious that there is plenty of mental causation. Suppose you see a friend, and this causes you to wave to him: how? Something like this: light is reflected from him onto your retina; impulses travel up your optic nerve; your striate cortex processes the information carried by them; you form (somehow) the belief that your friend is there; this makes you form the intention to greet your friend; that makes certain things happen in your motor systems; they cause your arm to rise . . . . Both physical and mental facts seem equally involved in this chain of causation. How then can a physicalism defined by causation exclude these apparently mental causes and effects?

It is indeed an old thought that mental causation is hard to make sense of, and especially causation linking the mental to the non-mental, because they seem to be so different. But why should that impress anyone who has learned from Hume that causation never "makes sense": that it is always a matter of fact, not of reason? Nothing in either Humean or other modern analyses of causation forces causes to be like their effects; nor does anything in them stop causes and effects being mental.

Take the requirement that token causes and effects be localized in space and time, so that they can be contiguous (or, if need be, dense or continuous) and so that one can precede the other. Token sensations and even token thoughts can certainly be localized enough for that (since localizing a token thought no more localizes its unlocalizable abstract content than localizing a red object localizes the abstract colour red). Nothing about the mental prevents people's token thoughts, feelings and sensations being wherever and whenever those people are, in order to be where they can have the immediate and therefore contiguous mental and non-mental causes and effects which they clearly appear to have.

Other common demands on causation are also just as easily met by mental as by non-mental causes and effects: for instance, the demand that causes be in the circumstances sufficient for their effects, or necessary (or both); or that they make their effects more probable than they would have been without them; or that causal relations instantiate laws. It is hard to see why any such condition should present any obstacle to the existence of mental causes and effects.

If there is a problem with mental causation, it lies in intentionality, the mind's capacity to represent aspects of the world. And intentionality is indeed often supposed to prevent mental phenomena from being, as such, physical. Thus Fodor:

> I suppose that sooner or later the physicists will complete the catalogue they've been compiling of the ultimate and irreducible properties of things. When they do, the likes of *spin, charm,* and *charge* will perhaps appear on their list. But *aboutness* surely won't; intentionality simply doesn't go that deep.[12]

But in the previous section, we have already disputed the pretensions of physics to provide all "the ultimate and irreducible properties of things". And no one impressed by our arguments will think it matters that intentionality goes less "deep" in this sense than spin and charge. For many non-mental (e.g. chemical and biological) properties will also not figure on the physicists' list; and if that does not impugn them or the entities they characterize, why should it impugn intentionality or the entities it characterizes?

But many philosophers would still agree with Fodor's subsequent comment that "the deepest motivation for intentional irrealism derives from a certain ontological intuition: that there is no place for intentional categories in a physicalist view of the world". Thus Field writes: "Any materialist who takes beliefs and desires at face value ... must show that the relations in question are not irreducibly mental."[13] If this intuition were correct, and there were independent reasons for accepting his "physicalist view of the world", then we would indeed have reason to deny the reality of intentionality, and thus much, if not all, of the mental. But as we shall see, the intuition is wrong.

What is the problem of intentionality supposed to be? Intentional states typically have three distinctive features: (1) they seem to be affected by, and to cause actions involving, distant object or events; (2) their ascription creates non-extensional contexts – sentences whose truth-value may alter when names or descriptions in them are replaced by others that apply to the same things; and (3) they can be about objects or events which do not exist. Suppose for example that (1) you read something about Santa Fe that makes you want to go there, which causes you to get on a plane and do so. But (2) you do not want to go to the most beautiful city in New Mexico, which Santa Fe is, because you do not know that it is. And (3) you could have wanted to go to Santa Fe even if, like Eldorado, it did not exist.

The challenge which (1) and (3) present is to explain how Santa Fe can cause you to act as you do when it is so far away, and need not even exist. No one believes that a city can have such effects directly at such distances – especially when it need not exist. Your action must be directly caused by some intrinsic property you actually have, not by your relations to distant and possibly non-existent objects, like Santa Fe, or to abstract ones like the possibly false proposition that it is in New Mexico.

But this does not mean that the causal powers of token thoughts and other mental states cannot depend on their contents: they can. All it means is that they must do so indirectly, via a mental representation, i.e. via some intrinsic non-relational property of the mental state (or of its owner). A token thought must have some such intrinsic property, correlated somehow with its content, to give it its right causes and effects. An instance of this property is, we may say, the local *causal surrogate* for that content.

But these intrinsic properties could still be mental. They could be sensations, or visual or other mental images or models – which need not, incidentally, be conscious.[14] And even if the compositional structure of thought requires these tokens to form a correspondingly complex ("syntactic") structure, they could still be images – like Shepard's shapes composed of images of cubes.[15] So the problem which thoughts pose for causation is *not* that they are mental and causation is not. It is that causation depends directly only on intrinsic properties, whereas the causal powers of token thoughts depend on their contents, which are not intrinsic.[16] This indeed shows that these contents need causal surrogates: but not because they are mental, since the surrogates could be mental too.

Moreover, the need for causal surrogates is by no means confined to psychology. They are needed throughout physical science. It is, for example, a standard function of physical fields to provide local causal surrogates for what would otherwise be unmediated action at a distance. But no one thinks that accepting Newtonian gravitational fields means denying the physical status, or the existence, of the Newtonian gravity they mediate.

In other parts of physics and chemistry, causal surrogates are needed also to bring about what would otherwise have to be backward causation. We noted earlier that Boyle's law makes the eventual pressure of an ideal gas sample double after its volume is suddenly halved at constant temperature. But that token equilibrium pressure, P, cannot directly affect the non-equilibrium processes which lead to it, since that would need backward causation. Moreover, P, like Santa Fe, need not even exist. The sample's volume may be altered again before it reaches equilibrium: but this cannot affect its behaviour before that. So the future P needs a causal surrogate *in the present* to make the sample head for P, just as Santa Fe needs one *in you* to make you head for it.

And as for this case, so for all systems that tend to stable equilibria: from simple pendulums to chemical and biological reactions of all kinds. The Gibbs' potentials of chemical thermodynamics, for example, are causal surrogates for the equilibria to which chemical systems tend:[17] equilibria whose existence and physical status they certainly do not impugn, any more than the field mechanisms of Newtonian gravity impugn it, or than the kinetics of gases refutes Boyle's law or shows that having a gas sample's volume does not really cause the doubling of its pressure. Why therefore should physiological or psychological accounts of how the contents of token thoughts produce their effects contradict them, or the causal explanations they give of our actions?

So much for the alleged problems posed by (1) and (3) for the ontological authority of intentional psychology. What about (2), the non-extensionality of ascriptions of intentional mental states? This does not exclude the mental from the physical either, since non-extensionality occurs in physics too.[18] This is because laws entail non-extensional conditions. Suppose for example that H and K are the genes that give us hearts and kidneys. The fact that we all have both does not make "anyone who had gene H would have a heart" entail either "anyone who had gene K would have a heart" or "anyone who had gene H would have a kidney".

The probabilistic laws of modern microphysics cannot be extensional for another reason too, because "$p(\ldots) = -$" is not extensional: for if it were, "a is the F" and the necessary truth "$p(a$ is $a) = 1$" would entail "$p(a$ is the $F)$

= 1", which it clearly does not, on any view of probability (take for example "F" = "next Prime Minister").

The non-extensionality of probability incidentally explains that of many singular causal instances of the contexts "... because ...", even in physics. This is because causation gives effects probabilities, if only subjective ones. Probabilistic accounts of causation make that explicit, and it is implicit even in deterministic accounts.[19] Effects of sufficient causes, for example, have probability 1; and effects of necessary ones would in their absence have probability 0. So "E because ..." must be non-extensional, since though a's being the F might give "E" a contingent probability, a's being a cannot. And "... because C" cannot be extensional either, because of its counterfactual implications: the probability of a necessary truth like "a is a" cannot depend on C, even if that of a true "a is the F" does.

These and other reasons convince us, *pace* Davidson and others, that even in physics singular causation never depends on, and mostly is not, an extensional causal relation between particulars.[20] But if causal contexts can be non-extensional anyway, they can perfectly well contain non-extensional contexts like "believes ...", "wants ...", "fears ...", etc.: as in "b fears that a is the F because a told her so" or "b does D because she wants a to be the F and believes he will be only if she does D". So we see no reason either to deny the causation which such sentences obviously report, or to suppose that it must be based on, or reduced to, any extensional causal relation – let alone a non-mental one that relates non-mental particulars.

In short, all the supposedly problematic features of intentional states are as endemic to physics, and in particular to non-mental causation, as they are to psychology. The notion of causation will thus not serve to define the physical (and hence ontologically authoritative) sciences in such a way as to exclude psychology. Defining the physical as the causal will not make physicalism a non-vacuous doctrine about the mind.

4 PSYCHOLOGICAL AND PSYCHOPHYSICAL LAWS

In order for the issue of physicalism to be a serious one, there has to be a principled distinction between the mental and the physical which explains why non-mental sciences have an ontological authority which psychology lacks. We have seen that neither causation nor reducibility to physics can provide such a distinction. But perhaps laws can. The ontological authority of science arguably rests on the laws it discovers, which tell us what kinds of things there are, and what properties and relations distinguish them. But many agree with Davidson that the mental is "anomalous": that strictly speaking there are no psychological or psychophysical laws.[21] If that were so, psychology would add nothing to our ontology of non-mental kinds, with their distinctive non-mental properties and relations.

But why should we deny that, for example, "All men are mortal" (a true psychophysical generalization limiting the sentience of members of our species) is a law? There are some bad reasons for denying it, which we shall not consider in detail. One is the idea that laws are necessarily true, which no generalizations about the mental ever are. Thus for McGinn, for mental terms to feature in laws is for "universal generalizations containing mental terms [to be] metaphysically necessary".[22] But, he argues (influenced by Kripke's well-known argument against the identity theory),[23] no non-analytic necessarily true generalizations link mental terms either to non-mental or to other mental terms.

Nor they do: but then none links the terms of physics to each other either. The laws of physics are not metaphysically necessary. We agree with Davidson that laws must be "supported by their instances" and "support counterfactual and subjunctive claims" ("if x were F it would be G").[24] But "All men are mortal" can clearly meet these conditions without being a necessary truth: the fact that something *would not* live for ever if it were human does not mean it *could not*, any more than "if we went we would go by bus" means we could not go by train. Nor therefore does the fact that the laws of physics meet these conditions show them to be necessary truths; and one of us has argued elsewhere that they are not.[25] So if terms had to feature in non-analytic necessary laws in order to count as physical, the terms of *physics* would not count, never mind those of psychology.

The law that all Fs are G entails only that anything *would* be G if it were F, not that it *must* be. (And the probabilistic law that all Fs have a chance p of being G, where $0 < p < 1$, does not even entail that – not even if it is a necessary truth.) The mere possibility of exceptions to psychological and psychophysical generalizations cannot therefore stop them being laws. And even if it could, even if laws did have to be both necessary and deterministic, how would one show without begging the question that a true generalization really could have exceptions? Not just by imagining them. We can all imagine light going faster in a vacuum than its actual speed c. This does not show that it really could go faster, still less that the constancy of c is not a law. And similarly in psychology. Anyone can imagine brine tasting like port: it can still be a law that to no one with our taste-buds would it ever taste anything like that.

Another bad reason for denying the existence of psychophysical laws is the so-called "variable realization" of mental states: the fact that "the range of physical states fit to realise a given mental state can be indefinitely various".[26] That cannot stop psychophysical generalizations being laws. For if it did, there would be hardly any laws in physics either. States like masses, volumes and temperatures are even more variously realized than mental states: one can have a gram or a litre of almost anything, at any one of an indenumerable infinity of temperatures.[27] So if variable realization does not rule out laws in mechanics and thermodynamics, it can hardly rule them out in psychology.

Nor should we be impressed by the inability of armchair reflection to excogitate psychological or psychophysical generalizations. Physics and chemistry are not excogitatable a priori, and we see no reason why psychology should be. It can take as much unobvious theory and experiment to discover the psychophysics of taste, or of vision,[28] or the unconscious psychology of inference,[29] as to uncover (say) the biochemistry of reproduction.

So in particular, Stich's failure to excogitate laws featuring intentional mental states does not mean there are not any.[30] The obvious explanation of our inability to state such laws in simple and exceptionless forms is that our intentional psychology is too complex and (probably) probabilistic. But so is the meteorology of hurricanes, and the quantum mechanics of large molecules. Their laws, for those very reasons, are not statable by us in simple and exceptionless forms. No one infers from this that there are no such laws; and the inference is no better in psychology.

Davidson himself does not use these arguments against the existence of psychological laws. His own argument goes as follows:

1   There are no strict psycho*physical* laws.
2   Singular causes and effects must instantiate strict laws.
3   The mental is not a "comprehensive closed" system, being affected by the non-mental, which does form such a system.

But by (1) these mental effects cannot instantiate strict psychophysical laws. So

4   "there are no strict laws at all on the basis of which we can predict and explain mental phenomena".[31]

The argument fails at every step. (1) is false, and not only because "All men are mortal" is a law. There are many more such laws, linking sensations – like pains, smells, tastes, and visual, aural and tactile sensations – to non-mental features of those who have them. There must be, because whole industries depend on them. Think of the laws which must underlie the reliable production and use of anaesthetics, scents, narcotics, sweeteners, coloured paints and lights, loudspeakers and soft cushions. And if Newton's laws of motion suffice to add masses and forces to our physical ontology, these laws must suffice to add to it the kinds of sensations that feature in them.

But even if there were no such psychophysical laws, this would not undermine the ontological authority of psychology. Even if no laws linked the mental to the non-mental, psychology could still have its own laws, defining its own mental ontology, on a par with that of chemistry (say). For as we saw in Section 2, chemistry's ontological authority does not depend on its being reducible to physics via physiochemical laws. Nor therefore can psychology's ontological authority depend on there being psychophysical laws.[32]

But as we have seen, our sensations are in fact subject to psychophysical laws, which themselves suffice to refute Davidson's denial that "there can be strict laws linking the mental and the [non-mental]";[33] since these laws may very well be "strict" (i.e. deterministic). Davidson is admittedly more interested in intentional states than in sensations; but the refutation still holds, since sensations are indisputably mental – as Davidson himself admits.[34]

So (1) is false. And so is (2): causes and effects need only instantiate probabilistic laws.[35] But can we not therefore make (2) true – and strengthen (4) – by deleting "strict" throughout? Indeed we can, and we should: but that will not help Davidson, since it only makes (1) even more incredible.

Nor does admitting probabilistic laws do anything to rescue (3). For whether causation needs strict or merely probabilistic laws, the non-mental no more forms a "comprehensive closed system" than the mental does.

For what does "a comprehensive closed system" mean? For Davidson, it means a system of "homonomic" laws, which "can hope to be precise, explicit and as exceptionless as possible" only because they draw their concepts "from a comprehensive closed theory". The non-mental sciences can provide such a theory, Davidson claims; but psychology cannot. Its generalizations are hopelessly "heteronomic": that is, they "may give us reason to believe there is a precise law at work, but one that can be stated only by shifting to a different vocabulary".[36]

But this distinction will not do, since physics itself is full of heteronomic laws. Take Newtonian mechanics, which defines Newtonian concepts of force and mass by saying how they combine to cause acceleration. But the laws of motion that do this do not form a closed theory. Indeed, without some further law relating force to other concepts, they form no testable theory at all. In the theory of Newton's *Principia*, the further law is the inverse square law of gravity. But that theory is not closed either. There are many other kinds of force: electrical, magnetic, viscous, etc. So as a law of net force, Newton's law of gravity is as hopelessly heteronomic as the laws of psychology: it can be made exceptionless only by provisos invoking alien concepts of electricity, etc.[37] And similarly for all the other laws of force. All are true only as laws of *kinds* of forces: gravitational, electrical, etc., which combine into net forces by vectorial addition. The theory of Newtonian mechanics is just the conjunction of all such laws, however diverse their other concepts, with Newton's laws of motion.

Newtonian mechanics has of course been superseded, but not because it was only a conjunction: for a conjunction, as we saw in Section 2, has all the unity a science needs. So our "comprehensive closed theory" can also be a simple conjunction: the conjunction of all true scientific theories and laws. But then to say, as Davidson does, that the non-mental sciences can supply this conjunction on their own is simply to deny the existence of psychological laws: which both begs the question and is refuted by the laws that we know link sensations to their non-mental causes.

So Davidson's argument (1)–(4) quite fails to show that there are no psychophysical or psychological laws. But this does not refute his claim that there are no laws linking *intentional* mental states. And for that claim Davidson gives a special argument, which rests mainly on two connected ideas: the "holism" of the intentional, and the "constitutive ideal of rationality".

The holism of intentional mental states amounts to their being conceptually interdependent, which sensations are not. The belief that *P*, for example, must inhibit the belief that not-*P*, and also the desire that *P* (people do not want what they think they already have). Again, neither belief nor desire can cause action on its own. To do that they must combine, and different combinations can cause the same action: I can say "*P*", for example, either because I believe it and want to speak truly or because I disbelieve it and want to lie. And there is no doubt that such familiar relations between beliefs, desires and actions do partly define them, and thus stop any laws involving them being wholly independent.

But these facts cannot stop there being such laws, because they too have Newtonian parallels. Newtonian force (f) and mass (m) are also conceptually interdependent, being partly defined by the relation $f = ma$, which stops laws involving them being independent of each other. And this relation too requires forces and masses to combine to produce their effects (accelerations) – a lets many combinations cause the same effect. So we can no more infer and force f or a mass m from the acceleration a they cause than we can infer a belief or a desire from the action they cause. In short, holism alone will not suffice to distinguish the intentional from the non-mental in a way that will show it to be anomalous – as Davidson again admits.[38]

What about Davidson's "constitutive ideal of rationality"? This is the idea that the relations between beliefs, desires and actions mentioned above partly define or constitute (hence "constitutive") what it is to be rational. For instance, the fact that the belief that P will generally inhibit the belief that not-P is one of the holistic truisms that help to define rationality: it is rational not to have obviously contradictory pairs of beliefs. Rationality is an ideal because thinkers can be more or less rational: they can fail to have the totality of their intentional states standing in all these "rational" relations.

This may all be true: but again it cannot rule out psychological laws since it too has a Newtonian parallel. Indeed everything that Davidson says is peculiar to "our use of the concepts of belief, desire and the rest" has a Newtonian parallel. Here it is:

> We must stand prepared, as the evidence [of accelerations induced by gravity, electricity, etc.] accumultates, to adjust our theory [of the forces and masses involved] in the light of considerations of cogency [satisfying Newton's laws]: the constitutive ideal of *rationality* [Newton's laws] partly controls each phase in the evolution of what must be an evolving theory. An arbitrary choice of translation scheme [from accelerations to forces] would preclude such opportunistic tempering of theory: put differently, *a right arbitrary choice of a translation manual* would be of a manual acceptable in the light of all possible evidence, and this *is a choice we cannot make*.[39]

We have italicized the two debatable analogies. First, *rationality*, which many think is a normative notion, constraining for example, what one *ought* to believe. Well, maybe it is, but a belief's rationality may still be a fact about it, for example, something that makes it probably true; with the constitutive ideal simply requiring beliefs to be so related to each other, and to their perceptual causes, that under normal conditions most of them *are* true. And that, far from preventing laws linking the contents of our beliefs to our surroundings and to the non-mental operation of our senses, positively requires there to be some such laws (if only probabilistic ones).

Secondly, the claim that no evidence can enable us to choose a right translation scheme: that is, one which correctly infers beliefs, desires, etc. from their perceptual causes and behavioural effects. But if this is to provide a disanalogy with mechanics, it cannot just mean that no evidence could entail the right theory. That is true in spades in Newtonian mechanics, even if forces are observable, since every ascription of a mass at any time t entails an indenumerable infinity of net accelerations under different net forces at t, none of which entails any other, and only one of which can be actual. How could intentional mental states be more underdetermined by the evidence for them than that?

Davidson, however, thinks that Quine's "indeterminacy of translation" shows that they must be.[40] He says that the anomalism of the mental "traces back" to the "central role of translation" and its indeterminacy. For if there is no determinate translation of sentences, there is no right statement of what they mean. So, since their meanings are the contents of the beliefs they would express, there is no right statement of those either: that is, beliefs (and a fortiori other intentional mental states) have no determinate contents. Contents, like sentence meanings, are not just underdetermined by evidence: they simply do not exist. And if they do not exist, they certainly cannot have instances which feature in laws.

But we deny the indeterminacy of translation, for familiar reasons.[41] As we have already seen, and many others have pointed out,[42] it cannot be entailed by the underdetermination of theories by evidence, or even Newtonian mechanics would have no laws. Nor, without begging the present question, can it be entailed by "Quine's claim that theories of translation are ... underdetermined even by the totality of truths expressible in terms of physics",[43] since psychological and psychophysical laws are *ex hypothesi* not so expressible. To base the indeterminacy of translation on that claim is to base it on what we saw in Section 2 is an untenable version – the reducibility-to-physics version – of the very physicalism it is being used to support.

We know of no other reason to deny a priori the existence of laws involving intentional mental states. But might not the totality of all true non-mental theories be *in fact* so comprehensive and closed as to preclude psychological and psychophysical laws? We do not see how. No amount of physics, for example, can stop mental states instantiating other laws as well. The other laws must of course be consistent with physics – but only because all truths must be consistent with each other. That truism gives no priority to physics, whose laws must equally be consistent with those of psychology.

But perhaps this reading of (3) may look more plausible as a thesis about *causation*, rather than about laws: and Davidson himself suggests that this is how he understands (3) when he says that "too much happens to affect the mental that is not itself a systematic part of the mental".[44]

For suppose physics did form a comprehensive causal system: so that laws of physics made each brain state or bodily movement b_2 of yours at any time t_2 be determined by your brain states at an earlier time t_1 (plus non-mental input between t_1 and t_2). How could your mental states between t_1 and t_2 also affect b_2 without violating these deterministic laws?

But now consider a parallel case. Suppose Kepler's laws made the Earth's orbital position p_2 at t_2 be determined by its position p_1 at t_1 (plus its velocity then, the input from space between t_1 and t_2). How, we might equally ask, could the Earth's positions between t_1 and t_2 also affect p_2 without violating Kepler's laws? Yet they must affect p_2 if p_1 does, for p_1 itself comes between t_2 and still earlier positions p_0 which, given Kepler's laws, also determine p_2. There's nothing special about t_1.

The solution to this puzzle lies in the counterfactual conditional (C) which this causal claim entails: if p_1 had been different, so would p_2 – but p_0 would not. In other words, what violates Kepler's laws is only (C)'s counterfactual antecedent. (C) itself does not violate them, and nor therefore does the causal claim which entails it: indeed Kepler's laws are what make (C), and hence the causal claim, true.

Similarly in our original case. Our mental states, intentional and otherwise, could – and would – affect our brain states and bodily movements even if the laws of physics made them all determined also by earlier brain states. The claim that a system thus constrained by non-mental laws must be closed, in the sense of being unaffectable by its mental states, simply does not follow – and it is not true.

5 SUPERVENIENCE

We have seen that neither laws nor causation deprive psychology of the ontological authority of non-mental sciences. But that still leaves one non-vacuous interpretation of physicalism. The last refuge of the modern physicalist is *supervenience*: the thesis that there is no change or difference without a non-mental change or difference. Two things will never change or differ in any way without also changing or differing in some non-mental way. The physical excludes the mental by being that on which everything else, including the mental, supervenes.

Supervenience is stronger than the trivial claim that everything extended in space has physical parts, but weaker than reductionism, since it says nothing about *which* non-mental difference will accompany any mental one: it does not entail the existence of any psychophysical laws. But it must be stronger than we have so far indicated. For given the multitude of changeable non-mental properties which any thing has (including its spatiotemporal location), all things that change or differ mentally are bound to change or differ in fact in some non-mental respect. So supervenience, to be serious, must mean more than that. The relevant range of non-mental respects must be restricted (at least by excluding spatiotemporal location), and the claim must be at least subjunctive – "Two things *would* never differ ..." – and arguably even stronger – "Two things *could* never differ ...."

However, to give supervenience a run for its money, we will take it as weakly as we can: in its subjunctive form, and with the relevant non-mental respects restricted as little as possible. Even so, we see no reason to believe it. The evidence for it cannot be empirical, since the prospect of ever finding two things, complex enough to have psychological properties, type-identical in every reasonable non-mental respect, is extremely slight, to say the least. The only remotely plausible argument for supervenience is one which appeals to the causal principle mentioned in Section 3, that there is no unmediated action at a distance. This means, as we saw there, that tokens of beliefs and other intentional mental states need intrinsic properties to act as causal surrogates for their contents. And if these properties are all non-mental, and sensations are likewise determined by their non-mental causes, then supervenience may well seem to follow.

But it does not. First, as we have already observed, the intrinsic properties which act as causal surrogates for the contents of token beliefs and other intentional states may very well be mental. And secondly, whether they are mental or not, beliefs will still not supervene on them. For two thinkers could easily have all the same intrinsic properties and still have different beliefs. This is an obvious moral of Putnam's "Twin Earth" stories:[45] the content of your Twin Earth duplicate's belief that water is wet differs from yours, because his (or her) water is XYZ and yours is H_2O. And similarly for indexical beliefs. If the content of "That's an elm" includes the tree you look at as you think it, it will differ for two people looking at different trees, even if they have all the same intrinsic properties.

The defender of supervenience might respond that this only shows that thoughts do not supervene on their thinkers' intrinsic properties. They might still supervene on those plus thinkers' non-mental (e.g. spatio-temporal) relations to other things, and those things' non-mental properties (being an elm, or H_2O). But that is not true either, as we can see by considering how thinkers make mistakes. Suppose for example that you and your intrinsically identical twin now look at the same elm, but that although this makes you think it is an elm, it makes him or her think it is an oak. Same intrinsic properties, same relations, same properties of the thing thought about: but different thoughts.

Again, the defender of supervenience might respond that in such a case there would always be some relevant non-mental difference: if not in your eyes, then in how the tree looks from your different viewpoints. But we doubt this. You and your twin might well differ in only mental respects: for example, in your beliefs about what elms look like – beliefs which need supervene on nothing present or non-mental, merely on the different mental effects trees have had on you in the past. And we see no non-question-begging reason to think that those effects must supervene on past non-mental differences.

On the other hand, your and your twin's past experiences do have present effects: they make you think "That's an elm", and your twin think "That's an oak". And being at a temporal distance, they cannot have those effects immediately: their effects must be mediated by some present intrinsic properties of you and of your twin. So perhaps your thoughts must supervene on your intrinsic properties after all?

Not so. For not only, as we have seen, may these mediating properties themselves be mental, but even if they are not, they need not differ just because their mental effects do. Causation need not, after all, be deterministic, and modern physics tells us that it often is not. So we have every reason to expect some indeterminism in the causal processes of our perception, our reasoning and our action: this being one way in which these processes can go wrong and make us make mistakes. But when causation is indeterministic, causes and effects will not supervene on each other. In short, modern physics gives us reason to deny the supervenience of the contents of our token thoughts on even the most extensive list of our other intrinsic and extrinsic properties and relations.

And as for thoughts, so for sensations. Their having non-mental causes or effects will not make them supervenient. On the contrary, if the relevant causation is somewhat indeterministic, sensations *cannot* supervene on their non-mental causes.

Yet again, however, the defenders of supervenience may reply that causation, unlike supervenience, takes time – and we agree.[46] Causes always precede their effects, whereas token thoughts and sensations are only supposed to supervene on *simultaneous* tokens of non-mental properties. So showing that they do not supervene on their earlier non-mental causes does not directly refute that claim.

But it does refute it indirectly. For suppose an intrinsic non-mental property P causes a mental property M indeterministically. (Say for example that one's chance of being M at t_2 is 0.9 if one has just been P (at t_1), and 0.1 if one has not.) Now suppose that at t_1 many people share *all* their intrinsic non-mental properties, including P. At t_2, therefore, most but not all of them will be M: that is, some pairs of people, atom-for-atom alike at t_1, will differ at t_2 in this mental respect.

Now let a and b be any such pair: at t_2, a is M and b is not. What about a's and b's intrinsic non-mental properties at t_2? Well, these may all be determined by a's and b's shared non-mental state at t_1. But if so, then they too will all be shared, and M will not supervene on them either. But M will not supervene on them anyway. For even if some relevant laws of physics are indeterministic, so that a's and b's state at t_1 does not *make* them share all their intrinsic non-mental properties at t_2, it still will not *stop* them doing so. On the contrary: given enough such as and bs, some will certainly differ mentally at t_2 without differing in any other way.

In other words, modern indeterministic physics must predict that some pairs of people, atom-for-atom alike in all non-mental respects, will differ in some simultaneous mental respects: and will do so precisely because the properties involved are causally related. In short, modern physics suggests that even the weakest serious form of supervenience, which is itself the weakest non-vacuous form of physicalism, is false. And physicalists can surely not expect a physicalism that is falsified by physics to be verified by anything else.

6 THE END

We have argued that no defensible definition of physicalism will deprive psychology of the ontological status of the non-mental sciences. In no non-vacuous sense is physicalism true. But this does not mean that we want to encourage a revival of Cartesian dualism. On the contrary, our arguments entail that there is no divide between the mental and the non-mental sufficient even to set physicalism up as a serious question, let alone as a serious answer to it. Physicalism is the wrong answer to an essentially trivial question. So it cannot begin to help philosophers of mind answer the serious questions about the mind and, above all, about intentionality: what enables some parts of the world (us) to think about other parts, including other people (and of course ourselves). And to those questions it is quite obvious that neither dualism nor physicalism has anything to contribute. The dualist does not even try to explain intentionality: he just takes it for granted, stipulating it into existence. And saying that minds are all physical no more helps to explain how some physical things can think than saying that all flesh is grass helps to explain the difference between carnivores and vegetarians. This, therefore, should really be the last paper on the subject of physicalism. But we fear it will not be.[47]

NOTES

1   C. Longuet-Higgins, "The failure of reductionism", in C. Longuet-Higgins *et al.*, *The Nature of Mind*, 16. Edinburgh, Edinburgh University Press.
2   *Pace* H. H. Field, *Science Without Numbers*, Oxford, Blackwell, 1980 and B. Stroud "The physical World", *Proceedings of the Aristotelian Society*, 1987: 264.
3   See e.g. C. G. Hempel, *Philosophy of Natural Science*, Englewood Cliffs, NJ, Prentice-Hall, 1966, ch. 8.
4   See M. Friedman, "Theoretical explanation", in R. Healey (ed.) *Reduction, Time and Reality*, Cambridge, Cambridge University Press, 1981.
5   H. Feigl, "Physicalism, unity of science and the foundations of psychology" (1963), in his *Inquiries & Provocations*, ed. R. Cohen, Dordrecht, Reidel, 1981: 315.
6   G. Schlesinger, *Method in the Physical Sciences*, London, Routledge & Kegan Paul, 1963, ch. 2.
7   A. S. Eddington, *The Nature of the Physical World*, Cambridge, Cambridge University Press, 1929: xi–xiv.
8   C. McGinn, *The Subjective View*, Oxford, Clarendon Press, 1983, ch. 7.
9   G. P. Hellman and F. W. Thompson, "Physicalism: ontology, determination and reduction", *Journal of Philosophy*, 1905.
10 W. V. O. Quine, "On what there is", in his *From a Logical Point of View*, Cambridge, Mass., Harvard University Press, 1953.
11 See J. A. Fodor "Special sciences", *Synthèse*, 1974 [ch. 2, this volume].
12 J. A. Fodor, *Psychosemantics: the problem of meaning in the philosophy of mind*, Cambridge, Mass., MIT Press, 1987: 97.
13 H. H. Field, "Mental representation", *Erkenntnis*, 1978: 78.
14 See P. N. Johnson-Laird, *Mental Models*, Cambridge, Cambridge University Press, 1983; R. N. Shepard and L. A. Cooper, *Mental Images and Their Transformations*, Cambridge, Mass., MIT Press, 1982.
15 Shepard and Cooper, ibid., ch. 3.
16 As one of us has shown in detail elsewhere: T. M. Crane, *The Content and Causation of Thought*, Cambridge University Ph.D. Dissertation, 1989.
17 K. G. Denbigh, *The Principles of Chemical Equilibrium*, Cambridge, Cambridge University Press, 1955: 76.
18 B. Enc, "Intentional states of mechanical systems", *Mind*, 1982.
19 E.g. D. H. Mellor, "On raising the chances of effects", in J. H. Fetzer (ed.) *Probability and Causality*, Dordrecht, Reidel, 1988; J. L. Mackie, "Causes and conditions" (1965), in E. Sosa (ed.) *Causation and Conditionals*, Oxford, Oxford University Press, 1975.

20 D. Davidson, "Causal relations" (1967), in his *Essays on Actions and Events*, Oxford, Clarendon Press, 1980; D. H. Mellor, "The singularly afecting facts of causation", in D. Pettit *et al.*, (eds) *Metaphysics and Morality*, Oxford, Blackwell, 1987.

21 D. Davidson, "Mental events" (1970), in his *Essays on Actions and Events*, Oxford, Clarendon Press, 1980.

22 C. McGinn, "Philosophical materialism", *Synthèse*, 1980: 187.

23 S. Kripke, "Naming and necessity", in D. Davidson and G. Harman (eds) *Semantics of Natural Languages*, Dordrecht, Reidel, 1972.

24 D. Davidson, "Mental Events": 217.

25 See D. H. Mellor, "Necessities and universals in natural laws", in D. H. Mellor (ed.) *Science, Belief & Behaviour*, Cambridge, Cambridge University Press, 1980; D. M. Armstrong, *What is a Law of Nature?*, Cambridge, Cambridge University Press, 1983.

26 C. McGinn, "Mental states, natural kinds, and psychophysical laws I", *Proceedings of the Aristotelian Society Supplementary Volume*, 1978: 197.

27 See M. Wilson, "What is this thing called 'pain'? – the philosophy of science behind the contemporary debate", *Pacific Philosophical Quarterly*, 1985: 235

28 D. Marr, *Vision*, San Francisco, Freeman, 1982.

29 P. N. Johnson-Laird, *Mental Models*.

30 S. Stich, *From Folk Psychology to Cognitive Science*, Cambridge, Mass., 1983, ch. 7.

31 D. Davidson, "Mental events": 224–5.

32 See W. Lycan, "Psychological laws", *Philosophical Topics*, 1981.

33 D. Davidson, "Mental events": 212.

34 Ibid., p. 211; see also his "Replies to essays", in B. Vermazen and M. Hintikka (eds) *Essays on Davidson: Actions and Events*, Oxford, Clarendon Press, 1985: 246.

35 See e.g. P. Suppes, "Davidson's views on psychology as a science", in B. Vermazen and M. Hintikka, (eds) *Essays on Davidson*; D. H. Mellor, "On raising the chances of effects", in Fetzer (ed.) *Probability and Causality*.

36 D. Davidson, "Mental events": 219.

37 See N. Cartwright, *How the Laws of Physics Lie*, Oxford, Clarendon Press, 1983, ch. 3.

38 "Mental events": 221; "Replies to Essays": 248.

39 "Mental events": 223.

40 W. V. O. Quine, *Word and Object*, Cambridge, Mass., MIT Press, 1960, ch. 2.; D. Davidson, "Mental events": 222.

41 See e.g. R. Kirk, *Translation Determined*, Oxford, Clarendon Press, 1986, pt III.

42 E.g. N. Chomsky, "Quine's empirical assumptions", in D. Davidson and J. Hintikka (eds) *Words and Objections*, Dordrecht, Reidel, 1969.

43 R. Kirk, *Translation Determined*: 136.

44 "Mental events": 224.

45 H. Putnam, "The meaning of 'meaning'", in his *Mind, Language and Reality*, Cambridge, Cambridge University Press, 1975. The moral is drawn explicitly by T. Burge, "Individualism and psychology", *Philosophical Review*, 1986.

46 D. H. Mellor, *Real Time*, Cambridge University Press, 1981, chs 9–10.

47 The material in this paper is derived partly from one author's Ph.D. dissertation (T. M. Crane, *Content and Causation of Thought*) and partly from material presented by the other author to meetings of the British Society for the Philosophy of Science, the Oxford University Philosophical Society, the Cambridge University PPE Workshop and to seminars at University College London, the University of Sussex, the University of California at Irvine, the

University of Wisconsin at Madison, Northwestern University and the History and Philosophy of Science Department in Cambridge. We are grateful for helpful comments and criticism made by many people on those occasions and in many private conversations and correspondence.

POSTSCRIPT

We have been accused of ignoring the most plausible versions of physicalism (Robinson 1991, Pettit 1993), of not taking account of the methodology of physical science (Smith 1992, Papineau 1993) and of giving an invalid argument against supervenience (Menuge 1993). We have rebutted some of these accusations in detail elsewhere (Crane 1993, Mellor 1993). Here we address more general issues.

Although all the doctrines we attacked have been explicitly advanced as physicalist, many of our physicalist critics now deny that they hold any of them. Their combination of Puritan zeal with Anglican equivocation does make our Hydra-headed opponents hard to pin down, but it also suggests a worship of the physical that owes more to emotion than to argument. We must however confess to ignoring one fashionable physicalist credo, the cry that all entities, if not reducible to physical ones, are at least *composed* of or *constituted* by them: i.e. that mental particulars, properties and facts are "nothing over and above" the physical entities which constitute them (see Charles and Lennon 1992 for versions of this view). Many physicalists seem surprised by our reluctance to be impressed by this modest proposal.

But how modest this proposal is depends on what "composed of" means. Agreeing with De Morgan that "great fleas have little fleas upon their backs to bite 'em, and little fleas have lesser fleas, [perhaps] *ad infinitum*", we admitted in our paper that "everything extended in space either is physical or has some physical parts", simply because the study of the smallest entities, including spacetime points, is traditionally assigned to physics departments. What we deny is that this is a serious reading of physicalism, unless these little points and parts are taken to be all there is. For *contra* Pettit (1993), non-physical fleas, such as our minds, are not made physical by having little physical fleas inside 'em: so either these non-physical entities do not exist or this so-called "physicalism" admits all we assert, namely that not everything is physical.

To this most physicalists reply that non-physical wholes depend on their physical parts: remove the latter and you remove the former. But so what? All wholes depend on their parts in this way: does that make our galaxy no more than the spacetime points it occupies and without which it would not exist? Moreover, as we observed, many parts depend just as much on the whole they are parts of: as, for example, each particle in a gas sample depends for its temperature on the mean kinetic energy of all the others; or as the colour of a small part of a painted surface depends on the colours that surround it. The supposed truisms of mereology do not show mental or physical wholes to be nothing more than their trivially physical smallest parts.

In any case the relevant relation between the mental and the physical is not that of wholes to parts. That is a relation between particulars, whereas physicalism is a thesis about properties. What our constitution theorists must therefore argue is that physical properties in some sense "constitute" mental ones. But in what sense? Two proposals have been made recently: that mental properties are related to physical ones (1) as determinables like colour are to their determinate values, like green (Yablo 1992), or (2) as a "role" is to a "realizer" of that role (Papineau 1993). Although we reject both these views, here we remark only that they both credit the world with containing more than a "true completed physics" would assert. Why then call these views physicalist? The only reason we can think of is to signal their inconsistency with Cartesian dualism. But it is bizarre to reduce physicalism to a mere denial of one of the most contentious theories of the mind there has ever been.

We do however have a diagnosis of why constitution theorists jump through so many hoops to say how mental and physical properties are related. We think it is because they take denying Cartesian minds to entail accepting some principle about the generality or universality of physics, such as the principle Papineau (1993) calls the "completeness" of physics – that all physical effects are completely determined by purely physical causes. Once accepted, this principle generates a seemingly hard but actually quite spurious problem of how to explain the reality and causal efficacy of mental entities. Our solution is to avoid raising the problem in the first place, by rejecting the principle. For as our paper shows, neither physics in particular nor the non-mental sciences in general are complete in any sense that poses any problem for mental causation. There would only be a problem if physical laws were so complete that adding mental laws would create a contradiction. But in that sense physics is not complete at all: for example, the physical laws which require our thoughts and actions to conserve energy and momentum are consistent with any number of psychological and psychophysical laws and consequent mental causation.

The vogue for constitution theories also exemplifies two other defects in recent physicalist literature. The first is that it deflects serious debate about the mind's place in nature into attempts to answer the silly question, "given that we must be physicalists, what sort of physicalists should we be?" All this produces is vague or vacuous formulations of physicalism, which do nothing to solve any real philosophical problems about the mind, such as those posed by consciousness and intentionality. The right approach is to start with those problems and see if their solutions require us to suppose that the mind is physical, and if so in what sense. These physicalists are like Christians or socialists posing such questions as "The Middle East: what should a Christian/socialist think?", to which the only sensible answer is: first think about the real problems of the Middle East and see if they demand, or even admit, Christian or socialist solutions.

The literature's second defect is its tendency to rely on a few talismanic words to ward off belief in spooks. Take "supervenience": despite all the effort put into defining all the possible versions of this vague idea, even physicalists are beginning to realize that it cannot on its own define a serious kind of physicalism (see Horgan 1993). We think the significance of "constitution" has been exaggerated in much the same way. It makes perfectly good sense to talk of the constitution of a particular thing or event by its spatial or spatiotemporal parts. But this, as we have noted, is not how the mental is related to the physical. Yet far from being discouraged by the obvious disanalogy, constitution theorists respond by claiming that, even though the precise notion of constitution here has yet to be formulated, they do know that the physical must "in some sense" constitute the mental. In short, as with "supervenience", they find solace in a physicalistically correct word, almost regardless of its meaning (see e.g. Pettit 1993: 215).

So much for today's physicalist orthodoxy. Other critics have complained that our paper did not adequately address its precursors. For instance, we did not discuss the arguments of David Lewis and others for various forms of identity theory. Thus Lewis (1966) argues that if mental states are defined in terms of their causal roles, and physics is "explanatorily adequate", then mental states must be physical states. But if we did not tackle this argument directly, we did tackle it indirectly, by attacking in our Section 2 its second premise, that physics is explanatorily adequate.

Similarly with the "overdetermination argument" for token identity (see Papineau 1990). This assumes that (1) some token physical effect has a token mental cause, (2) all physical effects have complete physical causes and (3) there is no causal overdetermination, and infers that the token mental cause is identical with some token physical cause. Here the premise we challenged was (2): we denied that all physical effects have physical causes which are complete in any sense that stops them also having different mental causes. To this we would now add that (3) is also false in any sense that would yield the conclusion, even if (2) were true. Take the members of a firing squad all firing at once, perhaps to try and absolve each other from the charge of causing the death of their victim, Don. Who then killed Don? Such cases do pose a problem for counterfactual analyses of causation, but that is no reason to pretend that they cannot occur. And in the mental case the problem need never arise if, as we have argued, psychophysical laws link mental and physical events and states. For then Don's wife Kim's distress and a state of her brain can both be sufficient causes of her collapse, since a psychophysical law can make each of these causes supervene on the other, thus making each such that, without it, Kim would not have collapsed. The problem of overdetermination, such as it is, arises only when two or more sufficient causes are nomologically independent, which the distinct mental and physical causes of Kim's collapse need not be. But even if they were independent, they would pose no worse a problem than the firing squad does – and the theory they would pose it for is not any non-physicalist theory of the mind but the counterfactual theory of causation.

These and other links between identity theories and our anti-physicalism are developed in more detail in Crane (forthcoming). Here we can only repeat that we have not yet found a serious version of physicalism that is immune to the arguments of our paper. This however brings us to the other common complaint about us, namely that we did not say what our own position is: dualist, non-reductionist, naturalist, anti-naturalist? To this complaint we must first reply that it misses our main point, which was to deny the significance of the problem to which physicalism, dualism and the rest offer solutions. However, to satisfy those who want a label for our view of the mind, we shall conclude by offering one.

Although we have explicitly rejected Cartesian dualism, we should not mind being called "dualists" if this implied no more than our belief that some mental items are not physical. But it implies more than this. In particular, it implies that we think the mental–physical distinction matters more than, say, chemical–electrical, biological–economic or thermal–gravitational distinctions. But we do not think it does. Accepting the existence of irreducibly mental entities does not make us divide empirical entities into just two significant classes: the mental and the physical. "Dualism" is therefore a misleading label for our view.

We should also quite like to call our view "naturalism", if all this meant was that minds are natural entities which can be studied by the natural science of psychology. For we are opposed not only to Cartesian dualism, but also to the view, popular with Wittgensteinians and others, that there cannot be a science of the mind. Unfortunately physicalists like Pettit (1993: 213) have recently hijacked "naturalism", originally applied in ethics to views identifying values like goodness with factual states like happiness, as a euphemism for "physicalism", which makes it even worse than "dualism" as a label for our view.

Pending redemption of the term "naturalism", we think the least bad label for our view is "egalitarian pluralism". There are many kinds of particulars, properties and facts, including physical, chemical, biological, psychological and social ones, none of which we see any *a priori* reason to believe more basic than any other. In particular, we see no philosophical reason to require or expect mental (or any other kind of) phenomena to have what Menuge calls a "deeper, purely physical explanation" (1993: 230). That is one of the two chief morals of our paper.

The other is contained in our final plea to philosophers of mind to waste less time on the question of physicalism. And here, although many still make ritual obeisances to the physical, we do see some hopeful signs. It is starting to dawn even on physicalists that solutions to the most important problems of the mind are not advanced by accepting – or by rejecting – physicalism. Current theories of content, for example, need assume nothing about the physical or non-physical nature of the mind. We do not of course foresee our present-day physicalists recanting; but we do see them, like Soviet philosophers towards the end of that regime, devoting themselves, after increasingly perfunctory incantations of their party dogma, to more serious issues in the philosophy of mind.

REFERENCES

Charles, David and Lennon, Kathleen (eds) (1992) *Reduction, Explanation and Realism*, Oxford: Clarendon Press.

Crane, Tim (1994) "Against physicalism" in Samuel Guttenplan (ed.) *A Companion to the Philosophy of Mind*, Oxford: Blackwell.

—— (1993) "Reply to Pettit", *Analysis* 53.

Horgan, Terence (1993) "From supervenience to superdupervenience: meeting the demands of a material world', *Mind* 102.

Lewis, David (1966) "An argument for the identity theory", *Journal of Philosophy* 67.

Mellor, D. H. (1993) "Supervenience? No chance! Reply to Menuge", *Analysis* 53.

Menuge, Angus (1993) "Supervenience, by chance? Reply to Crane and Mellor", *Analysis* 53.

—— (1990) "Why supervenience?" *Analysis* 50.

Papineau, David (1993) *Philosophical Naturalism*, Oxford: Blackwell.

Pettit, Philip "A definition of physicalism", *Analysis* 53.

Robinson, Don (1991) "On Crane and Mellor's argument against physicalism", *Mind* 100.

Smith, Peter (1992) "Modest reductions and the unity of science" in David Charles and Kathleen Lennon (eds) *Reduction, Explanation and Realism*, Oxford: Clarendon Press.

Yablo, Stephen (1992) "Mental causation", *Philosophical Review* 101.

Part II

Materialism and Mind

4   Sensations and Brain Processes

J. J. C. Smart

This paper[1] takes its departure from arguments to be found in U. T. Place's "Is consciousness a brain process?"[2] I have had the benefit of discussing Place's thesis in a good many universities in the United States and Australia, and I hope that the present paper answers objections to his thesis which Place has not considered and that it presents his thesis in a more nearly unobjectionable form. This paper is meant also to supplement the paper "The 'mental' and the 'physical,'" by H. Feigl,[3] which in part argues for a similar thesis to Place's.

Suppose that I report that I have at this moment a roundish, blurry-edged after-image which is yellowish towards its edge and is orange towards its center. What is it that I am reporting? One answer to this question might be that I am not reporting anything, that when I say that it looks to me as though there is a roundish yellowy-orange patch of light on the wall I am expressing some sort of *temptation*, the temptation to say that there *is* a roundish yellowy-orange patch on the wall (though I may know that there is not such a patch on the wall). This is perhaps Wittgenstein's view in the *Philosophical Investigations* (see §§ 367, 370). Similarly, when I "report" a pain, I am not really reporting anything (or, if you like, I am reporting in a queer sense of "reporting"), but am doing a sophisticated sort of wince. (See § 244: "The verbal expression of pain replaces crying and does not describe it." Nor does it describe anything else?)[4] I prefer most of the time to discuss an after-image rather than a pain, because the word "pain" brings in something which is irrelevant to my purpose: the notion of "distress". I think that "he is in pain" entails "he is in distress," that is, that he is in a certain agitation-condition.[5] Similarly, to say "I am in pain" may be to do more than "replace pain behavior": it may be partly to report something, though this something is quite nonmysterious, being an agitation-condition, and so susceptible of behavioristic analysis. The suggestion I wish if possible to avoid is a different one, namely that "I am in pain" is a genuine report, and that what it reports is an irreducibly psychical something. And similarly the suggestion I wish to resist is also that to say "I have a yellowish-orange after-image" is to report something irreducibly psychical.

Why do I wish to resist this suggestion? Mainly because of Occam's razor. It seems to me that science is increasingly giving us a viewpoint whereby organisms are able to be seen as physicochemical mechanisms:[6] it seems that even the behavior of man himself will one day be explicable in mechanistic terms. There does seem to be, so far as science is concerned, nothing in the world but increasingly complex arrangements of physical constituents. All except for one place: in consciousness. That is, for a full description of what is going on in a man you would have to mention not only the physical processes in his tissues, glands, nervous system, and so forth, but also his states of consciousness: his visual, auditory, and tactual sensations, his aches and pains. That these should be *correlated* with brain processes does not help, for to say that they are *correlated* is to say that they are something "over and above." You cannot correlate something with itself. You correlate footprints with burglars, but not Bill Sikes the burglar with Bill Sikes the burglar. So sensations, states of consciousness, do seem to be the one sort of thing left outside the physicalist picture, and for various reasons I just cannot believe that this can be so. That everything should be explicable in terms of physics (together of course with descriptions of the ways in which the parts are put together – roughly, biology is to physics as radio-engineering is to electromagnetism) except the occurrence of sensations seems to me to be frankly unbelievable. Such sensations would be "nomological danglers," to use Feigl's expression.[7] It is not often realized how odd would be the laws whereby these nomological danglers would dangle. It is sometimes asked, "Why can't there be psychophysical laws which are of a novel sort, just as the laws of electricity and magnetism were novelties from the standpoint of Newtonian mechanics?" Certainly we are pretty sure in the future to come across new ultimate laws of a novel type, but I expect them to relate simple constituents: for example, whatever ultimate particles are then in vogue. I cannot believe that ultimate laws of nature could relate simple constituents to configurations consisting of perhaps billions of neurons (and goodness knows how many billion billions of ultimate particles) all put together for all the world as though their main purpose in life was to be a negative feedback mechanism of a complicated sort. Such ultimate laws would be like nothing so far known in science. They have a queer "smell" to them. I am just unable to believe in the nomological danglers themselves, or in the laws whereby they would dangle. If any philosophical arguments seemed to compel us to believe in such things, I would suspect a catch in the argument. In any case it is the object of this paper to show that there are no philosophical arguments which compel us to be dualists.

The above is largely a confession of faith, but it explains why I find Wittgenstein's position (as I construe it) so congenial. For on this view there are, in a sense, no sensations. A man is a vast arrangement of physical particles, but there are not, over and above this, sensations or states of consciousness. There are just behavioral facts about this vast mechanism, such as that it expresses a temptation (behavior disposition) to say "there is a yellowish-red patch on the wall" or that it goes through a sophisticated sort of wince, that is, says "I am in pain." Admittedly Wittgenstein says that though the sensation "is not a something," it is nevertheless "not a nothing either" (§ 304), but this need only mean that the word "ache" has a use. An ache is a thing, but only in the innocuous sense in which the plain man, in the first paragraph of Frege's *Foundations of Arithmetic*, answers the question

"What is the number one?" by "a thing." It should be noted that when I assert that to say "I have a yellowish-orange after-image" is to express a temptation to assert the physical-object statement "There is a yellowish-orange patch on the wall," I mean that saying "I have a yellowish-orange after-image" is (partly) the exercise of the disposition[8] which is the temptation. It is not to *report* that I have the temptation, any more than is "I love you" normally a report that I love someone. Saying "I love you" is just part of the behavior which is the exercise of the disposition of loving someone.

Though for the reasons given above, I am very receptive to the above "expressive" account of sensation statements, I do not feel that it will quite do the trick. Maybe this is because I have not thought it out sufficiently, but it does seem to me as though, when a person says "I have an after-image," he *is* making a genuine report, and that when he says "I have a pain," he *is* doing more than "replace pain-behavior," and that "this more" is not just to say that he is in distress. I am not so sure, however, that to admit this is to admit that there are nonphysical correlates of brain processes. Why should not sensations just be brain processes of a certain sort? There are, of course, well-known (as well as lesser-known) philosophical objections to the view that reports of sensations are reports of brain processes, but I shall try to argue that these arguments are by no means as cogent as is commonly thought to be the case.

Let me first try to state more accurately the thesis that sensations are brain processes. It is not the thesis that, for example, "after-image" or "ache" means the same as "brain process of sort X" (where "X" is replaced by a description of a certain sort of brain process). It is that, in so far as "after-image" or "ache" is a report of a process, it is a report of a process that *happens to be* a brain process. It follows that the thesis does not claim that sensation statements can be *translated* into statements about brain processes.[9] Nor does it claim that the logic of a sensation statement is the same as that of a brain-process statement. All it claims is that in so far as a sensation statement is a report of something, that something is in fact a brain process. Sensations are nothing over and above brain processes. Nations are nothing "over and above" citizens, but this does not prevent the logic of nation statements being very different from the logic of citizen statements, nor does it insure the translatability of nation statements into citizen statements. (I do not, however, wish to assert that the relation of sensation statements to brain process statements is very like that of nation statements to citizen statements. Nations do not just *happen to be* nothing over and above citizens, for example. I bring in the "nations" example merely to make a negative point: that the fact that the logic of A-statements is different from that of B-statements does not insure that A's are anything over and above B's.)

REMARKS ON IDENTITY

When I say that a sensation is a brain process or that lightning is an electric discharge, I am using "is" in the sense of strict identity. (Just as in the – in this case necessary – proposition "7 is identical with the smallest prime number greater than 5.") When I say that a sensation is a brain process or that lightning is an electric discharge I do not mean just that the sensation is somehow spatially or temporally continuous with the brain process or that the lightning is just spatially or temporally continuous with the discharge. When on the other hand I say that the successful general is the same person as the small boy who stole the apples I mean only that the successful general I see before me is a time slice[10] of the same four-dimensional object of which the small boy stealing apples is an earlier time slice. However, the four-dimensional object which has the general-I-see-before-me for its late time slice is identical in the strict sense with the four-dimensional object which has the small-boy-stealing-apples for an early time slice. I distinguish these two senses of "is identical with" because I wish to make it clear that the brain-process doctrine asserts identity in the *strict* sense.

I shall now discuss various possible objections to the view that the processes reported in sensation statements are in fact processes in the brain. Most of us have met some of these objections in our first year as philosophy students. All the more reason to take a good look at them. Others of the objections will be more recondite and subtle.

Objection 1   Any illiterate peasant can talk perfectly well about his after-images or how things look or feel to him, or about his aches and pains, and yet he may know nothing whatever about neurophysiology. A man may, like Aristotle, believe that the brain is an organ for cooling the body without any impairment of his ability to make true statements about his sensations. Hence the things we are talking about when we describe our sensations cannot be processes in the brain.

Reply   You might as well say that a nation of slugabeds, who never saw the Morning Star or knew of its existence, or who had never thought of the expression "the Morning Star," but who used the expression "the Evening Star" perfectly well, could not use this expression to refer to the same entity as we refer to (and describe as) "the Morning Star."[11]

You may object that the Morning Star is in a sense not the very same thing as the Evening Star, but only something spatiotemporally continuous with it. That is, you may say that the Morning Star is not the Evening Star in the strict sense of "identity" that I distinguished earlier.

There is, however, a more plausible example. Consider lightning.[12] Modern physical science tells us that lightning is a certain kind of electrical discharge due to ionization of clouds of water vapor in the atmosphere. This, it is now believed, is what the true nature of lightning is. Note that there are not two things: a flash of lightning and an electrical discharge. There is one thing, a flash of lightning, which is described scientifically as an electrical discharge to the earth from a cloud of ionized water molecules. The case is not at all like that of explaining a footprint by reference to a burglar. We say that what lightning really is, what its true nature as revealed by science is, is an electrical discharge. (It is not the true nature of a footprint to be a burglar.)

To forestall irrelevant objections, I should like to make it clear that by "lightning" I mean the publicly observable physical object, lightning, not a visual sense-datum of lightning. I say that the publicly observable physical object lightning is in fact the electrical discharge, not just a correlate of it. The sense-datum, or rather the having of the sense-datum, the "look" of lightning, may well in my view be a correlate of the electrical discharge. For in my view it is a brain state *caused* by the lightning. But we should no more confuse sensations of lightning with lightning than we confuse sensations of a table with the table.

In short, the reply to Objection 1 is that there can be contingent statements of the form "A is identical with B," and a person may well know that something is an A without knowing that it is a B. An illiterate peasant might well be able to talk about his sensations without knowing about his brain processes, just as he can talk about lightning though he knows nothing of electricity.

Objection 2 It is only a contingent fact (if it is a fact) that when we have a certain kind of sensation there is a certain kind of process in our brain. Indeed it is possible, though perhaps in the highest degree unlikely, that our present physiological theories will be as out of date as the ancient theory connecting mental processes with goings on in the heart. It follows that when we report a sensation we are not reporting a brain process.

Reply The objection certainly proves that when we say "I have an after-image" we cannot *mean* something of the form "I have such and such a brain process." But this does not show that what we report (having an after-image) is not *in fact* a brain process. "I see lightning" does not *mean* "I see an electrical discharge." Indeed, it is logically possible (though highly unlikely) that the electrical discharge account of lightning might one day be given up. Again, "I see the Evening Star" does not *mean* the same as "I see the Morning Star," and yet "The Evening Star and the Morning Star are one and the same thing" is a contingent proposition. Possibly Objection 2 derives some of its apparent strength from a "Fido"–Fido theory of meaning. If the meaning of an expression were what the expression named, then of course it *would* follow from the fact that "sensation" and "brain process" have different meanings that they cannot name one and the same thing.

Objection 3[13] Even if Objections 1 and 2 do not prove that sensations are something over and above brain processes, they do prove that the qualities of sensations are something over and above the qualities of brain processes. That is, it may be possible to get out of asserting the existence of irreducibly psychic processes, but not out of asserting the existence of irreducibly psychic *properties*. For suppose we identify the Morning Star with the Evening Star. Then there must be some properties which logically imply that of being the Morning Star, and quite distinct properties which entail that of being the Evening Star. Again, there must be some properties (for example, that of being a yellow flash) which are logically distinct from those in the physicalist story.

Indeed, it might be thought that the objection succeeds at one jump. For consider the property of "being a yellow flash." It might seem that this property lies inevitably outside the physicalist framework within which I am trying to work (either by "yellow" being an objective emergent property of physical objects, or else by being a power to produce yellow sense-data, where "yellow," in this second instantiation of the word, refers to a purely phenomenal or introspectible quality). I must therefore digress for a moment and indicate how I deal with secondary qualities. I shall concentrate on color.

First of all, let me introduce the concept of a normal percipient. One person is more a normal percipient than another if he can make color discriminations that the other cannot. For example, if A can pick a lettuce leaf out of a heap of cabbage leaves, whereas B cannot though he can pick a lettuce leaf out of a heap of beetroot leaves, then A is more normal than B. (I am assuming that A and B are not given time to distinguish the leaves by their slight difference in shape, and so forth.) From the concept of "more normal than" it is easy to see how we can introduce the concept of "normal." Of course, Eskimos may make the finest discriminations at the blue end of the spectrum, Hottentots at the red end. In this case the concept of a normal percipient is a slightly idealized one, rather like that of "the mean sun" in astronomical chronology. There is no need to go into such subtleties now. I say that "This is red" means something roughly like "A normal percipient would not easily pick this out of a clump of geranium petals though he would pick it out of a clump of lettuce leaves." Of course it does not exactly mean this: a person might know the meaning of "red" without knowing anything about geraniums, or even about normal percipients. But the point is that a person can be *trained* to say "This is red" of objects which would not easily be picked out of geranium petals by a normal percipient, and so on. (Note that even a color-blind person can reasonably assert that something is red, though of course he needs to use another human being, not just himself, as his "color meter.") This account of secondary qualities explains their unimportance in physics. For obviously the discriminations and lack of discriminations made by a very complex neurophysiological mechanism are hardly likely to correspond to simple and nonarbitrary distinctions in nature.

I therefore elucidate colors as powers, in Locke's sense, to evoke certain sorts of discriminatory responses in human beings. They are also, of course, powers to cause sensations in human beings (an account still nearer Locke's). But these sensations, I am arguing, are identifiable with brain processes.

Now how do I get over the objection that a sensation can be identified with a brain process only if it has some phenomenal property, not possessed by brain processes, whereby one-half of the identification may be, so to speak, pinned down?

Reply My suggestion is as follows. When a person says, "I see a yellowish-orange after-image," he is saying something like this: "*There is something going on which is like what is going on when* I have my eyes open, am awake, and there is an orange illuminated in good light in front of me, that is, when I really see an orange." (And there is no reason why a person should not say the same thing when he is having a veridical sense-datum, so long as we construe "like" in the last sentence in such a sense that something can be like itself.) Notice that the italicized words, namely "there is something going on which is like what is going on when," are all quasilogical or topic-neutral words. This explains why the ancient Greek peasant's reports about his sensations can be neutral between dualistic metaphysics or my materialistic metaphysics. It explains how sensations can be brain processes and yet how a man who reports them need know nothing about brain processes. For he reports them only very abstractly as "something going on which is like what is going on when . . . ." Similarly, a person may say "someone is in the room," thus reporting truly that the doctor is in the room, even though he has never heard of doctors. (There are not two people in the room: "someone" *and* the doctor.) This account of sensation statements also explains the singular elusiveness of "raw feels" – why no one seems to be able to pin any properties on them.[14] Raw feels, in my view, are colorless for the very same reason that *something* is colorless. This does not mean that sensations do not have plenty of properties, for if they are brain processes they certainly have lots of neurological properties. It only means that in speaking of them as being like or unlike one another we need not know or mention these properties.

This, then, is how I would reply to Objection 3. The strength of my reply depends on the possibility of our being able to report that one thing is like another without being able to state the respect in which it is like. I do not see why this should not be so. If we think cybernetically about the nervous system we can envisage it as able to respond to certain likenesses of its internal processes without being able to do more. It would be easier to build a machine which would tell us, say on a punched tape, whether or not two objects were similar, than it would be to build a machine which would report wherein the similarities consisted.

Objection 4   The after-image is not in physical space. The brain process is. So the after-image is not a brain process.

Reply   This is an *ignoratio elenchi*. I am not arguing that the after-image is a brain process, but that the experience of having an after-image is a brain process. It is the *experience* which is reported in the introspective report. Similarly, if it is objected that the after-image is yellowy-orange, my reply is that it is the experience of seeing yellowy-orange that is being described, and this experience is not a yellowy-orange something. So to say that a brain process cannot be yellowy-orange is not to say that a brain process cannot in fact be the experience of having a yellowy-orange after-image. There is, in a sense, no such thing as an after-image or a sense-datum, though there is such a thing as the experience of having an image, and this experience is described indirectly in material object language, not in phenomenal language, for there is no such thing.[15] We describe the experience by saying, in effect, that it is like the experience we have when, for example, we really see a yellowy-orange patch on the wall. Trees and wallpaper can be green, but not the experience of seeing or imagining a tree or wallpaper. (Or if they are described as green or yellow this can only be in a derived sense.)

Objection 5 It would make sense to say of a molecular movement in the brain that it is swift or slow, straight or circular, but it makes no sense to say this of the experience of seeing something yellow.

Reply So far we have not given sense to talk of experiences as swift or slow, straight or circular. But I am not claiming that "experience" and "brain process" mean the same or even that they have the same logic. "Somebody" and "the doctor" do not have the same logic, but this does not lead us to suppose that talking about somebody telephoning is talking about someone over and above, say, the doctor. The ordinary man when he reports an experience is reporting that something is going on, but he leaves it open as to what sort of thing is going on, whether in a material solid medium or perhaps in some sort of gaseous medium, or even perhaps in some sort of nonspatial medium (if this makes sense). All that I am saying is that "experience" and "brain process" may in fact refer to the same thing, and if so we may easily adopt a convention (which is not a change in our present rules for the use of experience words but an addition to them) whereby it would make sense to talk of an experience in terms appropriate to physical processes.

Objection 6 Sensations are private, brain processes are *public*. If I sincerely say, "I see a yellowish-orange after-image," and I am not making a verbal mistake, then I cannot be wrong. But I can be wrong about a brain process. The scientist looking into my brain might be having an illusion. Moreover, it makes sense to say that two or more people are observing the same brain process but not that two or more people are reporting the same inner experience.

Reply This shows that the language of introspective reports has a different logic from the language of material processes. It is obvious that until the brain process theory is much improved and widely accepted there will be no *criteria* for saying "Smith has an experience of such-and-such a sort" *except* Smith's introspective reports. So we have adopted a rule of language that (normally) what Smith says goes.

Objection 7 I can imagine myself turned to stone and yet having images, aches, pains, and so on.

Reply I can imagine that the electrical theory of lightning is false, that lightning is some sort of purely optical phenomenon. I can imagine that lightning is not an electrical discharge. I can imagine that the Evening Star is not the Morning Star. But it is. All the objection shows is that "experience" and "brain process" do not have the same meaning. It does not show that an experience is not in fact a brain process.

This objection is perhaps much the same as one which can be summed up by the slogan: "What can be composed of nothing cannot be composed of anything."[16] The argument goes as follows: on the brain-process thesis the identity between the brain process and the experience is a contingent one. So it is logically possible that there should be no brain process, and no process of any other sort either (no heart process, no kidney process, no liver process). There would be the experience but no "corresponding" physiological process with which we might be able to identify it empirically.

I suspect that the objector is thinking of the experience as a ghostly entity. So it is composed of something, not of nothing, after all. On his view it is composed of ghost stuff, and on mine it is composed of brain stuff. Perhaps the counter-reply will be[17] that the experience is simple and uncompounded, and so it is not composed of anything after all. This seems to be a quibble, for, if it were taken seriously, the remark "What can be composed of nothing cannot be composed of anything" could be recast as an a priori argument against Democritus and atomism and for Descartes and infinite divisibility. And it seems odd that a question of this sort could be settled a priori. We must therefore construe the word "composed" in a very weak sense, which would allow us to say that even an indivisible atom is composed of something (namely, itself). The dualist cannot really say that an experience can be composed of nothing. For he holds that experiences are something over and above material processes, that is, that they are a sort of ghost stuff. (Or perhaps ripples in an underlying ghost stuff.) I say that the dualist's hypothesis is a perfectly intelligible one. But I say that experiences are not to be identified with ghost stuff but with brain stuff. This is another hypothesis, and in my view a very plausible one. The present argument cannot knock it down a priori.

Objection 8 The "beetle in the box" objection (see Wittgenstein, *Philosophical Investigations*, § 293). How could descriptions of experiences, if these are genuine reports, get a foothold in language? For any rule of language must have public criteria for its correct application.

Reply The change from describing how things are to describing how we feel is just a change from uninhibitedly saying "this is so" to saying "this looks so." That is, when the naïve person might be tempted to say, "There is a patch of light on the wall which moves whenever I move my eyes" or "A pin is being stuck into me," we have learned how to resist this temptation and say "It *looks as though* there is a patch of light on the wallpaper" or "It *feels as though* someone were sticking a pin into me." The introspective account tells us about the individual's state of consciousness in the same way as does "I see a patch of light" or "I feel a pin being stuck into me": it differs from the corresponding perception statement in so far as it withdraws any claim about what is actually going on in the external world. From the point of view of the psychologist, the change from talking about the environment to talking about one's perceptual sensations is simply a matter of disinhibiting certain reactions. These are reactions which one normally suppresses because one has learned that in the prevailing circumstances they are unlikely to provide a good indication of the state of the environment.[18] To say that something looks green to me is simply to say that my experience is like the experience I get when I see something that really is green. In my reply to Objection 3, I pointed out the extreme openness or generality of statements which report experiences. This explains why there is no language of private qualities. (Just as "someone," unlike "the doctor," is a colorless word.)[19]

If it is asked what is the difference between those brain processes which, in my view, are experiences and those brain processes which are not, I can only reply that it is at present unknown. I have been tempted to conjecture that the difference may in part be that between perception and reception (in D. M. MacKay's terminology) and that the type of brain process which is an experience might be identifiable with MacKay's active "matching response."[20] This, however, cannot be the whole story, because sometimes I can perceive something unconsciously, as when I take a handkerchief out of a drawer without being aware that I am doing so. But at the very least, we can classify the brain processes which are experiences as those brain processes which are, or might have been, causal conditions of those pieces of verbal behavior which we call reports of immediate experience.

I have now considered a number of objections to the brain-process thesis. I wish now to conclude with some remarks on the logical status of the thesis itself. U. T. Place seems to hold that it is a straight-out scientific hypothesis.[21] If so, he is partly right and partly wrong. If the issue is between (say) a brain-process thesis and a heart thesis, or a liver thesis, or a kidney thesis, then the issue is a purely empirical one, and the verdict is overwhelmingly in favor of the brain. The right sorts of things don't go on in the heart, liver, or kidney, nor do these organs possess the right sort of complexity of structure. On the other hand, if the issue is between a brain-or-liver-or-kidney thesis (that is, some form of materialism) on the one hand and epiphenomenalism on the other hand, then the issue is not an empirical one. For there is no conceivable experiment which could decide between materialism and epiphenomenalism. This latter issue is not like the average straight-out empirical issue in science, but like the issue between the nineteenth-century English naturalist Philip Gosse[22] and the orthodox geologists and paleontologists of his day. According to Gosse, the earth was created about 4,000 BC exactly as described in *Genesis*, with twisted rock strata, "evidence" of erosion, and so forth, and all sorts of fossils, all in their appropriate strata, just as if the usual evolutionist story had been true. Clearly this theory is in a sense irrefutable: no evidence can possibly tell against it. Let us ignore the theological setting in which Philip Gosse's hypothesis had been placed, thus ruling out objections of a theological kind, such as "what a queer God who would go to such elaborate lengths to deceive us." Let us suppose that it is held that the universe just *began* in 4,004 BC with the initial conditions just everywhere as they were in 4,004 BC, and in particular that our own planet began with sediment in the rivers, eroded cliffs, fossils in the rocks, and so on. No scientist would ever entertain this as a serious hypothesis, consistent though it is with all possible evidence. The hypothesis offends against the principles of parsimony and simplicity. There would be far too many brute and inexplicable facts. Why are pterodactyl bones just as they are? No explanation in terms of the evolution of pterodactyls from earlier forms of life would any longer be possible. We would have millions of facts about the world as it was in 4,004 BC that just have to be *accepted.*

The issue between the brain-process theory and epiphenomenalism seems to be of the above sort. (Assuming that a behavioristic reduction of introspective reports is not possible.) If it be agreed that there are no cogent philosophical arguments which force us into accepting dualism, and if the brain-process theory and dualism are equally consistent with the facts, then the principles of parsimony and simplicity seem to me to decide overwhelmingly in favor of the brain-process theory. As I pointed out earlier, dualism involves a large number of irreducible psychophysical laws (whereby the "nomological danglers" dangle) of a queer sort, that just have to be taken on trust, and are just as difficult to swallow as the irreducible facts about the paleontology of the earth with which we are faced on Philip Gosse's theory.

NOTES

1   This is a very slightly revised version of a paper which was first published in the *Philosophical Review,* LXVIII (1959), 141–56. Since that date there have been criticisms of my paper by J. T. Stevenson, *Philosophical Review,* L.XIX (1960), 505–10, to which I have replied in *Philosophical Review,* LXX (1961), 406–7, and by G. Pitcher and by W. D. Joske, *Australasian Journal of Philosophy,* XXXVIII (1960), 150–60, to which I have replied in the same volume of that journal, pp. 252–4.

2   *British Journal of Psychology,* XLVII (1956), 44–50.

3   *Minnesota Studies in the Philosophy of Science,* Vol. II (Minneapolis: University of Minnesota Press 1958), pp. 370–497.

4   Some philosophers of my acquaintance, who have the advantage over me in having known Wittgenstein, would say that this interpretation of him is too behavioristic. However, it seems to me a very natural interpretation of his printed words, and whether or not it is Wittgenstein's real view it is certainly an interesting and important one. I wish to consider it here as a possible rival both to the "brain process" thesis and to straight-out old-fashioned dualism.

5   See Ryle, *The Concept of Mind* (London: Hutchinson's University Library, 1949), p. 93.

6   On this point see Paul Oppenheim and Hilary Putnam, "Unity of science as a working hypothesis," in *Minnesota Studies in the Philosophy of Science,* Vol. II (Minneapolis: University of Minnesota Press, 1958), pp. 3–36.

7   Feigl, ibid., p. 428. Feigl uses the expression "nomological danglers" for the laws whereby the entities dangle: I have used the expression to refer to the dangling entities themselves.

8   Wittgenstein did not like the word "disposition." I am using it to put in a nutshell (and perhaps inaccurately) the view which I am attributing to Wittgenstein. I should like to repeat that I do not wish to claim that my interpretation of Wittgenstein is correct. Some of those who knew him do not interpret him in this way. It is merely a view which I find myself extracting from his printed words and which I think is important and worth discussing for its own sake.

9   See Place, ibid. pp. 44–5, and Feigl, ibid., p. 390, near top.

10 See J. H. Woodger, *Theory Construction,* International Encyclopedia of Unified Science, II, No. 5 (Chicago: University of Chicago Press, 1939), 38. I here

permit myself to speak loosely. For warnings against possible ways of going wrong with this sort of talk, see my note "Spatialising time," *Mind*, LXIV (1955), 239–41.

11   Cf. Feigl, ibid., p. 439.
12   See Place, ibid., p. 48; also Feigl, ibid., p. 438.
13   I think this objection was first put to me by Professor Max Black. I think it is the most subtle of any of those I have considered, and the one which I am least confident of having satisfactorily met.
14   See B. A. Farrell, "Experience," *Mind*, LIX (1950), 170–98.
15   Dr J. R. Smythies claims that a sense-datum language could be taught independently of the material object language ("A note on the fallacy of the 'phenomenological fallacy,'" *British Journal of Psychology*, XLVIII [1957], 141–4). I am not so sure of this: there must be some public criteria for a person having got a rule wrong before we can teach him the rule. I suppose someone might *accidentally* learn color words by Dr Smythies' procedure. I am not, of course, denying that we can learn a sense-datum language in the sense that we can learn to report our experience. Nor would Place deny it.
16   I owe this objection to Dr C. B. Martin. I gather that he no longer wishes to maintain this objection, at any rate in its present form.
17   Martin did not make this reply, but one of his students did.
18   I owe this point to Place, in correspondence.
19   The "beetle in the box" objection is, *if it is sound*, an objection to *any* view, and in particular the Cartesian one, that introspective reports are genuine reports. So it is no objection to a weaker thesis that I would be concerned to uphold, namely, that if introspective reports of "experiences" are genuinely reports, then the things they are reports of are in fact brain processes.
20   See his article "Towards an information-flow model of human behaviour," *British Journal of Psychology*, XLVII (1956), 30–43.
21   Ibid. For a further discussion of this, in reply to the original version of the present paper, see Place's note "Materialism as a scientific hypothesis," *Philosophical Review*, LXIX (1960), 101–4.
22   See the entertaining account of Gosse's book *Omphalos* by Martin Gardner in *Fads and Fallacies in the Name of Science*, 2nd edn (New York: Dover, 1957), pp. 124–7.

POSTSCRIPT

Though I mostly agree with what I said in "Sensations and brain processes" there are some minor changes and some elucidations that I should like to make.

Experiences (havings of sensations and images) seemed to be particularly recalcitrant to the behaviouristic approach of Gilbert Ryle, which I had previously espoused. At the time I wrote the article in question I still thought that beliefs and desires could be elucidated wholly in terms of hypothetical propositions about behaviour. I soon got persuaded by D. M. Armstrong that we should identify beliefs and desires with mental *states* which are contingently identified with brain states. I would have eventually come anyway to such a view because of my general realism and worries abut the semantics of the contrary to fact conditionals that play an essential part in a behaviouristic analysis. Beliefs and desires raise questions about intentionality. I can desire a unicorn but there are no unicorns to be desired. This is very odd. I cannot kick a football without there being a football to be kicked. Also I cannot kick a football without kicking some particular football. I can desire a bicycle but no particular one: any decent one will do. So "desire" does not work like "kick". The best way to deal with this seems to be Quine's: say something like "believes-true S" and "desires-true S" where S is a sentence. The sentence serves to individuate a mental state (brain state). Or I could use a predicate in the case of "I desire a unicorn": "I desire-true of myself 'possesses a unicorn'". (Unicorns may not exist but the predicate "possesses a unicorn" does. I shall not attempt here to defend this account against various objections that might come to mind.)

Another place in which I was too behaviouristic was in my account of colours. I would now identify the yellow colour of a lemon with a state of the surface of the lemon. It is a state (described "topic-neutrally" as between physicalist and non-physicalist accounts) but contingently identified with a physical state, admittedly a highly disjunctive and idiosyncratic state, of no interest presumably to (say) Alpha Centaurians who had very different visual systems, but a physical state nevertheless. Still, this physical state is identified by the discriminatory reactions of normal human percipients in normal light (e.g. cloudy Scottish daylight). See "On some criticisms of a physicalist theory of colours" in my *Essays Metaphysical and Moral* (Oxford: Basil Blackwell, 1987).

It has widely been supposed that the identity theory has been outmoded by "functionalism". This is the theory that mental entities are functionally described in terms of their inputs (stimuli) and outputs (behaviour). Thus a kidney might be described not anatomically but (say) as an organ that regulated water flow and cleaned body fluids of poisons. Then we could go on contingently to identify a kidney with a certain shaped piece of anatomy. Or at least in the case of humans and related mammals. Similarly a functionalist might deny that brain states in you and me need to be at all similar, so long as the functions are the same. Now it seems to me that the difference between identity theory and functionalism has been greatly exaggerated. My topic-neutral formula "What is going on in me is like what goes on in me when ..." is very like a functionalist description, though it asserts (what the functionalist at least would not deny) that the experience of toothache, say, is not something abstract, like a function, but is something *going on*. (So plausibly a brain process.)

The functionalist need not take sides on whether your brain process when you have a pain is similar or not to mine. It is not an all or nothing matter between the functionalist and me. I would expect some similarity. I would expect even more similarity between my present and past brain processes. Perhaps less between mine and a sheep's, but some all the same. Even if we were to make an electronic robot that could feel pain I would expect a similarity at least of an abstract sort (e.g. of wave form) between my brain process and the electronic one. So it is not an all or nothing issue. The same would apply to the distinction between so-called type–type identity theories and so-called token–token ones. A token–token identity theorist holds only that any individual experience is identical with some individual brain process, whereas a type–type theorist would hold that all experiences of a certain sort are identical with brain processes of a certain sort. If asked whether I was a type–type identity theorist I would say "Yes and no", depending on how abstract you allowed the similarities to be.

When we are aware of our inner experiences we are aware of patterns of similarity and difference between them. References to such patterns are "topic-neutral" and so also are descriptions in terms of topic-neutral words such as being intermittent or waxing and waning. I need to contend that we can be aware of salient similarities and differences without being able to say in what respects these similarities subsist, but this contention seems to me to be plausible. (See my article "Materialism", *Journal of Philosophy* LX (1936), 651–62.) Brain processes answer to these topic-neutral descriptions but also have neurophysiological descriptions of which we are unaware. Nevertheless if a sensation is identical with a brain process it must have all the properties of the brain process. (I would no longer speak of the need for a convention as I did in the reply to objection 6. The thing just follows from the logic of identity.)

Why then does it seem intuitive to us that a sensation has "spooky", non-physical, properties? D. M. Armstrong has suggested in his article "The headless woman illusion and the defence of materialism" (*Analysis* XXIX (1968), 48–9) that the trouble comes from confusing "I am not aware of my present experience as being neurophysiological" with the stronger "I am aware of my present experience as non-neurophysiological". The former is true and the latter is false: the true one is compatible with my experience in fact being neurophysiological.

I am now disposed to think of the identity theory as a straight-out scientific hypothesis (as U. T. Place did). In the final two paragraphs of my article I was being too empiricist. Ockham's Razor and considerations of simplicity are perfectly good scientific principles for deciding between hypotheses which are equally favoured by the empirical evidence. Of course philosophical clarification is needed also, but that is common in theoretical science too.

5 Mental Events

Donald Davidson

Mental events such as perceivings, rememberings, decisions, and actions resist capture in the nomological net of physical theory.[1] How can this fact be reconciled with the causal role of mental events in the physical world? Reconciling freedom with causal determinism is a special case of the problem if we suppose that causal determinism entails capture in, and freedom requires escape from, the nomological net. But the broader issue can remain alive even for someone who believes a correct analysis of free action reveals no conflict with determinism. *Autonomy* (freedom, self-rule) may or may not clash with determinism; *anomaly* (failure to fall under a law) is, it would seem, another matter.

I start from the assumption that both the causal dependence and the anomalousness of mental events are undeniable facts. My aim is therefore to explain, in the face of apparent difficulties, how this can be. I am in sympathy with Kant when he says,

> it is as impossible for the subtlest philosophy as for the commonest reasoning to argue freedom away. Philosophy must therefore assume that no true contradiction will be found between freedom and natural necessity in the same human actions, for it cannot give up the idea of nature any more than that of freedom. Hence even if we should never be able to conceive how freedom is possible, at least this apparent contradiction must be convincingly eradicated. For if the thought of freedom contradicts itself or nature ... it would have to be surrendered in competition with natural necessity.[2]

Generalize human actions to mental events, substitute anomaly for freedom, and this is a description of my problem. And of course the connection is closer, since Kant believed freedom entails anomaly.

Now let me try to formulate a little more carefully the "apparent contradiction" about mental events that I want to discuss and finally dissipate. It may be seen as stemming from three principles.

The first principle asserts that at least some mental events interact causally with physical events. (We could call this the Principle of Causal Interaction.) Thus, for example, if someone sank the *Bismarck*, then various mental events such as perceivings, notings, calculations, judgments, decisions, intentional actions, and changes of belief played a causal role in the sinking of the *Bismarck*. In particular, I would urge that the fact that someone sank the *Bismarck* entails that he moved his body in a way that was caused by mental events of certain sorts, and that this bodily movement in turn caused the *Bismarck* to sink.[3] Perception illustrates how causality may run from the physical to the mental: if a man perceives that a ship is approaching, then a ship approaching must have caused him to come to believe that a ship is approaching. (Nothing depends on accepting these as examples of causal interaction.)

Though perception and action provide the most obvious cases where mental and physical events interact causally, I think reasons could be given for the view that all mental events, ultimately perhaps through causal relations with other mental events, have causal intercourse with physical events. But if there are mental events that have no physical events as causes or effects, the argument will not touch them.

The second principle is that where there is causality, there must be a law: events related as cause and effect fall under strict deterministic laws. (We may term this the Principle of the Nomological Character of Causality.) This principle, like the first, will be treated here as an assumption, though I shall say something by way of interpretation.[4]

The third principle is that there are no strict deterministic laws on the basis of which mental events can be predicted and explained (the Anomalism of the Mental).

The paradox I wish to discuss arises for someone who is inclined to accept these three assumptions or principles, and who thinks they are inconsistent with one another. The inconsistency is not, of course, formal unless more premises are added. Nevertheless it is natural to reason that the first two principles, that of causal interaction, and that of the nomological character of causality, together imply that at least some mental events can be predicted and explained on the basis of laws, while the principle of the anomalism of the mental denies this. Many philosophers have accepted, with or without argument, the view that the three principles do lead to a contradiction. It seems to me, however, that all three principles are true, so that what must be done is to explain away the appearance of contradiction; essentially the Kantian line.

The rest of this paper falls into three parts. The first part describes a version of the identity theory of the mental and the physical that shows how the three principles may be reconciled. The second part argues that there cannot be strict psychophysical laws; this is not quite the principle of the anomalism of the mental, but on reasonable assumptions entails it. The last part tries to show that from the fact that there can be no strict psychophysical laws, and our other two principles, we can infer the truth of a version of the identity theory, that is, a theory that identifies at least some mental events with physical events. It is clear that this "proof" of the identity theory will be at best conditional, since two of its premises are unsupported, and the argument for the third may be found less than conclusive. But even someone unpersuaded of the truth of the premises may be interested to learn how they may be reconciled and that they serve to establish a version of the identity theory of the mental. Finally, if the argument is a good one, it should lay to rest the view, common to many friends and some foes of identity theories, that support for such theories can come only from the discovery of psychophysical laws.

I

The three principles will be shown consistent with one another by describing a view of the mental and the physical that contains no inner contradiction and that entails the three principles. According to this view, mental events are identical with physical events. Events are taken to be unrepeatable, dated individuals such as the particular eruption of a volcano, the (first) birth or death of a person, the playing of the 1968 World Series, or the historic utterance of the words, "You may fire when ready, Gridley." We can easily frame identity statements about individual events; examples (true or false) might be:

The death of Scott = the death of the author of *Waverley*;
The assassination of the Archduke Ferdinand = the event that started the
    First World War;
The eruption of Vesuvius in AD 79 = the cause of the destruction of
    Pompeii.

The theory under discussion is silent about processes, states, and attributes if these differ from individual events.

What does it mean to say that an event is mental or physical? One natural answer is that an event is physical if it is describable in a purely physical vocabulary, mental if describable in mental terms. But if this is taken to suggest that an event is physical, say, if some physical predicate is true of it, then there is the following difficulty. Assume that the predicate "x took place at Noosa Heads" belongs to the physical vocabulary; then so also must the predicate "x did not take place at Noosa Heads" belong to the physical vocabulary. But the predicate "x did or did not take place at Noosa Heads" is true of every event, whether mental or physical.[5] We might rule out predicates that are tautologically true of every event, but this will not help since every event is truly describable either by "x took place at Noosa Heads" or by "x did not take place at Noosa Heads." A different approach is needed.[6]

We may call those verbs mental that express propositional attitudes like believing, intending, desiring, hoping, knowing, perceiving, noticing, remembering, and so on. Such verbs are characterized by the fact that they sometimes feature in sentences with subjects that refer to persons, and are completed by embedded sentences in which the usual rules of substitution appear to break down. This criterion is not precise, since I do not want to include these verbs when they occur in contexts that are fully extensional ("He knows Paris," "He perceives the moon" may be cases), nor exclude them whenever they are not followed by embedded sentences. An altern-ative characterization of the desired class of mental verbs might be that they are psychological verbs as used when they create apparently nonextensional contexts.

Let us call a description of the form "the event that is M" or an open sentence of the form "event x is M" a *mental description* or a *mental open sentence* if and only if the expression that replaces "M" contains at least one mental verb essentially. (Essentially, so as to rule out cases where the description or open sentence is logically equivalent to one not containing mental vocabulary.) Now we may say that an event is mental if and only if it has a mental description, or (the description operator not being primitive) if there is a mental open sentence true of that event alone. Physical events are those picked out by descriptions or open sentences that contain only the physical vocabulary essentially. It is less important to characterize a physical vocabulary because relative to the mental it is, so to speak, recessive in determining whether a description is mental or physical. (There will be some comments presently on the nature of a physical vocabulary, but these comments will fall far short of providing a criterion.)

On the proposed test of the mental, the distinguishing feature of the mental is not that it is private, subjective, or immaterial, but that it exhibits what Brentano called intentionality. Thus intentional actions are clearly included in the realm of the mental along with thoughts, hopes, and regrets (or the events tied to these). What may seem doubtful is whether the criterion will include events that have often been considered paradigmatic of the mental. Is it obvious, for example, that feeling a pain or seeing an afterimage will count as mental? Sentences that report such events seem free from taint of nonextensionality, and the same should be true of reports of raw feels, sense data, and other uninterpreted sensations, if there are any.

However, the criterion actually covers not only the havings of pains and afterimages, but much more besides. Take some event one would intuitively accept as physical, let's say the collision of two stars in distant space. There must be a purely physical predicate "Px" true of this collision, and of others, but true of only this one at the time it occurred. This particular time, though, may be pinpointed as the same time that Jones notices that a pencil starts to roll across his desk. The distant stellar collision is thus *the* event x such that Px and x is simultaneous with Jones' noticing that a pencil starts to roll across his desk. The collision has now been picked out by a mental description and must be counted as a mental event.

This strategy will probably work to show every event to be mental; we have obviously failed to capture the intuitive concept of the mental. It would be instructive to try to mend this trouble, but it is not necessary for present purposes. We can afford Spinozistic extravagance with the mental since accidental inclusions can only strengthen the hypothesis that all mental events are identical with physical events. What would matter would be failure to include bona fide mental events, but of this there seems to be no danger.

I want to describe, and presently to argue for, a version of the identity theory that denies that there can be strict laws connecting the mental and the physical. The very possibility of such a theory is easily obscured by the way in which identity theories are commonly defended and attacked. Charles Taylor, for example, agrees with protagonists of identity theories that the sole "ground" for accepting such theories is the supposition that correlations or laws can be established linking events described as mental with events described as physical. He says, "It is easy to see why this is so: unless a given mental event is invariably accompanied by a given, say, brain process, there is no ground for even mooting a general identity between the two."[7] Taylor goes on (correctly, I think) to allow that there may be identity without correlating laws, but my present interest is in noticing the invitation to confusion in the statement just quoted. What can "a given mental event" mean here? Not a particular, dated, event, for it would not make sense to speak of an individual event being "invariably accompanied" by another. Taylor is evidently thinking of events of a given *kind*. But if the only identities are of kinds of events, the identity theory presupposes correlating laws.

One finds the same tendency to build laws into the statement of the identity theory in these typical remarks:

> When I say that a sensation is a brain process or that lightning is an electrical discharge, I am using 'is' in the sense of strict identity ... there are not two things: a flash of lightning and an electrical discharge. There is one thing, a flash of lightning, which is described scientifically as an electrical discharge to the earth from a cloud of ionized water molecules.[8]

The last sentence of this quotation is perhaps to be understood as saying that for every lightning flash there exists an electrical discharge to the earth from a cloud of ionized water molecules with which it is identical. Here we have an honest ontology of individual events and can make literal sense of identity. We can also see how there could be identities without correlating laws. It is possible, however, to have an ontology of events with the conditions of individuation specified in such a way that any identity implies a correlating law. Kim, for example, suggests that Fa and Gb "describe or refer to the same event" if and only if $a = b$ and the property of being F = the property of being G. The identity of the properties in turn entails that $(x) (Fx \leftrightarrow Gx)$.[9] No wonder Kim says:

> If pain is identical with brain state B, there must be a concomitance between occurrences of pain and occurrences of brain state B .... Thus, a necessary condition of the pain–brain stage B identity is that the two expressions "being in pain" and "being in brain state B" have the same extension .... There is no conceivable observation that would confirm or refute the identity but not the associated correlation.[10]

It may make the situation clearer to give a fourfold classification of theories of the relation between mental and physical events that emphasizes the independence of claims about laws and claims of identity. On the one hand there are those who assert, and those who deny, the existence of psychophysical laws; on the other hand there are those who say mental events are identical with physical and those who deny this. Theories are thus divided into four sorts: *Nomological monism*, which affirms that there are correlating laws and that the events correlated are one (materialists belong in this category); *nomological dualism*, which comprises various forms of parallel-ism, interactionism, and epiphenomenalism; *anomalous dualism*, which combines ontological dualism and the general failure of laws correlating the mental and the physical (Cartesianism). And finally there is *anomalous monism*, which classifies the position I wish to occupy.[11]

Anomalous monism resembles materialism in its claim that all events are physical, but rejects the thesis, usually considered essential to materialism, that mental phenomena can be given purely physical explanations. Anomalous monism shows an ontological bias only in that it allows the possibility that not all events are mental, while insisting that all events are physical. Such a bland monism, unbuttressed by correlating laws or conceptual economies, does not seem to merit the term "reductionism"; in any case it is not apt to inspire the nothing-but reflex ("Conceiving the *Art of the Fugue* was nothing but a complex neural event," and so forth).

Although the position I describe denies there are psychophysical laws, it is consistent with the view that mental characteristics are in some sense dependent, or supervenient, on physical characteristics. Such super-venience might be taken to mean that there cannot be two events alike in all physical respects but differing in some mental respect, or that an object cannot alter in some mental respect without altering in some physical respect. Dependence or supervenience of this kind does not entail reducibility through law or definition: if it did, we could reduce moral properties to descriptive, and this there is good reason to *believe* cannot be done; and we might be able to reduce truth in a formal system to syntactical properties, and this we *know* cannot in general be done.

This last example is in useful analogy with the sort of lawless monism under consideration. Think of the physical vocabulary as the entire vocabulary of some language L with resources adequate to express a certain amount of mathematics, and its own syntax. L′ is L augmented with the truth predicate "true-in-L," which is "mental." In L (and hence L′) it is possible to pick out, with a definite description or open sentence, each sentence in the extension of the truth predicate, but if L is consistent there exists no predicate of syntax (or the "physical" vocabulary), no matter how complex, that applies to all and only the true sentences of L. There can be no "psychophysical law" in the form of a biconditional, "(x) (x is true-in-L if and only if x is ø)" where "ø" is replaced by a "physical" predicate (a predicate of L). Similarly, we can pick out each mental event using the physical vocabulary alone, but no purely physical predicate, no matter how complex, has, as a matter of law, the same extension as a mental predicate.

It should now be evident how anomalous monism reconciles the three original principles. Causality and identity are relations between individual events no matter how described. But laws are linguistic; and so events can instantiate laws, and hence be explained or predicted in the light of laws, only as those events are described in one or another way. The principle of causal interaction deals with events in extension and is therefore blind to the mental–physical dichotomy. The principle of the anomalism of the mental concerns events described as mental, for events are mental only as described. The principle of the nomological character of causality must be read carefully: it says that when events are related as cause and effect, they have descriptions that instantiate a law. It does not say that every true singular statement of causality instantiates a law.[12]

II

The analogy just bruited, between the place of the mental amid the physical, and the place of the semantical in a world of syntax, should not be strained. Tarski provided that a consistent language cannot (under some natural assumptions) contain an open sentence "Fx" true of all and only the true sentences of that language. If our analogy were pressed, then we would expect a proof that there can be no physical open sentence "Px" true of all and only the events having some mental property. In fact, however, nothing I can say about the irreducibility of the mental deserves to be called a proof; and the kind of irreducibility is different. For if anomalous monism is correct, not only can every mental event be uniquely singled out using only physical concepts, but since the number of events that falls under each mental predicate may, for all we know, be finite, there may well exist a physical open sentence coextensive with each mental predicate, though to construct it might involve the tedium of a lengthy and uninstructive alternation. Indeed, even if finitude is not assumed, there seems no compelling reason to deny that there could be coextensive predicates, one mental and one physical.

The thesis is rather that the mental is nomologically irreducible: there may be *true* general statements relating the mental and the physical, statements that have the logical form of a law; but they are not *lawlike* (in a strong sense to be described). If by absurdly remote chance we were to stumble on the nonstochastic true psychophysical generalization, we would have no reason to believe it more than roughly true.

Do we, by declaring that there are no (strict) psychophysical laws, poach on the empirical preserves of science – a form of *hubris* against which philosophers are often warned? Of course, to judge a statement lawlike or illegal is not to decide its truth outright; relative to the acceptance of a general statement on the basis of instances, ruling it lawlike must be a priori. But such relative apriorism does not in itself justify philosophy, for in general the grounds for deciding to trust a statement on the basis of its instances will in turn be governed by theoretical and empirical concerns not to be distinguished from those of science. If the case of supposed laws linking the mental and the physical is different, it can only be because to allow the possibility of such laws would amount to changing the subject. By changing the subject I mean here: deciding not to accept the criterion of the mental in terms of the vocabulary of the propositional attitudes. This short answer cannot prevent further ramifications of the problem, however, for there is no clear line between changing the subject and changing what one says on an old subject, which is to admit, in the present context at least, that there is no clear line between philosophy and science. Where there are no fixed boundaries only the timid never risk trespass.

It will sharpen our appreciation of the anomological character of mental–physical generalizations to consider a related matter, the failure of definitional behaviorism. Why are we willing (as I assume we are) to abandon the attempt to give explicit definitions of mental concepts in terms of behavioral ones? Not, surely, just because all actual tries are conspicuously inadequate. Rather it is because we are persuaded, as we are in the case of so many other forms of definitional reductionism (naturalism in ethics, instrumentalism and operationalism in the sciences, the causal theory of meaning, phenomenalism, and so on – the catalog of philosophy's defeats), that there is system in the failures. Suppose we try to say, not using any mental concepts, what it is for a man to believe there is life on Mars. One line we could take is this: when a certain sound is produced in the man's presence ("Is there life on Mars?") he produces another ("Yes"). But of course this shows he believes there is life on Mars only if he understands English, his production of the sound was intentional, and was a response to the sounds as meaning something in English; and so on. For each discovered deficiency, we add a new proviso. Yet no matter how we patch and fit the nonmental conditions, we always find the need for an additional condition (provided he *notices*, *understands*, etc.) that is mental in character.[13]

A striking feature of attempts at definitional reduction is how little seems to hinge on the question of synonymy between definiens and definiendum. Of course, by imagining counterexamples we do discredit claims of synonymy. But the pattern of failure prompts a stronger conclusion: if we were to find an open sentence couched in behavioral terms and exactly coextensive with some mental predicate, nothing could reasonably persuade us that we had found it. We know too much about thought and behavior to trust exact and universal statements linking them. Beliefs and desires issue in behavior only as modified and mediated by further beliefs and desires, attitudes and attendings, without limit. Clearly this holism of the mental realm is a clue both to the autonomy and to the anomalous character of the mental.

These remarks apropos definitional behaviorism provide at best hints of why we should not expect nomological connections between the mental and the physical. The central case invites further consideration.

Lawlike statements are general statements that support counterfactual and subjunctive claims, and are supported by their instances. There is (in my view) no nonquestion-begging criterion of the lawlike, which is not to say there are no reasons in particular cases for a judgment. Lawlikeness is a matter of degree, which is not to deny that there may be cases beyond debate. And within limits set by the conditions of communication, there is room for much variation between individuals in the pattern of statements to which various degrees of nomologicality are assigned. In all these respects, nomologicality is much like analyticity, as one might expect since both are linked to meaning.

"All emeralds are green" is lawlike in that its instances confirm it, but "all emeralds are grue" is not, for "grue" means "observed before time t and green, otherwise blue," and if our observations were all made before t and uniformly revealed green emeralds, this would not be a reason to expect other emeralds to be blue. Nelson Goodman has suggested that this shows that some predicates, "grue" for example, are unsuited to laws (and thus a criterion of suitable predicates could lead to a criterion of the lawlike). But it seems to me the anomalous character of "All emeralds are grue" shows only that the predicates "is an emerald" and "is grue" are not suited to one another: grueness is not an inductive property of emeralds. Grueness *is* however an inductive property of entities of other sorts, for instance of emerires. (Something is an emerire if it is examined before *t* and is an emerald, and otherwise is a sapphire.) Not only is "All emerires are grue" entailed by the conjunction of the lawlike statements "All emeralds are green" and "All sapphires are blue," but there is no reason, as far as I can see, to reject the deliverance of intuition, that it is itself lawlike.[14] Nomological statements bring together predicates that we know a priori are made for each other – know, that is, independently of knowing whether the evidence supports a connection between them. "Blue," "red," and "green" are made for emeralds, sapphires, and roses; "grue," "bleen," and "gred" are made for sapphalds, emerires, and emeroses.

The direction in which the discussion seems headed is this: mental and physical predicates are not made for one another. In point of lawlikeness, psychophysical statements are more like "All emeralds are grue" than like "All emeralds are green."

Before this claim is plausible, it must be seriously modified. The fact that emeralds examined before *t* are grue not only is no reason to believe all emeralds are grue; it is not even a reason (if we know the time) to believe *any* unobserved emeralds are grue. But if an event of a certain mental sort has usually been accompanied by an event of a certain physical sort, this often is a good reason to expect other cases to follow suit roughly in proportion. The generalizations that embody such practical wisdom are assumed to be only roughly true, or they are explicitly stated in probabilistic terms, or they are insulated from counterexample by generous escape clauses. Their importance lies mainly in the support they lend singular causal claims and related explanations of particular events. The support derives from the fact that such a generalization, however crude and vague, may provide good reason to believe that underlying the particular case there is a regularity that could be formulated sharply and without caveat.

In our daily traffic with events and actions that must be foreseen or understood, we perforce make use of the sketchy summary generalization, for we do not know a more accurate law, or if we do, we lack a description of the particular events in which we are interested that would show the relevance of the law. But there is an important distinction to be made within the category of the rude rule of thumb. On the one hand, there are generalizations whose positive instances give us reason to believe the generalization itself could be improved by adding further provisos and conditions stated in the same general vocabulary as the original generalization. Such a generalization points to the form and vocabulary of the finished law: we may say that it is a *homonomic* generalization. On the other hand there are generalizations which when instantiated may give us reason to believe there is a precise law at work, but one that can be stated only by shifting to a different vocabulary. We may call such generalizations *heteronomic*.

I suppose most of our practical lore (and science) is heteronomic. This is because a law can hope to be precise, explicit, and as exceptionless as possible only if it draws its concepts from a comprehensive closed theory. This ideal theory may or may not be deterministic, but it is if any true theory is. Within the physical sciences we do find homonomic generalizations, generalizations such that if the evidence supports them, we then have reason to believe they may be sharpened indefinitely by drawing upon further physical concepts: there is a theoretical asymptote of perfect coherence with all the evidence, perfect predictability (under the terms of the system), total explanation (again under the terms of the system). Or perhaps the ultimate theory is probabilistic, and the asymptote is less than perfection; but in that case there will be no better to be had.

Confidence that a statement is homonomic, correctible within its own conceptual domain, demands that it draw its concepts from a theory with strong constitutive elements. Here is the simplest possible illustration; if the lesson carries, it will be obvious that the simplification could be mended.

The measurement of length, weight, temperature, or time depends (among many other things, of course) on the existence in each case of a two-place relation that is transitive and asymmetric: warmer than, later than, heavier than, and so forth. Let us take the relation *longer than* as our example. The law or postulate of transitivity is this:

(L) $L(x,y)$ and $L(y,z) \to L(x, z)$

Unless this law (or some sophisticated varient) holds, we cannot easily make sense of the concept of length. There will be no way of assigning numbers to register even so much as ranking in length, let alone the more powerful demands of measurement on a ratio scale. And this remark goes not only for any three items directly involved in an intransitivity: it is easy to show (given a few more assumptions essential to measurement of length) that there is no consistent assignment of a ranking to any item unless (L) holds in full generality.

Clearly (L) alone cannot exhaust the import of "longer than" – otherwise it would not differ from "warmer than" or "later than." We must suppose there is some empirical content, however difficult to formulate in the available vocabulary, that distinguishes "longer than" from the other two-place transitive predicates of measurement and on the basis of which we may assert that one thing is longer than another. Imagine this empirical content to be partly given by the predicate "$o(x,y)$". So we have this "meaning postulate":

(M) $o(x,y) \to L(x,y)$

that partly interprets (L). But now (L) and (M) together yield an empirical theory of great strength, for together they entail that there do not exist three objects a, b, and c such that $o(a,b)$, $o(b,c)$, and $o(c,a)$. Yet what is to prevent this happening if $o(x,y)$ is a predicate we can ever, with confidence, apply? Suppose we *think* we observe an intransitive triad; what do we say? We could count (L) false, but then we would have no application for the concept of length. We could say (M) gives a wrong test for length; but then it is unclear what we thought was the *content* of the idea of one thing being longer than another. Or we could say that the objects under observation are not, as the theory requires, *rigid* objects. It is a mistake to think we are forced to accept some one of these answers. Concepts such as that of length are sustained in equilibrium by a number of conceptual pressures, and theories of fundamental measurement are distorted if we force the decision, among such principles as (L) and (M): analytic or synthetic. It is better to say the whole set of axioms, laws, or postulates for the measurement of length is partly constitutive of the idea of a system of macroscopic, rigid, physical objects. I suggest that the existence of lawlike statements in physical science depends upon the existence of constitutive (or synthetic a priori) laws like those of the measurement of length within the same conceptual domain.

Just as we cannot intelligibly assign a length to any object unless a comprehensive theory holds of objects of that sort, we cannot intelligibly attribute any propositional attitude to an agent except within the framework of a viable theory of his beliefs, desires, intentions, and decisions.

There is no assigning beliefs to a person one by one on the basis of his verbal behavior, his choices, or other local signs no matter how plain and evident, for we make sense of particular beliefs only as they cohere with other beliefs, with preferences, with intentions, hopes, fears, expectations, and the rest. It is not merely, as with the measurement of length, that each case tests a theory and depends upon it, but that the content of a propositional attitude derives from its place in the pattern.

Crediting people with a large degree of consistency cannot be counted mere charity: it is unavoidable if we are to be in a position to accuse them meaningfully of error and some degree of irrationality. Global confusion, like universal mistake, is unthinkable, not because imagination boggles, but because too much confusion leaves nothing to be confused about and massive error erodes the background of true belief against which alone failure can be construed. To appreciate the limits to the kind and amount of blunder and bad thinking we can intelligibly pin on others is to see once more the inseparability of the question what concepts a person commands and the question what he does with those concepts in the way of belief, desire, and intention. To the extent that we fail to discover a coherent and plausible pattern in the attitudes and actions of others we simply forego the chance of treating them as persons.

The problem is not bypassed but given center stage by appeal to explicit speech behavior. For we could not begin to decode a man's sayings if we could not make out his attitudes towards his sentences, such as holding, wishing, or wanting them to be true. Beginning from these attitudes, we must work out a theory of what he means, thus simultaneously giving content to his attitudes and to his words. In our need to make him make sense, we will try for a theory that finds him consistent, a believer of truths, and a lover of the good (all by our own lights, it goes without saying). Life being what it is, there will be no simple theory that fully meets these demands. Many theories will effect a more or less acceptable compromise, and between these theories there may be no objective grounds for choice.

The heteronomic character of general statements linking the mental and the physical traces back to this central role of translation in the description of all propositional attitudes, and to the indeterminacy of translation.[15] There are no strict psychophysical laws because of the disparate commitments of the mental and physical schemes. It is a feature of physical reality that physical change can be explained by laws that connect it with other changes and conditions physically described. It is a feature of the mental that the attribution of mental phenomena must be responsible to the background of reasons, beliefs, and intentions of the individual. There cannot be tight connections between the realms if each is to retain allegiance to its proper source of evidence. The nomological irreducibility of the mental does not derive merely from the seamless nature of the world of thought, preference, and intention, for such interdependence is common to physical theory, and is compatible with there being a single right way of interpreting a man's attitudes without relativization to a scheme of translation. Nor is the irreducibility due simply to the possibility of many equally eligible schemes, for this is compatible with an arbitrary choice of one scheme relative to which assignments of mental traits are made. The point is rather that when we use the concepts of belief, desire, and the rest, we must stand prepared, as the evidence accumulates, to adjust our theory in the light of considerations of overall cogency: the constitutive ideal of rationality partly controls each phase in the evolution of what must be an evolving theory. An arbitrary choice of translation scheme would preclude such opportunistic tempering of theory; put differently, a right arbitrary choice of a translation manual would be of a manual acceptable in the light of all possible evidence, and this is a choice we cannot make. We must conclude, I think, that nomological slack between the mental and the physical is essential as long as we conceive of man as a rational animal.

III

The gist of the foregoing discussion, as well as its conclusion, will be familiar. That there is a categorial difference between the mental and the physical is a commonplace. It may seem odd that I say nothing of the supposed privacy of the mental, or the special authority an agent has with respect to his own propositional attitudes, but this appearance of novelty would fade if we were to investigate in more detail the grounds for accepting a scheme of translation. The step from the categorial difference between the mental and the physical to the impossibility of strict laws relating them is less common, but certainly not new. If there is a surprise, then, it will be to find the lawlessness of the mental serving to help establish the identity of the mental with that paradigm of the lawlike, the physical.

The reasoning is this. We are assuming, under the Principle of the Causal Dependence of the Mental, that some mental events at least are causes or effects of physical events; the argument applies only to these. A second Principle (of the Nomological Character of Causality) says that each true singular causal statement is backed by a strict law connecting events of kinds to which the events mentioned as cause and effect belong. Where there are rough, but homonomic, laws, there are laws drawing on concepts from the same conceptual domain and upon which there is no improving in point of precision and comprehensiveness. We urged in the last section that such laws occur in the physical sciences. Physical theory promises to provide a comprehensive closed system guaranteed to yield a standardized, unique description of every physical event couched in a vocabulary amenable to law.

It is not plausible that mental concepts alone can provide such a framework, simply because the mental does not, by our first principle, constitute a closed system. Too much happens to affect the mental that is not itself a systematic part of the mental. But if we combine this observation with the conclusion that no psychophysical statement is, or can be built into, a strict law, we have the Principle of the Anomalism of the Mental: there are no strict laws at all on the basis of which we can predict and explain mental phenomena.

The demonstration of identity follows easily. Suppose m, a mental event, caused p, a physical event; then under some description m and p instantiate a strict law. This law can only be physical, according to the previous paragraph. But if m falls under a physical law, it has a physical description; which is to say it is a physical event. An analogous argument works when a physical event causes a mental event. So every mental event that is causally related to a physical event is a physical event. In order to establish anomalous monism in full generality it would be sufficient to show that every mental event is cause or effect of some physical event; I shall not attempt this.

If one event causes another, there is a strict law which those events instantiate when properly described. But it is possible (and typical) to know of the singular causal relation without knowing the law or the relevant descriptions. Knowledge requires reasons, but these are available in the form of rough heteronomic generalizations, which are lawlike in that instances make it reasonable to expect other instances to follow suit without being lawlike in the sense of being indefinitely refinable. Applying these facts to knowledge of identities, we see that it is possible to know that a mental event is identical with some physical event without knowing which one (in the sense of being able to give it a unique physical description that brings it under a relevant law). Even if someone knew the entire physical history of the world, and every mental event were identical with a physical, it would not follow that he could predict or explain a single mental event (so described, of course).

Two features of mental events in their relation to the physical – causal dependence and nomological independence – combine, then, to dissolve what has often seemed a paradox, the efficacy of thought and purpose in the material world, and their freedom from law. When we portray events as perceivings, rememberings, decisions, and actions, we necessarily locate them amid physical happenings through the relation of cause and effect; but that same mode of portrayal insulates mental events, as long as we do not change the idiom, from the strict laws that can in principle be called upon to explain and predict physical phenomena.

Mental events as a class cannot be explained by physical science; particular mental events can when we know particular identities. But the explanations of mental events in which we are typically interested relate them to other mental events and conditions. We explain a man's free actions, for example, by appeal to his desires, habits, knowledge, and perceptions. Such accounts of intentional behavior operate in a conceptual framework removed from the direct reach of physical law by describing both cause and effect, reason and action, as aspects of a portrait of a human agent. The anomalism of the mental is thus a necessary condition for viewing action as autonomous. I conclude with a second passage from Kant:

> It is an indispensable problem of speculative philosophy to show that its illusion respecting the contradiction rests on this, that we think of man in a different sense and relation when we call him free, and when we regard him as subject to the laws of nature .... It must therefore show that not only can both of these very well co-exist, but that both must be thought *as necessarily united* in the same subject.[16]

NOTES

1   I was helped and influenced by Daniel Bennett, Sue Larson, and Richard Rorty, who are not responsible for the result. My research was supported by the National Science Foundation and the Center for Advanced Study in the Behavioral Sciences.

2   *Fundamental Principles of the Metaphysics of Morals*, trans, T. K. Abbott (London, 1909), pp. 75–6.

3   These claims are defended in my "Actions, reasons and causes," *The Journal of Philosophy* LX (1963), pp. 685–700 and in "Agency," a paper in the proceedings of the November, 1968, colloquium on Agent, Action, and Reason at the University of Western Ontario, London, Canada.

4   In "Causal relations," *The Journal of Philosophy* LXIV (1967), pp. 691–703, I elaborate on the view of causality assumed here. The stipulation that the laws be deterministic is stronger than required by the reasoning, and will be relaxed.

5   The point depends on assuming that mental events may intelligibly be said to have a location; but it is an assumption that must be true if an identity theory is, and here I am not trying to prove the theory but to formulate it.

6   I am indebted to Lee Bowie for emphasizing this difficulty.

7   Charles Taylor, "Mind–body identity, a side issue?" *The Philosophical Review* LXXVI (1967), p. 202.

8   J. J. C. Smart, "Sensations and brain processes," *The Philosophical Review* LXVIII (1959), pp. 141–56 [ch. 4, this volume]. The quoted passages are on pp. 163–5 of the reprinted version in *The Philosophy of Mind*, ed. V. C. Chappell (Englewood Cliffs, NJ, 1962). For another example, see David K. Lewis, "An argument for the identity theory," *The Journal of Philosophy* LXIII (1966), pp. 17–25. Here the assumption is made explicit when Lewis takes events as

universals (p. 17, footnotes 1 and 2). I do not suggest that Smart and Lewis are confused, only that their way of stating the identity theory tends to obscure the distinction between particular events and kinds of events on which the formulation of my theory depends.

9 Jaegwon Kim, "On the psycho-physical identity theory," *American Philosophical Quarterly* III (1966), p. 231.

10 Ibid., pp. 227–8. Richard Brandt and Jaegwon Kim propose roughly the same criterion in "The logic of the identity theory," *The Journal of Philosophy* LIV (1967), pp. 515–37. They remark that on their conception of event identity, the identity theory "makes a stronger claim than merely that there is a pervasive phenomenal–physical correlation" (p. 518). I do not discuss the stronger claim.

11 Anomalous monism is more or less explicitly recognized as a possible position by Herbert Feigl, "The 'mental' and the 'physical,'" in *Concepts, Theories and the Mind–Body Problem*, vol. II *Minnesota Studies in the Philosophy of Science* (Minneapolis, 1958); Sydney Shoemaker, "Ziff's other minds," *The Journal of Philosophy* LXII (1965), p. 589; David Randall Luce, "Mind–body identity and psycho–physical correlation," *Philosophical Studies* XVII (1966), pp. 1–7; Charles Taylor, "Mind–body identity," p. 207. Something like my position is tentatively accepted by Thomas Nagel, "Physicalism," *The Philosophical Review* LXXIV (1965), pp. 339–56, and briefly endorsed by P. F. Strawson in *Freedom and the Will*, ed. D. F. Pears (London, 1963), pp. 63–7.

12 The point that substitutivity of identity fails in the context of explanation is made in connection with the present subject by Norman Malcolm, "Scientific materialism and the identity theory," *Dialogue* III (1964–5), pp. 123–4. See also my "Actions, reasons and causes," *The Journal of Philosophy* LX (1963), pp. 696–9 and "The individuation of events" in *Essays in Honor of Carl G. Hempel*, ed. N. Rescher, et al. (Dordrecht, 1969).

13 The theme is developed in Roderick Chisholm, *Perceiving* (Ithaca, New York, 1957), ch. 11.

14 This view is accepted by Richard C. Jeffrey, "Goodman's query," *The Journal of Philosophy* LXII (1966), pp. 286 ff., John R. Wallace, "Goodman, logic, induction," same journal and issue, p. 318, and John M. Vickers, "Characteristics of projectible predicates," *The Journal of Philosophy* LXIV (1967), p. 285. On pp. 328–9 and 286–7 of these journal issues respectively Goodman disputes the lawlikeness of statements like "All emerires are grue." I cannot see, however, that he meets the point of my "Emeroses by other names," *The Journal of Philosophy* LXIII (1966), pp. 778–80.

15 The influence of W. V. O. Quine's doctrine of the indeterminacy of translation, as in ch. 2 of *Word and Object* (Cambridge, Mass., 1960), is, I hope, obvious. In § 45 Quine develops the connection between translation and the propositional attitudes, and remarks that "Brentano's thesis of the irreducibility of intentional idioms is of a piece with the thesis of indeterminacy of translation" (p. 221).

16 Op. cit., p. 76.

6   Philosophy and our Mental Life

Hilary Putnam

The question which troubles laymen, and which has long troubled philosophers, even if it is somewhat disguised by today's analytic style of writing philosophy, is this: are we made of matter or soul-stuff? To put it as bluntly as possible, are we just material beings, or are we "something more"? In this paper, I will argue as strongly as possible that this whole question rests on false assumptions. My purpose is not to dismiss the question, however, so much as to speak to the real concern which is behind the question. The real concern is, I believe, with the autonomy of our mental life.

People are worried that we may be debunked, that our behavior may be exposed as really explained by something mechanical. Not, to be sure, mechanical in the old sense of cogs and pulleys, but in the newer sense of electricity and magnetism and quantum chemistry and so forth. In this paper, part of what I want to do is to argue that this can't happen. Mentality is a real and autonomous feature of our world.

But even more important, at least in my feeling, is the fact that this whole question has nothing to do with our substance. Strange as it may seem to common sense and to sophisticated intuition alike, the question of the autonomy of our mental life does not hinge on and has nothing to do with that all too popular, all too old question about matter or soul-stuff. We could be made of Swiss cheese and it wouldn't matter.

Failure to see this, stubborn insistence on formulating the question as *matter or soul,* utterly prevents progress on these questions. Conversely, once we see that our substance is not the issue, I do not see how we can help but make progress.

The concept which is key to unravelling the mysteries in the philosophy of mind, I think, is the concept of *functional isomorphism.* Two systems are functionally isomorphic if *there is a correspondence between the states of one and the states of the other that preserves functional relations.* To start with computing machine examples, if the functional relations are just sequence relations, e.g. *state A is always followed by state B,* then, for F to be a functional isomorphism, it must be the case that state A is followed by state B in system 1 if and only if state $F(A)$ is followed by state $F(B)$ in system 2. If the functional relations are, say, data or print-out relations, e.g. *when print π is printed on the tape, system 1 goes into state A,* these must be preserved. *When* *print π is printed on the tape, system 2 goes into state F(A)*, if *F* is a functional isomorphism between system 1 and system 2. More generally, if *T* is a correct theory of the functioning of system 1, at the functional or psychological level, then an isomorphism between system 1 and system 2 must map each property and relation defined in system 2 in such a way that *T* comes out true when all references to system 1 are replaced by references to system 2, and all property and relation symbols in *T* are reinterpreted according to the mapping.

The difficulty with the notion of functional isomorphism is that it *presupposes the notion of a thing's being a functional or psychological description.* It is for this reason that, in various papers on this subject, I introduced and explained the notion in terms of Turing machines. And I felt constrained, therefore, to defend the thesis that *we* are Turing machines. Turing machines come, so to speak, with a normal form for their functional description, the so-called machine table – a standard style of program. But it does not seem fatally sloppy to me, although it is sloppy, if we apply the notion of functional isomorphism to systems for which we have no detailed idea at present what the normal form description would look like – systems like ourselves. The point is that even if we don't have any idea what a comprehensive psychological theory would look like, I claim that we know enough (and here analogies from computing machines, economic systems, games and so forth are helpful) to point out illuminating differences between any possible psychological theory of a human being, or even a functional description of a computing machine or an economic system, and a physical or chemical description. Indeed, Dennett and Fodor have done a great deal along these lines in recent books.

This brings me back to the question of *copper, cheese, or soul*. One point we can make immediately as soon as we have the basic concept of functional isomorphism is this: two systems can have quite different constitutions and be functionally isomorphic. For example, a computer made of electrical components can be isomorphic to one made of cogs and wheels. In other words, for each state in the first computer there is a corresponding state in the other, and, as we said before, the sequential relations are the same – if state *S* is followed by state *B* in the case of the electronic computer, state *A* would be followed by state *B* in the case of the computer made of cogs and wheels, and it doesn't matter at all that the *physical realizations* of those states are totally different. So a computer made of electrical components can be isomorphic to one made of cogs and wheels or to human clerks using paper and pencil. A computer made of one sort of wire, say copper wire, or one sort of relay, etc. will be in a different physical and chemical state when it computes than a computer made of a different sort of wire and relay. But the functional description may be the same.

We can extend this point still further. Assume that one thesis of materialism (I shall call it the "first thesis") is correct, and we are, as wholes, just material systems obeying physical laws. Then the second thesis of classical materialism cannot be correct – namely, our mental states, e.g. *thinking about next summer's vacation*, cannot be *identical* with any physical or chemical states. For it is clear from what we already know about computers etc., that whatever the program of the brain may be, it must be physically possible, though not necessarily feasible, to produce something with that same program but quite a different physical and chemical constitution. Then to identify the state in question with its physical or chemical realization would be quite absurd, given that that realization is in a sense quite accidental, from the point of view of psychology, anyway (which is the relevant science).[1] It is as if we met Martians and discovered that they were in all functional respects isomorphic to us, but we refused to admit that they could feel pain because their C fibers were different.

Now, imagine two possible universes, perhaps "parallel worlds", in the science fiction sense, in one of which people have good old fashioned souls, operating through pineal glands, perhaps, and in the other of which they have complicated brains. And suppose that the souls in the soul world are functionally isomorphic to the brains in the brain world. Is there any more sense to attaching importance to this difference than to the difference between copper wires and some other wires in the computer? Does it matter that the soul people have, so to speak, immaterial brains, and that the brain people have material souls? What matters is the common structure, the theory T of which we are, alas, in deep ignorance, and not the hardware, be it ever so ethereal.

One may raise various objections to what I have said. I shall try to reply to some of them.

One might, for example, say that if the souls of the soul people are isomorphic to the brains of the brain people, then their souls must be automata-like, and that's not the sort of soul we are interested in. "All your argument really shows is that there is no need to distinguish between a brain and an automaton-like soul." But what precisely does that objection come to?

I think there are two ways of understanding it. It might come to the claim that the notion of functional organization or functional isomorphism only makes sense for automata. But that is totally false. Sloppy as our notions are at present, we at least know this much, as Jerry Fodor has emphasized: we know that the notion of functional organization applies to anything to which the notion of a psychological theory applies. I explained the most general notion of functional isomorphism by saying that two systems are functionally isomorphic if there is an isomorphism that makes both of them models for the same psychological theory. (That is stronger than just saying that they are both models for the same psychological theory – they are isomorphic realizations of the same abstract structure.) To say that real old fashioned souls would not be in the domain of definition of the concept of functional organization or of the concept of functional isomorphisms would be to take the position that whatever we mean by the soul, it is something for which there can be no theory. That seems pure obscurantism. I will assume, henceforth, that it is not built into the notion of mind or soul or whatever that it is unintelligible or that there couldn't be a theory of it.

Secondly, someone might say more seriously that even if there is a theory of the soul or mind, the soul, at least in the full, rich old fashioned sense, is supposed to have powers that no mechanical system could have. In the latter part of this chapter I shall consider this claim.

If it is built into one's notions of the soul that the soul can do things that violate the laws of physics, then I admit I am stumped. There cannot be a soul which is isomorphic to a brain, if the soul can read the future clairvoyantly, in a way that is not in any way explainable by physical law. On the other hand, if one is interested in more modest forms of magic like telepathy, it seems to me that there is no reason in principle why we couldn't construct a device which would project subvocalized thoughts from one brain to another. As to reincarnation, if we are, as I am urging, a certain kind of functional structure (my identity is, as it were, my functional structure), there seems to be in principle no reason why that could not be reproduced after a thousand years or a million years or a billion years. Resurrection: as you know, Christians believe in resurrection in the flesh, which completely bypasses the need for an immaterial vehicle. So even if one is interested in those questions (and they are not my concern in this paper, although I am concerned to speak to people who have those concerns), even then one doesn't need an immaterial brain or soul-stuff.

So if I am right, and the question of matter or soul-stuff is really irrelevant to any question of philosophical or religious significance, why so much attention to it, why so much heat? The crux of the matter seems to be that both the Diderots of this world and the Descartes's of this world have agreed that if we are matter, then there is a physical explanation for how we behave, disappointing or exciting. I think the traditional dualist says *"wouldn't it be terrible if we turned out to be just matter, for then there is a physical explanation for everything we do"*. And the traditional materialist says *"if we are just matter, then there is a physical explanation for everything we do. Isn't that exciting!"* (It is like the distinction between the optimist and the pessimist: an optimist is a person who says "this is the best of all possible worlds"; and a pessimist is a person who says "you're right".)[2]

I think they are both wrong. I think Diderot and Descartes were both wrong in assuming that if we are matter, or our souls are material, then there is a physical explanation for our behavior.

Let me try to illustrate what I mean by a very simple analogy. Suppose we have a very simple physical system – a board in which there are two holes, a circle one inch in diameter and a square one inch high, and a cubical peg one-sixteenth of an inch less than one inch high. We have the following very simple fact to explain: *the peg passes through the square hole, and it does not pass through the round hole.*

In explanation of this, one might attempt the following. One might say that the peg is, after all, a cloud or, better, a rigid lattice of atoms. One might even attempt to give a description of that lattice, compute its electrical potential energy, worry about why it does not collapse, produce some quantum mechanics to explain why it is stable, etc. The board is also a lattice of atoms. I will call the peg "system A", and the holes "region 1" and "region 2". One could compute all possible trajectories of system A (there are, by the way, very serious questions about these computations, their effectiveness, feasibility, and so on, but let us assume this), and perhaps one could deduce from just the laws of particle mechanics or quantum electrodynamics that system *A* never passes through region 1, but that there is at least one trajectory which enables it to pass through region 2. Is this an explanation of the fact that the peg passes through the square hole and not the round hole?

Very often we are told that if something is made of matter, its behavior must have a physical explanation. And the argument is that if it is made of matter (and we make a lot of assumptions), then there should be a deduction of its behavior from its material structure. *What makes you call this deduction an explanation?*

On the other hand, if you are not "hipped" on the idea that *the* explanation must be at the level of the ultimate constituents, and that in fact the explanation might have the property that *the ultimate constituents don't matter,* that *only the higher level structure matters,* then there is a very simple explanation here. The explanation is that the board is rigid, the peg is rigid, and as a matter of geometrical fact, the round hole is smaller than the peg, the square hold is bigger than the cross-section of the peg. The peg passes through the hole that is large enough to take its cross-section, and does not pass through the hole that is too small to take its cross-section. That is a correct explanation whether the peg consists of molecules, or continuous rigid substance, or whatever. (If one wanted to amplify the explanation, one might point out the geometrical fact that a square one inch high is bigger than a circle one inch across.)

Now, one can say that in this explanation certain *relevant structural features of the situation* are brought out. The geometrical features are brought out. It is *relevant* that a square one inch high is bigger than a circle one inch around. And the relationship between the size and shape of the peg and the size and shape of the holes is *relevant.* It is *relevant* that both the board and the peg are *rigid* under transportation. And nothing else is relevant. The same explanation will go in any world (whatever the microstructure) in which those *higher level structural features* are present. In that sense *this explanation is autonomous.*

People have argued that I am wrong to say that the microstructural deduction is not an explanation. I think that in terms of the *purposes for which we use the notion of explanation,* it is not an explanation. If you want to, let us say that the deduction *is* an explanation, it is just a terrible explanation, and why look for terrible explanations when good ones are available?

Goodness is not a subjective matter. Even if one agrees with the positivists who saddled us with the notion of explanation as deduction from laws, one of the things we do in science is to look for laws. Explanation is superior not just subjectively, but *methodologically,* in terms of facilitating the aims of scientific inquiry, if it brings out relevant laws. An explanation is superior if it is more general.

Just taking those two features, and there are many many more one could think of, compare the explanation at the higher level of this phenomenon with the atomic explanation. The explanation at the higher level brings out the relevant geometrical relationships. The lower level explanation conceals those laws. Also notice that the higher level explanation applies to a much more interesting class of systems (of course that has to do with what we are interested in).

The fact is that we are much more interested in generalizing to other structures which are rigid and have various geometrical relations, than we are in generalizing to *the next peg that has exactly this molecular structure*, for the very good reason that there is not going to *be* a next peg that has exactly this molecular structure. So in terms of real life disciplines, real life ways of slicing up scientific problems, the higher level explanation is far more general, which is why it is *explanatory*.

We were only able to deduce a statement which is lawful at the *higher* level, that the peg goes through the hole which is larger than the cross-section of the peg. When we try to deduce the possible trajectories of "system *A*" from statements about the individual atoms, we use premises which are totally accidental – this atom is here, this carbon atom is there, and so forth. And that is one reason that it is very misleading to talk about a reduction of a science like economics to the level of the elementary particles making up the players of the economic game. In fact, their motions – buying this, selling that, arriving at an equilibrium price – these motions cannot be deduced from just the equations of motion. Otherwise they would be *physically necessitated*, not *economically necessitated*, to arrive at an equilibrium price. They play that game because they are particular systems with particular boundary conditions which are totally accidental from the point of view of physics. This means that the derivation of the laws of economics from *just* the laws of physics is *in principle* impossible. The derivation of the laws of economics from the laws of physics and *accidental statements about which particles were where when* by a Laplacian supermind might be in principle possible, but why want it? A few chapters of, e.g. von Neumann, will tell one far more about regularities at the level of economic structure than such a deduction ever could.

The conclusion I want to draw from this is that we do have the kind of autonomy that we are looking for in the mental realm. Whatever our mental functioning may be, there seems to be no serious reason to believe that it is *explainable* by our physics and chemistry. And what we are interested in is not: given that we consist of such and such particles, could someone have predicted that we would have this mental functioning? because such a prediction is not *explanatory*, however great a feat it may be. What we are interested in is: can we say at this autonomous level that since we have this sort of structure, this sort of program, it follows that we will be able to learn this, we will tend to like that, and so on? These are the problems of mental life – the description of this autonomous level of mental functioning – and that is what is to be discovered.

In previous papers, I have argued for the hypothesis that (1) a whole human being is a Turing machine, and (2) that psychological states of a human being are Turing machine states or disjunctions of Turing machine states. In this section I want to argue that this point of view was essentially wrong, and that I was too much in the grip of the reductionist outlook.

Let me begin with a technical difficulty. A *state* of a Turing machine is described in such a way that a Turing machine can be in exactly one state at a time. Moreover, memory and learning are not represented in the Turing machine model as acquisition of new states, but as acquisition of new information printed on the machine's tape. Thus, if human beings have any states at all which resemble Turing machine states, those states must (1) be states the human can be in at any time, independently of learning and memory; and (2) be *total* instantaneous states of the human being – states which determine, together with learning and memory, what the next state will be, as well as totally specifying the present condition of the human being ("totally" from the standpoint of psychological theory, that means).

These characteristics establish that *no* psychological state in any customary sense can be a Turing machine state. Take a particular kind of pain to be a "psychological state". If I *am* a Turing machine, then my present "state" must determine not only whether or not I am having that particular kind of pain, but also whether or not I am about to say "three", whether or not I am hearing a shrill whine, etc. So the psychological state in question (the pain) is not the same as my "state" in the sense of *machine state*, although it is possible (so far) that my machine state *determines* my psychological state. Moreover, *no* psychological theory would pretend that having a pain of a particular kind, being about to say "three", or hearing a shrill whine, etc., all belong to *one* psychological state, although there could well be a machine state characterized by the fact that I was in it only when simultaneously having that pain, being about to say "three", hearing a shrill whine, etc. So, even if I am a Turing machine, machine states are *not* the same as my psychological states. My description *qua* Turing machine (machine table) and my description *qua* human being (*via* a psychological theory) are descriptions at two totally different levels of organization.

So far it is still possible that a psychological state is a large disjunction (practically speaking, an almost infinite disjunction) of machine states, although no *single* machine state is a psychological state. But this is very unlikely when we move away from states like "pain" (which are almost *biological*) to states like "jealousy" or "love" or "competitiveness". Being jealous is certainly not an *instantaneous* state, and it depends on a great deal of information and on many learned facts and habits. But Turing machine states are instantaneous and are independent of learning and memory. That is, learning and memory may cause a Turing machine to go into a state, but the identity of the state does not depend on learning and memory, whereas, no matter what state I am in, identifying that state as "being jealous of X's regard for Y" involves specifying that I have learned that X and Y are persons and a good deal about social relations among persons. Thus jealousy can neither be a machine state nor a disjunction of machine states.

One might attempt to modify the theory by saying that being jealous = either being in State A and having tape c_1 *or* being in State A and having tape c_2 *or* ... being in State B and having tape d_1 *or* being in State B and having tape d_2 ... being in State Z and having tape y_1 ... *or* being in State Z and having tape y_n – i.e. define a psychological state as disjunction, the individual disjuncts being not Turing machine states, as before, but conjunctions of a machine state and a tape (i.e. a total description of the content of the memory bank). Besides the fact that such a description would be literally infinite, the theory is now without content, for the original purpose was to use the machine table as a model of a psychological theory, whereas it is now clear that the machine table description, although different from the description at the elementary particle level, is as removed from the description *via* a psychological theory as the physico-chemical description is.

What is the importance of machines in the philosophy of mind? I think that machines have both a positive and a negative importance. The positive importance of machines was that it was in connection with machines, computing machines in particular, that the notion of functional organization first appeared. Machines forced us to distinguish between an abstract structure and its concrete realization. Not that that distinction came into the world for the first time with machines. But in the case of computing machines, we could not avoid rubbing our noses against the fact that what we had to count as to all intents and purposes the same structure could be realized in a bewildering variety of different ways; that the important properties were not physical–chemical. That the machines made us catch on to the idea of functional organization is extremely important. The negative importance of machines, however, is that they tempt us to oversimplification. The notion of functional organization became clear to us through systems with a very restricted, very specific functional organization. So the temptation is present to assume that we must have that restricted and specific kind of functional organization.

Now I want to consider an example – an example which may seem remote from what we have been talking about, but which may help. This is not an example from the philosophy of mind at all. Consider the following fact. The earth does not go around the sun in a circle, as was once believed, it goes around the sun in an ellipse, with the sun at one of the foci, not in the center of the ellipse. Yet one statement which would hold true if the orbit was a circle and the sun was at the centre still holds true, surprisingly. That is the following statement: the radius vector from the sun to the earth sweeps out equal areas in equal times. If the orbit were a circle, and the earth were moving with a constant velocity, that would be trivial. But the orbit is not a circle. Also the velocity is not constant – when the earth is farthest away from the sun, it is going most slowly, when it is closest to the sun, it is going fastest. The earth is speeding up and slowing down. But the earth's radius vector sweeps out equal areas in equal times.[3] Newton deduced that law in his *Principia*, and his deduction shows that the only thing on which that law depends is that the force acting on the earth is in the direction of the sun. That is absolutely the only fact one needs to deduce that law. Mathematically it is equivalent to that law.[4] That is all well and good when the gravitational law is that every body attracts every other body according to an inverse square law, because then there is always a force on the earth in the direction of the sun. If we assume that we can neglect all the other bodies, that their influence is slight, then that is all we need, and we can use Newton's proof, or a more modern, simpler proof.

But today we have very complicated laws of gravitation. First of all, we say what is really going on is that the world lines of freely falling bodies in space-time are geodesics. And the geometry is determined by the mass–energy tensor, and the ankle bone is connected to the leg bone, etc. So, one might ask, how would a modern relativity theorist explain Kepler's law? He would explain it very simply. *Kepler's laws are true because Newton's laws are approximately true.* And, in fact, an attempt to replace that argument by a deduction of Kepler's laws from the field equations would be regarded as almost as ridiculous (but not quite) as trying to deduce that the peg will go through one hole and not the other from the positions and velocities of the individual atoms.

I want to draw the philosophical conclusion that Newton's laws *have a kind of reality in our world* even though they are not *true*. The point is that it will be necessary to appeal to Newton's laws in order to explain Kepler's laws. Methodologically, I can make that claim at least plausible. One remark – due to Alan Garfinkel – is that *a good explanation is invariant under small perturbations of the assumptions.* One problem with deducing Kepler's laws from the gravitational field equations is that if we do it, tomorrow the gravitational field equations are likely to be different. Whereas the explanation which consists in showing that whichever equation we have implies Newton's equation to a first approximation is invariant under even moderate perturbations, quite big perturbations, of the assumptions. One might say that every explanation of Kepler's laws "passes through" Newton's laws.

Let me come back to the philosophy of mind, however. If we assume a thorough atomic structure of matter, quantization and so forth, then, at first blush, it looks as if *continuities* cannot be relevant to our brain functioning. Mustn't it all be discrete? Physics says that the deepest level is discrete.

There are two problems with this argument. One is that there are continuities even in quantum mechanics, as well as discontinuities. But ignore that, suppose quantum mechanics were a thoroughly discrete theory.

The other problem is that if that were a good argument, it would be an argument against the utilizability of the model of air as a continuous liquid, which is the model on which aeroplane wings are constructed, at least if they are to fly at anything less than supersonic speeds. There are two points: one is that a discontinuous structure, a discrete structure, can approximate a continuous structure. The discontinuities may be irrelevant, just as in the case of the peg and the board. The fact that the peg and the board are not continuous solids is irrelevant. One can say that the peg and the board only approximate perfectly rigid continuous solids. But if the error in the approximation is irrelevant to the level of description, so what? It is not just that discrete systems can approximate continuous systems; the fact is that the system may behave in the way it does *because* a continuous system would behave in such and such a way, and the system approximates a continuous system.

This is not a Newtonian world. Tough. Kepler's law comes out true because the sun–earth system approximates a Newtonian system. And the error in the approximation is quite irrelevant at that level.

This analogy is not perfect because physicists are interested in laws to which the error in the approximation is relevant. It seems to me that in the psychological case the analogy is even better, that continuous models (for example, Hull's model for rote learning which used a continuous potential) could perfectly well be correct, whatever the ultimate structure of the brain is. We cannot deduce that a digital model has to be the correct model from the fact that ultimately there are neurons. The brain may work the way it does because it approximates some system whose laws are best conceptualized in terms of continuous mathematics. What is more, the errors in that approximation may be irrelevant at the level of psychology.

What I have said about *continuity* goes as well for many other things. Let us come back to the question of the soul people and the brain people, and the isomorphism between the souls in one world and the brains in the other. One objection was, if there is a functional isomorphism between souls and brains, wouldn't the souls have to be rather simple? The answer is no. Because brains can be essentially infinitely complex. A system with as many degrees of freedom as the brain can imitate to within the accuracy relevant to psychological theory any structure one can hope to describe. It might be, so to speak, that the ultimate physics of the soul will be quite different from the ultimate physics of the brain, but that at the level we are interested in, the level of functional organization, the same description might go for both. And also that that description might be formally incompatible with the actual physics of the brain, in the way that the description of the air flowing around an aeroplane wing as a continuous incompressible liquid is *formally incompatible with the actual structure of the air.*

Let me close by saying that these examples support the idea that our substance, what we are made of, places almost no first order restrictions on our form. And that what we are really interested in, as Aristotle saw,[5] is form and not matter. *What is our intellectual form?* is the question, not what the matter is. And whatever our substance may be, soul-stuff, or matter or Swiss cheese, it is not going to place any interesting first order restrictions on the answer to this question. It may, of course, place interesting higher order restrictions. Small effects may have to be explained in terms of the actual physics of the brain. But when we are not even at the level of an *idealized* description of the functional organization of the brain, to talk about the importance of small perturbations seems decidedly premature. My conclusion is that we have what we always wanted – an autonomous mental life. And we need no mysteries, no ghostly agents, no *élan vital* to have it.

NOTES

This paper was presented as a part of a Foerster symposium on "Computers and the Mind" at the University of California (Berkeley) in October, 1973. I am indebted to Alan Garfinkel for comments on earlier versions of this paper.
1   Even if it were not physically possible to realize human psychology in a creature

made of anything but the usual protoplasm, DNA, etc., it would still not be correct to say that psychological states are identical with their physical realizations. For, as will be argued below, such an identification has no *explanatory* value *in psychology*. On this point, compare Fodor (1968).

2   Joke credit: Joseph Weizenbaum.
3   This is one of Kepler's Laws.
4   Provided that the two bodies – the sun and the earth – are the whole universe. If there are other forces, then, of course, Kepler's law cannot be *exactly* correct.
5   E.g. Aristotle says: 'we can wholly dismiss as unnecessary the question whether the soul and the body are one: it is as meaningless to ask whether the wax and the shape given to it by the stamp are one, or generally the matter of a thing and that of which it is the matter.' (See *De Anima*, 412 a6–b9.)

REFERENCE

Fodor, J. (1968) *Psychological Explanation*, New York: Random House.

7 The Myth of Nonreductive Materialism

Jaegwon Kim

I

Reductionism of all sorts has been out of favor for many years. Few among us would now seriously entertain the possibility that ethical expressions are definable, or reducible in some broader sense, in terms of "descriptive" or "naturalistic" expressions. I am not sure how many of us can remember, in vivid enough detail, the question that was once vigorously debated as to whether so-called "physical-object statements" are translatable into statements about the phenomenal aspects of perceptual experience, whether these are conceived as "sense data" or as some manner of "being appeared to". You may recall the idea that concepts of scientific theories must be reduced, via "operational definitions", to intersubjectively performable procedures whose results can be ascertained through observation. This sounded good – properly tough-minded and hard-nosed – but it didn't take long for philosophers and scientists to realize that a restrictive constraint of this sort was neither enforceable nor necessary – not necessary to safeguard science from the threat of metaphysics and pseudo-science. These reductionisms are now nothing but museum pieces.

In philosophy of mind, too, we have gone through many reductionisms; some of these, such as logical behaviorism, have been defunct for many years; others, most notably the psychoneural identity theory, have been repeatedly declared dead; and still others, such as versions of functionalism, are still hanging on, though with varying degrees of difficulty. Perhaps as a result of the singular lack of success with which our earlier reductionist efforts have been rewarded, a negative image seems to have emerged for reductionisms in general. Many of us have the feeling that there is something rigid and narrow-minded about reductionist strategies. Reductionisms, we tend to feel, attempt to impose on us a monolithic, strait-jacketed view of the subject matter, the kind of cleansed and tidy picture that appeals to those obsessed with orderliness and discipline. Perhaps this impression has something to do with the reductionists' ritual incantations of slogans like "parsimony", "simplicity", "economy", and "unity", all of them virtues of a rather puritanical sort. Perhaps, too, reductionisms are out of step with the intellectual style of our times: we strive for patterns of life and thought that are rich in diversity and complexity and tolerant of disagreement and multiplicity. We are apt to think that the real world is a messy place and resists any simplistic drive, especially one carried on from the armchair, toward simplification and unification. In fact, the word "reductionism" seems by now to have acquired a negative, faintly disreputable flavor – at least in philosophy of mind. Being a reductionist is a bit like being a logical positivist or member of the Old Left – an aura of doctrinaire naivete hangs over such a person.

At any rate, reductionism in the mind–body problem has been out of fashion for two decades; it has been about that long since the unexpectedly early demise of the psychoneural identity theory, a doctrine advertised by its proponents as the one that was in tune with a world view adequately informed by the best contemporary science. Surprisingly, the abandonment of psychoneural reductionism has not led to a resurgence of dualism. What is curious, at least in terms of the expectations set by the earlier mind–body debates, is the fact that those who renounced reductionism have stayed with physicalism. The distinctive feature of the mind–body theories that have sprung up in the wake of the identity theory is the belief, or hope, that one can be an honest-to-goodness physicalist without at the same time being a reductionist. In fact, a correct and realistic view of science as it is practiced will show us, the new physicalists assure us, that as an account of the "cross-level" relation between theories, classical reductionism is untenable everywhere, not just about the psychophysical relation. The leading idea in all this has been the thought that we can assuage our physicalist qualms by embracing "ontological physicalism",[1] the claim that all that exists in spacetime is physical, but, at the same time, accept "property dualism", a dualism about psychological and physical attributes, insisting that psychological concepts or properties form an irreducible, autonomous domain. The issue I want to explore here is whether or not a robust physicalist can, consistently and plausibly, swear off reductionism – that is, whether or not a substantial form of physicalism can be combined with the rejection of psychophysical reduction.

To lay my cards on the table, I will argue that a middle-of-the-road position of the sort just described is not available. More specifically, I will claim that a physicalist has only two genuine options, eliminativism and reductionism. That is, if you have already made your commitment to a version of physicalism worthy of the name, you must accept the reducibility of the psychological to the physical, or, failing that, you must consider the psychological as falling outside your physicalistically respectable ontology. Of course, you might decide to reconsider your commitment to physicalism; but I will not here consider what dualist alternatives there might be which are still live options for us. So if I am right, the choices we face concerning the mind–body problem are rather stark: there are three – dualism, reductionism, and eliminativism.

II

Pressures from two sources have been largely responsible, I believe, for the decline of reductionism in philosophy of mind, a decline that began in the late 1960s. One was Donald Davidson's "anomalism of the mental", the doctrine that there are no precise or strict laws about mental events.[2]

According to Davidson, the mental is anomalous not only in that there are no laws relating mental events to other mental events but none relating them to physical events either. This meant that no nomological linkages between the mental and the physical were available to enable the reduction of the former to the latter. The second antireductionist pressure came from a line of argument based on the phenomenon of "multiple realizability" of mental states which Hilary Putnam forcefully brought to philosophical attention, claiming that it directly refuted the reductive materialism of Smart and Feigl.[3] Jerry Fodor and others have developed this idea as a general antireductionist argument, advancing the claim that the "special sciences", such as psychology, sociology, and economics, are in general irreducible to physical theory, and that reductive materialism, or "type identity theory", is generally false as a theory about science.[4] Earlier physicalists would have regarded the irreducibility as evidence showing the mental to be beyond the pale of a scientifically respectable ontology; that is, they would have inferred eliminativism from the irreducibility. This in fact was Quine's response to the problem of intentionality.[5] But not for the latter-day physicalists: for them, the irreducibility only meant that psychology, and other special sciences, are "autonomous", and that a physicalist can, in consistency and good conscience, accept the existence of these isolated autonomous domains within science.

Let us begin with Davidson. As noted, the anomalism of the mental can be thought of as the conjunction of two claims: first, the claim that there are no purely psychological laws, that is, laws connecting psychological events with other psychological events, and second, the claim that there are no laws connecting psychological events with physical events. The second claim, which we might call "psychophysical anomalism", is what underlies Davidson's argument against reductionism. The argument is simple and direct: the demise of analytical behaviorism scotched the idea that the mental could be definitionally reduced to the physical. Further, psychophysical anomalism shows that a nomological reduction of the mental isn't in the offing either. The implicit assumption about reduction in this argument is one that is widely shared: reduction of one theory to another requires the derivation of the laws of the reduced theory from those of the reducer, and for this to be possible, terms of the first theory must be appropriately connected via "bridge principles", with those of the second. And the bridge principles must be either conceptually underwritten as definitions, or else express empirical lawlike correlations ("bridge laws" or "theoretical identities").[6]

This is all pretty straightforward. What was striking was the further philosophical conclusions Davidson inferred from these considerations. Far from deriving some sort of dualism, he used them to argue for a materialist monism. His argument is well known, but it bears repeating. Mental events, Davidson observed, enter into causal relations with physical events.[7] But causal relations must be backed by laws: that is, causal relations between individual events must instantiate lawful regularities. Since there are no laws about the mental, either psychophysical or purely psychological, any causal relation involving a mental event must instantiate a physical law, from which it follows that the mental event has a physical description, or falls under a physical event kind. From this it further follows that the event is a physical event. For an event is physical (or mental) if it falls under a physical event kind (or a mental event kind).

It follows then that all events are physical events – on the assumption that every event enters into at least one causal relation. This assumption seems entirely unproblematic, for it only leaves out events that are both *causeless* and *effectless*. If there are any such events, it is difficult to see how their existence can be known to us; I believe we could safely ignore them. So imagine a Davidsonian universe of events: all these events are physical events, and some of them are also mental. That is to say, all events have physical properties, and some have mental properties as well. Such is Davidson's celebrated "anomalous monism".

Davidson's ontology recognizes individual events as spatiotemporal particulars. And the principal structure over these events is causal structure; the network of causal relations that interconnect events is what gives intelligible structure to this universe of events. What role does mentality play, on Davidson's anomalous monism, in shaping this structure? The answer: none whatever.

For anomalous monism entails this: the very same network of causal relations would obtain in Davidson's world if you were to redistribute mental properties over its events any way you like; you would not disturb a single causal relation if you randomly and arbitrarily reassigned mental properties to events, or even removed mentality entirely from the world. The fact is that under Davidson's anomalous monism, mentality does no causal work. Remember: on anomalous monism, events are causes or effects only as they instantiate physical laws, and this means that an event's mental properties make no causal difference. And to suppose that altering an event's mental properties would also alter its physical properties and thereby affect its causal relations is to suppose that psychophysical anomalism, a cardinal tenet of anomalous monism, is false.[8]

Anomalous monism, therefore, permits mental properties no causal role, not even in relation to other mental properties. What does no causal work does no explanatory work either; it may as well not be there – it's difficult to see how we could miss it if it weren't there at all. That there are in this world just these mental events with just these mental characteristics is something that makes no causal difference to anything. On anomalous monism, that an event falls under a given mental kind is a causally irrelevant fact; it is also something that is entirely inexplicable in causal terms. Given all this, it's difficult to see what point there is in recognizing mentality as a feature of the world. I believe that it we push anomalous monism this way, we will find that it is a doctrine virtually indistinguishable from outright eliminativism.

Thus, what we see is this: anomalous monism, rather than giving us a form of nonreductive physicalism, is essentially a form of eliminativism. Unlike eliminativism, it allows mentality to exist; but mentality is given no useful work and its occurrence is left wholly mysterious and causally inexplicable. This doesn't strike me as a form of existence worth having. In this respect, anomalous monism does rather poorly even in comparison with epiphenomenalism as a realism about the mental. Epiphenomenalism gives the mental a place in the causal network of events; the mind is given a well-defined place, if not an active role, in the causal structure of the world.

These observations highlight the importance of *properties*; for it is in terms of properties and their interrelations that we make sense of certain concepts that are crucial in this context, such as law, causality, explanation, and dependence. Thus, the anomalousness of mental properties has far-reaching consequences within Davidson's framework: within it, anomalous properties are causally and explanatorily impotent, and it is doubtful that they can have any useful role at all. The upshot is that we don't get in Davidson's anomalous monism a plausible form of nonreductive physicalism; his anomalous monism comes perilously close to eliminativism.[9]

III

Let us now turn to the multiple realizability (or "compositional plasticity") of psychological events and its implications for psychophysical reduction. In a passage that turned out to have a profound impact on the discussions of the mind–body problem, Putnam wrote:[10]

> Consider what the brain-state theorist has to do to make good his claims. He has to specify a physical–chemical state such that *any* organism (not just a mammal) is in pain if and only if (a) it possesses a brain of a suitable physical–chemical structure; and (b) its brain is in that physical–chemical state. This means that the physical–chemical state in question must be a possible state of a mammalian brain, a reptilian brain, a mollusc's brain (octopuses are mollusca, and certainly feel pain), etc. At the same time, it must *not* be a possible (physically possible) state of the brain of any physically possible creature that cannot feel pain. Even if such a state can be found, it must be nomologically certain that it will also be a state of the brain of any extraterrestrial life that may be found that will be capable of feeling pain before we can even entertain the supposition that it may *be* pain.

This paragraph helped bring on an unexpectedly early demise of the psychoneural identity theory of Smart and Feigl and inspired a new theory of the mental, functionalism, which in spite of its assorted difficulties is still the most influential position on the nature of the mental.[11] Putnam's basic point is that any psychological event-type can be "physically realized" or "instantiated" or "implemented" in endlessly diverse ways, depending on the physical–biological nature of the organism or system involved, and that this makes it highly implausible to expect the event to correlate uniformly with, and thus be identifiable with, some "single" type of neural or physical state. This idea has been used by Fodor to formulate a general anti-reductionist argument, whose gist can be quickly summarized.

As we have seen, reduction of one theory to another is thought to require the derivation of the laws of the reduced theory from the laws of the reducer via "bridge laws". If a predicate of the theory being reduced has a nomologically coextensive predicate in the reducing theory, the universally quantified biconditional connecting the two predicates will be available for use as a bridge law.[12] Let us say that the vocabulary of the reduced theory is "strongly connected" with that of the reducing theory if such a biconditional bridge law correlates each predicate of the former with a predicate of the latter. It is clear that the condition of strong connectibility guarantees reduction (on the assumption that the theory being reduced is a true theory). For it would enable us to rewrite basic laws of the target theory in the vocabulary of the reducer, using these biconditional laws in effect as definitions. Either these rewrites are derivable from the laws of the reducing theory, or else they can be added as additional basic laws. In the latter case, the reducer theory has been expanded; but that does not diminish the ontological and conceptual import of the reductive procedure.

But what multiple realization puts in doubt, according to the anti-reductionist, is precisely the strong connectibility of mental predicates vis-à-vis physical–neural predicates. For any psychological property, there is in principle an endless sequence of nomologically possible physical states such that, though each of them "realizes" or "implements" it, none of them will by itself be coextensive with it. Why can't we take the *disjunction* of these physical states as the physical coextension of the mental property? Putnam somewhat disdainfully dismisses this move, saying only that "this does not have to be taken seriously".[13] I think there are some complex issues here about disjunctive predicates vs. disjunctive properties, complexity of predicates vs. that of properties, etc.; but these are likely to be contentious issues that can only distract us at present.[14] So let us go along with Putnam here and disregard the disjunctive solution to the multiple realization problem.

In rejecting the disjunction move, however, Putnam appears to be assuming this: *a physical state that realizes a mental event is at least nomologically sufficient for it.* For if this assumption were rejected, the disjunction move couldn't even get started. This generates laws of the form "Pi → M", where M is a mental state and Pi is a physical state that realizes it. Thus, where there is multiple realization, there must be psychophysical laws, each specifying a physical state as nomologically sufficient for the given mental state. Moreover, Putnam's choice of examples in the quotation above, which are either biological species or determinate types of physical structures ("extraterrestrials"), and his talk of "species-specificity" and "species-independence"[15] suggest that he is thinking of laws of a somewhat stronger form, "Si → (M ↔ Pi)", which, *relative to species or structure* Si, specifies a physical state, Pi, as *both necessary and sufficient* for the occurrence of mental state M. A law of this form states that any organism or system, belonging to a certain species, is such that it has the given mental property at a time if and only if it is in a certain specified physical state at that time. We may call laws of this form "species-specific biconditional laws".

In order to generate laws of this kind, biological species may turn out to be too wide; individual differences in the localization of psychological functions in the brain are well known. Moreover, given the phenomena of learning and maturation, injuries to the brain, and the like, the neural structure that subserves a psychological state or function may change for an individual over its lifetime. What is important then is that these laws are relative to physical–biological structure-types, although for simplicity I will continue to put the matter in terms of species. The substantive theoretical assumption here is the belief that for each psychological state there are physical–biological structure types, at a certain level of description or specification, that generate laws of this form. I think an assumption of this kind is made by most philosophers who speak of multiple realizations of psychological states, and it is in fact a plausible assumption for a physicalist to make.[16] Moreover, such an assumption seems essential to the very idea of a physical realization; what else could "physical realization" mean?

So what I am saying is this: the multiple realization argument perhaps shows that the strong connectibility of mental properties vis-à-vis physical properties does not obtain: however, it *presupposes* that *species-specific strong connectibility* does hold. Merely to defeat the antireductionist argument, I need not make this second claim; all I need is the weaker claim that the phenomenon of multiple realization is *consistent* with the species-specific strong connectibility, and it seems to me that that is plainly true.

The point of all this is that the availability of species-specific biconditional laws linking the mental with the physical breathes new life into psycho-physical reductionism. Unlike species-independent laws, these laws cannot buy us a *uniform* or *global* reduction of psychology, a reduction of every psychological state to a uniform physical–biological base across all actual and possible organisms; however, these laws will buy us a series of *species-specific* or *local* reductions. If we had a law of this form for each psychological state-type for humans, we would have a physical reduction of human psychology; this reduction would tell us how human psychology is physically implemented, how the causal connections between our psychological events and processes work at the physical–biological level, what biological subsystems subserve our cognitive capacities and functions, and so forth. This is reduction in a full-blown sense, except that it is limited to individuals sharing a certain physical–biological structure. I believe "local reductions" of this sort are the rule rather than the exception in all of science, not just in psychology.[17] In any case, this is a plausible picture of what in fact goes on in neurobiology, physiological psychology, and cognitive neuroscience. And it seems to me that any robust physicalist must expect, and demand, the possibility of local reductions of psychology just in this sense.[18]

Thus, the conclusion we must draw is that the multiple realizability of the mental has no antireductionist implications of great significance; on the contrary, it entails, or at least is consistent with, the local reducibility of psychology, local relative to species or physical structure-types. If psycho-logical states are multiply realized, that only means that we shall have multiple local reductions of psychology. The multiple realization argument, if it works, shows that a global reduction is not in the offing; however, local reductions are reduction enough, by any reasonable scientific standards and in their philosophical implications.

IV

Some have looked to the idea of "supervenience" for a formulation of physicalism that is free of reductionist commitments. The promise of supervenience in this area appears to have been based, at least in part, on the historical circumstance that some prominent ethical theorists, such as G. E. Moore and R. M. Hare, who constructed classic arguments against naturalistic reductionism in ethics, at the same time held the view that moral properties are "supervenient" upon descriptive or naturalistic properties. So why not think of the relation between psychological and physical properties in analogy with the relation, as conceived by these ethical theorists, between moral and descriptive properties? In each instance, the supervenient properties are in some substantive sense dependent on, or determined by, their subvenient, base properties and yet, it is hoped, irreducible to them. This was precisely the line of thinking that appears to have prompted Davidson to inject supervenience into the discussion of the mind–body problem. He wrote:[19]

> Although the position I describe denies there are psychophysical laws, it is consistent with the view that mental characteristics are in some sense dependent, or supervenient, on physical characteristics. Such super-venience might be taken to mean that there cannot be two events alike in all physical respects but differing in some mental respects, or that an object cannot alter in some mental respect without altering in some physical respect. Dependence or supervenience of this kind does not entail reducibility through law or definition: if it did, we could reduce moral properties to descriptive, and this there is good reason to *believe* cannot be done . . .

Although Davidson himself did not pursue this idea further, many other philosophers have tried to work this suggestive idea into a viable form of nonreductive materialism.

The central problem in implementing Davidson's suggestion has been that of defining a supervenience relation that will fill the twin requirements he set forth: first, the relation must be *nonreductive*; that is, a given domain can be supervenient on another without being reducible to it. Second, the relation must be one of *dependence*: if a domain supervenes on another, there must be a sturdy sense in which the first is dependent on the second, or the second determines the first. But it has not been easy to find such a relation. The main difficulty has been this: if a relation is weak enough to be nonreductive, it tends to be too weak to serve as a dependence relation; conversely, when a relation is strong enough to give us dependence, it tends to be too strong – strong enough to imply reducibility.

I will not rehearse here the well known arguments pro and con concerning various supervenience relations that have been proposed. I will instead focus on one supervenience relation that has seemed to several philosophers[20] to hold the most promise as a nonreductive dependency relation, viz., "global supervenience". The generic idea of supervenience is that things that are indiscernible in respect of the "base" (or "subvenient") properties cannot differ in respect of the supervenient properties. Global supervenience applies this consideration to "worlds", giving us the following formulation of psychophysical supervenience:

> Worlds that are indiscernible in all physical respects are indiscernible in mental respects; in fact, physically indiscernible worlds are one and the same world.

Thus, any world that is just like this world in all physical details must be just like it in all psychological respects as well. This relation of supervenience is appropriately called "global" in that worlds rather than individuals within worlds are compared for discernibility or indiscernibility in regard to sets of properties. What is it for two worlds to be physically, or mentally, indiscernible? For simplicity let us assume that the same individuals exist in all the worlds:[21] We may then say that two worlds are indiscernible with respect to a set of properties just in case these properties are distributed over individuals in the same way in the two worlds.

It can be shown that, as hoped, the global supervenience of the mental on the physical does not entail the existence of psychophysical laws;[22] thus, global supervenience is consistent with the nomological irreducibility of the mental to the physical. The only question then is whether it yields an appropriate relation of dependency between the mental and the physical, one that is strong enough to qualify it as a physicalism. The answer, I will argue, is in the negative.

We may begin by observing that the global supervenience of the mental permits the following: imagine a world that differs from the actual world in some minute physical detail. We may suppose that in that world one lone hydrogen atom somewhere in deep space is slightly displaced relative to its position in this world. This world with one wayward hydrogen atom could, consistently with the global supervenience of the mental, be as different as you please from the actual world in any mental respect (thus, in that world nothing manifests mentality, or mentality is radically redistributed in other ways). The existence of such a world and other similarly aberrant worlds does not violate the constraints of global supervenience; since they are not physically indiscernible from the actual world, they could, under global supervenience, differ radically from this world in psychological characteristics.[23]

If that doesn't convince you of the weakness of global supervenience as a determination or dependency relation, consider this: it is consistent with global supervenience for there to be two organisms in our actual world which, though wholly indiscernible physically, are radically different in mental respects (say, your molecule-for-molecule duplicate is totally lacking in mentality). This is consistent with global supervenience because there might be no other possible world that is just like this one physically and yet differing in some mental respect.[24]

It seems to me that indiscernibility considerations at the global level, involving whole worlds, are just too coarse to give us the kind of dependency relation we should demand if the mental is truly dependent on the physical. Like it or not, we treat individuals, and perhaps also aggregates of individuals smaller than total worlds, as psychological units, and it seems to me that if psychophysical determination or dependence means anything, it ought to mean that the psychological nature of each such unit is wholly determined by its physical nature. That is, dependency or determination must hold at the local as well as the global level.

Moreover, talk of whole worlds in this connection, unless it is anchored in determinative relations obtaining at the local level, has little verifiable content; it is difficult to see how there can be empirical evidence for the global supervenience thesis that is not based in evidence about specific psychophysical dependencies – dependencies and correlations between specific psychological and physical properties. In fact, it seems to me that we must look to local dependencies for an *explanation* of global super-venience as well as its evidence. Why is it the case that no two worlds can exist that are indiscernible physically and yet discernible psychologically? Or why is it the case that "physical truths determine all the truths,"[25] as some prefer to put it? I think this is a legitimate question to raise, and as far as I can see the only answer, other than the response that it is a brute, unexplainable metaphysical fact, is in terms of local correlations and dependencies between specific mental and physical properties. If the global supervenience of the mental on the physical were to be proposed as an unexplainable fact that we must accept on faith, I doubt that we need to take the proposal seriously. Specific psychophysical dependencies holding for individuals, and other proper parts of the world, are both evidence for, and an explanatory ground of, global supervenience.

The trouble is that once we begin talking about correlations and dependencies between specific psychological and physical properties, we are in effect talking about psychophysical laws, and these laws raise the specter of unwanted physical reductionism. Where there are psycho-physical laws, there is always the threat, or promise, of psychophysical reduction. We must conclude that supervenience is not going to deliver to us a viable form of nonreductive materialism.

V

So far I have reviewed three influential formulations of nonreductive materialism – Davidson's anomalous monism, the Putnam–Fodor doctrine of psychological autonomy, and supervenient physicalism – and found each of them wanting either as a materialism or as an antireductionism. In this final section, I want to advance a direct argument to show why the prospects for a nonreductive physicalism are dim.

Let us first of all note that nonreductive physicalism is not to be a form of eliminativism; that is, it acknowledges the mental as a legitimate domain of entities. What sort of entities? Here let us, for convenience, make use of the Davidsonian scheme of individual events, thinking of mentality to be exhibited as properties of these events. Thus, as a noneliminativist, the nonreductive physicalist believes that there are events in her ontology that have mental properties (e.g., being a pain, being a belief that snow is cold, etc.). I argued earlier, in discussing Davidson's anomalous monism, that if your noneliminativism is to be more than a token gesture, you had better find some real causal work for your mental properties. The fact that a given event is a mental event of a certain kind must play some causal–explanatory role in what other events occur and what properties they have. Thus, I am supposing that a nonreductive physicalist is a mental realist, and that to be a mental realist, your mental properties must be *causal properties* – properties in virtue of which an event enters into causal relations it would otherwise not have entered into.

Let me now make another assumption: psychophysical causation takes place – that is, some mental events cause physical events. For example, a sudden sharp pain felt in my hand causes a jerky withdrawal of the hand. It is true that in Davidsonian domain all events are physical; that is, every event has some physical property. But when I say that mental events cause physical events, something stronger is intended, namely that an event, *in virtue of its mental property*, causes another event to have a certain physical property. I believe that this assumption will be granted by most of us – it will be granted by anyone who believes that at least sometimes our limbs move because we have certain desires and beliefs.[26] When I walk to the water fountain for a drink of water, my legs move in the way they do in part because of my desire for water and my belief that there is water to be had at the water fountain.

There is a further assumption that I believe any physicalist would grant. I call this "the causal closure of the physical domain"; roughly, it says this: *any physical event that has a cause at time t has a physical cause at t.* This is the assumption that if we trace the causal ancestry of a physical event, we need never go outside the physical domain. To deny this assumption is to accept the Cartesian idea that some physical events have only nonphysical causes, and if this is true there can in principle be no complete and self-sufficient physical theory of the physical domain. If the causal closure failed, our physics would need to refer in an essential way to nonphysical causal agents, perhaps Cartesian souls and their psychic properties, if it is to give a complete account of the physical world. I think most physicalists would find that picture unacceptable.

Now we are ready to derive some consequences from these assumptions. Suppose that a certain event, in virtue of its mental property, causes a physical event. The causal closure of the physical domain says that this physical event must also have a physical cause. We may assume that this physical cause, in virtue of its physical property, causes the physical event. The following question arises: *What is the relationship between these two causes, one mental and the other physical?* Each is claimed to be a cause of the physical effect. There are two initial possibilities that we can consider.

First, when we are faced with two purported causes of a single event, we could entertain the possibility that each is only a *partial cause*, the two together making up a full or sufficient cause, as when a car crash is said to be caused by the driver's careless braking and the icy condition of the road.

Applied to our case, it says that the mental cause and the physical cause are each only a partial cause, and that they *together* make up one sufficient cause. This seems like an absurd thing to say, and in any case it violates the causal closure principle in that it regards the mental event as a necessary constituent of a full cause of a physical event; thus, on this view, a full causal story of how this physical event occurs must, at least partially, go outside the physical domain.

Could it be that the mental cause and the physical cause are each an *independent sufficient* cause of the physical effect? The suggestion then is that the physical effect is *overdetermined*. So if the physical cause hadn't occurred, the mental cause by itself would have caused the effect. This picture is again absurd: from what we know about the physiology of limb movement, we must believe that if the pain sensation causes my hand to withdraw, the causal chain from the pain to the limb motion must somehow make use of the causal chain from an appropriate central neural event to the muscle contraction; it makes no sense to think that there was an independent, perhaps telekinetic, causal path from the pain to the limb movement. Moreover, the overdetermination idea seems to violate the causal closure principle as well: in the counterfactual situation in which the physical cause does not occur, the closure principle is violated. For the idea that the mental and the physical cause are each an independent sufficient cause involves the acceptance of the counterfactual that if the physical cause had not occurred, the mental cause would have occurred and caused the physical effect. This is in violation of the causal closure principle.

These two ways of looking at the situation are obvious nonstarters. We need a more plausible answer to the question, how are the mental cause and the physical cause of the single physical effect related to each other? Given that any physical event has a physical cause, how is a mental cause *also* possible? This I call "the problem of causal–explanatory exclusion", for the problem seems to arise from the fact that a cause, or causal explanation, of an event, when it is regarded as a full, sufficient cause or explanation, appears to *exclude* other *independent* purported causes or causal explanations of it.[27]

At this point, you might want to protest: why all this beating around the bush? Why not just say the mental cause and the physical cause are one and the same? Identification simplifies ontology and gets rid of unwanted puzzles. Consider saying that there are in this glass two distinct substances, H_2O and water; that is, consider saying that water and H_2O co-occur everywhere as a matter of law but that they are distinct substances nonetheless. This would invite a host of unwanted and unnecessary puzzles: given that what is in the glass weighs a total of ten ounces, how much of the weight is to be attributed to the water and how much to the H_2O? By dropping a lighted match in the glass, I extinguish it. What caused it? Was it the water or the H_2O? Were they each only a partial cause, or was the extinguishing of the match overdetermined? The identification of the water and the H_2O puts all these questions to rest in a single stroke: there is here one thing, not two. The identity solution can work similar magic in our present case: the pain *is* a neural state – here there is one cause, not two.

The limb motion was caused by the pain, that is to say, by a neural state. The unwanted puzzles vanish.

All this is correct. But what does the identity solution involve? Remember that what is for us at issue is the causal efficacy of *mental properties* of events vis-à-vis their physical properties. Thus, the items that need to be identified are properties – that is, we would need to identify mental properties with physical properties. If this could be done, that would be an excellent way of vindicating the causal powers of mentality.

But this is precisely the route that is barred to our nonreductivist friends. The identification of mental properties with physical properties is the heart of reductionist "type physicalism". These property identities would serve as bridge laws par excellence, enabling a derivational reduction of psychology to physical theory. The identities entail psychophysical correlations of biconditional form, stable over possible, or nomologically possible, worlds, and this, we have been told, is excluded by Davidson's mental anomalism and Putnam's multiple realization argument. So the identity solution is out of the question for the nonreductive materialist. Is there any other way to respond to the causal exclusion problem, a way that falls short of identifying mental and physical attributes?

There is one, but it isn't something that would be palatable to the nonreductivist. I believe that the only way other than the identity solution is to give a general account of causal relations involving macro-events as "supervenient causal relations", causal relations that are supervenient on micro-causal processes. You put a kettle of water on the stove and turn on the burner; and soon the water starts to boil. Heating the water caused it to boil. That is a causal relation at the macro-level. It is natural to think of this causal relation as supervenient on certain underlying causal processes at the micro-level. The heating of water supervenes on the increasing kinetic energy of water molecules, and when their mean kinetic energy reaches a certain level, water molecules begin to move in turbulence, some of them being ejected into the air. Boiling is a macro-state that supervenes on just these micro-processes. A sharp pain causes an anxiety attack five seconds later. What's going on? Again, it is tempting, and natural, to think thus: the pain is supervenient on a certain underlying neural activity, and this neural event causes another neural event to occur. The anxiety attack occurs because it is supervenient on this second neural event.

The general model of supervenient causation applied to macro-causal relations is this: macro-event **m** is a cause or effect of event **E** in virtue of the fact that **m** is supervenient on some micro-event, **n**, which is a cause or effect of event **E**.[28] The suggestion then is that we use this model to explain mental causation: a mental event is a cause, or an effect, of another event in virtue of the fact that it is supervenient on some physical event standing in an appropriate causal relation to this event. Thus, mental properties are seen as deriving their causal potential from the physical properties on which they supervene. That is the main idea.

But what sort of supervenience relation is involved in this picture? Global supervenience we considered above obviously will not do; it does not give us a way of speaking of supervenience of specific mental properties on specific physical properties, since it only refers to indiscernibility holding for worlds. Supervenient causation in my sense requires talk of specific mental properties supervening on specific physical base properties, and this is possible only if there are laws correlating psychological with physical properties. This is what I have called elsewhere "strong supervenience", and it can be argued plausibly that supervenience of this strength entails the possibility of reducing the supervenient to the subvenient.[29] I will spare you the details here, but the fact that this form of supervenience directly involves psychophysical laws would be enough to give pause to any would-be nonreductive physicalist. I am not entirely certain that this supervenience solution will suffice; that is, I am not certain that anything short of the identity solution will resolve the exclusion problem. However, I believe that it is the only alternative to explore if, for whatever reason, you are unwilling or unable to go for psychophysical attribute identities. But I doubt that this solution will be found acceptable by the nonreductivist any more than the identity solution.

If nonreductive physicalists accept the causal closure of the physical domain, therefore, they have no visible way of accounting for the possibility of psychophysical causation. This means that they must either give up their antireductionism or else reject the possibility of psychophysical causal relations. The denial of psychophysical causation can come about in two ways: first, you make such a denial because you don't believe there are mental events; or second, you keep faith with mental events even though you acknowledge that they never enter into causal transactions with physical processes, constituting their own autonomous causal world. So either you have espoused eliminativism, or else you are moving further in the direction of dualism, a dualism that posits a realm of the mental in total causal isolation from the physical realm. This doesn't look to me much like materialism.

Is the abandonment of the causal closure of the physical domain an option for the materialist? I think not: to reject the closure principle is to embrace irreducible nonphysical causes of physical phenomena. It would be a retrogression to Cartesian interactionist dualism, something that is definitive of the *denial* of materialism.

Our conclusion, therefore, has to be this: nonreductive materialism is not a stable position. There are pressures of various sorts that push it either in the direction of outright eliminativism or in the direction of an explicit form of dualism.[30]

NOTES

1 Throughout I will be using "physicalism" and "materialism" (and their cognates) interchangeably; similarly, "mental" and "psychological".
2 See Davidson, "Mental events" in *Essays on Actions and Events* (Oxford: Oxford University Press, 1980) [ch. 5, this volume]. This paper was first published in 1970.
3 See Putnam, "The nature of mental states" in *Mind, Language and Reality: Philosophical Papers*, vol. II (Cambridge: Cambridge University Press, 1975). This article was first published in 1967.

4   Jerry Fodor, "Special sciences, or the disunity of science as a working hypothesis", *Synthese* 28 (1974): 97–115 [ch. 2, this volume]. See also Richard Boyd, "Materialism without reductionism: what physicalism does not entail", *Readings in Philosophy of Psychology*, ed. Ned Block (Cambridge: Harvard University Press, 1980).

5   As it is the response of some recent eliminativists; see, e.g., Paul Churchland, "Eliminative materialism and the propositional attitudes", *Journal of Philosophy* 78 (1981): 67–90 [ch. 8, this volume].

6   The classic source on reduction is Ernest Nagel, *The Structure of Science* (New York: Harcourt, Brace & World, 1961), ch. 11.

7   Actually the argument can proceed with a weaker premise to the effect that mental events enter into causal relations, either with physical events or with other mental events.

8   Davidson says in "Mental events" that he believes in the "supervenience" of the mental on the physical, and this does introduce a constraint on the distribution of physical properties when the distribution of mental properties is altered. This, however, does not detract substantively from the point being made here. For one, it remains true, on the notion of supervenience Davidson favors (which corresponds to "weak supervenience"; see his "Reply to essays X–XII" in *Essays on Davidson: Actions and Events*, ed. Bruce Vermazen and Merrill B. Hintikka (Oxford: Oxford University Press, 1985)), that the removal of *all* mental properties from events of this world would have no consequence whatever on how physical properties are distributed over them. For another, the supervenience of the mental is best regarded as an independent thesis, and my present remarks only concern the implications of anomalous monism. I consider the supervenience view below in IV.

9   Davidson's overall views of the mental are richer and more complex than the present discussion might seem to indicate. I believe that they contain some distinctly dualistic elements; for a discussion of this aspect of Davidson, see my "Psychophysical laws" in Ernest LePore and Brian McLaughlin, eds., *Actions and Events: Perspectives on the Philosophy of Donald Davidson* (Oxford: Blackwell, 1984). There have been some interesting recent attempts, which I cannot discuss here, to reconcile anomalous monism and the possibility of mental causation; see, e.g., Ernest LePore and Barry Loewer, "Mind matters", *Journal of Philosophy* 84 (1987): 630–42; Brian McLaughlin, "Type epiphenomenalism, type dualism, and the causal priority of the physical", forthcoming; Terence Horgan, "Mental quasation", forthcoming.

10   Putnam, "The nature of mental states".

11   Putnam himself has abandoned functionalism; see his *Representation and Reality* (Cambridge: MIT Press, 1988), chs 5 and 6.

12   There are some complex logical and ontological details we are leaving out here. See, for details, Robert L. Causey, *Unity of Science* (Dordrecht: Reidel, 1977).

13   "The nature of mental states", p. 437.

14   Note also that derivational reduction does not *require* strong connectibility; any set of bridge laws, of whatever form and strength, will do as long as it enables the required derivation. But this obviously depends on the strength of the two theories involved, and there seems to be little of interest that is sufficiently general to say about this. There are also philosophical considerations for thinking that biconditionals and attribute identities are important in reduction. Cf. Lawrence Sklar, "Types of inter-theoretic reduction", *British Journal for the Philosophy of Science* 18 (1967): 109–24.

15 "The nature of mental states", p. 437.

16 Ned Block says, "Most functionalists are willing to allow ... that for each type of pain-feeling organism, there is (perhaps) a single type of physical state that realizes pain in that type of organism", in his "Introduction: what is functionalism?" in Block, ed., *Readings in Philosophy of Psychology*, vol. 1 (Cambridge: Harvard University Press, 1980), p. 172. Such a law would have exactly the form under discussion.

17 See on this point Berent Enc, "In defense of the identity theory", *Journal of Philosophy* 80 (1983): 279–98.

18 This point, and some related points, are elaborated in my "Disunity of psychology as a working hypothesis?", forthcoming.

19 "Mental events", in Davidson, *Essays on Actions and Events*, p. 214 [ch. 5, this volume].

20 Including Terence Horgan in his "Supervenience and microphysics", *Pacific Philosophical Quarterly* 63 (1982): 29–43; John Haugeland in "Weak supervenience", *American Philosophical Quarterly* 19 (1982): 93–103; John Post in *The Faces of Existence* (Ithaca: Cornell University Press, 1987); and Bradford Petrie, "Global supervenience and reduction", *Philosophy and Phenomenological Research* 48 (1987): 119–30. The model-theoretic notion of determination worked out by Geoffrey Hellman and Frank Thompson, in "Physicalism: ontology, determination, and reduction", *Journal of Philosophy* 72 (1975): 551–64, is closely related to global supervenience.

21 Even with this simplifying assumption certain complications arise; however, we may disregard them for the present purposes. For further details see my "Supervenience for multiple domains", *Philosophical Topics* 16 (1988): 129–50.

22 At least not in a straightforward way. See my "'Strong' and 'global' supervenience revisited", *Philosophy and Phenomenological Research* 48 (1987): 315–26.

23 This particular difficulty can be largely met by formulating global supervenience in terms of *similarity* between worlds rather than indiscernibility. See my "'Strong' and 'global' supervenience revisited".

24 This shows that global supervenience is consistent with the failure of "weak supervenience". See my "'Strong' and 'global' supervenience revisited".

25 See Hellman and Thompson, "Physicalism: ontology, determination, and reduction"; Post, *The Faces of Existence*.

26 For a forceful statement of this point see Fred Dretske, *Explaining Behavior: Reasons in a World of Causes* (Cambridge: MIT Press, 1988).

27 This idea is developed in greater detail in my "Mechanism, purpose, and explanatory exclusion", *Philosophical Perspectives* 3 (1989).

28 For critical discussions of this model, see Brian McLaughlin, "Event supervenience and supervenient causation", *Southern Journal of Philosophy* 22, *The Spindel Conference Supplement on Supervenience* (1984): 71–91; Peter Menzies, "Against causal reductionism", *Mind* 97 (1988): 560–74.

29 I am putting the point somewhat tentatively here because it involves several currently contentious issues. For a general argument for this point, see my "Concepts of supervenience", *Philosophy and Phenomenological Research* 45 (1984): 153–76; especially, section III; and "Supervenience as a philosophical concept", forthcoming in *Metaphilosophy*. However, this argument makes use of infinite disjunctions and conjunctions (actually, infinite disjunctions are all one needs; see "Supervenience as a philosophical concept"). If the argument is found objectionable because of this feature, it could be supplemented with an argument modeled on my argument in section III above against the Putnam–Fodor antireductionist thesis. This means that the supervenience relation

needed for the model of supervenient causation sketched here must require that each supervenient property have a *nomologically coextensive base property relative to the given physical structure*. There are, I believe, plausible considerations in favor of this stronger supervenience relation as a basis for the concept of supervenient causation (or the reduction of causal relations); however, I cannot go into the details here.

30   My thanks to Richard Brandt, Sydney Shoemaker, and Ernest Sosa for helpful comments on earlier versions, and to David Benfield, Barry Loewer, and Brian McLaughlin for discussing with me some of the topics of this paper.

8   Eliminative Materialism and the Propositional Attitudes

Paul M. Churchland

Eliminative materialism is the thesis that our common-sense conception of psychological phenomena constitutes a radically false theory, a theory so fundamentally defective that both the principles and the ontology of that theory will eventually be displaced, rather than smoothly reduced, by completed neuroscience. Our mutual understanding and even our introspection may then be reconstituted within the conceptual framework of completed neuroscience, a theory we may expect to be more powerful by far than the common-sense psychology it displaces, and more substantially integrated within physical science generally. My purpose in this paper is to explore these projections, especially as they bear on (1) the principal elements of common-sense psychology: the propositional attitudes (beliefs, desires, etc.), and (2) the conception of rationality in which these elements figure.

This focus represents a change in the fortunes of materialism. Twenty years ago, emotions, qualia, and "raw feels" were held to be the principal stumbling blocks for the materialist program. With these barriers dissolving,[1] the locus of opposition has shifted. Now it is the realm of the intentional, the realm of the propositional attitude, that is most commonly held up as being both irreducible to the ineliminable in favor of anything from within a materialist framework. Whether and why this is so, we must examine.

Such an examination will make little sense, however, unless it is first appreciated that the relevant network of common-sense concepts does indeed constitute an empirical theory, with all the functions, virtues, *and perils* entailed by that status. I shall therefore begin with a brief sketch of this view and a summary rehearsal of its rationale. The resistance it encounters still surprises me. After all, common sense has yielded up many theories. Recall the view that space has a preferred direction in which all things fall; that weight in an intrinsic feature of a body; that a force-free moving object will promptly return to rest; that the sphere of the heavens turns daily; and so on. These examples are clear, perhaps, but people seem willing to concede a theoretical component within common sense only if (1) the theory and the common sense involved are safely located in antiquity, and (2) the relevant theory is now so clearly false that its speculative nature is inescapable. Theories are indeed easier to discern under these circumstances. But the vision of hindsight is always 20/20. Let us aspire to some foresight for a change.

1 WHY FOLK PSYCHOLOGY IS A THEORY

Seeing our common-sense conceptual framework for mental phenomena as a theory brings a simple and unifying organization to most of the major topics in the philosophy of mind, including the explanation and prediction of behavior, the semantics of mental predicates, action theory, the other-minds problem, the intentionality of mental states, the nature of introspection, and the mind–body problem. Any view that can pull this lot together deserves careful consideration.

Let us begin with the explanation of human (and animal) behavior. The fact is that the average person is able to explain, and even predict, the behavior of other persons with a facility and success that is remarkable. Such explanations and predictions standardly make reference to the desires, beliefs, fears, intentions, perceptions, and so forth, to which the agents are presumed subject. But explanations presuppose laws – rough and ready ones, at least – that connect the explanatory conditions with the behavior explained. The same is true for the making of predictions, and for the justification of subjunctive and counterfactual conditional concerning behavior. Reassuringly, a rich network of common-sense laws can indeed be reconstructed from this quotidean commerce of explanation and anticipation; its principles are familiar homilies; and their sundry functions are transparent. Each of us understands others, as well as we do, because we share a tacit command of an integrated body of lore concerning the lawlike relations holding among external circumstances, internal states, and overt behavior. Given its nature and functions, this body of lore may quite aptly be called "folk psychology."[2]

This approach entails that the semantics of the terms in our familiar mentalistic vocabulary is to be understood in the same manner as the semantics of theoretical terms generally: the meaning of any theoretical term is fixed or constituted by the network of laws in which it figures. (This position is quite distinct from logical behaviorism. We deny that the relevant laws are analytic, and it is the lawlike connections generally that carry the semantic weight, not just the connections with overt behavior. But this view does account for what little plausibility logical behaviorism did enjoy.)

More importantly, the recognition that folk psychology is a theory provides a simple and decisive solution to an old skeptical problem, the problem of other minds. The problematic conviction that another individual is the subject of certain mental states is not inferred deductively from his behavior, nor is it inferred by inductive analogy from the perilously isolated instance of one's own case. Rather, that conviction is a singular *explanatory hypothesis* of a perfectly straightforward kind. Its function, in conjunction with the background laws of folk psychology, is to provide explanations/predictions/understanding of the individual's continuing behavior, and it is credible to the degree that it is successful in this regard over competing hypotheses. In the main, such hypotheses are successful, and so the belief that others enjoy the internal states comprehended by folk psychology is a reasonable belief.

Knowledge of other minds thus has no essential dependence on knowledge of one's own mind. Applying the principles of our folk psychology to our behavior, a Martian could justly ascribe to us the familiar run of mental states, even though his own psychology were very different from ours. He would not, therefore, be "generalizing from his own case."

As well, introspective judgments about one's own case turn out not to have any special status or integrity anyway. On the present view, an introspective judgment is just an instance of an acquired habit of conceptual response to one's internal states, and the integrity of any particular response is always contingent on the integrity of the acquired conceptual framework (theory) in which the response is framed. Accordingly, one's *introspective* certainty that one's mind is the seat of beliefs and desires may be as badly misplaced as was the classical man's *visual* certainty that the star-flecked sphere of the heavens turns daily.

Another conundrum is the intentionality of mental states. The "propositional attitudes," as Russell called them, form the systematic core of folk psychology; and their uniqueness and anomalous logical properties have inspired some to see here a fundamental contrast with anything that mere physical phenomena might conceivably display. The key to this matter lies again in the theoretical nature of folk psychology. The intentionality of mental states here emerges not as a mystery of nature, but as a structural feature of the concepts of folk psychology. Ironically, those same structural features reveal the very close affinity that folk psychology bears to theories in the physical sciences. Let me try to explain.

Consider the large variety of what might be called "numerical attitudes" appearing in the conceptual framework of physical science: "... has a $mass_{kg}$ of n", "... has a velocity of n", "... has a $temperature_K$ of n", and so forth. These expressions are predicate-forming expressions: when one substitutes a singular term of a number into the place held by "n", a determinate predicate results. More interestingly, the relations between the various "numerical attitudes" that result are precisely the relations between the numbers "contained" in those attitudes. More interesting still, the argument place that takes the singular terms for numbers is open to quantification. All this permits the expression of generalizations concerning the lawlike relations that hold between the various numerical attitudes in nature. Such laws involve quantification over numbers, and they exploit the mathematical relations holding in that domain. Thus, for example,

(1) (x) (f) (m) [$((x$ has a mass of $m)$ & $(x$ suffers a net force of $f))$
$\supset (x$ accelerates at $f/m)]$

Consider now the large variety of propositional attitudes: "... believes that p", "... desires that p", "... fears that p", "... is happy that p", etc. These expressions are predicate-forming expressions also. When one substitutes a singular term for a proposition into the place held by "p", a determinate predicate results, e.g., "... believes that Tom is tall." (Sentences do not generally function as singular terms, but it is difficult to escape the idea that when a sentence occurs in the place held by "p", it is there functioning as or like a singular term. On this, more below.) More interestingly, the relations between the resulting propositional attitudes are characteristically the relations that hold between the propositions "contained" in them, relations such as entailment, equivalence, and mutual inconsistency. More interesting still, the argument place that takes the singular terms for propositions is open to quantification. All this permits the expression of generalizations concerning the lawlike relations that hold among propositional attitudes. Such laws involve quantification over propositions, and they exploit various relations holding in that domain. Thus, for example,

(2) (x) (p) [$(x$ fears that $p)$ ⊃ $(x$ desires that ~ $p)$]

(3) (x) (p) [$(x$ hopes that $p)$ & $(x$ discovers that $p)$)
$$⊃ (x \text{ is pleased that } p)]$$

(4) (x) (p) (q) [$(x$ believes that $p)$ & $(x$ believes that (if p then q)))
$$⊃ (\text{barring confusion, distraction, etc., } x \text{ believes that } q)]$$

(5) (x) (p) (q) [$(x$ desires that $p)$ & $(x$ believes that (if q then p))
& $(x$ is able to bring it about that q))
$$⊃ (\text{barring conflicting desires or preferred strategies,} \\ x \text{ brings it about that } q)]^3$$

Not only is folk psychology a theory, it is so *obviously* a theory that it must be held a major mystery why it has taken until the last half of the twentieth century for philosophers to realize it. The structural features of folk psychology parallel perfectly those of mathematical physics; the only difference lies in the respective domain of abstract entities they exploit – numbers in the case of physics, and propositions in the case of psychology.

Finally, the realization that folk psychology is a theory puts a new light on the mind–body problem. The issue becomes a matter of how the ontology of one theory (folk psychology) is, or is not, going to be related to the ontology of another theory (completed neuroscience); and the major philosophical positions on the mind–body problem emerge as so many different anticipations of what future research will reveal about the intertheoretic status and integrity of folk psychology.

The identity theorist optimistically expects that folk psychology will be smoothly *reduced* by completed neuroscience, and its ontology preserved by dint of transtheoretic identities. The dualist expects that it will prove *ir*reducible to completed neuroscience, by dint of being a nonredundant description of an autonomous, nonphysical domain of natural phenomena. The functionalist also expects that it will prove irreducible, but on the quite different grounds that the internal economy characterized by folk psychology is not, in the last analysis, a law-governed economy of natural states, but an abstract organization of functional states, an organization instantiable in a variety of quite different material substrates. It is therefore irreducible to the principles peculiar to any of them.

Finally, the eliminative materialist is also pessimistic about the prospects for reduction, but his reason is that folk psychology is a radically inadequate account of our internal activities, too confused and too defective to win survival through intertheoretic reduction. On his view it will simply be displaced by a better theory of those activities.

Which of these fates is the real destiny of folk psychology, we shall attempt to divine presently. For now, the point to keep in mind is that we shall be exploring the fate of a theory, a systematic, corrigible, speculative *theory*.

2 WHY FOLK PSYCHOLOGY MIGHT (REALLY) BE FALSE

Given that folk psychology is an empirical theory, it is at least an abstract possibility that its principles are radically false and that its ontology is an illusion. With the exception of eliminative materialism, however, none of the major positions takes this possibility seriously. None of them doubts the basic integrity or truth of folk psychology (hereafter, "FP"), and all of them anticipate a future in which its laws and categories are conserved. This conservatism is not without some foundation. After all, FP does enjoy a substantial amount of explanatory and predictive success. And what better grounds than this for confidence in the integrity of its categories?

What better grounds indeed? Even so, the presumption in FP's favor is spurious, born of innocence and tunnel vision. A more searching examination reveals a different picture. First, we must reckon not only with FP's successes, but with its explanatory failures, and with their extent and seriousness. Second, we must consider the long-term history of FP, its growth, fertility, and current promise of future development. And third, we must consider what sorts of theories are *likely* to be true of the etiology of our behavior, given what else we have learned about ourselves in recent history. That is, we must evaluate FP with regard to its coherence and continuity with fertile and well-established theories in adjacent and overlapping domains – with evolutionary theory, biology, and neuroscience, for example – because active coherence with the rest of what we presume to know is perhaps the final measure of any hypothesis.

A serious inventory of this sort reveals a very troubled situation, one which would evoke open skepticism in the case of any theory less familiar and dear to us. Let me sketch some relevant detail. When one centers one's attention not on what FP can explain, but on what it cannot explain or fails even to address, one discovers that there is a very great deal. As examples of central and important mental phenomena that remain largely or wholly mysterious within the framework of FP, consider the nature and dynamics of mental illness, the faculty of creative imagination, or the ground of intelligence differences between individuals. Consider our utter ignorance of the nature and psychological functions of sleep, that curious state in which a third of one's life is spent. Reflect on the common ability to catch an outfield fly ball on the run, or hit a moving car with a snowball. Consider the internal construction of a 3-D visual image from subtle differences in the 2-D array of stimulations in our respective retinas. Consider the rich variety of perceptual illusions, visual and otherwise. Or consider the miracle of memory, with its lightning capacity for relevant retrieval. On these and many other mental phenomena, FP sheds negligible light.

One particularly outstanding mystery is the nature of the learning process itself, especially where it involves large-scale conceptual change, and especially as it appears in its pre-linguistic or entirely nonlinguistic form (as in infants and animals), which is by far the most common form in nature. FP is faced with special difficulties here, since its conception of learning as the manipulation and storage of propositional attitudes founders on the fact that how to formulate, manipulate, and store a rich fabric of propositional attitudes is itself something that is learned, and is only one among many acquired cognitive skills. FP would thus appear constitutionally incapable of even addressing this most basic of mysteries.[4]

Failures on such a large scale do not (yet) show that FP is a false theory, but they do move that prospect well into the range of real possibility, and they do show decisively that FP is *at best* a highly superficial theory, a partial and unpenetrating gloss on a deeper and more complex reality. Having reached this opinion, we may be forgiven for exploring the possibility that FP provides a positively misleading sketch of our internal kinematics and dynamics, one whose success is owed more to selective application and forced interpretation on our part than to genuine theoretical insight on FP's part.

A look at the history of FP does little to allay such fears, once raised. The story is one of retreat, infertility, and decadence. The presumed domain of FP used to be much larger than it is now. In primitive cultures, the behavior of most of the elements of nature were understood in intentional terms. The wind could know anger, the moon jealousy, the river generosity, the sea fury, and so forth. These were not metaphors. Sacrifices were made and auguries undertaken to placate or divine the changing passions of the gods. Despite its sterility, this animistic approach to nature has dominated our history, and it is only in the last two or three thousand years that we have restricted FP's literal application to the domain of the higher animals.

Even in this preferred domain, however, both the content and the success of FP have not advanced sensibly in two or three thousand years. The FP of the Greeks is essentially the FP we use today, and we are negligibly better at explaining human behavior in its terms than was Sophocles. This is a very long period of stagnation and infertility for any theory to display, especially when faced with such an enormous backlog of anomalies and mysteries in its own explanatory domain. Perfect theories, perhaps, have no need to evolve. But FP is profoundly imperfect. Its failure to develop its resources and extend its range of success is therefore darkly curious, and one must query the integrity of its basic categories. To use Imre Lakatos' terms, FP is a stagnant or degenerating research program, and has been for millennia.

Explanatory success to date is of course not the only dimension in which a theory can display virtue or promise. A troubled or stagnant theory may merit patience and solicitude on other grounds; for example, on grounds that it is the only theory or theoretical approach that fits well with other theories about adjacent subject matters, or the only one that promises to reduce to or be explained by some established background theory whose domain encompasses the domain of the theory at issue. In sum, it may rate credence because it holds promise of theoretical integration. How does FP rate in this dimension?

It is just here, perhaps, that FP fares poorest of all. If we approach *homo sapiens* from the perspective of natural history and the physical sciences, we can tell a coherent story of his constitution, development, and behavioral capacities which encompasses particle physics, atomic and molecular theory, organic chemistry, evolutionary theory, biology, physiology, and materialistic neuroscience. That story, though still radically incomplete, is already extremely powerful, outperforming FP at many points even in its own domain. And it is deliberately and self-consciously coherent with the rest of our developing world picture. In short, the greatest theoretical synthesis in the history of the human race is currently in our hands, and parts of it already provide searching descriptions and explanations of human sensory input, neural activity, and motor control.

But FP is no part of this growing synthesis. Its intentional categories stand magnificently alone, without visible prospect of reduction to that larger corpus. A successful reduction cannot be ruled out, in my view, but FP's explanatory impotence and long stagnation inspire little faith that its categories will find themselves neatly reflected in the framework of neuroscience. On the contrary, one is reminded of how alchemy must have looked as elemental chemistry was taking form, how Aristotelean cosmology must have looked as classical mechanics was being articulated, or how the vitalist conception of life must have looked as organic chemistry marched forward.

In sketching a fair summary of this situation, we must make a special effort to abstract from the fact that FP is a central part of our current *lebenswelt*, and serves as the principal vehicle of our interpersonal commerce. For these facts provide FP with a conceptual inertia that goes far beyond its purely theoretical virtues. Restricting ourselves to this latter dimension, what we must say is that FP suffers explanatory failures on an epic scale, that it has been stagnant for at least twenty-five centuries, and that its categories appear (so far) to be incommensurable with or orthogonal to the categories of the background physical science whose long-term claim to explain human behavior seems undeniable. Any theory that meets this description must be allowed a serious candidate for outright elimination.

We can of course insist on no stronger conclusion at this stage. Nor is it my concern to do so. We are here exploring a possibility, and the facts demand no more, and no less, than it be taken seriously. The distinguishing feature of the eliminative materialist is that he takes it very seriously indeed.

3 ARGUMENTS AGAINST ELIMINATION

Thus the basic rationale of eliminative materialism: FP is a theory, and quite probably a false one; let us attempt, therefore, to transcend it.

The rationale is clear and simple, but many find it uncompelling. It will be objected that FP is not, strictly speaking, an *empirical* theory; that it is not false, or at least not refutable by empirical considerations; and that it ought not or cannot be transcended in the fashion of a defunct empirical theory. In what follows we shall examine these objections as they flow from the most popular and best-founded of the competing positions in the philosophy of mind: functionalism.

An antipathy toward eliminative materialism arises from two distinct threads running through contemporary functionalism. The first thread concerns the *normative* character of FP, or at least of that central core of FP which treats of the propositional attitudes. FP, some will say, is a characterization of an ideal, or at least praiseworthy mode of internal activity. It outlines not only what it is to have and process beliefs and desires, but also (and inevitably) what it is to be rational in their administration. The ideal laid down by FP may be imperfectly achieved by empirical humans, but this does not impugn FP as a normative characterization. Nor need such failures seriously impugn FP even as a descriptive characterization, for it remains true that our activities can be both usefully and accurately understood as rational *except for* the occasional lapse due to noise, interference, or other breakdown, which defects empirical research may eventually unravel. Accordingly, though neuroscience may usefully augment it, FP has no pressing need to be displaced, even as a descriptive theory; nor could it be replaced, qua normative characterization, by any descriptive theory of neural mechanisms, since rationality is defined over propositional attitudes like beliefs and desires. FP, therefore, is here to stay.

Daniel Dennett has defended a view along these lines.[5] And the view just outlined gives voice to a theme of the property dualists as well. Karl Popper and Joseph Margolis both cite the normative nature of mental and linguistic activity as a bar to their penetration or elimination by any descriptive/materialist theory.[6] I hope to deflate the appeal of such moves below.

The second thread concerns the *abstract* nature of FP. The central claim of functionalism is that the principles of FP characterize our internal states in a fashion that makes no reference to their intrinsic nature or physical constitution. Rather, they are characterized in terms of the network of causal relations they bear to one another, and to sensory circumstances and overt behavior. Given its abstract specification, that internal economy may therefore be realized in a nomically heterogeneous variety of physical systems. All of them may differ, even radically, in their physical constitution, and yet at another level, they will all share the same nature. This view, says Fodor, "is compatible with very strong claims about the ineliminability of mental language from behavioral theories."[7] Given the real possibility of multiple instantiations in heterogeneous physical substrates, we cannot eliminate the functional characterization in favor of any theory peculiar to one such substrate. That would preclude our being able to describe the (abstract) organization that any one instantiation shares with all the others. A functional characterization of our internal states is therefore here to stay.

This second theme, like the first, assigns a faintly stipulative character to FP, as if the onus were on the empirical systems to instantiate faithfully the organization that FP specifies, instead of the onus being on FP to describe faithfully the internal activities of a naturally distinct class of empirical systems. This impression is enhanced by the standard examples used to illustrate the claims of functionalism – mousetraps, valve-lifters, arithmetical calculators, computers, robots, and the like. These are artifacts, constructed to fill a preconceived bill. In such cases, a failure of fit between the physical system and the relevant functional characterization impugns only the former, not the latter. The functional characterization is thus removed from empirical criticism in a way that is most unlike the case of an empirical theory. One prominent functionalist – Hilary Putnam – has argued outright that FP is not a corrigible theory at all.[8] Plainly, if FP is construed on these models, as regularly it is, the question of its empirical integrity is unlikely ever to pose itself, let alone receive a critical answer.

Although fair to some functionalists, the preceding is not entirely fair to Fodor. On his view the aim of psychology is to find the *best* functional characterization of ourselves, and what that is remains an empirical question. As well, his argument for the ineliminability of mental vocabulary from psychology does not pick out current FP in particular as ineliminable. It need claim only that *some* abstract functional characterization must be retained, some articulation or refinement of FP perhaps.

His estimate of eliminative materialism remains low, however. First, it is plain that Fodor thinks there is nothing fundamentally or interestingly wrong with FP. On the contrary, FP's central conception of cognitive activity – as consisting in the manipulation of propositional attitudes – turns up as the central element in Fodor's own theory on the nature of thought (*The Language of Thought, op. cit.*). And second, there remains the point that, whatever tidying up FP may or may not require, it cannot be displaced by any naturalistic theory of our physical substrate, since it is the abstract functional features of his internal states that make a person, not the chemistry of his substrate.

All of this is appealing. But almost none of it, I think, is right. Functionalism has too long enjoyed its reputation as a daring and *avant garde* position. It needs to be revealed for the short-sighted and reactionary position it is.

4 THE CONSERVATIVE NATURE OF FUNCTIONALISM

A valuable perspective on functionalism can be gained from the following story. To begin with, recall the alchemists' theory of inanimate matter. We have here a long and variegated tradition, of course, not a single theory, but our purposes will be served by a gloss.

The alchemists conceived the "inanimate" as entirely continuous with animated matter, in that the sensible and behavioral properties of the various substances are owed to the ensoulment of baser matter by various spirits or essences. These nonmaterial aspects were held to undergo development, just as we find growth and development in the various souls of plants, animals, and humans. The alchemist's peculiar skill lay in knowing how to seed, nourish, and bring to maturity the desired spirits enmattered in the appropriate combinations.

On one orthodoxy, the four fundamental spirits (for "inanimate" matter) were named "mercury," "sulphur," "yellow arsenic," and "sal ammoniac." Each of these spirits was held responsible for a rough but characteristic syndrome of sensible, combinatorial, and causal properties. The spirit mercury, for example, was held responsible for certain features typical of metallic substances – their shininess, liquefiability, and so forth. Sulphur was held responsible for certain residual features typical of metals, and for those displayed by the ores from which running metal could be distilled. Any given metallic substance was a critical orchestration principally of these two spirits. A similar story held for the other two spirits, and among the four of them a certain domain of physical features and transformations was rendered intelligible and controllable.

The degree of control was always limited, of course. Or better, such prediction and control as the alchemists possessed was owed more to the manipulative lore acquired as an apprentice to a master, than to any genuine insight supplied by the theory. The theory followed, more than it dictated, practice. But the theory did supply some rhyme to the practice, and in the absence of a developed alternative it was sufficiently compelling to sustain a long and stubborn tradition.

The tradition had become faded and fragmented by the time the elemental chemistry of Lavoisier and Dalton arose to replace it for good. But let us suppose that it had hung on a little longer – perhaps because the four-spirit orthodoxy had become a thumb-worn part of everyman's common sense – and let us examine the nature of the conflict between the two theories and some possible avenues of resolution.

No doubt the simplest line of resolution, and the one which historically took place, is outright displacement. The dualistic interpretation of the four essences – as immaterial spirits – will appear both feckless and unnecessary given the power of the corpuscularian taxonomy of atomic chemistry. And a reduction of the old taxonomy to the new will appear impossible, given the extent to which the comparatively toothless old theory cross-classifies things relative to the new. Elimination would thus appear the only alternative – *unless* some cunning and determined defender of the alchemical vision has the wit to suggest the following defense.

Being "ensouled by mercury," or "sulphur," or either of the other two so-called spirits, is actually a *functional* state. The first, for example, is defined by the disposition to reflect light, to liquefy under heat, to unite with other matter in the same state, and so forth. And each of these four states is related to the others, in that the syndrome for each varies as a function of which of the other three states is also instantiated in the same substrate. Thus the level of description comprehended by the alchemical vocabulary is abstract: various material substances, suitably "ensouled," can display the features of a metal, for example, or even of gold specifically. For it is the total syndrome of occurrent and causal properties which matters, not the corpuscularian details of the substrate. Alchemy, it is concluded, comprehends a level of organization in reality distinct from and irreducible to the organization found at the level of corpuscularian chemistry.

This view might have had considerable appeal. After all, it spares alchemists the burden of defending immaterial souls that come and go; it frees them from having to meet the very strong demands of a naturalistic reduction; and it spares them the shock and confusion of outright elimination. Alchemical theory emerges as basically all right! Nor need they appear too obviously stubborn or dogmatic in this. Alchemy as it stands, they concede, may need substantial tidying up, and experience must be our guide. But we need not fear its naturalistic displacement, they remind us, since it is the particular orchestration of the syndromes of occurrent and causal properties which makes a piece of matter gold, not the idiosyncratic details of its corpuscularian substrate. A further circumstance would have made this claim even more plausible. For the fact is, the alchemists *did* know how to make gold, in this relevantly weakened sense of "gold," and they could do so in a variety of ways. Their "gold" was never as perfect, alas, as the "gold" nurtured in nature's womb, but what mortal can expect to match the skills of nature herself?

What this story shows is that it is at least possible for the constellation of moves, claims, and defenses characteristic of functionalism to constitute an outrage against reason and truth, and to do so with a plausibility that is frightening. Alchemy is a terrible theory, well-deserving of its complete elimination, and the defense of it just explored is reactionary, obfuscatory, retrograde, and wrong. But in historical context, that defense might have seemed wholly sensible, even to reasonable people.

The alchemical example is a deliberately transparent case of what might well be called "the functionalist strategem," and other cases are easy to imagine. A cracking good defense of the phlogiston theory of combustion can also be constructed along these lines. Construe being highly phlogisticated and being dephlogisticated as functional states defined by certain syndromes of causal dispositions; point to the great variety of natural substrates capable of combustion and calxification; claim an irreducible functional integrity for what has proved to lack any natural integrity; and bury the remaining defects under a pledge to contrive improvements. A similar recipe will provide new life for the four humors of medieval medicine, for the vital essence or archeus of pre-modern biology, and so forth.

If its application in these other cases is any guide, the functionalist strategem is a smokescreen for the preservation of error and confusion. Whence derives our assurance that in contemporary journals the same charade is not being played out on behalf of FP? The parallel with the case of alchemy is in all other respects distressingly complete, right down to the parallel between the search for artificial gold and the search for artificial intelligence!

Let me not be misunderstood on this last point. Both aims are worthy aims: thanks to nuclear physics, artificial (but real) gold is finally within our means, if only in submicroscopic quantities; and artificial (but real) intelligence eventually will be. But just as the careful orchestration of superficial syndromes was the wrong way to produce genuine gold, so may the careful orchestration of superficial syndromes be the wrong way to produce genuine intelligence. Just as with gold, what may be required is that our science penetrate to the underlying *natural* kind that gives rise to the total syndrome directly.

In summary, when confronted with the explanatory impotence, stagnant history, and systematic isolation of the intentional idioms of FP, it is not an adequate or responsive defense to insist that those idioms are abstract, functional, and irreducible in character. For one thing, this same defense could have been mounted with comparable plausibility no matter *what* haywire network of internal states our folklore had ascribed to us. And for another, the defense assumes essentially what is at issue: it assumes that it is the intentional idioms of FP, plus or minus a bit, that express the *important* features shared by all cognitive systems. But they may not. Certainly it is wrong to assume that they do, and then argue against the possibility of a materialistic displacement on grounds that it must describe matters at a level that is different from the important level. This just begs the question in favor of the older framework.

Finally, it is very important to point out that eliminative materialism is strictly *consistent* with the claim that the essence of a cognitive system resides in the abstract functional organization of its internal states. The eliminative materialist is not committed to the idea that the correct account of cognition *must* be a naturalistic account, though he may be forgiven for exploring the possibility. What he does hold is that the correct account of cognition, whether functionalistic or naturalistic, will bear about as much resemblance to FP as modern chemistry bears to four-spirit alchemy.

Let us now try to deal with the argument, against eliminative materialism, from the normative dimension of FP. This can be dealt with rather swiftly, I believe.

First, the fact that the regularities ascribed by the intentional core of FP are predicated on certain logical relations among propositions is not by itself grounds for claiming anything essentially normative about FP. To draw a relevant parallel, the fact that the regularities ascribed by the classical gas law are predicated on arithmetical relations between numbers does not imply anything essentially normative about the classical gas law. And logical relations between propositions are as much an objective matter of abstract fact as are arithmetical relations between numbers. In this respect, the law

(4) (x) (p) (q) [$((x$ believes that $p)$ *&* $(x$ believes that (if p then $q)))$
$\supset$ (barring confusion, distraction, etc., x believes that $q)$]

is entirely on a par with the classical gas law

(6) (x) (P) (V) (μ) [$((x$ has a pressure $P)$ *&* $(x$ has a volume $V)$
& $(x$ has a quantity $\mu))$ $\supset$ (barring very high pressure or density,
x has a temperature of $PV/\mu R)$]

A normative dimension enters only because we happen to *value* most of the patterns ascribed by FP. But we do not value all of them. Consider

(7) (x) (p) [$((x$ desires with all his heart that $p)$ *&* $(x$ learns that $\sim p))$
$\supset$ (barring unusual strength of character,
x is shattered that $\sim p)$]

Moreover, and as with normative convictions generally, fresh insight may motivate major changes in what we value.

Second, the laws of FP ascribe to us only a very minimal and truncated rationality, not an ideal rationality as some have suggested. The rationality characterized by the set of all FP laws falls well short of an ideal rationality. This is not surprising. We have no clear or finished conception of ideal rationality anyway; certainly the ordinary man does not. Accordingly, it is just not plausible to suppose that the explanatory failures from which FP suffers are owed primarily to human failure to live up to the ideal standard it provides. Quite to the contrary, the conception of rationality it provides appears limping and superficial, especially when compared with the dialectical complexity of our scientific history, or with the ratiocinative virtuosity displayed by any child.

Third, even if our current conception of rationality – and more generally, of cognitive virtue – is largely constituted within the sentential/propositional framework of FP, there is no guarantee that this framework is adequate to the deeper and more accurate account of cognitive virtue which is clearly needed. Even if we concede the categorial integrity of FP, at least as applied to language-using humans, it remains far from clear that the basic parameters of intellectual virtue are to be found at the categorial level comprehended by the propositional attitudes. After all, language use is something that is learned, by a brain already capable of vigorous cognitive activity; language use is acquired as only one among a great variety of learned manipulative skills; and it is mastered by a brain that evolution has shaped for a great many functions, language use being only the very latest and perhaps the least of them. Against the background of these facts, language use appears as an extremely peripheral activity, as a biologically idiosyncratic mode of social interaction which is mastered thanks to the versatility and power of a more basic mode of activity. Why accept then, a theory of cognitive activity that models its elements on the elements of human language? And why assume that the fundamental parameters of intellectual virtue are or can be defined over the elements at this superficial level?

A serious advance in our appreciation of cognitive virtue would thus seem to *require* that we go beyond FP, that we transcend the poverty of FP's conception of rationality by transcending its propositional kinematics entirely, by developing a deeper and more general kinematics of cognitive activity, and by distinguishing within this new framework which of the kinematically possible modes of activity are to be valued and encouraged (as more efficient, reliable, productive, or whatever). Eliminative materialism thus does not imply the end of our normative concerns. It implies only that they will have to be reconstituted at a more revealing level of understanding, the level that a matured neuroscience will provide.

What a theoretically informed future might hold in store for us, we shall now turn to explore. Not because we can foresee matters with any special clarity, but because it is important to try to break the grip on our imagination held by the propositional kinematics of FP. As far as the present section is concerned, we may summarize our conclusions as follows. FP is nothing more and nothing less than a culturally entrenched theory of how we and the higher animals work. It has no special features that make it empirically invulnerable, no unique functions that make it irreplaceable, no special status of any kind whatsoever. We shall turn a skeptical ear then, to any special pleading on its behalf.

5 BEYOND FOLK PSYCHOLOGY

What might the elimination of FP actually involve – not just the comparatively straightforward idioms for sensation, but the entire apparatus of propositional attitudes? That depends heavily on what neuroscience might discover, and on our determination to capitalize on it. Here follow three scenarios in which the operative conception of cognitive activity is progressively divorced from the forms and categories that characterize natural language. If the reader will indulge the lack of actual substance, I shall try to sketch some plausible form.

First suppose that research into the structure and activity of the brain, both fine-grained and global, finally does yield a new kinematics and correlative dynamics for what is now thought of as cognitive activity. The theory is uniform for all terrestrial brains, not just human brains, and it makes suitable conceptual contact with both evolutionary biology and non-equilibrium thermodynamics. It ascribes to us, at any given time, a set or configuration of complex states, which are specified within the theory as figurative "solids" within a four- or five-dimensional phase space. The laws of the theory govern the interaction, motion, and transformation of these "solid" states within that space, and also their relations to whatever sensory and motor transducers the system possesses. As with celestial mechanics, the exact specification of the "solids" involved and the exhaustive accounting of all dynamically relevant adjacent "solids" is not practically possible, for many reasons, but here also it turns out that the obvious approximations we fall back on yield excellent explanations/predictions of internal change and external behavior, at least in the short term. Regarding long-term activity, the theory provides powerful and unified accounts of the learning process, the nature of mental illness, and variations in character and intelligence across the animal kingdom as well as across individual humans.

Moreover, it provides a straightforward account of "knowledge," as traditionally conceived. According to the new theory, any declarative sentence to which a speaker would give confident assent is merely a one-dimensional *projection* – through the compound lens of Wernicke's and Broca's areas onto the idiosyncratic surface of the speaker's language – a one-dimensional projection of a four- or five-dimensional "solid" that is an element in his true kinematical state. (Recall the shadows on the wall of Plato's cave.) Being projections of that inner reality, such sentences do carry significant information regarding it and are thus fit to function as elements in a communication system. On the other hand, being *sub*dimensional projections, they reflect but a narrow part of the reality projected. They are therefore *un*fit to represent the deeper reality in all its kinematically, dynamically, and even normatively relevant respects. That is to say, a system of propositional attitudes, such as FP, must inevitably fail to capture what is going on here, though it may reflect just enough superficial structure to sustain an alchemylike tradition among folk who lack any better theory. From the perspective of the newer theory, however, it is plain that there simply are no law-governed states of the kind FP postulates. The real laws governing our internal activities are defined over different and much more complex kinematical states and configurations, as are the normative criteria for developmental integrity and intellectual virtue.

A theoretical outcome of the kind just described may fairly be counted as a case of elimination of one theoretical ontology in favor of another, but the success here imagined for systematic neuroscience need not have any sensible effect on common practice. Old ways die hard, and in the absence of some practical necessity, they may not die at all. Even so, it is not inconceivable that some segment of the population, or all of it, should become intimately familiar with the vocabulary required to characterize our kinematical states, learn the laws governing their interactions and behavioral projections, acquire a facility in their first-person ascription, and displace the use of FP altogether, even in the marketplace. The demise of FP's ontology would then be complete.

We may now explore a second and rather more radical possibility. Everyone is familiar with Chomsky's thesis that the human mind or brain contains innately and uniquely the abstract structures for learning and using specifically human natural languages. A competing hypothesis is that our brain does indeed contain innate structures, but that those structures have as their original and still primary function the organization of perceptual experience, the administration of linguistic categories being an acquired and additional function for which evolution has only incidentally suited them.[9] This hypothesis has the advantage of not requiring the evolutionary saltation that Chomsky's view would seem to require, and there are other advantages as well. But these matters need not concern us here. Suppose, for our purposes, that this competing view is true, and consider the following story.

Research into the neural structures that fund the organization and processing of perceptual information reveals that they are capable of administering a great variety of complex tasks, some of them showing a complexity far in excess of that shown by natural language. Natural languages, it turns out, exploit only a very elementary portion of the available machinery, the bulk of which serves far more complex activities beyond the ken of the propositional conceptions of FP. The detailed unraveling of what that machinery is and of the capacities it has makes it plain that a form of language far more sophisticated than "natural" language, though decidedly "alien" in its syntactic and semantic structures, could also be learned and used by our innate systems. Such a novel system of communication, it is quickly realized, could raise the efficiency of information exchange between brains by an order of magnitude, and would enhance epistemic evaluation by a comparable amount, since it would reflect the underlying structure of our cognitive activities in greater detail than does natural language.

Guided by our new understanding of those internal structures, we manage to construct a new system of verbal communication entirely distinct from natural language, with a new and more powerful combinatorial grammar over novel elements forming novel combinations with exotic properties. The compounded strings of this alternative system – call them "übersätze" – are not evaluated as true or false, nor are the relations between them remotely analogous to the relations of entailment, etc., that hold between sentences. They display a different organization and manifest different virtues.

Once constructed, this "language" proves to be learnable; it has the power projected; and in two generations it has swept the planet. Everyone uses the new system. The syntactic forms and semantic categories of so-called "natural" language disappear entirely. And with them disappear the propositional attitudes of FP, displaced by a more revealing scheme in which (of course) übersätzenal attitudes" play the leading role. FP again suffers elimination.

This second story, note, illustrates a theme with endless variations. There are possible as many different "folk psychologies" as there are possible differently structured communication systems to serve as models for them.

A third and even stranger possibility can be outlined as follows. We know that there is considerable lateralization of function between the two cerebral hemispheres, and that the two hemispheres make use of the information they get from each other by way of the great cerebral commissure – the corpus callosum – a giant cable of neurons connecting them. Patients whose commissure has been surgically severed display a variety of behavioral deficits that indicate a loss of access by one hemisphere to information it used to get from the other. However, in people with callosal agenesis (a congenital defect in which the connecting cable is simply absent), there is little or no behavioral deficit, suggesting that the two hemispheres have learned to exploit the information carried in other less direct pathways connecting them through the subcortical regions. This suggests that, even in the normal case, a developing hemisphere *learns* to make use of the information the cerebral commissure deposits at its doorstep. What we have then, in the case of a normal human, is two physically distinct cognitive systems (both capable of independent func-tion) responding in a systematic and learned fashion to exchanged information. And what is especially interesting about this case is the sheer amount of information exchanged. The cable of the commissure consists of $\approx$ 200 million neurons,[10] and even if we assume that each of these fibers is capable of one of only two possible states each second (a most conservative estimate), we are looking at a channel whose information capacity is $> 2 \times 10^8$ binary bits/second. Compare this to the < 500 bits/second capacity of spoken English.

Now, if two distinct hemispheres can learn to communicate on so impressive a scale, why shouldn't two distinct brains learn to do it also? This would require an artificial "commissure" of some kind, but let us suppose that we can fashion a workable transducer for implantation at some site in the brain that research reveals to be suitable, a transducer to convert a symphony of neural activity into (say) microwaves radiated from an aerial in the forehead, and to perform the reverse function of converting received microwaves back into neural activation. Connecting it up need not be an insuperable problem. We simply trick the normal processes of dendretic arborization into growing their own myriad connections with the active microsurface of the transducer.

Once the channel is opened between two or more people, they can learn (*learn*) to exchange information and coordinate their behavior with the same intimacy and virtuosity displayed by your own cerebral hemispheres. Think what this might do for hockey teams, and ballet companies, and research teams! If the entire population were thus fitted out, spoken language of any kind might well disappear completely, a victim of the "why crawl when you can fly?" principle. Libraries become filled not with books, but with long recordings of exemplary bouts of neural activity. These constitute a growing cultural heritage, an evolving "Third World," to use Karl Popper's terms. But they do not consist of sentences or arguments.

How will such people understand and conceive of other individuals? To this question I can only answer, "In roughly the same fashion that your right hemisphere 'understands' and 'conceives of' your left hemisphere – intimately and efficiently, but not propositionally!"

These speculations, I hope, will evoke the required sense of untapped possibilities, and I shall in any case bring them to a close here. Their function is to make some inroads into the aura of inconceivability that commonly surrounds the idea that we might reject FP. The felt conceptual strain even finds expression in an argument to the effect that the thesis of eliminative materialism is incoherent since it denies the very conditions presupposed by the assumption that it is meaningful. I shall close with a brief discussion of this very popular move.

As I have received it, the reductio proceeds by pointing out that the statement of eliminative materialism is just a meaningless string of marks or noises, unless that string is the expression of a certain *belief*, and a certain *intention* to communicate, and a *knowledge* of the grammar of the language, and so forth. But if the statement of eliminative materialism is true, then there are no such states to express. The statement at issue would then be a meaningless string of marks or noises. It would therefore *not* be true. Therefore it is not true. QED.

The difficulty with any nonformal reductio is that the conclusion against the initial assumption is always no better than the material assumptions invoked to reach the incoherent conclusion. In this case the additional assumptions involve a certain theory of meaning, one that presupposes the integrity of FP. But formally speaking, one can as well infer, from the incoherent result, that this theory of meaning is what must be rejected. Given the independent critique of FP leveled earlier, this would even seem the preferred option. But in any case, one cannot simply assume that particular theory of meaning without begging the question at issue, namely, the integrity of FP.

The question-begging nature of this move is most graphically illustrated by the following analogue, which I owe to Patricia Churchland.[11] The issue here, placed in the seventeenth century, is whether there exists such a substance as *vital spirit*. At the time, this substance was held, without significant awareness of real alternatives, to be that which distinguished the animate from the inanimate. Given the monopoly enjoyed by this conception, given the degree to which it was integrated with many of our other conceptions, and given the magnitude of the revisions any serious alternative conception would require, the following refutation of any anti-vitalist claim would be found instantly plausible.

> The anti-vitalist says that there is no such thing as vital spirit. But this claim is self-refuting. The speaker can expect to be taken seriously only if his claim cannot. For if the claim is true, then the speaker does not have vital spirit and must be *dead*. But if he is dead, then his statement is a meaningless string of noises, devoid of reason and truth.

The question-begging nature of this argument does not, I assume, require elaboration. To those moved by the earlier argument, I commend the parallel for examination.

The thesis of this paper may be summarized as follows. The propositional attitudes of folk psychology do not constitute an unbreachable barrier to the advancing tide of neuroscience. On the contrary, the principled displacement of folk psychology is not only richly possible, it represents one of the most intriguing theoretical displacements we can currently imagine.

NOTES

An earlier draft of this paper was presented at the University of Ottawa, and to the *Brain, Mind, and Person* colloquium at SUNY/Oswego. My thanks for the suggestions and criticisms that have informed the present version.

1   See Paul Feyerabend, "Materialism and the mind–body problem," *Review of Metaphysics*, XVII, 1, 65 (September 1963): 49–66; Richard Rorty, "Mind–body identity, privacy, and categories," *ibid.*, XIX. 1, 73 (September 1965): 24–54; and my *Scientific Realism and the Plasticity of Mind* (New York: Cambridge University Press, 1979).

2   We shall examine a handful of these laws presently. For a more comprehensive sampling of the laws of folk psychology, see my *Scientific Realism and Plasticity of Mind*, ch. 4. For a detailed examination of the folk principles that underwrite action explanations in particular, see my "The logical character of action explanations," *Philosophical Review*, LXXIX, 2 (April 1970): 214–36.

3   Staying within an objectual interpretation of the quantifiers, perhaps the simplest way to make systematic sense of expressions like ⌜x believes that p⌝ and closed sentences formed therefrom is just to construe whatever occurs in the nested position held by "p," "q," etc. as there having the function of a singular term. Accordingly, the standard connectives, as they occur between terms in that nested position, must be construed as there functioning as operators that form compound singular terms from other singular terms, and not as sentence operators. The compound singular terms so formed denote the appropriate compound propositions. Substitutional quantification will of course under-write a different interpretation, and there are other approaches as well. Especially appealing is the prosentential approach of Dorothy Grover, Joseph Camp, and Nuel Belnap, "A prosentential theory of truth," *Philosophical Studies*, XXVII, 2 (February 1975): 73–125. But the resolution of these issues is not vital to the present discussion.

4   A possible response here is to insist that the cognitive activity of animals and infants is linguaformal in its elements, structures, and processing right from birth. J. A. Foder, in *The Language of Thought* (New York: Cromwell, 1975), has erected a positive theory of thought on the assumption that the innate forms

of cognitive activity have precisely the form here denied. For a critique of Fodor's view, see Patricia Churchland, "Fodor on language learning," *Synthese*, xxxviii, 1 (May 1978): 149–59.

5   Most explicitly in "Three kinds of intentional psychology", but this theme of Dennett's goes all the way back to his "Intentional systems," this JOURNAL, LXVIII, 4 (Feb. 25, 1971): 87–106; reprinted in his *Brainstorms* (Montgomery, Vt.: Bradford Books, 1978).

6   Popper, *Objective Knowledge* (New York: Oxford, 1972); with J. Eccles, *The Self and Its Brain* (New York: Springer Verlag, 1978). Margolis, *Persons and Minds* (Boston: Reidel, 1978).

7   *Psychological Explanation* (New York: Random House, 1968), p. 116.

8   "Robots: machines or artificially created life?", this JOURNAL, LXI, 21 (Nov. 12, 1964): 668–91, pp. 675, 681 ff.

9   Richard Gregory defends such a view in "The grammar of vision," *Listener*, LXXXIII, 2133 (February 1970): 242–6; reprinted in his *Concepts and Mechanisms of Perception* (London: Duckworth, 1975), pp. 622–9.

10 M. S. Gazzaniga and J. E. LeDoux, *The Integrated Mind* (New York: Plenum Press, 1975).

11 "Is determinism self-refuting?", *Mind*, 90 (1981), 99–101.

POSTSCRIPT: EVALUATING OUR SELF CONCEPTION

The realization that all of human knowledge is speculative and provisional is a highly liberating insight. It is also well founded. We have the repeated empirical lessons of our own intellectual history to press the point upon us. And at both the intentional and the neural levels we have sufficient theoretical insight into the nature of human cognition to explain why its speculative and provisional character is almost certainly inevitable. This recognition encourages a modest humility about the ultimate integrity of our current conceptions and convictions, while it fosters a modest optimism about our cognitive prospects in the centuries to come.

Such liberal cognitive sentiments are widespread in the current philosophical climate. Indeed, they are almost universal. But for some philosophers they are sorely tested when the question at issue is the possible displacement of our familiar *self* conception – a conception that portrays each human as a self-conscious rational economy of propositional attitudes. Like the self-proclaimed liberal family confronting the unexpectedly alien dinner guest (and potential son-in-law!), the discomfort level gets elevated to unseemly heights and prior principle tends to evaporate in a flurry of contrived evasions. Such "bad faith" or "inauthenticity," I shall argue here, dominates current discussions of eliminative materialism.

Not all resistance is of this inauthentic kind. Some philosophers are prepared to accept and even to insist on the theoretical character of our common-sense folk psychology (FP), while maintaining that, on the whole, the empirical evidence still indicates that FP, *qua* theory, is at least roughly *true*. This approach at least locates the issue where it should be located – in the empirical trenches. There is no bad faith shown here. Fodor (1990) is a clear example of this position, as is Devitt (1990), Horgan and Woodward (1985), and Clark (1990).

Nor is one bound to accept the "liberal cognitive sentiments" sketched above. It is still possible, perhaps, to argue for some kind of Kantian inevitability about the framework features of FP, or some Cartesian incorrigibility in our capacity for introspection. There need be nothing inauthentic about declining eliminative materialism (EM) if one declines the epistemology that makes it possible. If one is thus, shall we say, a Child of an Earlier Era, this may seem paleolithic and regrettable to some of us, but it is not bad faith for such a philosopher to insist on some special epistemological status for FP.

Neither of these positions will be the prime target of this essay, though I am deeply interested in both. I wish rather to focus on a series of objections to EM that profess to remain *faithful* to the contemporary epistemological perspective of my first paragraph while still contriving some way for our current self conception to *evade* the standards of epistemological evaluation that naturally go with that perspective. These, I submit, are the genuinely *in*authentic objections. They have achieved some currency and they need unmasking. Let us take them in turn.

1 THE "FUNCTIONAL KINDS" OBJECTION

This objection proceeds from the not implausible conjecture that the taxonomy of psychological kinds embedded in FP is most accurately construed as a taxonomy of functional kinds rather than of genuinely natural kinds. It is then pointed out, quite correctly, that the ontological integrity of functional kinds – such as *chair, mousetrap* or *bungalow* – is not contingent on their finding a smooth intertheoretic reduction to some natural science of the underlying substrate (because the relevant functional properties might be realizable in a variety of substrates with a variety of dynamical resources). The conclusion is then drawn that FP has nothing to fear from any future failure to find a smooth explanatory reduction within, say, computational neuroscience. The principle, "Reduce, or be eliminated," on which EM is said to rest, is rejected as unacceptable.

One will find straightforward versions of this objection in Putnam (1988) and Searle (1992). It is a popular objection and it is sufficiently obvious that my original 1981 paper on EM addressed it at some length showing the ease of constructing a parallel "vindication" of the dear departed Alchemical Kinds). I stand by that original response, but let me here try a more direct approach.

In fact, the case for EM rests on no such overblown principle as "Reduce, or be eliminated," at least if this is interpreted as a demand for a type–type reduction. Such a draconian principle would banish all functional kinds at once. But the defender of EM is neither ignorant of nor hostile to the existence of functional kinds. The worry is not that FP kinds are too much like the (legitimately functional) kinds *chair* and *bungalow*; the worry is that FP kinds are too much like the (genuinely uninstantiated) kinds *phlogiston* and *caloric fluid*.

The primary worry, in other words, is that FP is a radically *false* representation of the kinematical and dynamical reality within each of us. One relevant *symptom* of FP's radical falsity would be its inevitable failure to find even a rough or disjunctive reduction within an explanatorily superior neuroscientific successor theory. Further symptoms of possible falsity would be FP's explanatory, predictive, and manipulative failures. Taken together, such symptoms could constitute a serious empirical case against FP, as they might against any other theory. That case will have to be evaluated as a whole, with the matter of reductive relations to neuroscience (or their absence) being but one very important part of it. Focusing our attention on the ontological status of chairs and bungalows simply deflects our attention away from the need and the obligation to pursue that broad empirical evaluation of FP. And it misrepresents the rationale behind EM.

It misleads in a further respect. The physical tokens of any functional kind are typically manufactured to meet our functional specifications and typically there is no intelligible question of whether our functional concept is adequate to the behavioral reality the manufactured object displays. No one feels a need to evaluate our concept *paring knife*, for example, in order to see if it lives up to the structural and behavioral reality of real paring knives. The onus of match is entirely in the other direction. Casting FP kinds as functional kinds implicitly portrays them as having a similar "authority" and empirical "invulnerability."

But human beings and animals are not artifacts. We are natural objects. Accordingly, while our internal economy may indeed be an abstract, high-level functional economy, realizable in many other substrates, *it remains a wholly empirical question whether our current FP conception of that internal economy is an accurate representation of its real structure.* Let us agree then that FP kinds are abstractly functional. This changes the situation in no relevant way. The issue of their collective descriptive integrity must still be addressed. The objection from functional kinds, as outlined above, is just a smoke screen that obscures our continuing obligation to evaluate the empirical integrity of FP and to compare its virtues and failings with competing representations of what cognitive activity consists in. It cannot serve as a *defense* of FP against real or prospective empirical criticisms.

2 THE "SELF-DEFEATING" OBJECTION

I am unsure who originated this one. Rudder-Baker (1987) has certainly pressed it home at greatest length, but many others have urged it in many forms, beginning with the audience at the very first public presentation of my 1981 paper, in draft, in 1980, at the University of Ottawa. A purely *a priori* objection, it dismisses EM as incoherent on grounds that, in arguing, stating, or embracing its case, it must presuppose the integrity of the very conceptual framework it proposes to eliminate. Consider, for example, the evident conflict between the eliminativist's apparent *belief* that FP is false, and his concurrent claim that there *are no* beliefs.

These and many other "pragmatic paradoxes" do indeed attend the eliminativist's current position. But they signal only the depth and far-reaching character of the conceptual revolution that EM would have us contemplate, not some flaw within EM itself. Logically, the situation is entirely foursquare. Assume Q (the framework of FP assumptions); argue legitimately from Q and other empirical premises to the conclusion that not-Q; and then conclude not-Q by the principle of *reductio ad absurdum.* (We get (Q→ not-Q) by conditional proof, which reduces to (not-Q v not-Q), which reduces to (not-Q).)

If the "self-defeating" objection were correct in this instance, it would signal a blanket refutation of all formal *reductios*, because they all "presuppose what they are trying to deny." Such a demonstration would be a major contribution to logic, and not just to the philosophy of mind. A more balanced opinion, I suggest, is that this venerable principle of argument is threatened neither in general, nor in the case at issue.

Let us concede then, or even insist, that current FP permits no coherent or tension-free denial of itself within its own theoretical vocabulary. As we have just seen, this buys it no proof against empirical criticism. Moreover, a *new* psychological framework – appropriately grounded in computational neuroscience, perhaps – need have no such limitation where the coherent denial of FP is concerned. We need only construct it, and move in. We can then express criticisms of FP that are entirely free of internal conflicts. This was the aim of EM in the first place. (For a particularly penetrating analysis of this objection by a non-eliminativist, see Devitt 1990).

The overdrawn character of this objection shows itself in one further respect: if it were legitimate, it could be elsewhere employed to prove far too much. To see this, suppose that humankind had used – for understanding what we now call "cognition" – a conceptual framework quite different from and much less successful than our current FP. (At some point in our distant evolutionary past, we must have done so.) It uses "gruntal attitudes," let us suppose, rather than propositional attitudes.

Suppose now that some forward-looking group sets about to develop a new and better conception, one that shapes up in content and structure rather like our current FP. Contemplating the shortcomings of their older conception, and the explanatory promise of the very different new framework, these people (let us call them "eliminative intentionalists") suggest that the older framework be dismissed entirely and the new one be adopted, even in the marketplace.

But alas! A "self-defeating" objection precisely parallel to that observed above can here be constructed that will (a) block, as strictly incoherent, any attempt to reject the older framework, and (b) demand of any new cognitive theory that it be consistent with the older theory already in place. Ironically, that relocated Rudder-Baker objection would then be blocking the adoption of our current propositional-attitude FP!

In fact, such an objection could be mounted to block the displacement of any conceptual framework for cognition whatever, since the same awkwardness – formulating a rejection of a framework within the framework itself – will arise *whatever* conception of cognition one happens to be using. The objection here at issue is an empty and essentially conservative objection, in that it can be used to protect, against radical overthrow, any framework that enjoys the irrelevant distinction of being the framework in use at that time.

3 THE "WHAT COULD FALSIFY IT?" OBJECTION

The more modest one's imagination, the more impressive this objection is likely to seem, which should put one on guard immediately. There is more than a whiff of an *argumentum ad ignorantiam* about this objection ("I cannot imagine how FP could be falsified; therefore, it isn't a falsifiable theory"). Let me try to sustain this diagnosis by meeting the objection head on, by trying to repair the very ignorance that makes it plausible.

The objector's question is rhetorical, of course, and gets its force by placing an unreasonable demand on one's imagination. With theories of the complexity and broad scope of FP, it is *in general* difficult or impossible to cite any single experiment or observation that would refute the theory at one blow. If we have learned anything from Duhem, Quine, Lakatos, and Kuhn, it is that theories, especially theories of broad scope and complexity, tend to die of slow empirical strangulation rather than by quick observational guillotine. This is triply true if the theory is also vague, incomplete, and festooned with *ceteris paribus* clauses, as FP most famously is.

Even so, theories can have severe empirical pressure put on them, by chronic poor performance in a proprietary domain (cf. Ptolemaic astronomy); by incompatibility with closely neighboring theories that are performing extremely well (cf. Vitalism *vis-à-vis* metabolic chemistry and molecular biology); by poor extension to domains continuous with but outside the domain of initial performance (cf. Newtonian mechanics in strong gravitational fields or high relative velocities); and finally, by the occasional empirical result carefully contrived to discriminate in some important way between competing alternatives (cf. Eddington's eclipse expedition, or the comparative statistical trials of Freudian vs other forms of psychotherapy). All but the last mode of pressure require significant periods of time for the empirical pressure to accumulate, and tests of the last kind are relatively rare, often hard to think of, usually difficult to set up, and regularly ambiguous in their outcomes even so.

Can we imagine pressures of these four prototypical kinds building up on FP? Not only can we, but the relevant pressures are already there. Some of us think we can hear the edifice creaking even as we discuss the matter. FP's explanatory success in predicting and explaining belief acquisition, practical deliberation, emotional reaction, and physical behavior is far from zero, to be sure, but it is even farther from the possible limit of 100 percent success in the capacity to predict and explain all such activities. "The complexity of human cognition allows no more than a rough grasp of even its major activities," it is said in exculpation. Perhaps so. But that is the same apologia deployed by astrologers. And FP's marginal performance in its proprietary domains is now at least twenty centuries in evidence. This is chronically poor performance by any measure.

FP is also under pressure from computational neuroscience, whose portrayal of the fundamental kinematics and dynamics of human and animal cognition is profoundly different from the propositional-attitude psychology of FP. The brain's computational activity is no longer the smooth-walled mystery it used to be. We are now contemplating the high-dimensional vector of neuronal activation-levels as the fundamental mode of *representation* in the brain. And we are now contemplating the vector-to-vector transformation, via vast matrices of synaptic connections, as the fundamental mode of *computation* in the brain (more on this below). Propositions and inferences are there in the brain only in some profoundly hidden and undiscovered form, or only in some small and uniquely human subsystem, if they are there at all.

We cannot yet insist that no accommodation will be found. Nor can we insist that computational neuroscience (CN) has things right. But CN is a robustly progressive and expansionist research program. And undeniably there is a *prima facie* failure-of-fit between the relevant ontologies and their correlative dynamics. Here is a second dimension of empirical pressure on FP. This, incidentally, is the substance of the worry, cited earlier, that FP will fail to find a smooth reduction within a more penetrating successor or substrate theory.

FP is subject to a third dimension of empirical pressure in its failure to extend successfully to adjacent domains. FP functions best for normal, adult, language-using humans in mundane situations. Its explanatory and predictive performance for prelinguistic children and animals is decidedly poorer. And its performance for brain-damaged, demented, drugged, depressed, manic, schizophrenic, or profoundly stressed humans is pathetic. Many attempts have been made to extend FP into these domains. Freud's attempt is perhaps the most famous. They have all been conspicuous failures.

The fourth dimension of empirical pressure is the hardest to address, for the reasons outlined earlier. I shall stick my neck out even so, if only to illustrate some relevant possibilities. One way to perform an empirical test of the hypothesis that the cognition of humans and the higher animals is an inference-rule-governed dance of propositional attitudes is to construct an artifactual system that deliberately and unquestionably *does* conduct its "cognitive" affairs in *exactly* that way. The purpose is to see if such a system can then display, in real time, all of the cognitive capacities that humans and the higher animals display.

A positive result would be highly encouraging for the hypothesis, though not decisive, because of the possibility that there is more than one way to achieve such cognitive capacities, and the possibility that the human and the artifact achieve them differently. On the other hand, persistently *negative* results in this experiment would augur very darkly for the hypothesis under test. If the relevant cognitive capacities never emerge from such a system, no matter how we tinker with it, or if they never emerge from it in anything remotely like real time, despite a blazing computational speed advantage on the part of the machine (a factor of roughly 10^6 with electronic machines over biological brains), then we have a gathering case that such a system is not in fact a reconstruction of our own computational strategy, a gathering case that our own system, and that of animals, must be using some quite different strategy.

The reader will perceive that I cite this example not just because it is a possible empirical test of the hypothesis at issue, but also because the AI community has in effect been performing and re-performing this test for something close to a quarter century now. The results have been persistently negative in just the way feared. The results are indecisive, to be sure. But there is widespread acknowledgment of and celebrated disappointment in the decreasing cognitive returns generated in the classical fashion from machines of ever-increasing speed and power. This is empirical evidence relevant to the hypothesis cited above, and it certainly isn't positive.

All told then, it is indeed possible for FP to suffer disconfirmatory empirical pressure. It does so in four different dimensions, and the pressure is the more powerful for being negative in all four. It is at least arguable that FP is approaching the brink of falsification already.

4 THE "IT SERVES QUITE DIFFERENT PURPOSES" OBJECTION

This line of argument was first pressed by Wilkes (1984), and finds further expression in Hannan (1989). Both philosophers claim that the conceptual framework of FP is used for a vast range of "nonscientific" purposes beyond the prototypically "theoretical purpose of describing the ultimate nature of human psychological organization" (Hannan). The idea here is that FP is up to a different game, is deployed in pursuit of different goals, from the game or the goals of a typical scientific theory. The leading examples of FP's "nontheoretical" functions concern the many practical activities that humans engage in and the many mundane purposes they address.

These premises about the manifold practical functions of FP are all true. Yet the conclusions drawn therefrom betray a narrow and cartoonish conception of what theories are and what they do. The stereotype of an abstract propositional description invented for the purpose of deep explanation far from the concerns of practical life may be popular, but it is not remotely accurate. Theory is regularly an intimate part and constituting element of people's second-by-second practical lives. Consider the role of circuit theory in the practical day of an electronics engineer designing radios, TVs, and stereos. Consider the role of geometry in the working day of a carpenter. Musical theory in the working day of a composer or jazz musician. Chemical theory in the working day of a drug engineer. Medical theory in the day of a physician. Optics in the day of a camera lens designer. Computer science in the day of a programmer. Metallurgy, mechanics, and simple thermal physics in the day of a blacksmith.

Such cases should not be set aside as the exceptional and occasional intrusions of theory into the alien realm of practice. Our best (Kuhn 1962) and most recent (Churchland 1989, ch. 9) accounts of what learning a theory amounts to portray the process as much less the memorizing of doctrine and much more the slow acquisition and development of a host of diverse *skills* – skills of perception, categorization, analogical extension, physical manipulation, evaluation, construction, analysis, argument, computation, anticipation, and so forth. Becoming a physical chemist, for example, is very much a matter of being socialized into a community of practice with shared goals, values, techniques, and equipment. Sustaining enhanced practice is what theories typically do, at least for those who have internalized the relevant theories.

Once they have been internalized, of course, they no longer seem like theories, in the sense of the false stereotype here at issue. Yet theories they remain, how ever much they have become the implicit engine of intricate mundane practice. In the case of FP, we have what is no doubt the most thoroughly internalized theory any human ever acquires. Small wonder it serves the diverse practical purposes mentioned by Wilkes and Hannan. Idle spectators excepted, that is what theories are for.

In sum, the claim that FP is an empirical theory is entirely consistent with – indeed it is explanatory of – the intricate practical life enjoyed by its adepts. It is typical of theoretical adepts that their practical activities, and their practical worlds, are transformed by the relevant acquisition of knowledge. So it is with children who master FP in the normal course of socialization.

As regards immunity to elimination, we should observe that practices can be displaced just as well as theories, and for closely related reasons. Becoming a medieval alchemist, for example, was a matter of learning an inseparable mix of theory and practice. But when modern chemistry began to flower, the medieval practice was displaced almost in its entirety. Current chemical practice would be unintelligible to an alchemist. And given the spectacular power of modern chemistry, no one defends or mourns the passing of the alchemist's comparatively impotent practice, intricate and dear to him though it was.

This intimate connection of theory with practice has another side. The objection at issue wrongly characterizes the eliminativist as willing to turn her back on the intricacies of social practice in favor of an austere concern with new and abstract theory. But nothing could be further from the truth. The positive idea behind the projected displacement of FP is the hope of a comparably superior social practice rooted in a comparably superior account of human cognition and mental activity. If better chemical theory can sustain better chemical practice, then better psychological theory can sustain better social practice. A deeper understanding of the springs of human behavior may thus permit a deeper level of cognitive interaction, moral insight, and mutual care. Accordingly, a genuinely worthy scientific replacement for FP need not be "dehumanizing," as so many fear. More likely it will be just the reverse. Perversity of practice is a chronic feature of our social history. Think of trial by ordeal, purification by fire, absolution by ritual, and rehabilitation by exorcism or, currently, by long imprisonment in the intimate company of other sociopaths. Against such dark and impotent practices, any source of light should be welcomed.

5 THE "NO EXISTING ALTERNATIVES" OBJECTION

Near the close of her 1989 paper, Hannan remarks,

> even if all conceptual schemes, including the conceptual scheme
> embodying the notion of rationality, are vulnerable to revision and
> overthrow, we have no possible way to reject rationality and propositional
> attitude concepts until replacement concepts are suggested. And at this
> point, no replacement concepts have been suggested . . . . in the absence
> of plausible replacements for these concepts, or even the hint that such
> replacements might be on the horizon, don't we have ample reason to
> bet against the eliminativist?

I doubt Hannan is misled on the point, but it is worth emphasizing that no
one is suggesting that we move out of our current house before we have
constructed a new one that invites us to move in. What EM urges is only the
poverty of our current home, the pressing need to explore the construction
of one or more new ones, and the probability that we will eventually move
in to one of them.

On two other points, however, I believe Hannan is importantly misled.
The latter quotation embodies an argument of the form, "If FP is currently
the only boat afloat, isn't this ample reason to expect that it will continue
to be the only boat afloat?" The response is straightforward. No, it isn't
ample reason to expect that. On the other hand, it is ample reason for
immediately gathering as much driftwood as we can, and for beginning the
construction of alternative boats, if only to foster illuminating comparisons
with our current vehicle, which after all is leaking at every seam.

The former quotation embodies a far more important misconception.
Here in 1993, we *do* have some very specific and highly promising
"replacement" concepts under active exploration. They are now the prime
focus of several new journals and they have been under vigorous exploration for over a decade at several centers of cognitive and neuroscientific
research. These are the ideas mentioned briefly in (3) above. I can give only
the flavor of this new approach here, but that much is quickly done.

One of the basic ideas of this new approach has some instances already
familiar to you. Consider the momentary picture on your TV screen. That
representation of some distant scene is a *pattern* of brightness levels across
a large *population* of tiny pixels – about 200,000 of them on a standard set.
A coherent *sequence* of such patterns represents the behavior of that distant
portion of the world over time.

A very similar case, this time in you, is the momentary pattern of
activation levels across the 100 million light-sensitive cells of your retina.
The temporal sequence of such patterns represents the unfolding external
world. A further example is the activation pattern, and the sequences
thereof, across the millions of auditory cells in the cochlea of your inner
ear. Here, of course, the "semantics" of the representation is not "pictorial"
as in the case of vision. The information-preserving transformation from
external world to internal representation is quite different in these two
cases, and different again in the other modalities.

Proprietary patterns of activation across the cellular populations of your many other sensory modalities complete the story of peripheral world-representation. *Prima facie*, there is nothing "propositional" about any of these representations, either in their various "syntaxes" or in their diverse "semantics."

These intricate patterns – or *activation vectors*, as they are called – are projected inwards from the periphery, along crowded axonal highways, to secondary cell populations within the brain called the primary sensory cortices, one for each of the sensory modalities. Here too, representation consists in the pattern of activation levels across the cortical population of neurons, patterns provoked by the arriving sensory vectors.

But the patterns at this level are not mere repetitions of the original patterns at the sensory periphery. Those patterns have been transformed during their journey to the cortical populations. They get transformed mainly by the vast filter of synaptic connections they have to traverse in order to stimulate the cortical population. The result is typically a *new* pattern across the cortical canvas, a principled *transformation* of the original sensory pattern.

Such transformations illustrate the second major idea of the new approach. *Computation* over these vectorial representations consists in their principled transformation by the vast matrix of tiny synaptic connections that intervene between any two neuronal populations. Such a process, note well, performs a prodigious number of elementary computations all at once, since each of the (possibly 10^{12}) synaptic connections does its job at the same time as all the other connections in the same matrix. This is called "massively parallel processing" and it provides us with a robust explanation of how animals can perform their extraordinary feats of computation in real time despite having "wetware" that is millions of times slower than the electronic hardware of conventional computers.

An intuitive way to think of such transformations is as follows. Consider a pictorial image projected through a nonuniform lens, or reflected from a deformed mirror. The image that comes out is quite different from the image that went in. And by configuring the surface of the lens/mirror to suit our purposes, we can produce any general transformation in the image we desire. Here the input and output images correspond to the input and output activation patterns, and the lens or mirror corresponds to the matrix of synaptic connections. Learning, incidentally, consists in modifying the configuration of synaptic connections. Learning, in other words, modifies the way we transform patterns.

The several cortical populations project in turn to further cell populations, and those to populations further still, until eventually the receiving population consists of motor cells, cells whose patterned activity is transformed by the muscle spindles into coherent bodily movement of some kind. Thus do we complete the basics of our new conception of how the nervous system works, from perception through cognition to organized behavior. It is here a stick-figure portrait, to be sure, but you will find it richly articulated in many directions in the literature. Patricia Churchland's and Terry Sejnowski's (1992) book provides an accessible and richly illustrated entry into the current state of research. My (1989) book attempts to draw out some of its consequences for epistemology and the philosophy of science.

What is important for the issues of this paper is that the relevant sciences have indeed articulated fertile and systematic theories concerning representation and computation in the brain. From the perspective of those theories, the most general and fundamental form of representation in the brain has nothing discernible to do with propositions, and the most general and fundamental form of computation in the brain has nothing discernible to do with inferences between propositions. The brain appears to be playing a different game from the game that FP ascribes to it.

6 CONCLUDING REMARKS

Despite the occasional polemics, the primary lesson of this paper is not that FP is already doomed, or that our current social practices are about to be swept away. The primary lesson is that we must confront the issue of the descriptive integrity and explanatory efficacy of folk psychology for what it is: an empirical question. How computational neuroscience and connectionist AI will fare in the coming years remains to be seen. How those research programs will explain our undoubted capacity for language and logic remains to be worked out. Whether folk psychological categories will find some kinematical and dynamical role within the new framework remains a strictly open question. In all of this there is plenty of empirical evidence to mull over, and ample room for reasonable people to disagree. It is an exciting period of theoretical and empirical evaluation. It would be inauthentic not to enjoy it for what it is.

REFERENCES

Churchland, Paul (1981) "Eliminative materialism and the propositional attitudes," *Journal of Philosophy*, 78, 67–90.
—— (1989) *A Neurocomputational Perspective: The Nature of Mind and the Structure of Science*, Cambridge: MIT Press.
Churchland, Patricia and Sejnowski, T. (1992) *The Computational Brain*, Cambridge: MIT Press.
Clark, A. (1990) *Microcognition*, Cambridge: MIT Press.
Devitt, M. (1990) "Transcendentalism about content," *Pacific Philosophical Quarterly* 71, 247–63.
Fodor, J. (1990) *A Theory of Content and Other Essays*, Cambridge: MIT Press.
Hannan, B. (1989) "Don't stop believing: the case against eliminative materialism," *Review of Metaphysics*.
Horgan, T. and Woodward, J. (1985) "Folk psychology is here to stay," *Philosophical Review* XCIV, 197–220.
Kuhn, T. (1962) *The Structure of Scientific Revolutions*, Chicago: University of Chicago Press.
Putnam, H. (1988) *Representation and Reality*, Cambridge: MIT Press.
Rudder-Baker, L. (1987) *Saving Belief: A Critique of Physicalism*, Princeton: Princeton University Press.

Searle, J. (1992) *The Rediscovery of the Mind*, Cambridge: MIT Press.
Wilkes, K. (1984) "Pragmatics in science and theory in common sense," *Inquiry*, 27, 339–61.

9   What Mary Didn't Know

Frank Jackson

Mary is confined to a black-and-white room, is educated through black-and-white books and through lectures relayed on black-and-white television. In this way she learns everything there is to know about the physical nature of the world. She knows all the physical facts about us and our environment, in a wide sense of "physical" which includes everything in *completed* physics, chemistry, and neurophysiology, and all there is to know about the causal and relational facts consequent upon all this, including of course functional roles. If physicalism is true, she knows all there is to know. For to suppose otherwise is to suppose that there is more to know than every physical fact, and that is just what physicalism denies.

Physicalism is not the noncontroversial thesis that the actual world is largely physical, but the challenging thesis that it is entirely physical. This is why physicalists must hold that complete physical knowledge is complete knowledge simpliciter. For suppose it is not complete: then our world must differ from a world, $W(P)$, for which it is complete, and the difference must be in nonphysical facts; for our world and $W(P)$ agree in all matters physical. Hence, physicalism would be false at our world [though contingently so, for it would be true at $W(P)$].[1]

It seems, however, that Mary does not know all there is to know. For when she is let out of the black-and-white room or given a color television, she will learn what it is like to see something red, say. This is rightly described as *learning* – she will not say "ho, hum." Hence, physicalism is false. This is the knowledge argument against physicalism in one of its manifestations.[2] This note is a reply to three objections to it mounted by Paul M. Churchland.[3]

1 THREE CLARIFICATIONS

The knowledge argument does not rest on the dubious claim that logically you cannot imagine what sensing red is like unless you have sensed red. Powers of imagination are not to the point. The contention about Mary is not that, despite her fantastic grasp of neurophysiology and everything else physical, she *could not imagine*, what it is like to sense red; it is that, as a matter of fact, she *would not know*. But if physicalism is true, she would know; and no great powers of imagination would be called for. Imagination is a faculty that those who *lack* knowledge need to fall back on.

Secondly, the intensionality of knowledge is not to the point. The argument does not rest on assuming falsely that, if S knows that a is F and if $a = b$, then S knows that b is F. It is concerned with the nature of Mary's total body of knowledge before she is released: is it complete, or do some facts escape it? What is to the point is that S may know that a is F and *know* that $a = b$, yet arguably not know that b is F, by virtue of not being sufficiently logically alert to follow the consequences through. If Mary's lack of knowledge were at all like this, there would be no threat to physicalism in it. But it is very hard to believe that her lack of knowledge could be remedied merely by her explicitly following through enough logical consequences of her vast physical knowledge. Endowing her with great logical acumen and persistence is not in itself enough to fill in the gaps in her knowledge. On being let out, she will not say "I could have worked all this out before by making some more purely logical inferences."

Thirdly, the knowledge Mary lacked which is of particular point for the knowledge argument against physicalism is *knowledge about the experiences of others*, not about her own. When she is let out, she has new experiences, color experiences she has never had before. It is not, therefore, an objection to physicalism that she learns *something* on being let out. Before she was let out, she could not have known facts about her experience of red, for there were no such facts to know. That physicalist and nonphysicalist alike can agree on. After she is let out, things change; and physicalism can happily admit that she learns this; after all, some physical things will change, for instance, her brain states and their functional roles. The trouble for physicalism is that, after Mary sees her first ripe tomato, she will realize how impoverished her conception of the mental life of *others* has been *all along*. She will realize that there was, all the time she was carrying out her laborious investigations into the neurophysiologies of others and into the functional roles of their internal states, something about these people she was quite unaware of. All along their experiences (or many of them, those got from tomatoes, the sky, ...) had a feature conspicuous to them but until now hidden from her (in fact, not in logic). But she knew all the physical facts about them all along; hence, what she did not know until her release is not a physical fact about their experiences. But it is a fact about them. That is the trouble for physicalism.

2 CHURCHLAND'S THREE OBJECTIONS

(i) Churchland's first objection is that the knowledge argument contains a defect that "is simplicity itself" (23). The argument equivocates on the sense of "knows about". How so? Churchland suggests that the following is "a conveniently tightened version" of the knowledge argument:

(1) Mary knows everything there is to know about brain states and their properties.
(2) It is not the case that Mary knows everything there is to know about sensations and their properties.

Therefore, by Leibniz's law,

(3) Sensations and their properties ≠ brain states and their properties (23).

Churchland observes, plausibly enough, that the type or kind of knowledge involved in premise 1 is distinct from the kind of knowledge involved in premise 2. We might follow his lead and tag the first "knowledge by description," and the second "knowledge by acquaintance"; but, whatever the tags, he is right that the displayed argument involves a highly dubious use of Leibniz's law.

My reply is that the displayed argument may be convenient, but it is not accurate. It is not the knowledge argument. Take, for instance, premise 1. The whole thrust of the knowledge argument is that Mary (before her release) does *not* know everything there is to know about brain states and their properties, because she does not know about certain qualia associated with them. What is complete, according to the argument, is her knowledge of matters physical. A convenient and accurate way of displaying the argument is:

(1)′ Mary (before her release) knows everything physical there is to know about other people.

(2)′ Mary (before her release) does not know everything there is to know about other people (because she *learns* something about them on her release).

Therefore,

(3)′ There are truths about other people (and herself) which escape the physicalist story.

What is immediately to the point is not the kind, manner, or type of knowledge Mary has, but *what* she knows. What she knows beforehand is ex hypothesi everything physical there is to know, but is it everything there is to know? That is the crucial question.

There is, though, a relevant challenge involving questions about kinds of knowledge. It concerns the *support* for premise 2′. The case for premise 2′ is that Mary learns something on her release, she acquires knowledge, and that entails that her knowledge beforehand (*what* she knew, never mind whether by description, acquaintance, or whatever) was incomplete. The challenge, mounted by David Lewis and Laurence Nemirow, is that on her release Mary does *not* learn something or acquire knowledge in the relevant sense. What Mary acquires when she is released is a certain representational or imaginative ability; it is knowledge how rather than knowledge that. Hence, a physicalist can admit that Mary acquires something very significant of a knowledge kind – which can hardly be denied – without admitting that this shows that her earlier factual knowledge is defective. She knew all *that* there was to know about the experiences of others beforehand, but lacked an ability until after her release.[4]

Now it is certainly true that Mary will acquire abilities of various kinds after her release. She will, for instance, be able to imagine what seeing red is like, be able to remember what it is like, and be able to understand why her friends regarded her as so deprived (something which, until her release, had always mystified her). But is it plausible that that is *all* she will acquire? Suppose she received a lecture on skepticism about other minds while she was incarcerated. On her release she sees a ripe tomato in normal conditions, and so has a sensation of red. Her first reaction is to say that she now knows more about the kind of experiences others have when looking at ripe tomatoes. She then remembers the lecture and starts to worry. Does she really know more about what their experiences are like, or is she indulging in a wild generalization from one case? In the end she decides she does know, and that skepticism is mistaken (even if, like so many of us, she is not sure how to demonstrate its errors). What was she to-ing and fro-ing about – her abilities? Surely not; her representational abilities were a known constant throughout. What else then was she agonizing about than whether or not she had gained factual knowledge of others? There would be nothing to agonize about if ability was *all* she acquired on her release.

I grant that I have no *proof* that Mary acquires on her release, as well as abilities, factual knowledge about the experiences of others – and not just because I have no disproof of skepticism. My claim is that the knowledge argument is a valid argument from highly plausible, though admittedly not demonstrable, premises to the conclusion that physicalism is false. And that, after all, is about as good an objection as one could expect in this area of philosophy.

(ii) Churchland's second objection (24–5) is that there must be something wrong with the argument, for it proves too much. Suppose Mary received a special series of lectures over her black-and-white television from a full-blown dualist, explaining the "laws" governing the behavior of "ectoplasm" and telling her about qualia. This would not affect the plausibility of the claim that on her release she learns something. So if the argument works against physicalism, it works against dualism too.

My reply is that lectures about qualia over black-and-white television do not tell Mary all there is to know about qualia. They may tell her some things about qualia, for instance, that they do not appear in the physicalist's story, and that the quale we use "yellow" for is nearly as different from the one we use "blue" for as is white from black. But why should it be supposed that they tell her everything about qualia? On the other hand, it is plausible that lectures over black-and-white television might in principle tell Mary everything in the physicalist's story. You do not need color television to learn physics or functionalist psychology. To obtain a good argument against dualism (attribute dualism; ectoplasm is a bit of fun), the premise in the knowledge argument that Mary has the full story according to physicalism before her release, has to be replaced by a premise that she has the full story according to dualism. The former is plausible; the latter is not. Hence, there is no "parity of reasons" trouble for dualists who use the knowledge argument.

(iii) Churchland's third objection is that the knowledge argument claims "that Mary could not even *imagine* what the relevant experience would be like, despite her exhaustive neuroscientific knowledge, and hence must still be missing certain crucial information" (25), a claim he goes on to argue against.

But, as we emphasized earlier, the knowledge argument claims that Mary would not know what the relevant experience is like. What she could imagine is another matter. If her knowledge is defective, despite being all there is to know according to physicalism, then physicalism is false, whatever her powers of imagination.

NOTES

I am much indebted to discussions with David Lewis and with Robert Pargetter.

1   The claim here is not that, if physicalism is true, only what is expressed in explicitly physical language is an item of knowledge. It is that, if physicalism is true, then if you know everything expressed or expressible in explicitly physical language, you know everything. *Pace* Terence Horgan, "Jackson on physical information and qualia," *Philosophical Quarterly*, xxxiv, 135 (April 1984): 147–52.

2   Namely, that in my "Epiphenomenal qualia," ibid., xxxii, 127 (April 1982): 127–36. See also Thomas Nagel, "What is it like to be a bat?' *Philosophical Review*, lxxxiii, 4 (October 1974): 435–50, and Howard Robinson, *Matter and Sense* (New York: Cambridge, 1982).

3   "Reduction, qualia, and the direct introspection of brain states," *Journal of Philosophy*, lxxxii, 1 (January 1985): 8–28. Unless otherwise stated, future page references are to this paper.

4   See Laurence Nemirow, review of Thomas Nagel, *Mortal Questions, Philosophical Review*, lxxxix, 3 (July 1980): 473–7, and David Lewis, "Postscript to 'Mad pain and Martian pain'," *Philosophical Papers*, vol. 1 (New York: Oxford, 1983). Churchland mentions both Nemirow and Lewis, and it may be that he intended his objection to be essentially the one I have just given. However, he says quite explicitly (bottom of p. 23) that his objection does not need an "ability" analysis of the relevant knowledge.

POSTSCRIPT

Materialism is a doctrine in metaphysics. It is a claim about what there is and what it is like. The knowledge argument turns on an epistemological claim, namely, that no story about our world told purely in physical terms – the kind of terms that appear in the materialists' or physicalists' preferred account of the world and its nature – could enable one to deduce the phenomenal nature of psychological states. How is a doctrine in metaphysics supposed to be threatened by a doctrine about the impossibility of a certain sort of deduction?

Many have asked this question, and what follows is the sketch of my reply. (The matter is discussed at much greater length, in the context of a general discussion of the role of conceptual analysis in metaphysics, in "Armchair metaphysics", in *Philosophy in Mind*, ed. John O'Leary Hawthorne and Michaelis Michael, Philosophical Studies, Kluwer, forthcoming.) My reply comes in three stages. I give the first two stages in outline only, as I take it that they involve by now familiar points. I spend a little more time on the third.

The first point to note is that metaphysical theses that make a claim to completeness commit their holders to supervenience theses. Here is how the point applies in the case of materialism. Consider any possible world that is a minimal physical duplicate of our world. It is, that is, exactly like ours in every physical respect: it is physical individual, property and relation exactly like our world, and moreover it contains nothing extra; it contains nothing more than it has to in order to be physically exactly like our world. (We can count the necessarily existing entities, if there are any, that all worlds have in common as trivially physical for our purposes here.) Materialists who hold that materialism is a complete account of our world, or a complete account of our world as far as the mind is concerned – materialists who are, that is, not some kind of dual attribute dualist – must hold that these minimal physical duplicates are psychological duplicates of our world. They must, that is, hold the following supervenience thesis

> (S) Any world that is a minimal physical duplicate of our world is a psychological duplicate of our world.

For suppose that (S) is false. Then there is a difference in psychological nature between our world and some minimal physical duplicate of it. But then either our world contains some psychological nature that the minimal physical duplicate does not, or the minimal physical duplicate contains some psychological nature that our world does not. The second is impossible because the extra nature would have to be non-physical (as our world and the duplicate are physically identical), and the minimal physical duplicate contains no non-physical nature by definition. (Perhaps it will be objected that a minimal physical duplicate contains nothing more than it *has* to in order to be a physical duplicate of our world, and that this allows as a possibility that it has some non-physical nature provided that that nature is necessitated by its physical nature. But its physical nature is exactly the same as our world's. Hence, if this physical nature necessitates some non-physical nature, our world must have some non-physical nature and materialism is false. We could stop right here.) But if our world contains some psychological nature that the duplicate does not, this nature must be non-physical (as our world and the duplicate are physically identical). But then materialism would be false. For our world would contain some non-physical psychological nature, and so materialism's claim to completeness concerning at least the psychological nature of our world would be false. Hence, if the supervenience thesis is false, materialism is false – that is to say, materialism is committed to the supervenience thesis.

The second point to note is that supervenience theses expressed in terms of quantifications over possible worlds, as is (S), yield entailment theses. We can think of a statement as telling a story about how things are, and as being true inasmuch as things are the way the story says they are. Let Ø be the statement that tells the rich, complex and detailed physical story that is true at the actual world and all and only the minimal physical duplicates of the actual world, and false elsewhere. Let Ω be any true statement entirely about the psychological nature of our world: Ω is true at our world, and every world at which Ω is false differs in some psychological way from our world. If (S) is true, every world at which Ø is true is a psychological duplicate of our world. But then every world at which Ø is true is a world at which Ω is true – that is, Ø entails Ω.

Hence, despite the fact that materialism is a doctrine in metaphysics, it is by virtue of its claim to completeness committed to the entailment of the psychological way things are, including of course the phenomenal way they are, by a rich enough, purely physical story about the way they are.

What has this to do with the possibility of deducing the psychological way things are from the physical way things are? What, that is, has it to do with what I contend that the Mary case shows cannot be done? The answer depends on what should be said about the necessary *a posteriori*, a controversial matter to which I now turn.

Consider

> (A) H_2O covers most of the planet.
>   Therefore, water covers most of the planet.

Is this argument valid? It is valid in one sense. Every possible world where the premise is true is a world where the conclusion is true. The premise entails the conclusion according to the notion of entailment we pre-supposed above, the notion of entailment elucidated in terms of being necessarily truth preserving. This is because the conditional "If H_2O covers most of the planet, then water covers most of the planet" is necessarily true. The argument, though, is invalid in the sense that it is not possible to deduce *a priori* the conclusion from the premise. This is because "If H_2O covers most of the planet, then water covers most of the planet" is *a posteriori*. (The necessary *a posteriori* status of the conditional follows from the famous necessary *a posteriori* status of "Water = H_2O".) As we might put it: the premise necessitates, logically determines, or strictly implies, the conclusion, but it does not *a priori* entail it.

It might well be thought (and has been by many) that this argument provides a model for a materialist to view the relationship between the physical way things are and the psychological way things are. A rich enough story about the physical way our world is logically determines the psycho-logical way it is, but does not *a priori* entail the psychological way it is. The idea is that a view of this kind respects the result that materialists must hold that the psychological way things are supervenes on the physical way they are, without forcing them to admit the possibility of *a priori* deducing the psychological way things are from the physical way they are. Hence, runs the suggestion, materialists can sidestep the challenge posed by the knowledge argument. What Mary knows logically determines or fixes all there is to know about the psychological way things are, including the sensory or phenomenal way they are, but it does not enable her, even in principle, to deduce the psychological way things are.

I think this suggestion rests on a misunderstanding of what we learnt from Saul Kripke about the necessary *a posteriori*. In a nutshell my reply is that we learnt about *two* things together: the necessary *a posteriori*, and the contingent *a priori*, and when we bear this in mind, we see that a *rich enough* story about the H_2O way things are *a priori* entails the water way things are, despite the fact that "H_2O covers most of the planet" does not *a priori* entail that water covers most of the planet. I will make the crucial point with a simple, made-up example.

Suppose that I introduce the word "Fred" as a (rigid) name for the shape of the largest object next door – that is to say, I explain what the word is to mean in these very terms – and let us suppose that that object is, as it happens, square. The statement (schema) "If X is square, then X is Fred" will be necessarily true, for it is true in every world by virtue of the fact that "Fred" is a rigid designator of squareness (together, of course, with the fact that "square" is a rigid designator). But it will not be *a priori*. Mere understanding of the words that make it up plus logical acumen cannot by themselves reveal whether the statement is true or false. Hence

(B)   X is square.
        Therefore, X is Fred.

will be valid in the necessarily truth-preserving sense but not in the *a priori* deducibility sense. This, though, does not mean that there is no argument from the square way things are to the Fred way they are that is valid in the *a priori* deducibility sense. For "If X has the shape of the largest object next door, then X is Fred" is contingent *a priori*. It is contingent because it is false in worlds where the largest object next door is not square. It is *a priori* because understanding the word "Fred" is enough to tell you that it is true: the very way I explained the use I was giving the word "Fred" tells you that any object with the shape of the largest object next door is Fred. Now consider

(B+)   X is square.
        The largest object next door is square.
        Therefore, X is Fred.

This argument is valid in both the necessarily truth-preserving sense and the *a priori* deducibility sense. It is necessarily truth preserving because, as already noted, (B) is. It allows an *a priori* deduction of the conclusion from the premises because the two premises together *a priori* entail that X has the shape of the largest object next door, and "If X has the shape of the largest object next door, then X is Fred" is, as already noted, *a priori*. That is to say, a rich enough story about the square way things are – the story given in the two premises of (B+) taken together – *a priori* entails the Fred way they are.

The same general picture applies, it seems to me, to the relationship between the H_2O way things are and the water way things are. Our understanding of "Water" is as a rigid designator whose reference is fixed by "the stuff that fills the water role", where the water role is spelt out in terms of, say (the details are to some extent controversial and indeterminate, as is inevitable with a real-life example in place of a made-up one), satisfying most of: being an odorless and colorless liquid, falling from the sky, being called "water" by experts, being necessary to life on the planet, filling the oceans, and so on. The combination of the fact that "water" and "H_2O" are rigid designators with its being *a posteriori* that H_2O fills the water role, explains why statements like "Water is H_2O" and "If H_2O covers most of the planet, water covers most of the planet", are necessary *a posteriori*. The fact that we understand "water" as being a rigid designator of that which fills the water role means that statements like "Water = the stuff that fills the water role" and "If what fills the water role covers most of the planet, water covers most of the planet" are contingent *a priori*. But then it follows that although argument (A) is not valid in the *a priori* deducibility sense, the following supplementation of it is valid in both the *a priori* deducibility sense and the necessarily truth-preserving sense:

(A+) H_2O covers most of the planet.
        H_2O fills the water role.
        Therefore, water covers most of the planet.

Hence, a *rich enough* story about the H_2O way things are does enable the *a priori* deduction of the water way things are.

The same goes for the other well-known examples of the necessary *a posteriori*. As Kripke noted when he argued that "Heat is molecular motion" is necessary *a posteriori*, this view goes hand in hand with the view that something like "Heat causes such and such sensations" is contingent *a priori*. (Saul Kripke, *Naming and Necessity*, Basil Blackwell, Oxford, 1980, see esp. pp. 132ff. Actually, heat is not always molecular motion, and water is arguably not H_2O so much as sufficiently large aggregations of H_2O molecules; but in the interests of simplicity we fudge.) But then a rich enough story about molecular motion does yield the facts about heat. True, a limited story about molecular motion, one that tells you which substances have a good deal of it but not much else, does not tell you much about heat, despite necessitating the facts about heat. But a story that includes the way molecular motion causes various sensations and whatever else is involved in fixing the reference of "heat" will tell you all there is to know about heat.

I think that the materialist has to say the same thing about the relationship between the physical way the world is and the psychological way the world is. A partial story about the physical way the world is might logically necessitate the psychological way the world is without enabling an *a priori* deduction of the psychological way the world is. It might be like the partial stories about H_2O, and squareness encapsulated in the premises of arguments like (A) and (B), above. They necessitate, without *a priori* entailing, the facts about, respectively, water, and Fred. But the materialist is committed to a complete or near enough complete story about the physical way the world is enabling in principle the *a priori* deduction of the psychological way the world is. Materialism about the mind is like what we might call "H_2O-ism" about water. Someone who knows where all the H_2O is *and* enough else about H_2O – that it fills the sea, gets tagged "water" by experts, its molecules move past each other reasonably freely, and so and so forth – knows all there is to know about water, and this is crucial to H_2O-ism being, as it is, true. There is nothing more to the water way our world is than the H_2O way it is. In the same way, I think it is crucial for the truth of materialism (materialism proper, not some covert form of dual attribute theory of mind) that knowing a rich enough story about the physical nature of our world is tantamount to knowing the psychological story about our world.

Finally, I should point out that there is a much shorter way of making plausible the knowledge argument's presumption that materialism is committed to the *a priori* deducibility of our psychological nature from our and our environment's physical nature.

It is implausible that there are facts about very simple organisms that cannot be deduced *a priori* from enough information about their physical nature and how they interact with their environments, physically described. The physical story about amoeba and their interactions with their environments is the whole story about amoeba. Mary would not lack any knowledge about them. But according to materialism, we differ from amoeba essentially only in complexity of ingredients and their arrangement. It is hard to see how that kind of difference could generate important facts about us that in principle defy our powers of deduction, and the fact that we have a phenomenal psychology is certainly an important fact about us. Think of the charts in biology classrooms showing the evolutionary progression from single-celled creatures on the far left to the higher apes and humans on the far right: where in that progression can the materialist plausibly claim that failure of *a priori* deducibility of important facts about us emerges? Or, if it comes to that, where in the development of each and every one of us from a zygote could the materialist plausibly locate the place where there emerge important facts about us that cannot be deduced from the physical story about us?

Part III

Materialism and Meaning

10 Things and their Place in Theories

W. V. O. Quine

I

Our talk of external things, our very notion of things, is just a conceptual apparatus that helps us to foresee and control the triggering of our sensory receptors in the light of previous triggering of our sensory receptors. The triggering, first and last, is all we have to go on.

In saying this I too am talking of external things, namely, people and their nerve endings. Thus what I am saying applies in particular to what I am saying, and is not meant as skeptical. There is nothing we can be more confident of than external things – some of them, anyway – other people, sticks, stones. But there remains the fact – a fact of science itself – that science is a conceptual bridge of our own making, linking sensory stimulation to sensory stimulation; there is no extrasensory perception.

I should like now to consider how this bridging operation works. What does it mean to assume external objects? And what about objects of an abstract sort, such as numbers? How do objects of both sorts help us in developing systematic connections between our sensory stimulations?

The assuming of objects is a mental act, and mental acts are notoriously difficult to pin down – this one more than most. Little can be done in the way of tracking thought processes except when we can put words to them. For something objective that we can get our teeth into we must go after the words. Words accompany thought for the most part anyway, and it is only as thoughts are expressed in words that we can specify them.

If we turn our attention to the words, then what had been a question of assuming objects becomes a question of verbal *reference* to objects. To ask what the *assuming* of an object consists in is to ask what *referring* to the object consists in.

We refer by using words, and these we learn through more or less devious association with stimulations of our sensory receptors. The association is direct in cases where the word is learned by ostension. It is thus that the child learns to volunteer the word "milk", or to assent if the word is queried, in the conspicuous presence of milk; also to volunteer the word so as to induce the presence of milk.

The mechanism in such a case is relatively clear and simple, as psychological mechanisms go. It is the conditioning of a response. To call it objective reference, however, is premature. Learning the expression "milk" in this way, by direct association with appropriate stimulations, is the same in principle as learning the sentence "It's windy" or "It's cold" or "It's raining" by direct association with appropriate stimulations. It is we in our adult ontological sophistication that recognize the word "milk" as referring to an object, a substance, while we are less ready to single out an object of reference for "It's windy" or "It's cold" or "It's raining". This is the contrast that we need eventually to analyze if we are to achieve a satisfactory analysis of what to count as objective reference; and it is not a contrast that obtrudes in the primitive phase of learning by ostension. The word "milk", when uttered in recognition or when queried and assented to, is best regarded at first as a sentence on a par with "It's windy", "It's cold", and the rest; it is as if to say "It's milk". It is a one-word sentence. All of these examples are *occasion* sentences, true on some occasions of utterance and false on others. We are conditioned to assent to them under appropriate stimulation. There is no call to read into them, as yet, any reference to objects.

The view of sentences as primary in semantics, and of names or other words as dependent on sentences for their meaning, is a fruitful idea that began perhaps with Jeremy Bentham's theory of fictions. What Bentham observed was that you have explained any term quite adequately if you have shown how all contexts in which you propose to use it can be paraphrased into antecedently intelligible language. When this is recognized, the philosophical analysis of concepts or explication of terms comes into its own. Sentences come to be seen as the primary repository of meaning, and words are seen as imbibing their meaning through their use in sentences.

Recognition of sentences as primary has not only expedited philosophical analysis; it has also given us a better picture of how language is actually learned. First we learn short sentences, next we get a line on various words through their use in those sentences, and then on that basis we manage to grasp longer sentences in which those same words recur. Accordingly the development leading from sensory stimulation to objective reference is to be seen as beginning with the flat conditioning of simple occasion sentences to stimulatory events, and advancing through stages more forthrightly identifiable with objective reference. We have still to consider what the distinguishing traits of these further stages might be.

As long as the word "milk" can be accounted for simply as an occasion sentence on a par with "It's raining", surely nothing is added by saying that it is a name of something. Nothing really is said. Similarly for "sugar", "water", "wood". Similarly even for "Fido" and "Mama". We would be idly declaring there to be designata of the words, counterparts, shadows, one apiece: danglers, serving only as honorary designata of expressions whose use as occasion sentences would continue as before.

The outlook changes when individuative words emerge: words like "chair" and "dog". These differ from the previous examples in the complexity of what has to be mastered in learning them. By way of mastery of any of those previous words, all that was called for was the ability to pass a true–false test regarding points or neighborhoods taken one at a time. It is merely a question, in the case of Fido or milk, of what visible points are on Fido or on milk and what ones are not. To master "dog" or "chair", on the other hand, it is not enough to be able to judge of each visible point whether it is on a dog or chair; we have also to learn where one dog or chair leaves off and another sets in.

In the case of such words, individuative ones, the idea of objective reference seems less trivial and more substantial. The word "dog" is taken to denote each of many things, each dog, and the word "chair", each chair. It is no longer an idle one-to-one duplication, a mirroring of each word in an object dreamed up for that exclusive purpose. The chairs and dogs are indefinite in number and individually, for the most part, nameless. The "Fido"–Fido principle, as Ryle called it, has been transcended.

However, this contrast between the individuatives and the previous words does not become detectable until a further device has become available: predication. The contrast emerges only when we are in a position to compare the predication "Fido is a dog" with the predication "Milk is white". Milk's being white comes down to the simple fact that whenever you point at milk you point at white. Fido's being a dog does not come down to the simple fact that whenever you point at Fido you point at a dog: it involves that and more. For whenever you point at Fido's head you point at a dog, and yet Fido's head does not qualify as a dog.

It is in this rather subtle way that predication creates a difference between individuative terms and others. Prior to predication, such words as "dog" and "chair" differ in no pertinent way from "milk" and "Fido"; they are simple occasion sentences that herald, indifferently, the presence of milk, Fido, dog, chair.

Thus reference may be felt to have emerged when we take to predicating individuative terms, as in "Fido is a dog". "Dog" then comes to qualify as a general term denoting each dog, and thereupon, thanks again to the predication "Fido is a dog", the word "Fido" comes at last to qualify as a singular term naming one dog. In view then of the analogy of "Milk is white" to "Fido is a dog", it becomes natural to view the word "milk" likewise as a singular term naming something, this time not a body but a substance.

In *Word and Object* and *The Roots of Reference* I have speculated on how we learn individuative terms, predication, and various further essentials of our language. I will not go further into that, but will merely remind you of what some of these further essentials are. Along with singular predication, as in "Milk is white" and "Fido is a dog", we want plural predication: "Dogs are animals". Along with monadic general terms, moreover, such as "dog" and "animal", we want dyadic ones, such as "part of", "darker than", "bigger than", and "beside"; also perhaps triadic and higher. Also we want predication of these polyadic terms, at least in the singular: thus "Mama is bigger than Fido", "Fido is darker than milk". Also we want the truth functions – "not", "and", "or" – by means of which to build compound sentences.

Now a further leap forward, as momentous as predication, is the *relative clause*. It is a way of segregating what a sentence says about an object, and packaging it as a complex general term. What the sentence

Mont Blanc is higher than the Matterhorn but the Matterhorn is steeper

says about the Matterhorn is packaged in the relative clause:

object that is not as high as Mont Blanc but is steeper.

Predicating this of the Matterhorn carries us back in effect to the original sentence.

The grammar of relative clauses can be simplified by rewriting them in the "such that" idiom:

object x such that Mont Blanc is higher than x but x is steeper.

This keeps the word order of the original sentence. The "x" is just a relative pronoun written in mathematical style. We can change the letter to avoid ambiguity in case one relative clause is embedded in another.

The relative clause serves no purpose in singular predication, since such predication just carries us back to a sentence of the original form. Where it pays off is in plural predication. Without relative clauses, the use of plural predication is cramped by shortage of general terms. We could still say "Dogs are animals" and perhaps "Small dogs are amusing animals", but it is only with the advent of relative clauses that we can aspire to such heights as "Whatever is salvaged from the wreck belongs to the state". It becomes:

Objects x such that x is salvaged from the wreck are objects x such that x belongs to the state.

In general, where "Fx" and "Gx" stand for any sentences that we are in a position to formulate about x, relative clauses open the way to the plural predication:

Objects x such that Fx are objects x such that Gx.

Once we have this equipment, we have the full benefit of universal and existential quantification. This is evident if we reflect that "$(x)Fx$" is equivalent to "(x) (if not Fx then Fx)" and hence to:

Objects x such that not Fx are objects x such that Fx.

I said that reference may be felt to emerge with the predicating of individuatives. However, it is better seen as emerging by degrees. Already at the start the sentences "Fido" and "Milk", unlike "It's raining", are learned by association with distinctively salient portions of the scene. Typically the salience is induced by pointing. Here already, in the selectivity of salience, is perhaps a first step toward the eventual namehood of "Fido" and "Milk". Predications such as "Milk is white" further enhance this air of objective reference, hinging as they do on a coinciding of saliences. Thus contrast the predication "Milk is white" with "When night falls the lamps are lit". "When" here is a connection comparable to the truth functions; it just happens to deliver standing sentences rather than occasion sentences when applied to occasion sentences. "Milk is white" likewise can be viewed as a standing sentence compounded of the occasion sentences "Milk" and "White", but it says more than "When there is milk there is white"; it says "*Where* there is milk there is white". The concentration on a special part of the scene is thus doubly emphasized, and in this I sense further rumblings of objective reference.

Predications such as "Milk is white" still afford, even so, little reason for imputing objective reference. As already remarked, we might as well continue to use the purported names as occasion sentences and let the objects go. A finite and listed ontology is no ontology.

Predication of individuatives, next, as in "Fido is a dog", heightens reference in two ways. The concentration on a special part of the scene is emphasized here more strongly still than in "Milk is white", since Fido is required not merely to be contained in the scattered part of the world that is made up of dog; he is required to fill one of its discrete blobs. And the more telling point, already noted, is that "dog" transcends the "Fido"–Fido principle; dogs are largely nameless.

Even at this stage, however, the referential apparatus and its ontology are vague. Individuation goes dim over any appreciable time interval. Thus consider the term "dog". We would recognize any particular dog in his recurrences if we noticed some distinctive trait in him; a dumb animal would do the same. We recognize Fido in his recurrences in learning the occasion sentence "Fido", just as we recognize further milk and sugar in learning "Milk" and "Sugar". Even in the absence of distinctive traits we will correctly concatenate momentary canine manifestations as stages of the same dog as long as we keep watching. After any considerable lapse of observation, however, the question of identity of unspecified dogs simply does not arise – not at the rudimentary stage of language learning. It scarcely makes sense until we are in a position to say such things as that in general if *any* dog undergoes such and such then in due course that *same* dog will behave thus and so. This sort of general talk about long-term causation becomes possible only with the advent of quantification or its equivalent, the relative clause in plural predication. Such is the dependence of individuation, in the time dimension, upon relative clauses; and it is only with full individuation that reference comes fully into its own.

With the relative clause at hand, objective reference is indeed full blown. In the relative clause the channel of reference is the relative pronoun "that" or "which", together with its recurrences in the guise of "it", "he", "her", and so on. Regimented in symbolic logic, these pronouns give way to bound variables of quantification. The variables range, as we say, over all objects; they admit all objects as values. To assume objects of some sort is to reckon objects of that sort among the values of our variables.

II

What objects, then, do we find ourselves assuming? Certainly bodies. The emergence of reference endowed the occasion sentences "Dog" and "Animal" with the status of general terms denoting bodies, and the occasion sentences "Fido" and "Mama" with the status of singular terms designating bodies.

We can see how natural it is that some of the occasion sentences ostensively learned should have been such as to foreshadow bodies, if we reflect on the social character of ostension. The child learns the occasion sentence from the mother while they view the scene from their respective vantage points, receiving somewhat unlike presentations. The mother in her childhood learned the sentence in similarly divergent circumstances. The sentence is thus bound to be versatile, applying regardless of angle. Thus it is that the aspects of a body in all their visual diversity are naturally gathered under a single occasion sentence, ultimately a single designation.

We saw how the reification of milk, wood, and other substances would follow naturally and closely on that of bodies. Bodies are our paradigmatic objects, but analogy proceeds apace; nor does it stop with substances. Grammatical analogy between general terms and singular terms encourages us to treat a general term as if it designated a single object, and thus we are apt to posit a realm of objects for the general terms to designate: a realm of properties, or sets. What with the nominalizing also of verbs and clauses, a vaguely varied and very untidy ontology grows up.

The common man's ontology is vague and untidy in two ways. It takes in many purported objects that are vaguely or inadequately defined. But also, what is more significant, it is vague in its scope; we cannot even tell in general which of these vague things to ascribe to a man's ontology at all, which things to count him as assuming. Should we regard grammar as decisive? Does every noun demand some array of denotata? Surely not; the nominalizing of verbs is often a mere stylistic variation. But where can we draw the line?

It is a wrong question; there is no line to draw. Bodies are assumed, yes; they are the things, first and foremost. Beyond them there is a succession of dwindling analogies. Various expressions come to be used in ways more or less parallel to the use of the terms for bodies, and it is felt that corresponding objects are more or less posited, *pari passu*; but there is no purpose in trying to mark an ontological limit to the dwindling parallelism.

My point is not that ordinary language is slipshod, slipshod though it be. We must recognize this grading off for what it is, and recognize that a fenced ontology is just not implicit in ordinary language. The idea of a boundary between being and nonbeing is a philosophical idea, an idea of technical science in a broad sense. Scientists and philosophers seek a comprehensive system of the world, and one that is oriented to reference even more squarely and utterly than ordinary language. Ontological concern is not a correction of a lay thought and practice; it is foreign to the lay culture, though an outgrowth of it.

We can draw explicit ontological lines when desired. We can regiment our notation, admitting only general and singular terms, singular and plural predication, truth functions, and the machinery of relative clauses; or, equivalently and more artificially, instead of plural predication and relative clauses we can admit quantification. Then it is that we can say that the objects assumed are the values of the variables, or of the pronouns. Various turns of phrase in ordinary language that seemed to invoke novel sorts of objects may disappear under such regimentation. At other points new ontic commitments may emerge. There is room for choice, and one chooses with a view to simplicity in one's overall system of the world.

More objects are wanted, certainly, than just bodies and substances. We need all sorts of parts or portions of substances. For lack of a definable stopping place, the natural course at this point is to admit as an object the material content of any portion of space-time, however irregular and discontinuous and heterogeneous. This is the generalization of the primitive and ill-defined category of bodies to what I call physical objects.

Substances themselves fall into place now as physical objects. Milk, or wood, or sugar, is the discontinuous four-dimensional physical object comprising all the world's milk, or wood, or sugar, ever.

The reasons for taking the physical objects thus spatio-temporally, and treating time on a par with space, are overwhelming and have been adequately noted in various places.[1] Let us pass over them and ponder rather the opposition to the four-dimensional view; for it is a curiosity worth looking into. Part of the opposition is obvious misinterpretation: the notion that time is stopped, change is denied, and all is frozen eternally in a fourth dimension. These are the misgivings of unduly nervous folk who over-estimate the power of words. Time as a fourth dimension is still time, and differences along the fourth dimension are still changes; they are merely treated more simply and efficiently than they otherwise might be.

Opposition has proceeded also from the venerable doctrine that not all the statements about the future have truth values now, because some of them remain, as of now, causally undetermined. Properly viewed, however, determinism is beside the point. The question of future truths is a matter of verbal convenience and is as innocuous as Doris Day's tautological fatalism "Che sarà sarà".

Another question that has been similarly linked to determinism, wrongly and notoriously, is that of freedom of the will. Like Spinoza, Hume, and so many others, I count an act as free insofar as the agent's motives or drives are a link in its causal chain. Those motives or drives may themselves be as rigidly determined as you please.

It is for me an ideal of pure reason to subscribe to determinism as fully as the quantum physicists will let me. But there are well-known difficulties in the way of rigorously formulating it. When we say of some event that it is determined by present ones, shall we mean that there is a general conditional, true but perhaps unknown to us, whose antecedent is instantiated by present events and whose consequent is instantiated by the future event in question? Without some drastic limitations on complexity and vocabulary, determinism so defined is pretty sure to boil down to "Che sarà sarà" and to afford at best a great idea for a song. Yet the idea in all its vagueness retains validity as an ideal of reason. It is valid as a general injunction: look for mechanisms.

This has been quite a spray, or spree, of philosophical miscellany. Let us now return to our cabbages, which is to say, our newly generalized physical objects. One of the benefits that the generalization confers is the accom-modation of events as objects. An action or transaction can be identified with the physical objects consisting of the temporal segment or segments of the agent or agents for the duration. Misgivings about this approach to events have been expressed, on the grounds that it does not distinguish two acts that are performed simultaneously, such as walking and chewing gum. But I think that all the distinctions that need to be drawn can be drawn, still, at the level of general terms. Not all walks are gum chewings, nor vice versa, even though an occasional one may be. Some things may be said of an act on the score of its being a walk, and distinctive things may be said of it on the score of its being a chewing of gum, even though it be accounted one and the same event. There are its crural features on the one hand and its maxillary features on the other.

A reason for being particularly glad to have accommodated events is Davidson's logic of adverbs,[2] for Davidson has shown to my satisfaction that quantification over events is far and away the best way of construing adverbial constructions.

Our liberal notion of physical objects brings out an important point about identity. Some philosophers propound puzzles as to what to say about personal identity in cases of split personality or in fantasies about metempsychosis or brain transplants. These are not questions about the nature of identity. They are questions about how we might best construe the term "person". Again there is the stock example of the ship of Theseus, rebuilt bit by bit until no original bit remained. Whether we choose to reckon it still as the same ship is a question not of "same" but of "ship"; a question of how we choose to individuate that term over time.

Any coherent general term has its own principle of individuation, its own criterion of identity among its denotata. Often the principle is vague, as the principle of individuation of persons is shown to be by the science-fiction examples; and a term is as vague as its principle of individuation.

Most of our general terms individuate by continuity considerations, because continuity favors causal connections. But even useful terms, grounded in continuity, often diverge in their individuation, as witness the evolving ship of Theseus, on the one hand, and its original substance, gradually dispersed, on the other. Continuity follows both branches.

All this should have been clear without help of our liberal notion of physical object, but this notion drives the point home. It shows how empty it would be to ask, out of context, whether a certain glimpse yesterday and a certain glimpse today were glimpses of the same thing. They may or may not have been glimpses of the same body, but they certainly were glimpses of *a* same thing, a same physical object; for the content of any portion of space-time, however miscellaneously scattered in space and time that portion be, counts as a physical object.

The president or presidency of the United States is one such physical object, though not a body. It is a spatially discontinuous object made up of temporal segments, each of which is a temporal stage also of a body, a human one. The whole thing has its temporal beginning in 1789, when George Washington took office, and its end only at the final take-over, quite possibly more than two centuries later. Another somewhat similar physical object is the Dalai Lama, an example that has been invigorated by a myth of successive reincarnation. But the myth is unnecessary.

A body is a special kind of physical object, one that is roughly continuous spatially and rather chunky and that contrasts abruptly with most of its surroundings and is individuated over time by continuity of displacement, distortion, and discoloration. These are vague criteria, especially so in view of molecular theory, which teaches that the boundary of a solid is ill defined and that the continuity of a solid is only apparent and properly a matter of degree.

The step of generalization from body to physical object follows naturally, we saw, on the reification of portions of stuff. It follows equally naturally on molecular theory: if even a solid is diffuse, why stop there?

We can be happy not to have to rest existence itself on the vague notions of body and substance, as we would have to do if bodies and substances were our whole ontology. Specific individuatives such as "dog" or "desk" continue, like "body", to suffer from vagueness on the score of the micro-physical boundaries of their denotata, as well as vagueness on the score of marginal denotata themselves, such as makeshift desks and remote ancestors of dogs; but all this is vagueness only of classification and not of existence. All the variants qualify as physical objects.

Physical objects in this generous sense constitute a fairly lavish universe, but more is wanted – notably numbers. Measurement is useful in cookery and commerce, and in the fullness of time it rises to a nobler purpose: the formulation of quantitative laws. These are the mainstay of scientific theory, and they call upon the full resources of the real numbers. Diagonals call for irrationals, circumferences call for transcendentals. Nor can we rest with constants; we must quantify over numbers. Admitting numbers as values of variables means reifying them and recognizing numerals as names of them; and this is required for the sake of generality in our quantitative laws.

Measures have sometimes been viewed as impure numbers: nine miles, nine gallons. We do better to follow Carnap[3] in construing each scale of measurement as a polyadic general term relating physical objects to pure numbers. Thus "gallon xy" means that the presumably fluid and perhaps scattered physical object x amounts to y gallons, and "mile xyz" means that the physical objects x and y are z miles apart. Pure numbers, then, apparently belong in our ontology.

Classes do too, for whenever we count things we measure a class. If a statistical generality about populations quantifies over numbers of people, it has to quantify also over the classes whose numbers those are. Quantification over classes figures also in other equally inconspicuous ways, as witness Frege's familiar definition of ancestor in terms of parent: one's ancestors are the members shared by every class that contains oneself and the parents of its members.

Sometimes in natural science we are concerned explicitly with classes, or seem to be – notably in taxonomy. We read that there are over a quarter-million species of beetles. Here evidently we are concerned with a quarter-million classes and, over and above these, a class of all these classes. However, we can economize here. Instead of talking of species in this context, we can make do with a dyadic general term applicable to beetles: "conspecific". To say that there are over a quarter-million species is equivalent to saying that there is a class of over a quarter-million *beetles* none of which are conspecific. This still conveys impressive information, and it still requires reification of a big class, but a class only of beetles and not of classes.

This way of dodging a class of classes is not always available. It worked here because species are mutually exclusive.

Note the purely auxiliary role of classes in all three examples. In counting things we are more interested in the things counted than in their class. In the genealogical example the concern is with people, their parentage and ancestry; classes entered only in deriving the one from the other. In the example of the beetles, classes were indeed out in the open – even inordinately so, I argued. But even so, it is because of an interest still strictly in beetles, not classes, that one says there are so many species. The statement tells us that beetles are highly discriminate in their mating. It conveys this sort of information, but more precisely, and it makes auxiliary reference to classes as a means of doing so. Limited to physical objects though our interests be, an appeal to classes can thus be instrumental in pursuing those interests. I look upon mathematics in general in the same way, in its relation to natural science. But to view classes, numbers, and the rest in this instrumental way is not to deny having reified them; it is only to explain why.

III

So we assume abstract objects over and above the physical objects. For a better grasp of what this means, let us consider a simple case: the natural numbers. The conditions we need to impose on them are simple and few: we need to assume an object as first number and an operator that yields a unique new number whenever applied to a number. In short, we need a progression. Any progression will do, for the following reasons. The fundamental use of natural numbers is in measuring classes: in saying that a class has n members. Other serious uses prove to be reducible to this use. But any progression will serve *this* purpose; for we can say that a class has n members by saying that its members are in correlation with the members of the progression up to n – not caring which progression it may be.

There are ways of defining specific progressions of classes, no end of ways. When we feel the need of natural numbers we can simply reach for members of one of these progressions instead – whichever one comes handy. On the basis of natural numbers, in turn, it is possible with the help of classes to define the ratios and the irrational numbers in well-known ways. On one such construction they turn out to be simply certain classes of natural numbers. So, when we feel the need of ratios and irrationals, we can simply reach for appropriate subclasses of one of the progressions of classes. We need never talk of numbers, though in practice it is convenient to carry over the numerical jargon.

Numbers, then, except as a manner of speaking, are by the board. We have physical objects and we have classes. Not just classes of physical objects, but classes of classes and so on up. Some of these higher levels are needed to do the work of numbers and other gear of applied mathematics, and one then assumes the whole hierarchy if only for want of a natural stopping place.

But now what are classes? Consider the bottom layer, the classes of physical objects. Every relative clause or other general term determines a class, the class of those physical objects of which the term can be truly predicated. Two terms determine the same class of physical objects just in case the terms are true of just the same physical objects. Still, compatibly with all this we could reconstrue every class systematically as its complement and then compensate for the switch by reinterpreting the dyadic general term "member of" to mean what had been meant by "not a member of". The effects would cancel and one would never know.

We thus seem to see a profound difference between abstract objects and concrete ones. A physical object, one feels, can be pinned down by pointing – in many cases, anyway, and to a fair degree. But I am persuaded that this contrast is illusory.

By way of example, consider again my liberalized notion of a physical object as the material content of any place-time, any portion of space-time. This was an intuitive explanation, intending no reification of space-time itself. But we could just as well reify those portions of space-time and treat of them instead of the physical objects. Or, indeed, call them physical objects. Whatever can be said from the old point of view can be paraphrased to suit the new point of view, with no effect on the structure of scientific theory or on its links with observational evidence. Wherever we had a predication "x is a P", said of a physical object x, we would in effect read "x is the place-time of a P"; actually we would just reinterpret the old "P" as "place-time of a P", and rewrite nothing.

Space separately, or place anyway, is an untenable notion. If there were really places, there would be absolute rest and absolute motion; for change of place would be absolute motion. However, there is no such objection to place-times or space-time.

If we accept a redundant ontology containing both physical objects and place-times, then we can indeed declare them distinct; but even then, if we switch the physical objects with their place-times and then compensate by reinterpreting the dyadic general term "is the material content of" to mean "is the place-time of" and vice versa, no one can tell the difference. We could choose either interpretation indifferently if we were translating from an unrelated language.

These last examples are unnatural, for they work only if the empty place-times are repudiated and just the full ones are admitted as values of the variables. If we were seriously to reconstrue physical objects as place-times, we would surely enlarge our universe to include the empty ones and thus gain the simplicity of a continuous system of coordinates.

This change in ontology, the abandonment of physical objects in favor of pure space-time, proves to be more than a contrived example. The elementary particles have been wavering alarmingly as physics progresses. Situations arise that curiously challenge the individuality of a particle, not only over time, but even at a single time. A field theory in which states are ascribed directly to place-times may well present a better picture, and some physicists think it does.

At this point a further transfer of ontology suggests itself: we can drop the space-time regions in favor of the corresponding classes of quadruples of numbers according to an arbitrarily adopted system of coordinates. We are left with just the ontology of pure set theory, since the numbers and their quadruples can be modeled within it. There are no longer any physical objects to serve as individuals at the base of the hierarchy of classes, but there is no harm in that. It is common practice in set theory nowadays to start merely with the null class, form its unit class, and so on, thus generating an infinite lot of classes, from which all the usual luxuriance of further infinites can be generated.

One may object to thus identifying the world with the output of so arbitrarily chosen a system of coordinates. On the other hand, one may condone this on the ground that no numerically specific coordinates will appear in the laws of truly theoretical physics, thanks to the very arbitrariness of the coordinates. The specificity of the coordinates would make itself known only when one descends to coarser matters of astronomy, geography, geology, and history, and here it is perhaps appropriate.

We have now looked at three cases in which we interpret or reinterpret one domain of objects by identifying it with part of another domain. In the first example, numbers were identified with some of the classes in one way or another. In the second example, physical objects were identified with some of the place-times, namely, the full ones. In the third example, place-times were identified with some of the classes, namely, classes of quadruples of numbers. In each such case simplicity is gained, if to begin with we had been saddled with the two domains.

There is a fourth example of the same thing that is worth noting, for it concerns the long-debated dualism of mind and body. I hardly need say that the dualism is unattractive. If mind and body are to interact, we are at a loss for a plausible mechanism to the purpose. Also we are faced with the melancholy office of talking physicists out of their cherished conservation laws. On the other hand, an aseptic dualistic parallelism is monumentally redundant, a monument to everything multiplicacious that William of Ockham so rightly deplored. But now it is easily seen that dualism with or without interaction is reducible to physical monism, unless disembodied spirits are assumed. For the dualist who rejects disembodied spirits is bound to agree that for every state of mind there is an exactly concurrent and readily specifiable state of the accompanying body. Readily specifiable certainly; the bodily state is specifiable simply as the state of accompanying a mind that is in that mental state. But then we can settle for the bodily states outright, bypassing the mental states in terms of which I specified them. We can just reinterpret the mentalistic terms as denoting these correlated bodily states, and who is to know the difference?

This reinterpretation of mentalistic terms is reminiscent of the treatment of events that I suggested earlier, and it raises the same question of discrimination of concurrent events. But I would just propose again the answer that I gave then.

I take it as evident that there is no inverse option here, no hope of sustaining mental monism by assigning mental states to all states of physical objects.

These four cases of reductive reinterpretation are gratifying, enabling us as they do to dispense with one of two domains and make do with the other alone. But I find the other sort of reinterpretation equally instructive, the sort where we save nothing but merely change or seem to change our objects without disturbing either the structure or the empirical support of a scientific theory in the slightest. All that is needed in either case, clearly, is a rule whereby a unique object of the supposedly new sort is assigned to each of the old objects. I call such a rule of a proxy function. Then, instead of predicating a general term "P" of an old object x, saying that x is a P, we reinterpret x as a new object and say that it is the f of a P, where "f" expresses the proxy function. Instead of saying that x is a dog, we say that x is the lifelong filament of space-time taken up by a dog. Or, really, we just adhere to the old term "P", "dog", and reinterpret it as "f of a P", "place-time of a dog". This is the strategy that we have seen in various examples.

The apparent change is twofold and sweeping. The original objects have been supplanted and the general terms reinterpreted. There has been a revision of ontology on the one hand and of ideology, so to say, on the other; they go together. Yet verbal behavior proceeds undisturbed, warranted by the same observations as before and elicited by the same observations. Nothing really has changed.

The conclusion I draw is the inscrutability of reference. To say what objects someone is talking about is to say no more than how we propose to translate his terms into ours; we are free to vary the decision with a proxy function. The translation adopted arrests the free-floating reference of the alien terms only relatively to the free-floating reference of our own terms, by linking the two.

The point is not that we ourselves are casting about in vain for a mooring. Staying aboard our own language and not rocking the boat, we are borne smoothly along on it and all is well; "rabbit" denotes rabbits, and there is no sense in asking "Rabbits in what sense of 'rabbit'?" Reference goes inscrutable if, rocking the boat, we contemplate a permutational mapping of our language on itself, or if we undertake translation.

Structure is what matters to a theory, and not the choice of its objects. F. P. Ramsey urged this point fifty years ago, arguing along other lines, and in a vague way it had been a persistent theme also in Russell's *Analysis of Matter*. But Ramsey and Russell were talking only of what they called theoretical objects, as opposed to observable objects.

I extend the doctrine to objects generally, for I see all objects as theoretical. This is a consequence of taking seriously the insight that I traced from Bentham – namely, the semantic primacy of sentences. It is occasion sentences, not terms, that are to be seen as conditioned to stimulations. Even our primordial objects, bodies, are already theoretical – most conspicuously so when we look to their individuation over time. Whether we encounter the same apple the next time around, or only another one like it, is settled if at all by inference from a network of hypotheses that we have internalized little by little in the course of acquiring the non-observational superstructure of our language.

It is occasion sentences that report the observations on which science rests. The scientific output is likewise sentential: true sentences, we hope, truths about nature. The objects, or values of variables, serve merely as indices along the way, and we may permute or supplant them as we please as long as the sentence-to-sentence structure is preserved. The scientific system, ontology and all, is a conceptual bridge of our own making, linking sensory stimulation to sensory stimulation. I am repeating what I said at the beginning.

But I also expressed, at the beginning, my unswerving belief in external things – people, nerve endings, sticks, stones. This I reaffirm. I believe also, if less firmly, in atoms and electrons and in classes. Now how is all this robust realism to be reconciled with the barren scene that I have just been depicting? The answer is naturalism: the recognition that it is within science itself, and not in some prior philosophy, that reality is to be identified and described.

The semantical considerations that seemed to undermine all this were concerned not with assessing reality but with analyzing method and evidence. They belong not to ontology but to the methodology of ontology, and thus to epistemology. Those considerations showed that I could indeed turn my back on my external things and classes and ride the proxy functions to something strange and different without doing violence to any evidence. But all ascription of reality must come rather from within one's theory of the world; it is incoherent otherwise.

My methodological talk of proxy functions and inscrutability of reference must be seen as naturalistic too; it likewise is no part of a first philosophy prior to science. The setting is still the physical world, seen in terms of the global science to which, with minor variations, we all subscribe. Amid all this there are our sensory receptors and the bodies near and far whose emanations impinge on our receptors. Epistemology, for me, or what comes nearest to it, is the study of how we animals can have contrived that very science, given just that sketchy neural input. It is this study that reveals that displacements of our ontology through proxy functions would have measured up to that neural input no less faithfully. To recognize this is not to repudiate the ontology in terms of which the recognition took place.

We *can* repudiate it. We are free to switch, without doing violence to any evidence. If we switch, then this epistemological remark itself undergoes appropriate reinterpretation too; nerve endings and other things give way to appropriate proxies, again without straining any evidence. But it is a confusion to suppose that we can stand aloof and recognize all the alternative ontologies as true in their several ways, all the envisaged worlds as real. It is a confusion of truth with evidential support. Truth is immanent, and there is no higher. We must speak from within a theory, albeit any of various.

Transcendental argument, or what purports to be first philosophy, tends generally to take on rather this status of immanent epistemology insofar as I succeed in making sense of it. What evaporates is the transcendental question of the reality of the external world – the question whether or in how far our science measures up to the *Ding an sich.*

Our scientific theory can indeed go wrong, and precisely in the familiar way: through failure of predicted observation. But what if, happily and unbeknownst, we have achieved a theory that is conformable to every possible observation, past and future? In what sense could the world then be said to deviate from what the theory claims? Clearly in none, even if we can somehow make sense of the phrase "every possible observation". Our overall scientific theory demands of the world only that it be so structured as to assure the sequences of stimulation that our theory gives us to expect. More concrete demands are empty, what with the freedom of proxy functions.

Radical skepticism stems from the sort of confusion I have alluded to, but is not of itself incoherent. Science is vulnerable to illusion on its own showing, what with seemingly bent sticks in water and the like, and the skeptic may be seen merely as overreacting when he repudiates science across the board. Experience might still take a turn that would justify his doubts about external objects. Our success in predicting observations might fall off sharply, and concomitantly with this we might begin to be somewhat successful in basing predictions upon dreams or reveries. At that point we might reasonably doubt our theory of nature in even fairly broad outlines. But our doubts would still be immanent, and of a piece with the scientific endeavor.

My attitude toward the project of a rational reconstruction of the world from sense data is similarly naturalistic. I do not regard the project as incoherent, though its motivation in some cases is confused. I see it as a project of positing a realm of entities intimately related to the stimulation of the sensory surfaces, and then, with the help perhaps of an auxiliary realm of entities in set theory, proceeding by contextual definition to construct a language adequate to natural science. It is an attractive idea, for it would bring scientific discourse into a much more explicit and systematic relation to its observational checkpoints. My only reservation is that I am convinced, regretfully, that it cannot be done.

Another notion that I would take pains to rescue from the abyss of the transcendental is the notion of a matter of fact. A place where the notion proves relevant is in connection with my doctrine of the indeterminacy of translation. I have argued that two conflicting manuals of translation can both do justice to all dispositions to behavior, and that, in such a case, there is no fact of the matter of which manual is right. The intended notion of matter of fact is not transcendental or yet epistemological, not even a question of evidence; it is ontological, a question of reality, and to be taken naturalistically within our scientific theory of the world. Thus suppose, to make things vivid, that we are settling still for a physics of elementary particles and recognizing a dozen or so basic states and relations in which they may stand. Then when I say there is no fact of the matter, as regards, say, the two rival manuals of translation, what I mean is that both manuals are compatible with all the same distributions of states and relations over elementary particles. In a word, they are physically equivalent. Needless to say, there is no presumption of our being able to sort out the pertinent distributions of microphysical states and relations. I speak of a physical condition and not an empirical criterion.

It is in the same sense that I say there is no fact of the matter of our interpreting any man's ontology in one way or, via proxy functions, in another. Any man's, that is to say, except ourselves. We can switch our own ontology too without doing violence to any evidence, but in so doing we switch from our elementary particles to some manner of proxies and thus reinterpret our standard of what counts as a fact of the matter. Factuality, like gravitation and electric charge, is internal to our theory of nature.

NOTES

This is a revised and amplified version of "What is it all about?" an essay first published by the United Chapters of Phi Beta Kappa in *The American Scholar*, Winter 1980–1981. That essay was the Gail Caldwell Stine Memorial Lecture that I gave at Mount Holyoke College in April 1980 and soon afterward at Oakland University in Michigan, Uppsala University in Sweden, and the University of Iceland. The content derived largely from two of my four Immanuel Kant Lectures (Stanford University, February 1980) and developed out of lectures that I gave ten to twelve months earlier at Tallahassee, Ann Arbor, Berkeley, Los Angeles, Madison, Louvain-la-Neuve, Aix-en-Provence, and the Collège de France under such titles as "How and why to reify" and "Les étapes de la réification".

The present version incorporates substantial passages also from three other publications: "Whither physical objects?" (*Boston Studies in the Philosophy of Science*, vol. 39, pp. 497–504, copyright © 1976, D. Reidel Publishing Co., Dordrecht, Holland), "Facts of the matter" (R. Shahan, ed., *American Philosophy from Edwards to Quine*, Norman: University of Oklahoma Press, 1977), and "The variable and its place in reference" (Z.-van Straaten, ed., *Philosophical Subjects: Essays Presented to P. F. Strawson*, Oxford: Oxford University Press, 1980). Bits are drawn also from my replies to critics in three periodicals now in press: *Sintaxis* (Montevideo), the *Southwestern Journal of Philosophy*, and *Midwest Studies in Philosophy*.

1   E.g., in my *Word and object* (Cambridge, Mass.: MIT Press, 1960), pp. 170ff.
2   "The logical form of action sentences", in *Essays on Actions and Events* (Oxford: Clarendon Press, 1980), pp. 105–22.
3   *Physikalische Begriffsbildung* (Karlsruhe, 1926).

REFERENCES

Quine, W. V. O. (1960) *Word and Object*, Cambridge, Mass.: MIT Press.
——— (1974) *The Roots of Reference*, La Salle, Ill.: Open Court.
Russell, Bertrand (1927) *Analysis of Matter*, New York.

11 Physicalism and the Indeterminacy of Translation

Michael Friedman

I

Quine's thesis of the indeterminacy of translation is probably the most well known and most widely discussed thesis in contemporary philosophy. It seems to me, however, that despite its widespread discussion both the content of the thesis and the arguments for it remain relatively unclear. I think the main reason for this unclarity is that the thesis characteristically takes two different forms: (a) an *epistemological* form, in which it concerns the relation between translation manuals and the possible evidence or data which we use to choose between such manuals, and (b) an *ontological* form, in which it concerns the relation between translation manuals and "the totality of facts" or "the whole truth about nature" – it is this latter form which is expressed by saying that there is no fact of the matter about correct translation. Because the indeterminacy thesis takes two different forms, it is difficult to evaluate arguments for it. Is a given argument an argument for indeterminacy in the first sense or the second sense? Do arguments for indeterminacy in the first sense support indeterminacy in the second sense? Etc.

The first form of the indeterminacy thesis treats the issue from an epistemological or methodological point of view. The problem is the relationship between our data and methods for selecting translation manuals, on the one hand, and the translation manual we ultimately select, on the other. In this form, the thesis makes the claim that our data and methods do not determine a unique choice of translation. There will always be incompatible translation manuals equally well supported by the totality of our evidence. This epistemological reading of the indeterminacy thesis is supported by such passages from Quine as the following:

> The linguist's finished jungle-to-English manual has as its net yield an infinite *semantic correlation* of sentences .... Most of the semantic correlation is supported only by analytical hypotheses, in their extension beyond the zone where independent evidence ... is possible. That these unverifiable translations proceed without mishap must not be taken as pragmatic evidence of good lexicography, for mishap is impossible. ([5]: 71.)

> Yet one has only to reflect on the nature of possible data and methods to appreciate the indeterminacy. Sentences translatable outright, trans-latable by independent evidence of stimulatory occasions, are sparse and

must woefully under-determine the analytical hypotheses on which the translation of all further sentences depends. ([5]: 72.)

Many discussions of the indeterminacy thesis have assumed that the main philosophical problem raised by Quine's treatment of translation is this epistemological or methodological one. Thus, we have all heard philosophers debate about what are the correct "constraints" on the methodology of translation, whether the "principle of charity" is a good methodological principle, etc. Yet this methodological debate, interesting as it is in its own right, does not address itself to the whole problem – or even the main problem – raised by Quine's work. And this is for two reasons. First, Quine repeatedly states that his point is not an epistemological one. He is not claiming merely that we can never know which is the correct translation, but that there is no correct translation that we can either know or fail to know. There is no fact of the matter as to which translation is correct or incorrect:

> The point is not that we cannot be sure whether the analytical hypothesis is right, but that there is not even ... an objective matter to be right or wrong about. ([5]: 73.)

Second, as is well known, Quine holds a more general thesis of the underdetermination of theory. He holds that not only translation theory but all of science is epistemologically undetermined by our evidence. There will always be incompatible total scientific theories equally well supported by the totality of our evidence. But the indeterminacy thesis is supposed to distinguish translation theory from the rest of science; it is supposed to point out a special defect in such linguistic notions as meaning and reference. For example, in an often referred to passage from his reply to Chomsky in *Words and Objections*, Quine says:

> Though linguistics is of course a part of the theory of nature, the indeterminacy of translation is not just inherited as a special case of the under-determination of our theory of nature. It is parallel but additional. Thus, adopt for now my fully realistic attitude toward electrons and muons and curved space-time, thus falling in with the current theory of the world despite knowing that it is in principle methodologically under-determined. Consider, from this realistic point of view, the totality of truths of nature, known and unknown, observable and unobservable, past and future. The point about indeterminacy of translation is that it withstands even all this truth, the whole truth about nature. This is what I mean by saying that, where indeterminacy of translation applies, there is no real question of right choice; there is no fact of the matter even to *within* the acknowledged under-determination of a theory of nature. ([7]: 303.)

Thus, it is clear that Quine intends to be making something more than an epistemological claim in his thesis of the indeterminacy of translation. He wants to say that not only is translation not determined by all our *evidence*, it is not even determined by all the facts there are – not determined by all the *truths* about nature. Now, this strong claim is trivially false if we don't impose some kind of limitation on what can be part of the "totality of truths of nature" – otherwise, we can simply count our preferred translation manual as part of this totality. In Quine's case, the necessary limitation derives from his physicalism. He believes that physics is our most basic and fundamental theory of the world (our "ultimate parameter") and that the totality of truths about the entities dealt with by physics represents the totality of truths that there are. Therefore, since Quine believes that the totality of truths of nature = the totality of truths of physics, the ontological version of the indeterminacy thesis amounts to the claim that translation is not determined by the set of truths of physics. Translation theory is not determined by physical theory in the way chemical theory, for example, is determined by physical theory.

In this paper I concentrate mainly on the ontological version of the indeterminacy thesis. After attempting to further clarify the distinction between the two forms of the thesis in Section II, I go on in Section III to argue that Quine has not provided us with a reason for thinking that translation theory is undetermined (in the relevant sense) by the totality of physical facts. Quine has not provided us with a reason for thinking that linguistic theory is different from any other higher-level theory – like chemistry or biology – in this respect. In short, I try to show that one can accept Quine's physicalism without accepting the indeterminacy thesis. If I am right, the issue of indeterminacy is therefore independent of the dispute between Quine and the (anti-physicalistic) Frege–Church–Carnap tradition in semantics. As I suggest in Section IV, however, there is certainly an important historical connection between Quine's rejection of the Frege–Church–Carnap tradition, on the one hand, and his advocacy of the indeterminacy thesis, on the other.

II

As stated above, neither form of the indeterminacy thesis is very clear. What is the "totality of our evidence" and the "totality of truths of physics"? What does it mean for either of these totalities to "determine" a theory? Following some hints of Quine, I will try to state the two theses more precisely.

For simplicity, I adopt the fiction that our language is an interpreted first-order language whose domain of interpretation is the set of space-time points – so all predicates are predicates of space-time points. I also suppose that our physical theory is a definite first-order theory, with a definite set of primitive predicates. Finally, I will assume that our language contains a distinguished set of observational predicates, picked out, for example, as in Quine [6]: 86–9.

Now specify, for each observational predicate "Ox" and each space-time point q, whether "Ox" is true of q. (I ignore many-place predicates, but they can obviously be treated analogously.) Such a specification will be said to be a specification of *all possible evidence*. What is it for a theory to be epistemically determined by such a specification? Sometimes Quine writes as if "epistemically determines" just means "entails" – e.g., when he states the doctrine of the underdetermination of theory in the form: there are always incompatible theories which are each compatible with all possible evidence (cf., e.g., [8]: 179). In this form, the doctrine is of course trivially true for any theory that essentially contains non-observational predicates. At other times, Quine states the doctrine in the stronger form: there are incompatible theories which are each compatible with all possible evidence *and* equally in accordance with "the ideal organon of scientific method" (cf., e.g., [5]: 22). This stronger form of the doctrine suggests that Quine uses "epistemically determine" in such a way that a theory is epistemically determined just in case it is compatible with all possible evidence and there is no incompatible theory which is equally in accordance with "the ideal organon of scientific method." This latter sense of "epistemically determine" is clearly more interesting, although vaguer, than the first; but for present purposes it doesn't really matter which sense we use. So from now on I'll let "epistemically determine" be ambiguous as between the stronger and the weaker sense.

What about determination by the truths of physics? (Call this *ontological* determination.) We can start by specifying for each primitive predicate of physics "Px" and each space-time point q, whether "Px" is true of q (again, I ignore many-place predicates). Such a specification will be said to be a specification of *the totality of truths of physics*. What is it for a theory to be (ontologically) determined by such a specification? First of all, it is clear that one way a theory can be determined by physics is by being *reducible* to physics in the classical sense. A theory is reducible to physics in this sense if each predicate of the theory is coextensive with a predicate of physics and the laws of physics constrain the corresponding physical predicates to satisfy the theory. To be a little more precise: Let T_1 be physics, T_2 the theory to be reduced, and "F_1x", "$F_2 x$", ..., "F_nx" the primitive predicates of T_2. (I continue to ignore many-place predicates.) Let a *physical interpretation* be a mapping α which associates each "F_1x" with an open sentence containing only physical predicates, α ("F_1x") = "A_ix". For any sentence containing only predicates from among "F_1x", "F_2x", ..., "F_nx", we can define *truth under the interpretation* α and *satisfaction under* α – they are defined just like satisfaction and truth, except that the clause for *atomic* formulas now reads:

A sequence σ satisfies "F_ix" under α iff σ satisfies α ("F_ix").

Thus, T_2 is *strongly* (classically) *reducible* to T_1 *if there is a physical interpretation* α of T_2's primitive predicates such that for each predicate "F_ix" and each space-time point q, "F_1x" is true of q just in case α ("F_ix") is true of q (coextensiveness) and T_2 comes out true under α in every model of T_1.

However, it is also clear that there are more general ways in which a theory can be determined by physics. One such way emerges from the debate between identity theorists and functionalists in the philosophy of mind. The identity theorist argues that the relationship between mental and physical predicates is to be construed analogously to "theoretical identifications" like water = H_2O and temperature = mean kinetic energy. He thinks that mental predicates are explicitly definable in terms of physical predicates and, therefore, that psychology is strongly reducible to physics. The functionalist, on the other hand, argues against explicit definability. He argues, for example, that there is no one physical state that is always present when someone is in pain. To say that someone is in pain is to say that he is in some state or other which has the functional role characteristic of pain, and there are an indefinite number of distinct physical states that can play that functional role. Nevertheless, the functionalist thinks that each particular instance of a mental state is identical with some particular physical state; mental states are "realized" by particular physical states.

Can we make the kind of physical determination which the functionalist argues for more precise? The crucial difference between the identity theorist and the functionalist is that the identity theorist thinks that each mental predicate corresponds to a single physical predicate, while the functionalist thinks that each mental predicate corresponds to an indefinite number of physical predicates. Thus, it is natural to generalize the classical notion of reduction by associating each non-physical predicate, not with a single physical predicate, but with a *set* of physical predicates: Let "$F_1 x$", "$F_2 x$", ..., "$F_n x$" again be the primitive predicates of the theory to be reduced. Let a *physical realization* be a mapping β which associates each "$F_i x$" with a set of open sentences containing only physical predicates, β ("$F_i x$") = {"$A_i^1 x$", "$A_i^2 x$", ...}. For any sentence containing only predicates from among "$F_1 x$", "$F_2 x$", ..., "$F_n x$", we can define *truth under the realization* β and *satisfaction under* β – they are defined just like satisfaction and truth, except that the clause for *atomic* formulas now reads:

> A sequence σ satisfies "$F_i x$" under β iff there exists an "$A_i^j x$" ε β("$F_i x$") such that σ satisfies "$A_i^j x$".

Let us now define weak reducibility analogously to the above definition of strong reducibility: A theory is *weakly reducible* to physics if there is a physical realization β of its primitive predicates such that for each predicate "$F_i x$" and each space-time point q, "$F_i x$" is true of q just in case some "$A_i^j x$", in β("$F_i x$") is true of q ("$F_i x$" is not coextensive with any single physical predicate, but rather with a "disjunction" – possibly infinite – of physical predicates) and in every model of physics the theory comes out true under β.

I don't know if there are other kinds of physical determination besides these two kinds, if there are other kinds of physical determination besides what I have called weak and strong reduction. However, I hope that it will become clear in the course of my discussion that it is these two kinds of physical determination which are most relevant to what Quine says about the indeterminacy of translation. So from now on I will interpret "physical determination" as "weak or strong reduction" and interpret physicalism as the doctrine that all "respectable" predicates and theories must be weakly or strongly reducible to physics. Quine's complaint against linguistics and translation theory, then, is that they unlike other higher-level theories – fail to be (strongly or weakly) reducible to physics.

If all this is a fair interpretation of what Quine means by "being determined by all possible evidence" and "being determined by the totality of truths of nature" respectively, it follows that the two forms of the indeterminacy thesis are very different. First of all, the two forms of the thesis concern relations between different terms. The epistemological form of the thesis concerns a relation between translation theory and a specification for each *observational* predicate "Ox", and each space-time point q, whether "Ox" is true of q. The ontological form of the thesis concerns a relation between translation theory and an analogous specification for each *physical* predicate. Secondly, the relations referred to are different. The first version concerns a relation of epistemic determination (understood ambiguously as above); the second version concerns a non-epistemic relation of (weak or strong) reducibility.

Furthermore, although if we interpret "epistemically determines" as "entails" and assume that all observational predicates are physically determined, the ontological version of the thesis implies the epistemological version; the epistemological version definitely does not imply the ontological version. From the fact that a given theory is not epistemically determined by all observational truths, it by no means follows that it is not ontologically determined by all physical truths. Indeed, if Quine is right about the underdetermination of theory, there exist theories today which are ontologically determined but not epistemically determined. Chemical theory, for example, is, like all theory, not uniquely determined by all possible evidence; yet it is (strongly?) reducible to physics and is therefore ontologically determined – there is a fact of the matter about chemistry. Consequently, it would seem that arguments for the weaker, epistemological, version of the thesis do not go very far, if at all, towards supporting the stronger, ontological, version. Readers of *Word and Object* are therefore justifiably puzzled, I think, by the fact that most of Quine's discussion of translation is occupied with epistemological and methodological issues – issues which have no obvious connection with the more interesting question of whether there is a fact of the matter about translation, whether translation theory is physically determined. In fact, it is hard to find any passage in Quine's writings which is clearly an argument for the ontological version of the indeterminacy thesis. Nevertheless, I think Quine does have an argument for the claim that translation theory is not physically determined. I will examine it in the next section.

III

Quine's clearest and most explicit argument for the indeterminacy thesis is found in "On the reasons for indeterminacy of translation" [8]. There he uses the doctrine of underdetermination of theory to argue for indeterminacy in the following way. If underdetermination is true, there can be two incompatible total theories A and B formulable in our language which are both equally well supported by all possible true observation sentences of our language. Therefore, if we translate a foreign speaker's observation sentences – by matching their stimulus meanings with the stimulus meanings of our observation sentences – and thus determine which observation sentences (in our language) he accepts, we still haven't determined which theoretical sentences (in our language) he accepts. We are free to translate his theoretical sentences in such a way that he comes out as holding either theory *A* or theory *B*, because *A* and *B* are supported equally well by all possible observation sentences in the foreign speaker's language:

> Insofar as the truth of a physical theory is underdetermined by observables, the translation of the foreigner's physical theory is under-determined by translation of his observation sentences. If our physical theory can vary though all possible observations be fixed, then our translation of his physical theory can vary though our translations of all possible observation reports on his part be fixed. Our translation of his observation sentences no more fixes our translation of his physical theory than our own possible observations fix our own physical theory. ([8]: 179–80.)

This argument is a little more complicated than it first appears, because of the possible ambiguity of "fix". On the one hand, the observation sentences we accept do not epistemically determine for us (fix) the theoretical sentences we accept. On the other hand, the observation sentences the foreigner accepts do not epistemically determine for him (fix) the theoretical sentences he accepts. The conclusion Quine wants to derive from this is that our translation of the foreigner's observation sentences does not epistemically determine for us (fix) our translation of his theoretical sentences. It would seem that some such principle as: if S_1 does not epistemically determine S_2 for person P_1, then "P_1 believes S_1" does not epistemically determine "P_1 believes S_2" for person P_2, is required. In any case, I will assume that some such principle is plausible and that con-sequently Quine's argument that our translation of a foreign speaker's observation sentences does not epistemically determine (for us) our translation of his theoretical sentences is valid (given the assumption of the underdetermination of theory, of course).

How does the above argument support the indeterminacy thesis? Consider first the epistemological form of the thesis. The conclusion of the above argument is that our translation of a foreigner's observation sentences does not epistemically determine our translation of his theoret-ical sentences. What the (epistemological) indeterminacy thesis says is that all possible evidence does not epistemically determine our translation of his theoretical sentences. Now there are two important things to notice about the relation between all possible evidence, on the one hand, and the translation of observation sentences, on the other. First, the translation of observation sentences itself goes beyond all possible evidence in the strict sense – it is not determined by the totality of observational facts. Let us call a predicate "*Bx*" a *behavioral* predicate if "*Bx*" is true of *q* just in case there is an organism *O* at *q*, a stimulation σ, and an item of observable behavior β, such that if *O* were to receive σ, *O* would emit β. That is, "*Bx*" is a behavioral predicate just in case it attributes a behavioral disposition to some organism. In *Word and Object*, Quine shows that the translation of observation sentences is determined by behavioral facts, by the distribution of true behavioral predicates over space-time points. However, behavioral predicates are not themselves observational, nor are they determined by all possible observational facts (cf., e.g., [5]: 222–6). The attribution of a behavioral predicate essentially involves a (low-level) theoretical inference. Thus, Quine's conclusion is strictly stronger than the epistemological indeterminacy thesis as I have stated it. Not only is translation under-determined by the observational facts, it is not even determined by the totality of observational *and behavioral* facts.

Secondly, however, it is not clear that the translation of observation sentences exhausts the available evidence. Quine has shown (let us assume) that the translation of observation sentences does not determine the translation of theoretical sentences, and that the translation of observation sentences *is* determined by the observational + behavioral facts. To get the required conclusion – that the translation of theoretical sentences is *not* determined by the observational + behavioral facts – we need an additional premise to the effect that the translation of observation sentences is all the evidence that could possibly be relevant to the translation of theoretical sentences. And this is at least not obviously true – e.g., there could conceivably be non-linguistic behavioral facts that would be relevant to the translation of theoretical sentences. However, Quine himself certainly thinks that it is true:

> In order . . . to construe the foreigner's theoretical sentences we have to project analytical hypotheses, whose ultimate justification is substantially just that the implied observation sentences match up. ([8]: 179.)

Be this as it may, I will again assume that Quine has at least made this crucial claim plausible and that the above argument does support the epistemic version of the indeterminacy thesis (strengthened to include behavioral as well as strictly observational evidence as above).

What then of the non-epistemological form of the indeterminacy thesis? The first difficulty is that the argument I have been considering appears to deal exclusively with epistemic determination. However, we can immediately connect it up with ontological (reductive) determination if we assume that if a set of truths $\mathcal{S}$ ontologically determines a theory T, then $\mathcal{S}$ could, in principle anyway, epistemically determine T (since the truth and falsity of each sentence in T is settled by $\mathcal{S}$); and that consequently if $\mathcal{S}$ could not in principle epistemically determine T, then $\mathcal{S}$ does not ontologically determine T. The argument then gives us the result that the totality of observational + behavioral facts does not ontologically determine the translation of theoretical sentences (where determination by observational + behavioral facts is defined just like determination by physical facts, except that "observational or behavioral predicate" is substituted everywhere for "physical predicate"). The translation of theoretical sentences is not (strongly or weakly) reducible to facts about behavior, to facts about dispositions to assent and dissent given various sensory stimulations.

It seems to me that this last conclusion is both extremely plausible in its own right and quite well supported by Quine's arguments. However, it is still very far from the strong, ontological, form of the indeterminacy thesis. For, according to that form of the thesis, translation (of theoretical sentences) is not ontologically determined by any physical facts at all. And there are a lot more physical facts than facts about dispositions to assent and dissent given various sensory stimulations; there are a lot more physical facts than behavioral facts. (The set of observational + behavioral predicates is only a small fraction of the set of physically determined predicates.) Therefore, it would seem that if the argument we have been considering is to have any relevance to the strong indeterminacy thesis, we have to adopt some form of behaviorism about linguistics and translation theory. We have to suppose that the only physical facts that could be relevant to the reduction of translation theory to physics are behavioral facts. Furthermore, it seems clear that Quine himself holds such a behaviorist view of linguistics:

> When with Dewey we turn thus toward a naturalistic view of language and a behavioral view of meaning, what we give up is not just the museum figure of speech. We give up an assurance of determinacy .... When ... we recognize with Dewey that "meaning ... is primarily a property of behavior," we recognize that there are no meanings, nor likenesses nor distinctions of meaning, beyond what are implicit in people's dispositions to overt behavior. For naturalism the question whether two expressions are alike or unlike in meaning has no determinate answer, known or unknown, except insofar as the answer is settled in principle by people's speech dispositions, known or unknown. ([6]: 28–9).

If this is correct, then attempts like Harman's [2] to separate the indeterminacy thesis from behaviorism are misguided. Not only does Quine explicitly link his thesis to behaviorism, but without some sort of behavioristic assumption to the effect that the only facts that could be relevant to translation are behavioral facts, Quine's argument for the strong indeterminacy thesis is simply a *non-sequitur* – since the totality of physical facts ≠ the totality of behavioral facts. However, Harman is certainly right to insist that Quine's argument is not based on a general assumption of philosophical behaviorism – an assumption that *all* mental facts must be behavioristically reducible. Rather, Quine has special reasons for thinking that behaviorism is true for specifically *linguistic* facts. I will examine these reasons in what follows.

Let me first briefly review the situation. Quine wants to claim not only that there can be no grounds for choosing a unique correct translation, but that there is no objective fact to be right or wrong about. And what he means by this latter claim seems to be that there are no physical facts that determine what the correct translation is; translation theory is not determined by physics. However, the argument we have considered so far at most gives us the conclusion that there are no behavioral facts that determine what the correct translation is; translation theory is not determined by purely behavioral facts. Therefore, it is natural for someone (like myself) who agrees with Quine's physicalism but not with the indeterminacy thesis to suppose that there are other, physical but non-behavioral, facts which do determine translation, that there are non-behavioral physical facts to which translation theory is reducible. Plausible candidates for such facts are facts relating our uses of words to our internal (physiological) states, facts relating our uses of words to external physical objects (as so-called "causal" theories of reference suggest), etc. If Quine is to make a convincing case for indeterminacy, he must give us some reason to think that such non-behavioral facts are not relevant to reducing translation theory and that, consequently, since behavioral facts do not suffice to determine translation, nothing does.

I think Quine has several related arguments for the claim that only behavioral factors are relevant. The first appeals to the fact that one learns language on the basis of the observable behavior of others: In learning a language, all the facts one has access to are facts involving the observable behavior of speakers of the language. One doesn't have access to non-behavioral facts, such as facts about the speakers' internal neural states. If there were linguistic facts which were determined by non-behavioral factors (like internal neural states) but not by behavioral factors, these facts could not be learned in the course of acquiring a language. Therefore, all linguistic facts must be determined solely on the basis of observable behavior. This kind of argument is suggested by passages like the following:

> Meanings are, first and foremost, meanings of language. Language is a social art which we all acquire on the evidence solely of other people's overt behavior under publicly recognizable circumstances. Meanings, therefore, those very models of mental entities, end up as grist for the behaviorist's mill. Dewey was explicit on the point: "Meaning ... is not a psychic existence; it is primarily a property of behavior." ([6]: 26–7.)

> Language is a social art. In acquiring it we have to depend entirely on intersubjectively available cues as to what to say and when. Hence there is no justification for collating linguistic meanings, unless in terms of men's dispositions to respond overtly to socially observable stimulations. An effect of recognizing this limitation is that the enterprise of translation is found to be involved in a certain systematic indeterminacy .... ([5]: ix.)

At first sight, this argument appears to rest on a simple confusion between epistemic determination and ontological determination. From the premise that linguistic facts are epistemically determined by behavioral facts alone, it by no means follows that they must be ontologically determined by behavioral facts alone (unless we adopt an extremely strong version of "epistemically determines"). However, we can easily rephrase the argument in a way which doesn't confuse the two forms of determination (which doesn't require us to assume that epistemically determines = entails) as follows: All linguistic facts must be epistemically determined by behavioral factors alone, since these are all that are available in acquiring a language. Anything not epistemically determined by behavioral factors cannot be a linguistic fact, cannot be a fact about meaning. But we know from the epistemic indeterminacy thesis that the translation of theoretical sentences is not epistemically determined by behavioral factors; behavioral factors do not epistemically determine a unique, distinguished meaning for each theoretical sentence. Therefore, there are no linguistic facts determining the translation of theoretical sentences. Non-behavioral factors, like internal neural states, are consequently irrelevant to the translation of theoretical sentences. Non-behavioral facts cannot be *linguistic* facts.

I think what is wrong with this argument is the premise that linguistic facts must be epistemically determined by behavioral facts. It is certainly true that the only evidence we have available to us in acquiring language is the observable behavior of others; we learn language by something like an inference from other speakers' behavior. But it doesn't follow that this inference has to be epistemically determined (especially if we interpret "epistemically determines" in a very strong sense). On the contrary, it is plausible to view this inference as analogous to an inductive or theoretical inference and, as such, subject to the usual inductive or theoretical underdetermination. (In this connection, remember that even the attribution of behavioral dispositions involves a theoretical inference.) We learn language on the basis of other people's observable behavior, and we learn facts about electrons on the basis of the behavior of ordinary observable objects. In neither case is the former epistemically determined (much less ontologically determined) by the latter. Thus, the fact that we learn language on the *basis* of observable behavior gives us no reason to think that all linguistic facts must be epistemically (or ontologically) *determined* by facts about behavior.

A second Quinean argument again starts from the fact that one learns language by a social process which establishes conditioned relations between one's linguistic behavior and sensory stimulations. According to this argument, one has successfully mastered a language – one can communicate in that language – when the conditioned relations between one's linguistic behavior and sensory stimulations match up sufficiently with those of other speakers of the language. Now, non-behavioral factors (internal physiological states, "causal" relations to external objects, etc.) can vary arbitrarily as long as these conditioned relations are preserved. Such other factors, therefore, cannot be linguistically relevant; they cannot be relevant to the physical determination of translation. Quine appears to give a version of this argument in the following passage:

> The sort of meaning that is basic to translation, and to the learning of one's own language, is necessarily empirical [= behavioral] meaning and nothing more. A child learns his first words and sentences by hearing and using them in the presence of appropriate stimuli. These must be external stimuli, for they must act both on the child and on the speaker from whom he is learning. Language is socially inculcated and controlled; the inculcation and control turn strictly on the keying of sentences to shared stimulation. Internal factors may vary *ad libitum* without prejudice to communication as long as the keying of language to external stimuli is undisturbed. Surely one has no choice but to be an empiricist [= behaviorist] so far as one's theory of linguistic meaning is concerned. ([6]: 81.)

In this passage, Quine refers only to non-behavioral internal facts, but he would presumably make the same point about non-behavioral external facts like "causal" relations with external objects.

I don't think this argument is convincing. First of all, it at most shows that translation is not *strongly* determined by non-behavioral physical facts, that linguistic notions like meaning and reference are not explicitly definable in terms of non-behavioral physical predicates. The possibility remains open that such linguistic notions are *weakly* determined by nonbehavioral physical predicates, and that translation theory is therefore *weakly* reducible to physics. Suppose it were true that non-behavioral factors vary freely from speaker to speaker, and even vary from occasion to occasion with the same speaker. It would follow that linguistic notions could not be defined in terms of such non-behavioral factors, for different non-behavioral factors would underlie the same linguistic behavior at different times. However, we could still consistently suppose that each instance of linguistic behavior is determined by some physical, but non-behavioral, fact about the speaker. We could suppose that linguistic behavior is weakly, but not strongly, determined by physical facts. To return to the analogy with the philosophy of mind, Quine's argument shows at most that notions like meaning and reference have to be understood *functionally* relative to physical predicates, not that they have to be understood *behavioristically*. Note that the functionalist is no more a behaviorist than the identity theorist is. He does not expect that any interesting part of human behavior (including linguistic behavior) can be understood in purely behavioral terms.

Secondly, I don't think that Quine's argument even establishes that translation is not *strongly* determined by non-behavioral factors, that linguistic notions are not explicitly definable in terms of physical ones. For, in this connection, the crucial question is not whether non-behavioral factors could in principle vary arbitrarily, but whether they do in fact. Imagine for a moment that translation theory is at least weakly reducible to physics, so that there are physical predicates which realize such linguistic notions as meaning and reference. The only remaining question for the issue of strong reducibility is whether the physical predicates which realize the linguistic predicates vary from case to case or not. If the physical predicates vary sufficiently, linguistics will fail to be strongly reducible to physics; if not, linguistics will be strongly reducible. Nothing at all follows from the mere *possibility* that the physical predicates vary arbitrarily.

Imagine someone arguing that chemical structure cannot be relevant to explaining the observable properties of tap water, river water, sea water, etc., because it is in principle possible for such chemical structure to vary arbitrarily from case to case as long as the same observable properties are preserved. This would obviously be a *non sequitur*. For, first, even if chemical structure does vary arbitrarily, it may still be relevant to explaining the observable properties of water. It may weakly determine the properties of water even if it doesn't strongly determine them. Second, the issue is not what is in principle possible but what is in fact the case. And, as a matter of fact, all instances of water do share a similar chemical structure, a chemical structure which explains the similarity in their observable properties. I think the case of linguistics and translation theory is analogous. The issue is whether such non-behavioral factors as internal physiological states and external relations with physical objects are relevant to explaining linguistic behavior, and thus relevant to reducing translation theory to a physical basis. From the claim that such factors *may* vary arbitrarily while linguistic behavior is preserved, it by no means follows that they *do*. And even if non-behavioral factors do vary arbitrarily, it doesn't follow that they can't be relevant to explaining linguistic behavior and physically determining linguistic theory.

Thus, it seems to me that the central issue underlying the debate over whether there is a fact of the matter about translation is an empirical one – it is not something that can be settled by philosophical argument. The issue is whether there are non-behavioral physical facts which are sufficient to (weakly or strongly) reduce linguistics and translation theory to physical science. At best, therefore, what Quine is doing is betting on the future course of science. Quine is betting that science will not uncover such facts and that consequently only behavioral facts will prove explanatorily relevant. Quine's opponents are betting that science will uncover such facts. Given Quine's general philosophical orientation, it should perhaps not be too disturbing that the thesis of indeterminacy of translation turns out to be a guess as to the future progress of science. What is more disturbing is that it seems we have been given no reason for preferring Quine's guess to its opposite.

IV

Quine's attitude towards most of linguistic theory, particularly towards such semantical notions as meaning and reference, is basically one of skepticism. This skepticism has both epistemological and ontological motivations. On the one hand, Quine despairs of finding evidence that would enable one to decide between alternative, mutually incompatible imputations of meanings or of referents. On the other hand, he despairs of finding physical facts to which such notions as meaning and reference can be (weakly or strongly) reduced – in the way that, for example, there are physical facts to which such chemical notions as valence can be reduced. And, for a physicalist, if there are no physical facts underlying a given area of discourse, there are no objective facts at all. As I indicated above, I think that the second, ontologically motivated, form of skepticism is the most serious form, especially since I am in sympathy with Quine's physicalism. I also think – and I have tried to show above – that Quine's direct arguments for this kind of skepticism are far from conclusive. Nevertheless, it seems to me that Quinean skepticism becomes both understandable and plausible when viewed in its historical context.

In pre-Quinean philosophy of language, we find two main traditions. First, there is the verificationist tradition, which views the connection between language and sense experience as the most important semantical relation. Second, there is the Frege–Church–Carnap tradition, which explains the semantical properties of language by postulating such entities as concepts and propositions – where these latter are thought of as either irreducibly mental entities or abstract entities. Now, as a naturalist, Quine clearly could not be happy with this latter type of approach, because of its promiscuous postulation of scientifically unrespectable entities. (Quine, of course, is not opposed to postulating abstract entities *per se*. He thinks – reluctantly – that we should postulate all mathematical entities necessary for the mathematics of physics. Because of his physicalism, however, he would oppose the postulation of any *special* abstract entities – like concepts or propositions – which are not part of the ontology required by physical science.) On the other hand, the prospects for making scientific sense out of the verificationist approach to language appeared distinctly better. In fact, I think that one of Quine's major contributions is the way he shows how to put the verificationist tradition into a naturalistic setting – by means of the behavioral concepts of stimulus meaning, observation sentence, etc. However, Quine also saw what none of the earlier verificationists did, namely, that a consistent and physicalistically respectable verificationism (i.e., behaviorism) leads to skepticism about semantics, leads to the indeterminacy of translation and the inscrutability of reference (cf. [6]: 80–1).

If this is correct, Quine's naturalism led him to verificationism, and his naturalized verificationism led him to skepticism. Since I think that a naturalistic approach to language is salutary, I think that if we want to reject Quinean skepticism, we should reject his verificationism, not his physicalism. According to Quine, the only semantically relevant physical facts are behavioral ones – facts relating linguistic behavior to sensory stimulation – and these facts are insufficient to make sense of such traditional linguistic notions as meaning and reference. If we want to reject skepticism but retain naturalism, we have to look for other, possibly non-behavioral, physical facts to which these semantic notions can plausibly be (weakly or strongly) reduced. This latter type of program can be looked at as a type of "reductive physicalism" in contrast to Quine's "eliminative physicalism." (As these labels suggest, I view this issue as importantly analogous to the dispute between "reductive materialism" and "eliminative materialism" in the philosophy of mind – and I classify both identity theorists and functionalists as "reductive materialists", since both think that mental states are realized by physical states. The "reductive materialist" thinks that mental states and properties are identified with, or at least realized by, physical states and properties; the "eliminative materialist" thinks that mental states and properties do not have such a physical basis and that they should therefore be eliminated from scientific discourse. Similarly, the "reductive physicalist" in semantics thinks that semantic notions are scientifically respectable, for they are (weakly or strongly) reducible to purely physical ones; the "eliminative physicalist" – Quinean skeptic – thinks that semantic notions are not physicalistically reducible and that they are therefore not scientifically respectable.)

What would such a "reductive physicalism" look like? I think that one kind of answer is suggested by recent work on so-called "causal" theories of reference. According to this type of view, there are physical relations between our uses of words and physical objects in virtue of which words refer to the objects that they do refer to. There are physical relations between our use of the word "Socrates" and Socrates in virtue of which "Socrates" refers to Socrates; there are physical relations between our use of the word "red" and red things in virtue of which "red" applies to red things, etc. This type of view contrasts with the traditional Frege–Church–Carnap theory according to which reference is determined by the (non-physical) sense of an expression. It also contrasts with the Quinean skeptical approach according to which the only semantically relevant physical relations between words and non-linguistic entities relate our uses of words to sensory stimulations, stimulus meanings. Since different referents can yield the same stimulus meanings, we end up with the doctrine of inscrutability of reference. On the other hand, if we look at things from the point of view of a broader physicalism, the possibility of referential determinacy is restored. Thus, for example, if we suppose that the reference relation can be reduced to a certain physical relation R, we may find that R holds between a given tribe's use of the word "gavagai" and rabbits, while R does not hold between their use of the word "gavagai" and rabbit stages. (An analogous possibility exists if reference is realized, not by a single physical relation R, but by a set of physical relations $\{R_1, R_2, \ldots\}$.) This would give an objective sense to saying that "gavagia" refers to rabbits but not rabbit stages.

It is tempting for critics of this kind of physicalistic view of reference to adopt a "put up or shut up" attitude, to demand more information about the nature of this mysterious relation R (or about the set of mysterious relations $\{R_1, R_2, \ldots\}$ if weak reducibility is preferred) before taking the view seriously. This attitude, I think, is mistaken. Spelling out the precise nature of such a relation (or set of relations) is not a job for philosophers. Actually carrying out a physicalistic reduction of semantic notions like reference, if it is to be carried out at all, is a task for empirical scientists – for linguists and psychologists. (For this reason I don't think it is particularly helpful to call the view I am considering a "causal" theory of reference. Not only is the notion of causal connection itself notoriously unclear, but we are simply not in a position today to have much of a theory about the reference relation – just as we are not in a position today to have much of a theory about the brain processes underlying our psychological states. What is important – and I think the contrast with Quine's views shows this – is that reference is seen as a *physical* relation between our uses of words and the objects they refer to.) What a philosophical proponent of this kind of program can do is: (1) try to disarm philosophical arguments purporting to show that the intended reduction is in principle impossible (like the Quinean argument I considered above purporting to show that only behavioral facts could be semantically relevant), (2) argue that it is plausible that semantic notions should be so reducible, (3) argue that looking at semantic notions from a "reductive physicalist" point of view illuminates traditional philosophical issues – notably the concept of truth (cf. [1]), (4) try to show that such a point of view contrasts favorably with other philosophical attitudes towards semantics (cf., e.g., [3], [4]). Again, I think the analogy with the philosophy of mind is helpful. It is not up to the philosophical defender of "reductive materialism" to say precisely which neurophysiological states are to be identified with (are to realize) which mental states. What he can do, rather, is argue for the possibility and plausibility of the envisioned reduction, argue that looking at things from his point of view illuminates traditional disputes in the philosophy of mind, argue that his point of view contrasts favorably with other philosophical views such as dualism and analytical behaviorism, etc.

In conclusion, I think that Quine's skeptical attitude towards semantics is best seen as falling naturally into one of three important traditions in the philosophy of language. The verificationist tradition, of which Quine's views are a natural extension, sees the connection between language and sense-experience as centrally, and perhaps exclusively, important for semantics. The Frege–Church–Carnap tradition sees the postulation of special abstract entities such as concepts and propositions as necessary for understanding language. The theory-of-reference type of approach sees the (physical) relation between language and physical objects as centrally important. My own sympathies are obvious. Because I share Quine's naturalism, I find the Frege–Church–Carnap tradition barren and unfruitful, while the theory-of-reference approach impresses me as the most promising. Nevertheless, it is certainly true that I have here given the reader no grounds for choosing one of the three approaches over the others. What I have attempted to do, however, is show that Quine has not given us a reason to think we have no choice but skepticism.[1]

NOTE

1   I am indebted to discussions with and advice from Hartry Field, Warren D. Goldfarb, Robert Harding, and David Hills.

REFERENCES

[1]   Field, H., "Tarski's theory of truth," *Journal of Philosophy* 69(1972): 347–75.
[2]   Harman, G., "An introduction to 'Translation and meaning'," in *Words and Objections*, ed. by D. Davidson and J. Hintikka (Dordrecht: D. Reidel, 1969): 14–26.
[3]   Kripke, S., "Naming and necessity," in *Semantics of Natural Language*, ed. by D. Davidson and G. Harman (Dordrecht: D. Reidel, 1972): 253–355.
[4]   Putnam, H., "Meaning and reference," *Journal of Philosophy* 70 (1973): 699–711.
[5]   Quine, W. V., *Word and Object* (Cambridge, Mass.: MIT Press, 1960).
[6]   ——, *Ontological Relativity and Other Essays* (New York: Columbia University Press, 1969).
[7]   ——, "Reply to Chomsky," in *Words and Objections*, ed. by D. Davidson and J. Hintikka (Dordrecht: D. Reidel, 1969): 302–11.
[8]   ——, "On the reasons for indeterminacy of translation," *Journal of Philosophy* 67(1970): 178–83.

12 Why There Isn't a Ready-made World

Hilary Putnam

Two ideas that have become a part of our philosophical culture stand in a certain amount of conflict. One idea, which was revived by Moore and Russell after having been definitely sunk by Kant and Hegel (or so people thought), is metaphysical realism, and the other is that there are no such things as intrinsic or "essential" properties. Let me begin by saying a word about each.

What the metaphysical realist holds is that we can think and talk about things as they are, independently of our minds, and that we can do this by virtue of a "correspondence" relation between the terms in our language and some sorts of mind-independent entities. Moore and Russell held the strange view that *sensibilia* (sense data) are such *mind-independent* entities: a view so dotty, on the face of it, that few analytic philosophers like to be reminded that this is how analytic philosophy started. Today material objects are taken to be paradigm mind-independent entities, and the "correspondence" is taken to be some sort of causal relation. For example, it is said that what makes it the case that I refer to chairs is that I have causally interacted with them, and that I would not utter the utterances containing the word "chair" that I do if I did not have causal transactions "of the appropriate type" with chairs. This complex relationship – being connected with x by a causal chain of the appropriate type – between my word (or way of using the word) and x constitutes the relevant *correspondence* between my word and x. On this view, it is no puzzle that we can refer to physical things, but reference to numbers, sets, moral values, or anything not "physical" is widely held to be problematical if not actually impossible.

The second doctrine, the doctrine that there are no essential properties, is presaged by Locke's famous rejection of "substantial forms". Locke rejected the idea that the terms we use to classify things (e.g., "man" or "water") connote properties which are in any sense the "real essences" of those things. Whereas the medievals thought that the real essence of water was a so-called substantial form, which exists both in the thing and (*minus* the matter) in our minds, Locke argued that what we have in our minds is a number of conventional marks (e.g., being liquid) which we have put together into a descriptive idea because of certain interests we have, and that any assumption that these marks are the "real essence" of anything we classify under the idea is unwarranted.

Later empiricists went further and denied there was any place for the notion of an essence at all. Here is a typical way of arguing this case: "Suppose a piece of clay has been formed into a statue. We are sure the piece of clay would not be what it is (a piece of clay) if it were dissolved, or separated into its chemical elements, or cut into five pieces. We can also say the *statue* would not be what it is (*that* statue) if the clay were squeezed into a ball (or formed into a different statue). But the piece of clay and the statue are *one* thing, not two. What this shows is that it only makes sense to speak of an "essential property" of something *relative to a description*. Relative to the description "that statue", a certain shape is an essential property of the object; relative to the description "that piece of clay", the shape is *not* an essential property (but being clay is). The question "what are the essential properties of the thing *in itself*" is a nonsensical one."

The denial of essences is also a denial of intrinsic structure: an electron in my body has a certain electrical charge, but on the view just described it is a mistake to think that having that charge is an "intrinsic" property of the object (except *relative to the description* "electron") in a way in which the property of being a part of my body is not. In short, it is (or was until recently) commonly thought that

> A thing is not related to any one of its properties (or relations) any more "intrinsically" than it is to any of its other properties or relations.

The problem that the believer in metaphysical realism (or "transcendental realism" as Kant called it) has always faced involves the notion of "correspondence". There are many different ways of putting the signs of a language and the things in a set S in correspondence with one another, in fact infinitely many if the set S is infinite (and a very large finite number if S is a large finite set). Even if the "correspondence" has to be a reference relation and we specify which *sentences* are to correspond to *states of affairs which actually obtain*, it follows from theorems of model theory that there are still infinitely many ways of *specifying* such a correspondence.[1] How can we pick out any *one* correspondence between our words (or thoughts) and the supposed mind-independent things *if we have no direct access to the mind-independent things*? (German philosophy almost always began with a particular answer to this question – the answer "we can't" – after Kant.)

One thing is clear: an act of will (or intention) won't work. I can't simply *pick* one particular correspondence C and *will* (or stipulate) that C is to be the designated correspondence relation, because in order to do that I would need *already* to be able to *think about* the correspondence C – and C, being a relation to things which are external and mind-independent, is itself something outside the mind, something "external"! In short, if the mind does not have the ability to grasp external things or forms directly, then no *mental* act can give it the ability to single out a correspondence (or anything else external, for that matter).

But if the denial of intrinsic properties is correct, then no external thing or event is connected to any one relation it may have to other things (including our thoughts) in a way which is special or essential or intrinsic. If the denial of intrinsic properties is right, then it is not more essential to a mental event that it stand in a relation C_1 to any object x than it is that it stands in any other relation C_2 to any other object y. Nor is it any more essential to a non-mental object that it stand in a relation C to any one of my thoughts than it is that it stand in any one of a myriad other relations to any one of my other thoughts. On such a view, no relation C is metaphysically singled out as *the* relation between thoughts and things; reference becomes an "occult" phenomenon.

The tension or incompatibility between metaphysical realism and the denial of intrinsic properties has not gone unnoticed by modern materialists. And for this reason we now find many materialists employing a metaphysical vocabulary that smacks of the fourteenth century: materialists who talk of "causal powers", of "built-in" similarities and dissimilarities between things in nature, even materialists who speak unabashedly of *essences*. In this lecture I want to ask if this modern mixture of materialism and essentialism *is consistent*; and I shall argue that it *isn't*.

WHY I FOCUS ON MATERIALISM

The reason I am going to focus my attack on materialism is that materialism is the only *metaphysical* picture that has contemporary "clout". Metaphysics, or the enterprise of describing the "furniture of the world", the "things in themselves" apart from our conceptual imposition, has been rejected by many analytic philosophers (though *not*, as I remarked, by Russell), and by all the leading brands of continental philosophy. Today, apart from relics, it is virtually only materialists (or "physicalists", as they like to call themselves) who continue the traditional enterprise.

It was not always thus. Between the tenth and twelfth centuries the metaphysical community which included the Arabic Averroes and Avicenna, the Jewish Maimonides, and the Angelic Doctor in Paris disagreed on many questions, creation in particular. It was regarded as a hard issue whether the world always existed obeying the same laws (the doctrine ascribed to Aristotle), or was created from pre-existing matter (the doctrine ascribed to Plato) or was created *ex nihilo* (the Scriptural doctrine). But the existence of a supersensible Cause of the contingent and moving sensible things was taken to be *demonstrable*. Speculative reason could *know* there was an Uncaused Cause.

When I was seven years old the question "If God made the world, then who made God?" struck me one evening with vivid force. I remember pacing in circles around a little well for hours while the awful regress played itself out in my mind. If a medieval theologian had been handy, he would have told me that God was self-caused. He might have said God was the *ens necessarium*. I don't know if it would have helped; today philosophers would say that the doctrine of God's "necessary" existence invokes a notion of "necessity" which is incoherent or unintelligible.

The issue does, in a covert way, still trouble us. Wallace Matson (1967) ended a philosophic defense of atheism with the words, "Still, why *is* there something rather than nothing?". The doctrine that "you take the universe you get" (a remark Steven Weinberg once made in a discussion) sounds close to saying it's some sort of metaphysical *chance* (we might just as well have *anything*). The idea of a super-sensible Cause outside of the universe leads at once to the question that troubled me when I was seven. We don't even have the comfort of thinking of the universe as a kind of *ens necessarium*: *it* only came into existence a few billion years ago!

This situation was summed up by Kant: Kant held that the whole enterprise of trying to *demonstrate* the existence and nature of a super-sensible world by speculation leads only to antinomies. (The universe *must* have a cause; but *that* cause would have to have a cause; but an infinite regress is no explanation and self-causation is impossible...) Today, as I remarked, only a few relics would challenge this conclusion, which put an end to rationalism as well as to the medieval synthesis of Greek philosophy with revealed religion.

This decline of medieval philosophy was a long process which overlapped the decline of medieval science (with its substantial forms). Here too Kant summed up the issue for our culture: the medievals (and the rationalists) thought the mind had an intellectual intuition (*intellektuelle Anschauung*), a sort of perception that would enable it to perceive essences, substantial forms, or whatever. But there is no such faculty. "Nothing is in the mind that was not first in the senses *except the mind itself*", as Kant put it, quoting Leibnitz.

Again, no one but a few relics challenge *this* conclusion. But Kant drew a bold corollary, and this corollary is hotly disputed to the present day.

The corollary depends upon a claim that Kant made. The claim can be illustrated by a famous observation of Wittgenstein's. Referring to the "duck–rabbit" illusion (the figure that can be seen as either a duck or a rabbit), Wittgenstein remarked that while the physical image is capable of being seen either way, no "mental image" is capable of being seen either way: the "mental image" is always unambiguously a duck image or a rabbit image (*Philosophical Investigations* II, XI, 194–6). It follows that "mental images" are really very different from physical images such as line drawings and photographs. We might express this difference by saying the interpretation is *built in* to the "mental image"; the mental image is a *construction*.

Kant made the same point with respect to *memory*. When I have a memory of an experience this is not, contrary to Hume, *just* an image which "resembles" the earlier experience. To be a memory the interpretation has to be "built in": the interpretation that this is a *past* experience of *mine*. Kant (1933, "Transcendental Deduction") argues that the notion of the *past* involves causality and that causality involves laws and objects (so, according to Kant, does the assignment of all these experiences to *myself*). Past experiences are not directly available; saying we "remember" them is saying we have succeeded in constructing a version with causal relations and a continuing self in which they are located.

The corollary Kant drew from all this is that even experiences are in part constructions of the mind: I know what experiences I have and have had partly because I know what *objects* I am seeing and touching and have seen and touched, and partly because I know what *laws* these objects obey. Kant may have been overambitious in thinking he could specify the *a priori* constraints on the construction process; but the idea that all experience involves mental construction, and the idea that the dependence of physical object concepts and experience concepts goes *both* ways, continue to be of great importance in contemporary philosophy (of many varieties).

Since sense data and physical objects are interdependent constructions, in Kant's view, the idea that "all we know is sense data" is as silly as the idea that we can have knowledge of objects that goes beyond experience. Although Kant does not put it this way, I have suggested elsewhere (Putnam, 1981, ch. 3) that we can view him as rejecting the idea of truth as correspondence (to a mind-independent reality) and as saying that the only sort of truth we can have an idea of, or use for, is *assertibility* (by creatures with our rational natures) *under optimal conditions* (as determined by our sensible natures). Truth becomes a radically epistemic notion.

However, Kant remarks that the *desire* for speculative metaphysics, the desire for a theory of the furniture of the world, is deep in our nature. He thought we should abandon the enterprise of trying to have speculative knowledge of the "things in themselves" and sublimate the metaphysical impulse in the moral project of trying to make a more perfect world; but he was surely right about the strength of the metaphysical urge.

Contemporary materialism and scientism are a reflection of this urge in two ways. On the one hand, the materialism claims that physics is an approximation to a sketch of the one true theory, the true and complete description of the furniture of the world. (Since he often leaves out quantum mechanics, his picture differs remarkably little from Democritus': it's all atoms swerving in the void.) On the other hand, he meets the epistemological argument against metaphysics by claiming that we don't *need* an intellectual intuition to do *his* sort of metaphysics: his metaphysics, he says, is as open ended, as infinitely revisable and fallible, as science itself. In fact, it *is* science itself! (interpreted as claiming absolute truth, or, rather, claiming *convergence* to absolute truth). The appeal of materialism lies precisely in this, in its claim to be *natural* metaphysics, metaphysics within the bounds of science. That a doctrine which promises to gratify both our ambition (to know the noumena) and our caution (not to be unscientific) should have great appeal is hardly something to be wondered at.

This wide appeal would be reason enough to justify a critique of metaphysical materialism. But a second reason is this: metaphysical materialism has replaced positivism and pragmatism as the dominant contemporary form of scientism. Since scientism is, in my opinion, one of the most dangerous contemporary intellectual tendencies, a critique of its most influential contemporary form is a duty for a philosopher who views his enterprise as more than a purely technical discipline.

CAUSATION

What makes the metaphysical realist a *metaphysical* realist is his belief that there is somewhere "one true theory" (two theories which are true and complete descriptions of the world would be mere notational variants of each other). In company with a correspondence theory of truth, this belief in one true theory requires a *ready-made* world (an expression suggested in this connection by Nelson Goodman): the world itself has to have a "built-in" structure since otherwise theories with different structures might correctly "copy" the world (from different perspectives) and truth would lose its absolute (non-perspectival) character. Moreover, as I already remarked, "correspondence" between our symbols and something which has no determinate structure is hardly a well-defined notion.

The materialist metaphysician often takes *causal relations* as an example of built-in structure. Events have causes; objects have "causal powers". And he proudly proclaims his realism about these, his faith that they are "in" the world itself, in the metaphysical realist sense. Well, let us grant him that this is so, for the sake of argument: my question for the moment is not whether this sort of realism is justified, but whether it is really compatible with materialism. Is *causation* a physical relation?

In this discussion, I shall follow the materialist in ignoring quantum mechanics since it has *no* generally acceptable interpretation of the kind the realist advocates:[2] the standard (Copenhagen) interpretation makes essential reference to *observers*, and the materialist wants to imagine a physics in which the observer is simply another part of the system, as seen from a God's eye view. Physics is then a theory whose fundamental magnitudes are defined at all points in space and time; a property or relation is physically definable if it is definable in terms of these.[3]

I shall also assume that the fundamental magnitudes are basically the usual ones: if no restraint at all is placed on what counts as a possible "fundamental magnitude" in future physics, then *reference* or *soul* or *Good* could even be "fundamental magnitudes" in future physics! I shall not allow the naturalist the escape hatch of letting "future physics" mean we-know-not-what. Physicalism is only intelligible if "future physics" is supposed to resemble what *we* call "physics". The possibility of natural metaphysics (metaphysics within the bounds of science) is, indeed, not conclusively refuted by showing that present-day materialism cannot be a correct sketch of the one true (metaphysical) theory: but present-day materialism is, as already remarked, the view with clout.

Now if "*A* causes *B*" simply meant "whenever an *A*-type event happens, then a *B*-type event follows in time", "causes" would be physically definable. Many attempts have been made to give such a definition of causation – one which would apply to genuine causal laws while not applying to sequences we would regard as coincidental or otherwise non-causal. Few philosophers believe today that this is possible.

But let us assume that "causes" (in this sense) *is* somehow physically definable. A cause, in the sense this definition tries to capture, is a *sufficient* condition for its effect; whenever the cause occurs, the effect *must* follow (at least in a deterministic world). Following Mill, let us call such a cause a *total cause*. An example of a total cause at time t_0 of a physical event *e* occurring at a later time t_1 and a point *x* would be the entire distribution of values of the dynamical variables at time t_0 (inside a sphere *S* whose center is *x* and whose radius is sufficiently large so that events outside the sphere *S* could not influence events at *x* occurring at t_1 without having to send a signal to

x faster than light, which I assume, on the basis of relativity, to be impossible).

Mill pointed out that in ordinary language "cause" rarely (if ever) means "total cause". When I say "failure to put out the campfire caused the forest fire", I do *not* mean that the campfire's remaining lit during a certain interval was the *total cause* of the forest fire. Many other things – the dryness of the leaves, their proximity to the campfire, the temperature of the day, even the presence of oxygen in the atmosphere – are part of the *total* cause of the forest fire. Mill's point is that we regard certain parts of the total cause as "background", and refer only to the part of interest as "the" cause.

Suppose a professor is found stark-naked in a girl's dormitory room at midnight. His being naked in the room at midnight – ε, where ε is so small that he could neither get out of the room or put on his clothes between midnight – ε and midnight without moving faster than light, would be a "total cause" of his being naked in the girl's room at midnight; but no one would refer to this as the "cause" of his presence in the room in that state. On the other hand, when it is said that the presence of certain bodies of H_2O in our environment "causes" us to use the word "water" as we do, it is certainly *not* meant that the presence of H_2O is the "total cause". In its ordinary sense, "cause" can often be paraphrased by a locution involving *explain*; the presence of H_2O in our environment, our dependence on H_2O for life, etc., are "part of" the *explanation* of our having a word which we use as we use the word "water". The forest fire is *explained* (given background knowledge) by the campfire's not having been extinguished; but the professor's state at midnight – ε is not what we consider an *explanation* of the state of affairs at midnight.

When it is said that a word refers to x just in case the (use of the) word is connected to x by a "causal chain of the appropriate type", the notion of "causal chain" involved is that of an *explanatory* chain. Even if the notion of "total cause" *were* physically definable, it would not be possible to *use* it either in daily life or in philosophy; the notion the materialist really uses when he employs "causal chain", etc., in his philosophical explications is the intuitive notion of an *explanation*.

But this notion is certainly not physically definable. To see that it isn't, observe, first, that "explains" (and "caused", when it has the force of "explains why x happened") are abstract notions. Even when we imagine a possible world in which there are non-physical things or properties, we can conceive of these things and properties *causing* things to happen. A disembodied spirit would not have *mass* or *charge*, but (this is a conceptual question of course; I don't mean to suggest there *are* disembodied spirits) it could *cause* something (say, an emotional reaction in another spirit with which it communicated telepathically).

A definition of "caused" (in this "explanatory" sense) which was too "first order", too tied to the particular magnitudes which are the "fundamental magnitudes" of physics in *our* world, would make it *conceptually impossible* that a disembodied spirit (or an event involving magnitudes which are not "physical" in *our* world) could be a cause. This is why the suggested Humean definition of *total* cause – A is the (total) cause of B if and only if an A-type event is always followed in time by a *B*-type event – contained no *specific* physical term (except "time"): this definition *is* abstract enough to apply to possible worlds different from our own. (Although it fails even so.) Could there be an equally abstract (and more successful) definition of "cause" in the explanatory sense?

Imagine that Venusians land on Earth and observe a forest fire. One of them says, "*I* know what caused that – the atmosphere of the darned planet is saturated with oxygen."

What this vignette illustrates is that one man's (or extra-terrestrial's) "background condition" can easily be another man's "cause". What is and what is not a "cause" or an "explanation" depends on background knowledge and our reason for asking the question.

No purely *formal* relation between events will be sensitive to this relativity of explanatory arguments to background knowledge and interests.

Nelson Goodman has shown that no purely formal criterion can distinguish arguments which are intuitively sound inductive arguments from unsound arguments: for every sound inductive argument there is an unsound one of the very same form. The actual predicates occurring in the argument make the difference, and the distinction between "projectible" and "non-projectible" predicates is not a formal one. It is not difficult to show that the same thing is true of *explanations.* If we think of explanation as relation in "the world", then to define it one would need a predicate which could sort projectible from non-projectible properties; such a predicate could not be purely formal for then it would run afoul of Goodman's result, but it could not involve the particular fundamental magnitudes in *our* world in an essential way for then it would be open to counterexamples in other possible worlds.

"NON-HUMEAN" CAUSATION

Richard Boyd (1980) has suggested that the whole enterprise of *defining* causation was a mistake: physicalists should simply take the notion as a primitive one. He may only mean that to insist on a definition of "causes" (or anything else) in the standard formalism for mathematics and physics (which contains *names* for only countably many real numbers, etc.) is unreasonable: if so, this would not be an argument against expecting every *physical* property and relation to be definable in an *infinitary extension* of physics, a language which allows *infinitely long* names and sentences. (Indeed, if a property or relation is *not* physically definable even in this liberal sense, what is meant by calling it "physical"?) But he may have meant that one should literally take "causes" as an irreducible notion, one whose failure to be physically definable is not due to syntactic accidents, such as the limit on the length of formulas. But can a philosopher who accepts the existence of an irreducible phenomenon of *causation* call himself a materialist?

"Causes", we have just seen, is often paraphrasable as "explains". It rarely or never means "is the total cause of". When Boyd, for example, says that a certain micro-structure is a "causal power" (the micro-structure of sugar is a "causal power" in Boyd's sense, because it *causally explains* why sugar dissolves in water) he does not mean that the micro-structure in question is the *total cause* of the explained events (sugar will not dissolve in water if the water is *frozen*, for example, or if the water is already saturated with sugar, or if the water-cum-sugar is in an exotic quantum mechanical state). "Causal powers" are properties that *explain* something, given background conditions and given standards of salience and relevance.

A metaphysical view in which "causation" and "causal explanation" are built into the world itself is one in which explanation is wrenched out of what Professor Frederick Will (1974) has called "the knowledge institution", the inherited tradition which defines for us what is a background condition and what a salient variable parameter, and projected into the structure of reality. Boyd would probably reply that the "causal structure" of reality *explains* the success of the knowledge institution: our successful explanations simply copy the built-in causal structure.

Be that as it may, salience and relevance are attributes of thought and reasoning, not of nature. To project them into the realist's "real world", into what Kant called the *noumenal* world, is to mix objective idealism (or, perhaps, medieval Aristoteleanism) and materialism in a totally incoherent way. To say "materialism is *almost* true: the world is completely describable in the language of physics *plus* the one little added notion that some events intrinsically *explain* other events" would be ridiculous. This would not be a "near miss" for materialism, but a total failure. If events *intrinsically* explain other events, if there are saliencies, relevancies, standards of what are "normal" conditions, and so on, built into the world itself independently of minds, then the world is in many ways *like* a mind, or infused with something very much like reason. And if *that* is true, then materialism *cannot* be true. One can try to revive the project of speculative metaphysics, if one wishes: but one should not pass *this* sort of metaphysics off as (future) *physics*.

COUNTERFACTUALS AND "SIMILARITY"

Suppose I take a match from a new box of matches (in perfect condition), break it, and throw the pieces in the river. After all this, I remark, "If I had struck the match (instead of breaking it, etc.) it would have lit". Most of us would say, "true", or "probably true". But what does the statement actually assert?

A first stab at an explication might go as follows: the statement is true if it follows from physical laws (assume these to be given by a list – otherwise there are further problems about "laws") that if the match is struck (at an average (for me?) angle, with an average amount of force) against that striking surface, then, it ignites. But this doesn't work: even if we describe the match down to the atomic level, and ditto for the striking surface and the angle and force involved, there are still many other relevant variables unmentioned. (Notice the similarity to the problem of "cause" as "total cause": the statement "*A* caused *B*", and the statement "If *X* had happened, *Y* would have happened" have simple truth conditions when *all* the "background conditions" – and all the "laws" – are specified; but typically they *aren't* specified, and the speaker can't even conceive of *all* of them.) If no oxygen molecules happen to be near the top of the match, or if the entire match-cum-striking-surface-cum-atmosphere system is in a sufficiently strange quantum mechanical state, etc., then the match *won't* ignite (even if struck with that force, at that angle, etc.).

One is tempted to try: "It follows from the physical laws that if the match is struck against that surface (at the specified force and angle) and everything is *normal* then the match ignites", but this brings the very strange predicate "normal" into the story. Besides, maybe conditions *weren't* "normal" (in the sense of "average") at the time. (In infinitely many respects, conditions are *always* "abnormal": a truism from statistical theory). Or one is tempted to say: "It follows from the laws that if the match is struck against that surface (with the specified force and at the specified angle), and *everything else is as it actually was at the time,* then the match must ignite". But, as Nelson Goodman (1947) pointed out in a celebrated paper on this logical question, *everything* else *couldn't* be as it was at the time if the match were struck. The gravitational fields, the quantum mechanical state, the places where there were oxygen molecules in the air, and infinitely many other things *couldn't have been* "as they actually were at the time" if the match had been struck.

The reason I mention this is that David Lewis (in "Causation", *Journal of Philosophy* LXX, 1973), proposed to analyze "causes" using precisely this sort of contrary-to-fact conditional. The idea is that "*A* caused *B*" can be analyzed as "if *A* had *not* happened, *B would not have* happened".

Actually, this doesn't seem right. (Even if *A* caused *B*, there are situations in which it just isn't true that if *A* hadn't happened, *B* wouldn't have happened.)[4] But suppose it were right, or that, if it isn't right, contrary-to-fact conditionals can at any rate be used to explicate the notions that we wanted to use the notion of causality to explicate. How are the truth conditions for contrary-to-fact conditionals *themselves* to be explicated?

One famous materialist, John Mackie (1974), thinks contrary-to-fact conditionals aren't true or false. He regards them as ways of indicating what inferences are allowable in one's knowledge situation, rather than as asserting something true or false in the realist sense, independently of one's knowledge situation. "If I had struck that match it would have lit" indicates that my *knowledge situation* is such that (if I delete the information about what actually happened to the match) an inference from "the match was struck" to "the match ignited" would be *warranted*. The contrary-to-fact conditional signals the presence of what Wilfred Sellars calls a "material rule of inference". It has *assertibility conditions,* rather than truth conditions in the sense of absolute truth semantics.

Mackie, who follows Lewis in using counterfactuals to analyze "causes", concludes that *causation* (in the ordinary sense) is something *epistemic,* and not something in the world at all. But he believes there is another notion of causation, "mechanical causation", which is in the world. (It has to do with energy flow; as Mackie describes it, it is hard to see either what it is, or that it could be spelled out without using counterfactuals,[5] which would be fatal to Mackie's project of having a non-epistemic notion of causation.)

But Lewis, following Professor Robert Stalnaker, chooses to give *truth conditions* for contrary-to-fact conditionals. He postulates that there actually exist "other possible worlds" (as in science fiction), and that there is a "similarity metric" which determines how "near" or how "similar" any two possible worlds are (Lewis, 1973). A contrary-to-fact conditional, "If *X* had happened, then *Y* would have happened", is true just in case *Y* is *actually* true in all the *nearest* "parallel worlds" to the actual world in which *X* is actually true.

To me this smacks more of science fiction than of philosophy. But one thing is clear: a theory which requires an ontology of parallel worlds and a built-on "similarity metric" certainly does not have a *materialist* ontology. More important, it does not have a *coherent* ontology: not only is the actual existence of parallel worlds a dotty idea, but the idea of an *intrinsic* similarity metric, a metric highly sensitive to what we regard as relevant conditions, or normal conditions, one which gives weight to what sorts of features *we* count as similarities and dissimilarities between states of affairs, is one which once again implies that the world is like a mind, or imbued with something very much like reason. And if *this* is true, then it must have a (suitably metaphysical) *explanation*. Objective idealism can hardly be a *little bit* true. ("It's all physics, except that there's this similarity metric" just doesn't make *sense*.)

ESSENCES AND OBJECTS

In this philosophical culture, the denial of intrinsic or "essential" properties began with examples like the example of the thing whose shape is an "essential" property under *one* description ("that statue") but not under a different description ("that piece of clay"). One philosopher who thinks a wholly wrong moral was drawn from this example is Saul Kripke.

According to Kripke, the statue and the piece of clay are two objects, not one. The fact that the piece of clay has a model property, namely the property "being a thing which *could have been* spherical in shape", which the statue lacks (I assume this is not one of those contemporary statues) already proves the two objects cannot be identical, in Kripke's view.

Now, this sounds very strange at first hearing. If I put the statue on the scale, have I put *two objects* on the scale? If the piece of clay weighs 20 pounds and the statue weighs 20 pounds, why doesn't the scale read 40 and not 20 if both objects are on it right now? But what Kripke has in mind is not silly at all.

First of all, it also sounds strange to be told that a human being is not identical with the aggregation of the molecules in his body. Yet on a moment's reflection each of us is aware that he was not *that* aggregate of molecules a day ago. Seven years ago, precious few of those molecules were in my body. If after my death that exact set of molecules is assembled and placed in a chemical flask, it will be the same aggregation of molecules, but it won't be *me*. David Lewis (1976) has suggested that I and the aggregation of molecules are "identical for a period of time" in somewhat the way that

Highway 2 and Highway 16 can be "identical for a stretch"; as he points out, "identity for a time" is not strict logical identity. If *A* and *B* are identical in the strict sense, every property of *A* is a property of *B*; but it is not the case that every property of the aggregation of molecules is a property of *me*.

Just as we can recognize that I am not the same object as the aggregation of molecules in my body without denying that I *consist* of those molecules right now (the difference between the objects lies in the different statements that are true of them, not in their physical distinctness), so, one can agree with Kripke that the statue is not the same object as the piece of clay without denying that the piece of clay is the matter of the statue; once again the difference between the objects lies in the different statements that are true of them, not in their physical distinctness.

But now it begins to look as if objects, properly individuated, *do* have essences, do have *some* properties in a special way. Can Kripke's doctrine be of aid to materialism? (Kripke himself is quite averse to materialism, as is well known.)

A materialist whose ontology includes "possible worlds" might introduce suitable intensional objects by identifying them with functions taking possible worlds as arguments and space–time regions in those worlds as values. Thus, the statue would be the function defined on each possible world *Y* in which the statue exists, whose value on *Y* is the space–time region occupied by the statue in *Y*. This would, indeed, make the "statue" and the "piece of clay" different "objects" (different logical constructions) even if they occupy the same space–time region in the actual world, since there are other possible worlds in which they do not occupy the same space–time region.

But functions of this kind are standardly used in modern semantics to represent *concepts*. No one doubts that the *concept* "that statue" is a different *concept* from the *concept* "that piece of clay"; the question is whether there is some *individual* in the actual world to which one of these concepts *essentially* applies while the other only accidentally applies. The space–time region itself is *not* such an individual; and it is hard to see how a materialist is going to find one in *his* ontology.

Moreover, clever logical constructions are no answer to the philosophical difficulty. Doubtless one can come up with as many "objects" as one wants given "possible worlds" plus the resources of modern set theory; (the difficulty, indeed, is that one can come up with *too many*). Consider the metaphysical claim that my thoughts have some sort of intrinsic connection with external objects. If the events that take place in my brain are in a space–time region that has a set-theoretic connection with some abstract entity that involves certain external objects, then that same space–time region will have similar set-theoretic connections with some other abstract entities that involve some other external objects. To be sure, the materialist can say that my "thoughts" *intrinsically* involve certain external objects by *identifying them* (the thoughts) with one abstract entity and not with another; but if this identification is supposed to be a feature of reality itself, then there must really *be* essences in the world in a sense which pure set theory can't hope to explicate.

The difficulty is that Kripke individuates objects *by their modal properties*, by what they (essentially) *could* and *could not* be. Kripke's ontology *presupposes* essentialism; it can not be used to ground it. And modal properties are not, on the face of it, part of the materialist's furniture of the world.

But, I will be reminded, I have myself spoken of "essential properties" elsewhere (see Putnam, 1975*a*). I have said that there are possible worlds (possible *states* of the world, that is, not parallel worlds à la Lewis) in which some liquid other than H_2O has the taste of water (we might have different taste buds, for example), fills the lakes and rivers, etc., but no possible world in which *water* isn't H_2O. Once we have discovered what water is in the actual world, we have discovered its *nature*: is this not essentialism?

It *is* a sort of essentialism, but not a sort which can help the materialist. For what I have said is that it has long been our *intention* that a liquid should *count* as "water" only if it has the same composition as the paradigm examples of water (or as the majority of them). I claim that this was our intention even before we *knew* the ultimate composition of water. If I am right then, *given those referential intentions*, it was always impossible for a liquid other than H_2O to be water, even if it took empirical investigation to find it out. But the "essence" of water in *this* sense is the product of our use of the word, the kinds of referential intentions we have: this sort of essence is not "built into the world" in the way required by an *essentialist theory of reference itself* to get off the ground.

Similarly, Kripke has defended *his* essentialist theories by arguments which turn on speakers' referential intentions and practices; to date he has carefully refrained from trying to provide a metaphysical theory of reference (although he does seem to believe in mind-independent modal properties). I conclude that however one takes Kripke's theories (or mine); whether one takes them metaphysically, as theories of objective "essences" which are somehow "out there", or one takes them as theories of our referential practices and intentions, they are of no help to the materialist. On the metaphysical reading they are realist enough, but their realism is not of a materialist sort; on the purely semantical reading they *presuppose* the notion of reference, and cannot be used to support the metaphysical explanation of reference as intrinsic correspondence between thought and thing.

REFERENCE

Some metaphysical materialists might respond to what has been said by agreeing that, "*A* causes *B*" does *not* describe a simple "relation" between *A* and *B*. "All you're saying is that causal statements *rest on* a distinction between background conditions and differentiating factors, and I agree that this distinction isn't built into the things themselves, but is a reflection of the way we think about the things", such a philosopher might say. But here he has used the words "think about", i.e., he has appealed to the notion of *reference*.

The contemporary metaphysical materialist thinks about reference in the following way: the brain is a computer. Its computations involve *representations.* Some of these (perhaps all) are "propositional": they resemble sentences in an internal *lingua mentis.* (They have been called "sentence-analogs".) Some of them could be sentences in a public language, as when we engage in interior monolog. A person refers to something when, for example, the person thinks "the cat is on the mat" (the sentence-analog is "subvocalized") and the entire organism-cum-environment situation is such that the words "the cat" in the particular sentence-analog stand in a physical relation R (the relation of *reference*) to some cat and the words "the mat" stand in the relation R to some mat.

But what is this relation R? And what on earth could make anyone think it is a *physical* relation?

Well, there is *one* way in which *no one*, to my knowledge, would try to define R, and that is by giving a list of all possible reference situations. It is useful, however, to consider why not. Suppose someone proposed to define reference (for some set of languages, including "*lingua mentis*") thus:

> *X refers to Y if and only if X is a (token) word or word-analog and Y is an object or event and the entire situation (including the organism that produced X and the environment that contains Y) is S_1 or S_2 or S_3 or ... (infinite – possibly non-denumerably infinite – list of situations, described at the level of physics).*

There are (at least) three things wrong with this.

First, besides the fact that the list would have to be infinite, such a list would not tell us what the situations S_1, S_2, ... *had in common.* To define a physical property or relation by *listing* the situations in which it is found is not to say what it *is.* In fact, the materialists themselves object to *Tarski*'s definition of reference on just this ground: that Tarski defines primitive reference (for a fixed language), by a list of cases, and, as Hartry Field (1972*a*, p. 363) writes,

> Now, it would have been easy for a chemist, late in the last century, to have given a "valence definition" of the following form:
>
> (3) (E) (n) (E has valence $n \equiv E$ is potassium and n is +1, or ... or E is sulphur and n is –2)
>
> where in the blanks go a list of similar clauses, one for each element. But, though this is an extensionally correct definition of valence, it would not have been an acceptable reduction; and had it turned out that nothing else was possible – had all efforts to explain valence in terms of the structural properties of atoms proved futile – scientists would have eventually had to decide either (a) to give up valence theory, or else (b) to replace the hypothesis of physicalism by another hypothesis (chemicalism?). It is part of scientific methodology to resist doing (b); and I also think it is part of scientific methodology to resist doing (a) as long as the notion of valence is serving the purposes for which it was designed (i.e., as long as it is proving useful in helping us characterize chemical compounds in terms of their valences). But the methodology is not to resist (a) and (b) by giving lists like (3); the methodology is to look for a real reduction. This is a methodology that has proved extremely

fruitful in science, and I think we'd be crazy to give it up in linguistics. And I think we are giving up this fruitful methodology, unless we realize that we need to add theories of primitive reference to T_1 or T_2 if we are to establish the notion of truth as a physicalistically acceptable notion.

Secondly, it would be philosophically naive to think that such a list could answer any *philosophical* question about reference. For example, one could hold Quine's view, that there are definite *true* and *false* sentences[6] in science, but *no* determinate reference relation (the true sentences have infinitely many models, and there is no such thing as *the* model, in Quine's view), and still accept the list. Quine would simply say that the terms used to describe the situations S_1, S_2, ... etc. refer to different events in different models; thus the list, while correct in *each* admissible model, does not define a *determinate* reference relation (only a determinate reference relation *for each model*). Now Quine's view may be right, wrong, or meaningless; the question of the truth or falsity of metaphysical realism may be meaningful or meaningless (and if meaningful, may have a realist or a non-realist answer), but a list of cases (either this list or the one involved in the Tarskian truth definition referred to by Field), cannot speak to *this* issue. To think that it can is analogous to thinking (as G. E. Moore did) that one can refute Berkeley by holding up one's hand and saying "This is a material object. Therefore matter exists." This is, as Myles Burnyeat has put it, "to philosophize as if Kant had never existed". For better or worse, philosophy has gone second order.

Thirdly, the list is *too specific.* Reference is as "abstract" as causation. In possible worlds which contain individual things or properties which are not physical (in the sense of "physical$_2$":[7] not definable in terms of the fundamental magnitudes of the physics of the actual world), we could still *refer*: we could refer to disembodied minds, or to an emergent non-material property of Goodness, or to all sorts of things, in the appropriate worlds. But the relevant situations could not, by hypothesis, be completely described in terms of the fundamental magnitudes of the physics of *our* world. A definition of reference from which it followed that we could not refer to a non-physical magnitude if there were one is just *wrong*.

I know of only one realist who has sketched a way of defining reference which meets these difficulties, and that is David Lewis (1974). Lewis proposes to treat reference as a *functional* property of the organism-cum-environment situation.

Typical examples of functional properties come from the world of computers. Having a particular program, for example, is a functional (or in computer jargon a "software" property) as opposed to an ordinary first-order physical property (a "hardware" property). Functional properties are typically defined in batches; the properties or "states" in a typical batch (say, the properties that are involved in a given computer program) are characterized by a certain *pattern.* Each property has specified cause and effect relations to the other properties in the pattern and to certain non-functional properties (the "inputs" and "outputs" of the programs).

Lewis' suggestion is that *reference* is a member of such a batch of properties: not functional properties of the organism, but functional properties of the organism–environment system. If this could be shown, it would answer the question of what all the various situations in which something refers to something else "have in common": what they would have in common is something as abstract as a program, a scheme or formal pattern of cause–effect relationships. And if this could be shown, it would characterize reference in a way that makes it sufficiently abstract; the definition would not require any particular set of magnitudes to be the fundamental ones any more than the abstract description of a computer program does. Whether the second difficulty I noted would be met, I shall not attempt to judge.

The crucial point is that functional properties are defined *using the notions of cause and effect.* This is no problem for Lewis; Lewis believes he can define cause and effect using counterfactuals, and, as already mentioned, he gives truth conditions for counterfactuals in terms of a primitive notion of "similarity of possible worlds". Since he has a non-physical primitive in his system, he does not have to show that any of the notions he uses is physically definable. But the notion of "similarity of possible worlds" is not one to which the materialist is entitled; and neither is he entitled to counter-factuals or to the notion of "functional organization".

As Charles Fried remarked in his Tanner Lectures,[8] it is easy to *mistake* causality for a physical relation. *Act, smash, move,* etc. are causal verbs and describe events which are clearly physical. ("Smashed", for example, conveys two kinds of information: the information that *momentum* was transferred from one thing to another, which is purely physical informa-tion, and the information that the *breaking* of the second thing was *caused* by the momentum transfer.) As Fried points out, the causal judgment may be quite complicated in cases when both objects were in motion before the collision. Once one has made the error of taking causality to be a physical relation, it is easy to think that functional properties are simply higher-order physical properties (an error I myself once committed), and then to think that reference (and just about anything else) may be a functional property and hence physical. But once one sees this is an error, there is no vestige of a reason that I know of to think reference is a physical relation.

If the materialist cannot *define* reference, he can, of course, just take it as *primitive.* But reference, like causality, is a flexible, interest-relative notion: what we count as *referring* to something depends on background knowledge and our willingness to be charitable in interpretation. To read a relation so deeply human and so pervasively intentional into the world and to call the resulting metaphysical picture satisfactory (never mind whether or not it is "materialist") is absurd.

THE FAILURE OF NATURAL METAPHYSICS

As I've already pointed out, there are two traditional ways of attempting to overcome the obvious difficulties with a correspondence theory of truth. One way was to postulate a special mental power, an *intellektuelle Anschauung,* which gives the mind access to "forms". If the mind has direct access to the things in themselves, then there is no problem about how it can put them in correspondence with its "signs". The other way was to postulate a built-in structure of the world, a set of essences, and to say (what is certainly a dark saying) that this structure itself singles out *one* correspondence between signs and their objects. The two strategies were quite naturally related; if a philosopher believes in essences, he usually wants us to have epistemic access to them, and so he generally postulates an *intellektuelle Anschauung* to give us this access.

If all this is a failure, as Kant saw, where do we go from there? One direction, the only direction I myself see as making sense, might be a species of pragmatism (although the word "pragmatism" has always been so ill-understood that one despairs of rescuing the term), "internal" realism: a realism which recognizes a difference between "p" and "I think that p", between being *right*, and merely thinking one is right without locating that objectivity in either transcendental correspondence or mere consensus. Nelson Goodman has done a wonderful job of "selling" this point of view in *Ways of Worldmaking* (a book short enough to be read in an evening, and deep enough to be pondered for many). The other main direction – the one that does not make sense to me – is natural metaphysics, the tendency I have criticized here.

Goodman urges, shockingly, that we give up the notion of "*the* world". Although he speaks of us as making *many* worlds, he does not mean that there are many worlds in the David Lewis (or science fiction) sense, but that rightness is relative to medium and message. We make many versions; the standards of rightness that determine what is right and what is wrong are corrigible, relative to task and technique, but not *subjective*. The question this tendency raises is whether a narrow path can indeed be found between the swamps of metaphysics and the quicksands of cultural relativism and historicism; I shall say more about this in the next chapter.

The approach to which I have devoted this paper is an approach which claims that there *is* a "transcendental" reality in Kant's sense, one absolutely independent of our minds, that the regulative ideal of knowledge *is* to copy it or put our thoughts in "correspondence" with it, *but* (and this is what makes it "natural" metaphysics) we need no *intellektuelle Anschauung* to do this: the "scientific method" will do the job for us. "Metaphysics within the bounds of science alone" might be its slogan.

I can sympathize with the urge behind this view (I would not criticize it if I did not feel its attraction). I am not inclined to scoff at the idea of a noumenal ground behind the dualities of experience, even if all attempts to talk about it lead to antinomies. Analytic philosophers have always tried to dismiss the transcendental as nonsense, but it does have an eerie way of reappearing. (For one thing, almost every philosopher makes statements which contradict his own explicit account of what can be justified or known; this even arises in formal logic, when one makes statements about "all languages" which are barred by the prohibitions on self-reference. For another, almost everyone regards the statement that there is *no* mind-independent reality, that there are *just* the "versions", or there is just the "discourse", or whatever, as itself intensely paradoxical.) Because one cannot talk about the transcendent or even deny its existence without paradox, one's attitude to it must, perhaps, be the concern of religion rather than of rational philosophy.

The idea of a coherent theory of the noumena; consistent, systematic, and arrived at by "the scientific method" seems to me to be chimerical. True, a metaphysician could say "You have, perhaps, shown that *materialist* metaphysics is incoherent. If so, let us assume some primitive notions of an 'intentional' kind, say 'thinks about', or 'explains', and construct a scientific theory of *these* relations." But what reason is there to regard this as a reasonable program?

The whole history of science seems to accord badly with such dreams. Science as we know it has been anti-metaphysical from the seventeenth century on; and not just because of "positivistic interpretations". Newton was certainly no positivist; but he strongly rejected the idea that his theory of universal gravitation could or should be read as a description of metaphysically ultimate fact. (*"Hypotheses non fingo"* was a rejection of metaphysical "hypotheses", not of scientific ones.)

And Newton was certainly right. Suppose we lived in a Newtonian world, and suppose we could say with confidence that Newton's theory of gravity and Maxwell's theory of electromagnetism (referred to a privileged "ether frame") were perfectly accurate. Even then, these theories admit of a bewildering variety of empirically equivalent formulations; formulations which agree on the equations while disagreeing precisely on their metaphysical interpretation. There are action-at-a-distance versions of *both* electromagnetism and gravity; there are versions of both in which an extended physical agent, the field, mediates the interactions between distant bodies; there are even *space–time* versions of *Newtonian* gravitational theory. Philosophers today argue about which of these would be "right" in such a case; but I know of not a single first-rate physicist who takes an interest in such speculations.

The physics that has replaced Newton's has the same property. A theorist will say he is doing "field theory" while his fingers are drawing Feynman diagrams, diagrams in which field interactions are depicted as exchanges of *particles* (calling the particles "virtual" is, perhaps, a ghost of empiricist metaphysics). Even the statement that "the electron we measure is not the bare electron of the theory, but the bare electron surrounded by a cloud of virtual *particles*" counts as a statement of *field* theory, if you please! What used to be the metaphysical question of atom or vortex has become a question of the choice of a notation!

Worse still, from the metaphysician's point of view, the most successful and most accurate physical theory of all time, quantum mechanics, has *no* "realistic interpretation" that is acceptable to physicists. It is understood as a description of the world as *experienced by observers*; it does not even pretend to the kind of "absoluteness" the metaphysician aims at (which is not to say that, given time and ingenuity, one could not come up with any number of empirical equivalents which *did* pretend to be observer independent; it is just that physicists refuse to take such efforts seriously).

There is, then, nothing in the history of science to suggest that it either aims at or should aim at one single *absolute* version of "the world". On the contrary, such an aim, which would require science itself to decide which of the empirically equivalent successful theories in any given context was "really true", is contrary to the whole spirit of an enterprise whose strategy from the first has been to confine itself to claims with clear *empirical* significance. If metaphysics *is* ever revived as a culturally and humanly significant enterprise, it is far more likely to be along the lines of a Kurt Gödel or, perhaps, Saul Kripke – i.e., along the lines of those who *do* think, in spite of the history I cited, that we *do* have an *intellektuelle Anschauung* – than along the lines of natural metaphysics. But a successful revival along either line seems to be overwhelmingly unlikely.

NOTES

This was a lecture delivered at the University of California, Berkeley, on 27 April 1981. It was the first of two Howison Lectures on "The transcendence of reason".

1   In Putnam (1981) this result is extended to intensional logic; it is shown that even if we specify which sentences are to be true in each possible world, and not just in the actual world, the extensions of the extra-logical predicates are almost totally undetermined in almost all worlds.

2   I ignore here my *own* past attempts at a realist interpretation of quantum mechanics (using non-standard logic) for two reasons: they have never found much acceptance, and (more importantly) I no longer think quantum logic enables one to reconcile quantum mechanics with realism. (See chapter 14 of Putnam (1983)).

3   Strictly speaking, "if it is definable in terms of these, using, if necessary, constants for all real numbers and functions, infinite conjunctions and disjunctions, etc.": there is no philosophical significance to the question of whether a physical magnitude can be defined by a formula of finite length (or one containing a constant for some undefinable real number) from a metaphysical materialist's point of view.

4   These are situations in which *B* would have been produced by some other cause if *A* hadn't caused it. Another kind of counterexample: John and George are identical twins and have black hair. Is the following counterfactual true?

> "If John hadn't had black hair, George wouldn't have had black hair either."

> Everyone I've asked assures me it is. But then, on Lewis' theory it follows that

> "John's having black hair *caused* George to have black hair too"

> which is absurd.

5   If "mechanical causation" is simply momentum transfer, for example, then my flicking a virtually frictionless switch is *not* the "mechanical cause" of the light going on. Similarly, my putting my hand in front of a light is not the "mechanical cause" of the shadow. Such a narrow notion might be physical, but would be of no use in explicating *reference*. If, on the other hand, the switching case *is* a case of "mechanical causation", how does one characterize it without using the clause "the current *would not have* travelled to the light if the switch *had not been* moved", or some such subjunctive clause?

6 For Quine, this means true and false relative to our evolving doctrine; Quine rejects metaphysical realism and the idea of a unique "correspondence" between our terms and things in themselves. Quine's views are discussed in chapter 13 of Putnam (1983).

7 Paul Meehl and Wilfred Sellars (1956) introduced the terms "physical$_1$" and "physical$_2$". "Physical$_1$" properties are simply properties connected with space–time and with causal laws: thus a dualist could subscribe to the thesis "all properties are physical$_1$". "Physical$_2$" properties are physical in the sense used here.

8 "Is liberty possible?" *The Tanner Lectures on Human Values*, vol. 3. Cambridge 1982, pp. 89–135.

REFERENCES

Boyd, R. (1980) "Materialism without reductionism: what physicalism does not entail", in N. Block (ed.) *Readings in the Philosophy of Psychology*, Cambridge, Mass., 67–106.

Field, H. (1972) "Tarski's theory of truth", *Journal of Philosophy*, LXIX, 347–75.

Goodman, N. (1947) 'The problem of counterfactual conditionals', *Journal of Philosophy*, XLIV, 113–28.

—— (1978) *Ways of Worldmaking*, Indianapolis.

Kant, I. (1933) *The Critique of Pure Reason*, London.

Lewis, D. (1973) *Counterfactuals*, Oxford.

—— (1974) "Radical interpretation", *Synthese*, XXVII, 331–44.

—— (1976) "Survival and identity", in A. D. Rorty (ed.) *The Identity of Persons*, Berkeley, 17–40.

Mackie, J. (1974) *The Cement of the Universe*, Oxford.

Matson, W. (1967) *The Existence of God*, Ithaca, New York.

Meehl, P. and Sellars, W. (1956) "The concept of emergence", in H. Feigl and M. Scriven (eds.) *Minnesota Studies in the Philosophy of Science*, vol. 1, Minneapolis, 239–52.

Putnam, H. (1975a) 'The meaning of 'meaning' ", reprinted in Putnam (1975e).

—— (1975e) *Mind, Language and Reality: Philosophical Papers*, vol. 2, Cambridge.

—— (1981) *Reason, Truth and History*, Cambridge.

—— (1983) *Realism and Reason: Philosophical Papers*, vol. 3, Cambridge.

Will, F. L. (1974) *Induction and Justification*, Ithaca, New York.

Wittgenstein, L. W. (1953) *Philosophical Investigations*, Oxford.

13 Evolution, Error, and Intentionality

Daniel C. Dennett

Sometimes it takes years of debate for philosophers to discover what it is they really disagree about. Sometimes they talk past each other in long series of books and articles, never guessing at the root disagreement that divides them. But occasionally a day comes when something happens to coax the cat out of the bag. "Aha!" one philosopher exclaims to another, "so that's why you've been disagreeing with me, misunderstanding me, resisting my conclusions, puzzling me all these years!"

In the fall of 1985 I discovered what I took to be just such a submerged – perhaps even repressed – disagreement and guessed that it might take some shock tactics to push this embarrassing secret into the harsh glare of philosophical attention. There are few things more shocking to philosophers than strange bedfellows, so, in an earlier draft of this chapter which circulated widely in 1986, I drew up some deliberately oversimplified battle lines and picked sides – the good guys versus the bad guys. It worked. I was inundated with detailed, highly revealing responses from those I had challenged and from others who rose to the bait. By and large these reactions confirmed both my division of the field and my claims for its unacknowledged importance.

So constructive were the responses, however, even from those I had treated rather roughly – or misrepresented – in the earlier draft, that instead of just crowing "I told you so!" I should acknowledge at the outset that this heavily revised and expanded offspring of my earlier act of provocation owes a special debt to the comments of Tyler Burge, Fred Dretske, Jerry Fodor, John Haugeland, Saul Kripke, Ruth Millikan, Hilary Putnam, Richard Rorty, and Stephen Stich, and to many others, including especially Fred Adams, Peter Brown, Jerome Feldman, D. K. Modrak, Carolyn Ristau, Jonathan Schull, Stephen White, and Andrew Woodfield.

The Great Divide I want to display resists a simple, straightforward formulation, not surprisingly, but we can locate it by retracing the steps of my exploration, which began with a discovery about some philosophers' attitudes toward the interpretation of artifacts. The scales fell from my eyes during a discussion with Jerry Fodor and some other philosophers about a draft of a chapter of Fodor's *Psychosemantics* (1987). Scales often fall from my eyes when discussing things with Fodor, but this was the first time, so far as I can recall, that I actually found myself muttering "Aha!" under my breath. The chapter in question, "Meaning and the world order," concerns

Fred Dretske's attempts (1981, especially chapter 8; 1985, 1986) to solve the problem of misrepresentation. As an aid to understanding the issue, I had proposed to Fodor and the other participants in the discussion that we first discuss a dead simple case of misrepresentation: a coin-slot testing apparatus on a vending machine accepting a slug. "That sort of case is irrelevant," Fodor retorted instantly, "because after all, John Searle is right about one thing; he's right about artifacts like that. They don't have any intrinsic or original intentionality – only derived intentionality."

The doctrine of original intentionality is the claim that whereas some of our artifacts may have intentionality derived from us, we have original (or intrinsic) intentionality, utterly underived. Aristotle said that God is the Unmoved Mover, and this doctrine announces that we are Unmeant Meaners. I have never believed in it and have often argued against it. As Searle has noted, "Dennett . . . believes that nothing *literally* has any *intrinsic intentional* mental states" (1982, p. 57), and in the long-running debate between us (Searle 1980b, 1982, 1984, 1985; Dennett 1980b; Hofstadter and Dennett 1981; Dennett 1982, 1984, forthcoming c), I had assumed that Fodor was on my side on this particular point.

Did Fodor really believe that Searle is right about this? He said so. Dretske (1985) goes further, citing Searle's attack on artificial intelligence (Searle 1980b) with approval, and drawing a sharp contrast between people and computers:

> I lack specialized skills, knowledge and understanding, but nothing that is essential to membership in the society of rational agents. With machines, though, and this includes the most sophisticated modern computers, it is different. They *do* lack something that is essential.
>
> (p. 23)

Others who have recently struggled with the problem of misrepresentation or error also seemed to me to fall on Searle's side of the fence: in particular, Tyler Burge (1986) and Saul Kripke (1982, especially pp. 34ff). In fact, as we shall see, the problem of error impales all and only those who believe in original or intrinsic intentionality.

Are *original intentionality* and *intrinsic intentionality* the same thing? We will have to approach this question indirectly, by pursuing various attempts to draw a sharp distinction between the way our minds (or mental states) have meaning and the way other things do. We can begin with a familiar and intuitive distinction discussed by Haugeland. Our artifacts

> only have meaning because we give it to them; their intentionality, like that of smoke signals and writing, is essentially borrowed, hence *derivative*. To put it bluntly: computers themselves don't mean anything by their tokens (any more than books do) – they only mean what we say they do. Genuine understanding, on the other hand, is intentional "in its own right" and not derivatively from something else.
>
> (1981, pp. 32–3)

Consider an encyclopedia. It has derived intentionality. It contains information about thousands of things in the world, but only insofar as it is a device designed and intended for our use. Suppose we "automate" our encyclope-dia, putting all its data into a computer and turning its index into the basis for an elaborate question-answering system. No longer do we have to look up material in the volumes; we simply type in questions and receive answers. It might seem to naive users as if they were communicating with another person, another entity endowed with original intentionality, but we would know better. A question-answering system is still just a tool, and whatever meaning or aboutness we vest in it is just a by-product of our practices in using the device to serve our own goals. It has no goals of its own, except for the artificial and derived goal of "understanding" and "answering" our questions correctly.

But suppose we endow our computer with somewhat more autonomous, somewhat less slavish goals. For instance, a chess-playing computer has the (artificial, derived) goal of defeating its human opponent, of concealing what it "knows" from us, of tricking us perhaps. But still, surely, it is only our tool or toy, and although many of its internal states have a sort of aboutness or intentionality – e.g., there are states that represent (and hence are about) the current board positions, and processes that investigate (and hence are about) various possible continuations of the game – this is just derived intentionality, not original intentionality.

This persuasive theme (it is not really an argument) has convinced more than a few thinkers that no artifact could have the sort of intentionality we have. Any computer program, any robot we might design and build, no matter how strong the illusion we may create that it has become a genuine agent, could never be a truly autonomous thinker with the same sort of original intentionality we enjoy. For the time being, let us suppose that this is the doctrine of original intentionality, and see where it leads.

THE CASE OF THE WANDERING TWO-BITSER

I will now press my vending machine example – the example Fodor insisted was irrelevant – explicitly, for it makes vivid exactly the points of disagree-ment and casts several recent controversies (about "individualistic psycho-logy" and "narrow content," about error, about function) in a useful light. Consider a standard soft-drink vending machine, designed and built in the United States, and equipped with a transducer device for accepting and rejecting US quarters.[1] Let's call such a device a two-bitser. Normally, when a quarter is inserted into a two-bitser, the two-bitser goes into a state, call it Q, which "means" (note the scare-quotes) "I perceive/accept a genuine US quarter now." Such two-bitsers are quite clever and sophisticated, but hardly foolproof. They do "make mistakes" (more scare-quotes). That is, unmeta-phorically, sometimes they go into state Q when a slug or other foreign object is inserted in them, and sometimes they reject perfectly legal quarters – they fail to go into state Q when they are *supposed to*. No doubt there are detectable patterns in the cases of "misperception." No doubt at least some of the cases of "misidentification" could be predicted by someone with enough knowledge of the relevant laws of physics and design parameters of the two-bitser's transducing machinery, so that it would be just as much a matter of physical law that objects of kind *K* would put the device into state *Q* as that quarters would. Objects of kind *K* would be good "slugs" – reliably "fooling" the transducer.

If objects of kind *K* became more common in the two-bitser's normal environment, we could expect the owners and designers of two-bitsers to develop more advanced and sensitive transducers that would reliably discriminate between genuine US quarters and slugs of kind *K*. Of course trickier counterfeits might then make their appearance, requiring further advances in the detecting transducers, and at some point such escalation of engineering would reach diminishing returns, for there is no such thing as a *foolproof* mechanism. In the meantime, the engineers and users are wise to make do with standard, rudimentary two-bitsers, since it is not cost effective to protect oneself against negligible abuses.

The only thing that makes the device a quarter-detector rather than a slug-detector or a quarter-*or*-slug-detector is the shared intention of the device's designers, builders, owners, users. It is only in the environment or context of those users and their intentions that we can single out some of the occasions of state *Q* as "veridical" and others as "mistaken." It is only relative to that context of intentions that we could justify calling the device a two-bitser in the first place.

I take it that so far I have Fodor, Searle, Dretske, Burge, Kripke, et al. nodding their agreement: that's just how it is with such artifacts; this is a textbook case of derived intentionality, laid bare. And so of course it embarrasses no one to admit that a particular two-bitser, straight from the American factory and with "Model A Two-Bitser" stamped right on it, might be installed on a Panamanian soft-drink machine, where it proceeded to earn its keep as an accepter and rejecter of quarter-balboas, legal tender in Panama, and easily distinguished from US quarters by the design and writing stamped on them, but not by their weight, thickness, diameter, or material composition.

(I'm not making this up. I have it on excellent authority – Albert Erler of the Flying Eagle Shoppe, Rare Coins – that Panamanian quarter-balboas minted between 1966 and 1984 are indistinguishable from US quarters by standard vending machines. Small wonder, since they are struck from US quarter stock in American mints. And – to satisfy the curious, although it is strictly irrelevant to the example – the current official exchange rate for the quarter-balboa is indeed $.25!)

Such a two-bitser, whisked off to Panama (the poor man's Twin Earth), would still normally go into a certain physical state – the state with the physical features by which we used to identify state *Q* – whenever a US quarter or an object of kind *K* or a Panamanian quarter-balboa is inserted in it, but now a different set of such occasions count as the mistakes. In the new environment, US quarters count as slugs, as inducers of error, misperception, misrepresentation, just as much as objects of kind *K* do. After all, back in the United States a Panamanian quarter-balboa is a kind of slug.

Once our two-bitser is resident in Panama, should we say that the state we used to call *Q* still occurs? The physical state in which the device "accepts" coins still occurs, but should we now say that we should identify it as "realizing" a new state, *QB*, instead? Well, there is considerable freedom – not to say boredom – about what we should say, since after all a two-bitser is just an artifact, and talking about its perceptions and misperceptions, its veridical and nonveridical states – its intentionality, in short – is "just metaphor." The two-bitser's internal state, call it what you like, doesn't *really* (originally, intrinsically) mean either "US quarter here now" or "Panamanian quarter-balboa here now." It doesn't *really* mean anything. So Fodor, Searle, Dretske, Burge, and Kripke (*inter alia*) would insist.

The two-bitser was originally designed to be a detector of US quarters. That was its "proper function" (Millikan 1984), and, quite literally, its *raison d'etre*. No one would have bothered bringing it into existence had not this purpose occurred to them. And given that this historical fact about its origin licenses a certain way of speaking, such a device may be primarily or originally characterized as a two-bitser, a thing whose function is to detect quarters, so that *relative to that function* we can identify both its veridical states and its errors.

This would not prevent a two-bitser from being wrested from its home niche and pressed into service with a new purpose – whatever new purpose the laws of physics certify it would reliably serve – as a *K*-detector, a quarter-balboa-detector, a doorstop, a deadly weapon. In its new role there might be a brief period of confusion or indeterminacy. How long a track record must something accumulate before it is no longer a two-bitser, but rather a quarter-balboa-detector (a q-balber) – or a doorstop or a deadly weapon? On its very debut as a q-balber, after ten years of faithful service as a two-bitser, is its state already a *veridical* detection of a quarter-balboa, or might there be a sort of force-of-habit error of nostalgia, a mistaken identification of a quarter-balboa *as* a US quarter?

As described, the two-bitser differs strikingly from us in that it has no provision for memory of its past experiences – or even "memory" (in scare-quotes) for its past "experiences." But the latter, at least, could easily be provided, if it was thought to make a difference. To start with the simplest inroad into this topic, suppose the two-bitser (to refer to it by the name of its original baptism) is equipped with a counter, which after ten years of service stands at 1,435,792. Suppose it is not reset to zero during its flight to Panama, so that on its debut there the counter turns over to 1,435,793. Does this tip the balance in favor of the claim that it has not yet switched to the task of correctly identifying quarter-balboas? Would variations and complications on this theme drive your intuitions in different directions?

We can assure ourselves that nothing *intrinsic* about the two-bitser considered narrowly all by itself and independently of its prior history would distinguish it from a genuine q-balber, made to order on commission from the Panamanian government. Still, given its ancestry, is there not a problem about its function, its purpose, its meaning, on this first occasion when it goes into the state we are tempted to call *Q*? Is this a case of going into state *Q* (meaning "US quarter here now") or state *QB* (meaning "Panamanian quarter-balboa here now")? I would say, along with Millikan (1984), that whether its Panamanian debut counts as going into state *Q* or state *QB* depends on whether, in its new niche, it was *selected for* its capacity to detect quarter-balboas – literally selected, e.g., by the holder of the Panamanian Pepsi-Cola franchise. If it was so selected, then even though its new proprietors might have forgotten to reset its counter, its first "perceptual" act would count as a correct identification by a q-balber, for that is what it would *now* be *for*. (It would have acquired quarter-balboa detection as its proper function.) If, on the other hand, the two-bitser was sent to Panama by mistake, or if it arrived by sheer coincidence, its debut would mean nothing, though its utility might soon – immediately – be recognized and esteemed by the relevant authorities (those who could press it into service in a new role), and thereupon its *subsequent* states would count as tokens of *QB*.

Presumably Fodor et al. would be content to let me say this, since, after all, the two-bitser is just an artifact. It has no intrinsic, original intentionality, so there is no "deeper" fact of the matter we might try to uncover. This is just a pragmatic matter of how best to talk, when talking metaphorically and anthropomorphically about the states of the device.

But we part company when I claim to apply precisely the same morals, the same pragmatic rules of interpretation, to the human case. In the case of human beings (at least), Fodor and company are sure that such deeper facts do exist – even if we cannot always find them. That is, they suppose that, independently of the power of any observer or interpreter to discover it, there is always a fact of the matter about what a person (or a person's mental state) *really means*. Now we might call their shared belief a belief in *intrinsic* intentionality, or perhaps even *objective* or *real* intentionality. There are differences among them about how to characterize, and name, this property of human minds, which I will continue to call *original intentionality*, but they all agree that minds are unlike the two-bitser in this regard, and this is what I now take to be the most fundamental point of disagreement between Fodor and me, between Searle and me, between Dretske and me, between Burge and me, etc. Once it was out in the open many things that had been puzzling me fell into place. At last I understood (and will shortly explain) why Fodor dislikes evolutionary hypotheses almost as much as he dislikes artificial intelligence (see, e.g., "Tom Swift and his procedural grandmother" in Fodor 1981 and the last chapter of Fodor 1983); why Dretske must go to such desperate lengths to give an account of error; why Burge's "anti-individualism" and Kripke's ruminations on rule-following, which strike some philosophers as deep and disturbing challenges to their complacency, have always struck me as great labors wasted in trying to break down an unlocked door.

I part company with these others because although they might agree with me (and Millikan) about what one should say in the case of the transported two-bitser, they say that we human beings are not just fancier, more sophisticated two-bitsers. When we say that we go into the state of believing that we are perceiving a US quarter (or some genuine water as opposed to XYZ, or a genuine twinge of arthritis) this is no metaphor, no mere manner of speaking. A parallel example will sharpen the disagreement.

Suppose some human being, Jones, looks out the window and thereupon goes into the state of thinking he sees a horse. There may or may not be a horse out there for him to see, but the fact that he is in the mental state of thinking he sees a horse is not just a matter of interpretation (these others say). Suppose the planet Twin Earth were just like Earth, save for having schmorses where we have horses. (Schmorses look for all the world like horses, and are well-nigh indistinguishable from horses by all but trained biologists with special apparatus, but they aren't horses, any more than dolphins are fish.) If we whisk Jones off to Twin Earth, land of the schmorses, and confront him in the relevant way with a schmorse, then either he really is, still, provoked into the state of believing he sees a horse (a mistaken, nonveridical belief) or he is provoked by that schmorse into believing, for the first time (and veridically), that he is seeing a schmorse. (For the sake of the example, let us suppose that Twin Earthians call schmorses *horses* (*chevaux, Pferde*, etc.) so that what Jones or a native Twin Earthian *says to himself* – or others – counts for nothing). However hard it may be to determine exactly what state he is in, he is really in one or the other (or perhaps he really is in neither, so violently have we assaulted his cognitive system). Anyone who finds this intuition irresistible believes in original intentionality and has some distinguished company: Fodor, Searle, Dretske, Burge, and Kripke, but also Chisholm (1956, 1957), Nagel (1979, 1986), and Popper and Eccles (1977). Anyone who finds this intuition dubious if not downright dismissible can join me, the Churchlands (see especially Churchland and Churchland 1981), Davidson, Haugeland, Millikan, Rorty, Stalnaker, and our distinguished predecessors, Quine and Sellars, in the other corner (along with Douglas Hofstadter, Marvin Minsky, and almost everyone else in AI).

There, then, is a fairly major disagreement. Who is right? I cannot hope to refute the opposing tradition in the short compass of a chapter, but I will provide two different persuasions on behalf of my side: I will show what perplexities Fodor, Dretske, et al. entangle themselves in by clinging to their intuition, and I will provide a little thought experiment to motivate, if not substantiate, my rival view. First the thought experiment.

DESIGNING A ROBOT

Suppose you decided, for whatever reasons, that you wanted to experience life in the twenty-fifth century, and suppose that the only known way of keeping your body alive that long required it to be placed in a hibernation device of sorts, where it would rest, slowed down and comatose, for as long as you liked. You could arrange to climb into the support capsule, be put to sleep, and then automatically awakened and released in 2401. This is a time-honored science-fiction theme, of course.

Designing the capsule itself is not your only engineering problem, for the capsule must be protected and supplied with the requisite energy (for refrigeration or whatever) for over four hundred years. You will not be able to count on your children and grandchildren for this stewardship, of course, for they will be long dead before the year 2401, and you cannot presume that your more distant descendants, if any, will take a lively interest in your well-being. So you must design a supersystem to protect your capsule and to provide the energy it needs for four hundred years.

Here there are two basic strategies you might follow. On one, you should find the ideal location, as best you can foresee, for a fixed installation that will be well supplied with water, sunlight, and whatever else your capsule (and the supersystem itself) will need for the duration. The main drawback to such an installation or "plant" is that it cannot be moved if harm comes its way – if, say, someone decides to build a freeway right where it is located. The second alternative is much more sophisticated, but avoids this drawback: design a mobile facility to house your capsule along with the requisite sensors and early-warning devices so that it can move out of harm's way and seek out new energy sources as it needs them. In short, build a giant robot and install the capsule (with you inside) in it.

These two basic strategies are obviously copied from nature: they correspond roughly to the division between plants and animals. Since the latter, more sophisticated strategy better fits my purposes, we shall suppose that you decide to build a robot to house your capsule. You should try to design it so that above all else it "chooses" actions designed to further your best interests, of course. "Bad" moves and "wrong" turns are those that will tend to incapacitate it for the role of protecting you until 2401 – which is its sole *raison d'être*. This is clearly a profoundly difficult engineering problem, calling for the highest level of expertise in designing a "vision" system to guide its locomotion, and other "sensory" and locomotory systems. And since you will be comatose throughout and thus cannot stay awake to guide and plan its strategies, you will have to design it to generate its own plans in response to changing circumstances. It must "know" how to "seek out" and "recognize" and then exploit energy sources, how to move to safer territory, how to "anticipate" and then avoid dangers. With so much to be done, and done fast, you had best rely whenever you can on economies: give your robot no more discriminatory prowess than it will probably need in order to distinguish what needs distinguishing in its world.

Your task will be made much more difficult by the fact that you cannot count on your robot being the only such robot around with such a mission. If your whim catches on, your robot may find itself competing with others (and with your human descendants) for limited supplies of energy, fresh water, lubricants, and the like. It would no doubt be wise to design it with enough sophistication in its control system to permit it to calculate the benefits and risks of cooperating with other robots, or of forming alliances for mutual benefit. (Any such calculation must be a "quick and dirty" approximation, arbitrarily truncated. See Dennett, forthcoming b.)

The result of this design project would be a robot capable of exhibiting self-control, since you must cede fine-grained real-time control to your artifact once you put yourself to sleep.[2] As such it will be capable of deriving its own subsidiary goals from its assessment of its current state and the import of that state for its ultimate goal (which is to preserve you). These secondary goals may take it far afield on century-long projects, some of which may be ill advised, in spite of your best efforts. Your robot may embark on actions antithetical to your purposes, even suicidal, having been convinced by another robot, perhaps, to subordinate its own life mission to some other.

But still, according to Fodor et al., this robot would have no original intentionality at all, but only the intentionality it derives from its artifactual role as your protector. Its simulacrum of mental states would be just that – not *real* deciding and seeing and wondering and planning, but only *as if* deciding and seeing and wondering and planning.

We should pause, for a moment, to make sure we understand what this claim encompasses. The imagined robot is certainly vastly more sophisticated than the humble two-bitser, and perhaps along the path to greater sophistication we have smuggled in some crucial new capacity that would vouchsafe the robot our kind of original intentionality. Note, for instance, that our imagined robot, to which we have granted the power to "plan" new courses of actions, to "learn" from past errors, to form allegiances, and to "communicate" with its competitors, would probably perform very creditably in any Turing Test to which we subjected it (see Dennett 1985). Moreover, in order to do all this "planning" and "learning" and "communicating" it will almost certainly have to be provided with control structures that are rich in self-reflective, self-monitoring power, so that it will have a human-like access to its own internal states and be capable of reporting, avowing, and commenting upon what it "takes" to be the import of its own internal states. It will have "opinions" about what those states mean, and we should no doubt take those opinions seriously as very good evidence – probably the best evidence we can easily get – about what those states "mean" *metaphorically speaking* (remember: it's only an artifact). The two-bitser was given no such capacity to sway our interpretive judgments by issuing apparently confident "avowals".

There are several ways one might respond to this thought experiment, and we will explore the most promising in due course, but first I want to draw out the most striking implication of standing firm with our first intuition: no artifact, no matter how much AI wizardry is designed into it, has anything but derived intentionality. If we cling to this view, the conclusion forced upon us is that our own intentionality is exactly like that of the robot, for the science-fiction tale I have told is not new; it is just a variation on Dawkins's (1976) vision of us (and all other biological species) as "survival machines" designed to prolong the futures of our selfish genes. We are artifacts, in effect, designed over the eons as survival machines for genes that cannot act swiftly and informedly in their own interests. Our interests as we conceive them and the interests of our genes may well diverge – even though were it not for our genes' interests, we would not exist: their preservation is our original *raison d'être*, even if we can learn to ignore that goal and devise our own *summum bonum*, thanks to the intelligence our genes have installed in us. So our intentionality is derived from the intentionality of our "selfish" genes! *They* are the Unmeant Meaners, not us!

READING MOTHER NATURE'S MIND

This vision of things, while it provides a satisfying answer to the question of whence came our own intentionality, does seem to leave us with an embarrassment, for its derives our own intentionality from entities – genes – whose intentionality is surely a paradigm case of mere *as if* intentionality. How could the literal depend on the metaphorical? Moreover, there is surely this much disanalogy between my science-fiction tale and Dawkins's story: in my tale I supposed that there was conscious, deliberate, foresighted engineering involved in the creation of the robot, whereas even if we are, as Dawkins says, the product of a design process that has our genes as the primary beneficiary, that is a design process that utterly lacks a conscious, deliberate, foresighted engineer.

The chief beauty of the theory of natural selection is that it shows us how to eliminate this intelligent Artificer from our account of origins. And yet the process of natural selection is responsible for designs of great cunning. It is a bit outrageous to conceive of genes as clever designers; genes themselves could not be more stupid; *they* cannot reason or represent or figure out anything. They do not do the designing themselves; they are merely the beneficiaries of the design process. But then who or what does the designing? Mother Nature, of course, or more literally, the long, slow process of evolution by natural selection.

To me the most fascinating property of the process of evolution is its uncanny capacity to mirror *some* properties of the human mind (the intelligent Artificer) while being bereft of others. While it can never be stressed enough that natural selection operates with no foresight and no purpose, we should not lose sight of the fact that the process of natural selection has proven itself to be exquisitely sensitive to rationales, making myriads of discriminating "choices" and "recognizing" and "appreciating" many subtle relationships. To put it even more provocatively, when natural selection selects, it can "choose" a particular design *for one reason rather than another*, without ever consciously – or unconsciously! – "representing" either the choice or the reasons. (Hearts were chosen for their excellence as blood circulators, not for the captivating rhythm of their beating, though that *might* have been the reason something was "chosen" by natural selection.)

There is, I take it, no representation at all in the process of natural selection. And yet it certainly seems that we can give principled explanations of evolved design features that invoke, in effect, "what Mother Nature had in mind" when that feature was designed.[3]

Just as the Panamanian Pepsi-Cola franchise-holder can select the two-bitser *for* its talent at recognizing quarter-balboas, can adopt it *as* a quarter-balboa-detector, so evolution can select an organ *for* its capacity to oxygenate blood, can establish it *as* a lung. And it is only relative to just such design "choices" or evolution-"endorsed" purposes – *raisons d'être* – that we can identify behaviors, actions, perceptions, beliefs, or any of the other categories of folk psychology. (See Millikan 1984, 1986, for a forceful expression of this view.)

The idea that we are artifacts designed by natural selection is both compelling and familiar; some would go so far as to say that it is quite beyond serious controversy. Why, then, is it resisted not just by Creationists, but also (rather subliminally) by the likes of Fodor, Searle, Dretske, Burge, and Kripke? My hunch is because it has two rather unobvious implications that some find terribly unpalatable. First, if we are (just) artifacts, then what our innermost thoughts mean – and whether they mean anything at all – is something about which we, the very thinkers of those thoughts, have no special authority. The two-bitser turns into a q-balber without ever changing its inner nature; the state that used to mean one thing now means another. The same thing could in principle happen to us, if we are just artifacts, if our own intentionality is thus not original but derived. Those – such as Dretske and Burge – who have already renounced this traditional doctrine of privileged access can shrug off, or even welcome, that implication; it is the second implication that they resist: if we are such artifacts, not only have we no guaranteed privileged access to the deeper facts that fix the meanings of our thoughts, but *there are no such deeper facts*. Sometimes functional interpretation is obvious, that when it is not, when we go to read Mother Nature's mind, there is no text to be interpreted. When "the fact of the matter" about proper function is controversial – when more than one interpretation is well supported – there is no fact of the matter.

The tactic of treating evolution itself from the intentional stance needs further discussion and defense, but I want to approach the task indirectly. The issues will come into better focus, I think, if first we diagnose the resistance to this tactic – and its Siamese twin, the tactic of treating ourselves as artifacts – in recent work in philosophy of mind and language.

ERROR, DISJUNCTION, AND INFLATED INTERPRETATION

Dretske's attempt (1981, 1985, 1986) to deal with these issues invokes a distinction between what he calls *natural meaning* and *functional meaning*. Natural meaning (*meaning$_n$*) is defined in such a way as to rule out misrepresentation; what a particular ringing of the doorbell means$_n$ depends on the integrity of the circuit that causes the ringing. "When there is a short-circuit, the ring of the doorbell (regardless of what it was designed to indicate, regardless of what it normally indicates) does not indicate that the doorbutton is being depressed." "This is what it is *supposed* to mean$_n$, what it was *designed* to mean$_n$, what (perhaps) tokens of that type *normally* mean$_n$, but not what it *does* mean$_n$" (1986, p. 21).

It then falls to Dretske to define *functional meaning*, what it is for something to mean$_f$ that such-and-such, in such a way as to explain how a sign or state or event in some system can, on occasion, misrepresent something or "say" something false. But "if these functions are (what I shall call) *assigned* functions, then meaning$_f$ is tainted with the purposes, intentions and beliefs of those who assign the function from which meaning$_f$ derives its misrepresentational powers" (p. 22). Clearly, the meaning of the two-bitser's acceptance state Q is just such an assigned functional meaning, and Dretske would say of it: "That is the function we assign it, the reason it was built and the explanation for why it was built the way it was. Had our purposes been otherwise, it might have meant$_f$ something else" (p. 23).

Since merely *assigned* functional meaning is "tainted," Dretske must seek a further distinction. What he must characterize is the *natural* functions of the counterpart states of organisms, "functions a thing has which are independent of *our* interpretive intentions and purposes" (p. 25), so that he can then define natural functional meaning in terms of those functions.

> We are looking for what a sign is *supposed* to mean$_n$ where the "supposed to" is cashed out in terms of the function of that sign (or sign system) in the organism's *own* cognitive economy.
>
> (1986, p. 25)

The obvious way to go, as we saw in the last section, is to substitute for our interpretive intentions and purposes the intentions and purposes of the organism's designer, Mother Nature – the process of natural selection – and ask ourselves what, in *that* scheme, any particular type of signal or state is designed to signal, supposed to mean. Just as we would ultimately appeal to the engineers' rationales when deciding on the best account of representation and misrepresentation in our imagined survival-machine robot, so we can appeal to the discernible design rationales of natural selection in assigning content, and hence the power of *mis*representation, to event types in natural artifacts – organisms, ourselves included.

But although Dretske pays homage to those who have pursued that evolutionary path, and warily follows it some distance himself, he sees a problem. The problem is none other than the biological version of our question about what principled way there is to tell whether the state of the two-bitser (in some particular environment) means "quarter here now" or "quarter-balboa here now" or "thing of kind *F* or kind *G* or kind *K* here now." We must find an interpretation principle that assigns content, Dretske says, "without doing so by artificially *inflating* the natural functions of these systems" – while at the same time avoiding the too-deflationary principle which resolves all functional meaning into brute natural meaning, where misrepresentation is impossible.

Consider the classic case of what the frog's eye tells the frog's brain (Lettvin et al. 1959). Suppose we provoke a frog into catching and swallowing a lead pellet we toss at it (cf. Millikan 1986). If we interpret the signal coming from the eye as "telling" the frog that there is a fly flying toward it, then it is the eye that is passing mistaken information to the frog, whereas if we interpret that signal as merely signaling a dark moving patch on the retina, it is "telling the truth" and the error must be assigned to some later portion of the brain's processing (see Dennett 1969, p. 83). If we are strenuously minimal in our interpretations, the frog never makes a mistake, for every event in the relevant pathway in its nervous system can always be *de-interpreted* by adding disjunctions (the signal means something less demanding: fly *or* pellet *or* dark moving spot *or* slug of kind K *or* ...) until we arrive back at the brute meaning$_n$ of the signal type, where misrepresentation is impossible. No matter how many layers of transducers contribute to a signal's specificity, there will always be a deflationary interpretation of its meaning as meaning$_n$ unless we relativize our account to some assumption of the normal (Normal, in Millikan's sense) function (see Dennett 1969, section 9, "Function and content").

Dretske is worried about overendowing event types with content, attributing a more specific or sophisticated meaning to them than the facts dictate. But given the stinginess of Mother Nature the engineer, this otherwise laudable hermeneutical abstemiousness puts one at risk of failing to appreciate the "point," the real genius, of her inventions. A particularly instructive instance of the virtues of "inflationary" functional interpretation is Braitenberg's (1984) speculative answer to the question of why so many creatures – from fish to human beings – are equipped with special-purpose hardware that is wonderfully sensitive to visual patterns exhibiting symmetry around a vertical axis. There can be little doubt about what the deflationary description is of the content of these intricate transducers: they signal "instance of symmetry around vertical axis on the retina." But why? What is this for? The provision is so common that it must have a very general utility. Braitenberg asks what in the natural world (before there were church facades and suspension bridges) presents a vertically symmetrical view? Nothing in the plant world, and nothing in the terrain. Only this: other animals, *but only when they are facing the viewer!* (Rear views are often vertically symmetrical, but generally less strikingly so.) In other words, what a vertical-symmetry transducer tells one is (roughly) "someone is looking at you." Needless to say, this is typically a datum well worth an animal's attention, for the other creature, in whose cross-hairs the animal currently sits, may well be a predator – or a rival or a mate. And so it is not surprising that the normal effect of the symmetry detector's being turned ON is an immediate orientation reaction and (in the case of fish, for instance) preparation for flight. Is it inflationary to call this transducer a predator-detector? Or a predator-or-mate-or-rival-detector? If you were hired to design a fish's predator-detector, would you go for a more foolproof (but cumbersome, slow) transducer, or argue that this is really the very best sort of predator-detector to have, in which the false alarms are a small price to pay for its speed and its power to recognize relatively well-hidden predators?

Ecologically insignificant vertical symmetries count as *false* alarms only if we suppose the special-*purpose* wiring is *supposed* to "tell" the organism (roughly) "someone is looking at you." What *exactly* is the content of its deliverance? This quest for precision of content ascription, and for independence of interpretation, is the hallmark not only of Dretske's research program, but also of much of the theoretical work in philosophy of language and mind (the philosophical theory of meaning, broadly conceived). But at least in the case of the symmetry-detector (or whatever we want to call it) there is no "principled" answer to that, beyond what we can support by appeal to the functions we can discover and make sense of in this way, in the normal operation of the transducer in nature.

We saw in the case of human-designed artifacts that we could use our appreciation of the costs and benefits of various design choices to upgrade our interpretation of the two-bitser's discriminatory talent from mere disk-of-weight-w-and-thickness-t-and diameter-d-and material-m detection to quarter detection (or quarter-balboa detection, depending on the user's intentions). This is, if you like, the fundamental tactic of artifact hermeneutics. Why should Dretske resist the same interpretive principle in the case of natural functional meaning? Because it is not "principled" enough, in his view. It would fail to satisfy our yearning for an account of what the natural event *really* means, what it means under the aspect of "original" or "intrinsic" intentionality.[4]

In "Machines and the mental" (1985) Dretske claims that the fundamental difference between current computers and us is that while computers may process information by manipulating internal symbols of some sort, they have "no access, so to speak, to the *meaning* of these symbols, to the things the representations represent" (p. 26). This way of putting it suggests that Dretske is conflating two points: something's meaning something *to* or *for* a system or organism, and that system or organism's being in a position to know or recognize or intuit or introspect that fact from the inside.

> Unless these symbols have what we might call an *intrinsic* [my emphasis] meaning, a meaning they possess which is independent of our communicative intentions and purposes, then this meaning *must* be irrelevant to assessing what the machine is doing when it manipulates them.
>
> (1985, p. 28)

Dretske quite correctly insists that the meaning he is seeking for mental states must *make a real difference* in, and to, the life of the organism, but what he fails to see is that the meaning he seeks, while it is, in the case of an organism, independent of *our* intentions and purposes, is not independent of the intentions and purposes of Mother Nature, and hence is, in the end, just as derived and hence just as subject to indeterminacy of interpretation, as the meaning in our two-bitser.

Dretske attempts to escape this conclusion, and achieve "functional determination" in the face of threatened "functional indeterminacy," by devising a complicated story of how *learning* could make the crucial difference. According to Dretske, a learning organism can, through the process of repeated exposures to a variety of stimuli and the mechanism of associative learning, come to establish an internal state type that has a *definite, unique* function and hence functional meaning.

Confronted with our imagined robotic survival machine, Dretske's reaction is to suppose that in all likelihood some of its states do have natural (as to opposed to merely assigned) functional meaning, in virtue of the learning history of the survival machine's first days or years of service. "I think we could (logically) create an artifact that *acquired* original intentionality, but not one that (at the moment of creation, as it were) *had* it" (personal correspondence). The functions dreamed of, and provided for, by its engineers are only *assigned* functions – however brilliantly the engineers anticipated the environment the machine ends up inhabiting –

but once the machine has a chance to respond to the environment in a training or learning cycle, its states have at least the opportunity of acquiring natural (definite, unique) functional meaning – and not just the natural meaning in which misrepresentation is ruled out.

I will not present the details of this ingenious attempt because, for all its ingenuity, it won't work. Fodor (1987), in the chapter with which we began, shows why. First, it depends, as Fodor notes, on drawing a sharp line between the organism's learning period, when the internal state is developing its meaning, and the subsequent period when its meaning is held to be fixed. Misrepresentation is possible, on Dretske's view, only in the second phase, but any line we draw must be arbitrary. (Does a whistle blow, Fodor wonders, signalling the end of the practice session and the beginning of playing for keeps?) Moreover, Fodor notes (not surprisingly), Dretske's account cannot provide for the fixed natural functional meaning of any innate, unlearned representative states.

Dretske does not view this as a shortcoming. So much the worse for innate concepts, he says. "I don't think there are, or can be, innate concepts or beliefs .... Beliefs and desires, *reasons* in general (the sort of thing covered by the intentional stance), are (or so I would like to argue) invoked to explain patterns of behaviour that are acquired during the life history of the organism exhibiting the behavior (i.e., learned)" (personal correspondence).

The motivation for this stand can be brought out by considering an example. The first thing a baby cuckoo does when it hatches is to look around the nest for other eggs, its potential competitors for its adoptive parents' attention, and attempt to roll them over the edge. It surely has no inkling of the functional meaning of its activity, but that meaning is nevertheless there – *for* the organism and *to* the organism – unless we suppose by the latter phrase that the organism has to "have access" to that meaning, has to be in a position to reflect on it, or avow it, for instance. The rationale of the cuckoo's chillingly purposive activity is not in question; what remains to be investigated is to what extent the rationale is the fledgling's rationale and to what extent it is free-floating – merely what Mother Nature had in mind. For Dretske, however, this is an all-or-nothing question, and it is tied to his intuition that there must be unique and unequivocal (natural functional) meanings for mental states.

Dretske seems to be trying to do two things at one stroke: first, he wants to draw a principled (and all-or-nothing) distinction between free-floating and – shall we say? – "fully appreciated" rationales; and second, he wants to remove all interpretive slack in the specification of the "actual" or "real" meaning of any such appreciated meaning-states. After all, if we appeal to our introspective intuitions, that is just how it seems: not only is there something we mean by our thoughts – something utterly determinate even if sometimes publicly ineffable – but it is our recognition or appreciation of *that meaning* that explains what we thereupon do. There certainly is a vast difference between the extremes represented by the fledgling cuckoo and, say, the cool-headed and cold-blooded human murderer who "knows just what he is doing, and why," but Dretske wants to turn it into the wrong sort of difference. Echoing Searle, Dretske would sharply distinguish between syntax and semantics: in the human murderer, he would say, "it is the structure's having this meaning (its semantics), not just the structure that has this meaning (the syntax), which is relevant to explaining behavior" (personal correspondence; cf. Dretske 1985, p. 31). Even supposing Dretske could motivate the placement of such a threshold, dividing the spectrum of increasingly sophisticated cases into those where syntax does all the work and those where semantics comes unignorably into play, it is out of the question that the rigors of a learning history could break through *that* barrier, and somehow show an organism what its internal states "really meant."

Furthermore, *if* Dretske's learning-history move worked for learned representations, the very same move could work for innate representations "learned" by the organism's ancestors via natural selection over the eons. That is, after all, how we explain the advent of innate mechanisms – as arising out of a trial-and-error selection process over time. If, as Dretske supposes, "soft"-wiring can acquire natural functional meaning during an organisms's lifetime, thanks to its relations to environmental events, "hard"-wiring could acquire the same natural functional meaning over the lifetime of the species.

And again, when do we blow the whistle and freeze, for all future time, the meaning of such a designed item? What started out as a two-bitser can become a q-balber; what started out as a wrist bone can become a panda's thumb (Gould 1980), and what started out as an innate representation meaning one thing to an organism can come, over time in a new environment, to mean something else to that organism's progeny. (There are further problems with Dretske's account, some well addressed by Fodor, but I will pass over them.)

What, then, does Fodor propose in place of Dretske's account? He too is exercised by the need for an account of how we can pin an error on an organism. ("No representation without misrepresentation" would be a good Fodorian motto.) And like Dretske, he draws the distinction between derivative and original intentionality:

> I'm prepared that it should turn out that smoke and tree rings represent only relative to our interests in predicting fires and ascertaining the ages of trees, that thermostats represent only relative to our interest in keeping the room warm, and that English words represent only relative to our intention to use them to communicate our thoughts. I'm prepared, that is, that only mental states (hence, according to RTM [the Representational Theory of Mind], only mental representations) should turn out to have semantic properties *in the first instance*; hence, that a naturalized semantics should apply, strictu dictu, to mental representations only.
>
> (Fodor 1987, p. 99)

And then, like Dretske, he faces what he calls the disjunction problem. What principled or objective grounds can we have for saying the state means "quarter here now" (and hence is an error, when it occurs in perceptual response to a slug) instead of meaning "quarter *or* quarter-balboa *or* slug of kind K *or* . . ." (and hence, invariably, is not an error at all)? Fodor is no more immune than Dretske (or anyone else) to the fatal lure of teleology, of discovering what the relevant mechanism is "supposed to do," but he manfully resists:

> I'm not sure that this teleology/optimality account is false, but I do find it thoroughly unsatisfying . . . . I think maybe we can get a theory of error without relying on notions of optimality or teleology; and if we can, we should. All else being equal, the less Pop-Darwinism the better, surely.
>
> (Fodor 1987, pp. 105–6)

I appreciate the candor with which Fodor expresses his discomfort with appeals to evolutionary hypotheses. (Elsewhere he finds he must help himself to a bit of "vulgar Darwinism" to buttress an account he needs of the functions of transducers.) Why, though, should he be so unwilling to follow down the path? Because he sees (I gather) that the most one can ever get from any such story, however well buttressed by scrupulously gathered facts from the fossil record, etc., is a story with all the potential for indeterminacy that we found in the tale of the transported two-bitser. And Fodor wants real, original, intrinsic meaning – not for the states of artifacts, heavens knows, for Searle is right about them! – but for our own mental representations.

Does Fodor have an account that will work better than Dretske's? No. His is equally ingenious, and equally forlorn. Suppose, Fodor says, "I see a cow which, stupidly, I misidentify. I take it, say, to be a horse. So taking it causes me to effect the tokening of a symbol; viz., I say 'horse'." There is an asymmetry, Fodor argues, between the causal relations that hold between horses and "horse" tokenings on the one hand and between cows and "horse" tokenings on the other:

> In particular, misidentifying a cow as a horse wouldn't have led me to say "horse" *except that there was independently a semantic relation between "horse" tokenings and horses.* But for the fact that the word "horse" expresses the property of *being a horse* (i.e., but for the fact that one calls *horses* "horses", it would not have been *that* word that taking a cow to be a horse would have caused me to utter. Whereas, by contrast, since "horse" does mean *horse*, the fact that horses cause me to say "horse" does not depend upon there being semantic – or, indeed, any – connection between "horse" tokenings and cows.
>
> (Fodor 1987, pp. 107–8)

This doctrine of Fodor's then gets spelled out in terms of counterfactuals that hold under various circumstances. Again, without going into the details (for which see Akins, unpublished), let me just say that the trouble is that our nagging problem arises all over again. How does Fodor establish that, in his mental idiolect, "horse" means *horse* – and not *horse-or-other-quadruped-resembling-a-horse* (or something like that)? Either Fodor must go Searle's introspective route and declare that this is something he can just tell, from the inside, or he must appeal to the very sorts of design considerations, and the "teleology/optimality story" that he wants to resist. Those of us who have always loved to tell that story can only hope that he will come to acquire a taste for it, especially when he realizes how unpalatable and hard to swallow the alternatives are.

This brings me to Burge, who has also constructed a series of intuition pumps designed to reveal the truth to us about error. Burge has been arguing in a series of papers against a doctrine he calls *individualism*, a thesis about what facts settle questions about the content or meaning of an organism's mental states. According to individualism,

> an individual's intentional states and events (types and tokens) could not be different from what they are, given the individual's physical, chemical, neural, or functional histories, where these histories are specified nonintentionally and in a way that is independent of physical or social conditions outside the individual's body.
>
> (1986, p. 4)

Or in other words:

> The meaning or content of an individual's internal states could not be different from what it is, given the individual's *internal* history and constitution (considered independent of conditions outside its "body").

The falsehood of this thesis should not surprise us. After all, individualism is false of such simple items as two-bitsers. We changed the meaning of the two-bitser's internal state by simply moving it to Panama and giving it a new job to perform. Nothing structural or physical inside it changed, but the meaning of one of its states changed from Q to QB in virtue of its changed embedding in the world. In order to attribute meaning to functional states of an artifact, you have to depend on assumptions about what it is supposed to do, and in order to get any leverage about that, you have to look to the wider world of purposes and prowesses. Burge's anti-individualistic thesis is then simply a special case of a very familiar observation: functional characterizations are relative not only to the embedding environment, but also to assumptions about optimality of design. (See, e.g., Wimsatt (1974). Burge (1986) seems to appreciate this in footnote 18 on p. 35.)

Moreover, Burge supports his anti-individualism with arguments that appeal to just the considerations that motivated our treatment of the two-bitser. For instance, he offers an extended argument (ibid., pp. 41ff.) about a "person P who normally correctly perceives instances of a particular objective visible property O" by going into state O' and it turns out that in some circumstances, a different visible property, C, puts P into state O'. We can substitute "two-bitser" for "P", "Q" for "O'", "quarter" for "O", and "quarter-balboa" for "C", and notice that his argument is our old friend, without addition or omission.

But something is different: Burge leaves no room for indeterminacy of content; his formulations always presume that there is a fact of the matter about what something *precisely* means. And he makes it clear that he means to disassociate himself from the "stance-dependent" school of functional interpretation. He chooses to "ignore generalized arguments that mentalistic ascriptions are deeply indeterminate" (1986, p. 6) and announces his Realism by noting that psychology seems to presuppose the reality of beliefs and desires, and it seems to work. That is, psychology makes use of interpreted that-clauses, "– or what we might loosely call 'intentional content'." He adds, "I have seen no sound reason to believe that this use is merely heuristic, instrumentalistic, or second class in any other sense" (p. 8). That is why his thesis of anti-individualism seems so striking; he seems to be arguing for the remarkable view that *intrinsic* intentionality, *original* intentionality, is just as context sensitive as derived intentionality.

Although Burge, like Dretske and Fodor, is drawn inexorably to evolutionary considerations, he fails to see that his reliance on those very considerations must force him to give up his uncomplicated Realism about content. For instance, he champions Marr's (1982) theory of vision as a properly anti-individualistic instance of successful psychology without noticing that Marr's account is, like "engineering" accounts generally, dependent on strong (indeed too strong – see Ramachandran, 1985a,b) optimality assumptions that depend on making sense of *what Mother Nature had in mind* for various subcomponents of the visual system. Without the tactic I have been calling artifact hermeneutics, Marr would be bereft of any principle for assigning content. Burge himself enunciates the upshot of the tactic:

> The methods of individuation and explanation are governed by the assumption that the subject has adapted to his or her environment sufficiently to obtain veridical information from it under certain normal conditions. If the properties and relations that *normally* caused visual impressions were regularly different from what they are, the individual would obtain different information and have visual experiences with different intentional content.
>
> (1986, p. 35)

When we attribute content to some state or structure in Marr's model of vision, we must defend our attribution by claiming (in a paraphrase of Dretske on assigned functional meaning) that that is the function Mother Nature assigned this structure, the reason why it was built, and the explanation for why it was built the way it was. Had her purposes been otherwise, it might have meant$_f$ something else.

The method Burge endorses, then, must make the *methodological* assumption that the subject has adapted to his or her environment sufficiently so that when we come to assigning contents to the subject's states – when we adopt the intentional stance – the dictated attributions are those that come out veridical, *and useful.* Without the latter condition, Burge will be stuck with Fodor's and Dretske's problem of disjunctive dissipation of content, because you can always get veridicality at the expense of utility by adding disjuncts. Utility, however, is not an objective, determinate property, as the example of the two-bitser made clear. So contrary to what Burge assumes, he must relinquish the very feature that makes his conclusion so initially intriguing: his Realism about "intentional content," or in other words his belief that there is a variety of intrinsic or original intentionality that is not captured by our strategies for dealing with merely derived intentionality like that of the two-bitser.

The Realism about intentional content that Burge assumes, along with Fodor and the others, is also presupposed by Putnam, whose Twin Earth thought experiments (Putnam 1975) set the agenda for much recent work on these issues. We can see this clearly, now, by contrasting our two-bitser with a Putnamian example. In the case of the two-bitser, the laws of nature do not suffice to single out what its internal state *really means* – except on pain of making misrepresentation impossible. Relative to one rival interpretation or another, various of its moves count as errors, various of its states count as misrepresentations, but beyond the resources of artifact hermeneutics there are no deeper facts to settle disagreements.

Consider then the members of a Putnamian tribe who have a word, "glug," let us say, for the invisible, explosive gas they encounter in their marshes now and then. When we confront them with some acetylene, and they call it glug, are they making a mistake or not? All the gaseous hydrocarbon they have ever heretofore encountered, we can suppose, was methane, but they are unsophisticated about chemistry, so there is no ground to be discovered in their past behavior or current dispositions that would license a description of their glug-state as methane-detection *rather than* the more inclusive gaseous-hydrocarbon-detection. Presumably, gaseous hydrocarbon is a "natural kind" and so are its subspecies, acetylene, methane, propane, and their cousins. So the laws of nature will not suffice to favor one reading over the other. Is there a deeper fact of the matter, however, about what they *really mean* by "glug"? Of course once we educate them, they will have to *come* to mean one thing or the other by "glug", but in advance of these rather sweeping changes in their cognitive states, will there already be a fact about whether they believe the proposition that *there is methane present* or the proposition that *there is gaseous hydrocarbon present* when they express themselves by saying "Glug!"?

If, as seems likely, no answer can be wrung from exploitation of the intentional stance in their case, I would claim (along with Quine and the others on my side) that the meaning of their belief is simply indeterminate in this regard. It is not just that I can't tell, and they can't tell; there is nothing to tell. But Putnam, where he is being a Realist about intentional content, would hold that there is a further fact, however inaccessible to us interpreters, that settles the questions about which cases of glug identification don't merely *count as* but *really are* errors, given what "glug" really means. Is this deeper fact any more accessible to the natives than to us outsiders? Realists divide on that question.

Burge and Dretske argue against the traditional doctrine of privileged access, and Searle and Fodor are at least extremely reluctant to acknowledge that their thinking ever rests on any appeal to such an outmoded idea. Kripke, however, is still willing to bring this skeleton out of the closest. In Kripke's (1982) resurrection of Wittgenstein's puzzle about rule following, we find all our themes returning once more: a resistance to the machine analogy on grounds that meaning in machines is relative to "the intentions of the designer" (p. 34), and the immediately attendant problem of error:

How is it determined when a malfunction occurs? ... Depending on the intent of the designer, any particular phenomenon may or may not count as a machine malfunction .... Whether a machine ever malfunctions and, if so, when, is not a property of the machine itself as a physical object but is well defined only in terms of its program, as stipulated by its designer.

(pp. 34–5)

This familiar declaration about the relativity and derivativeness of machine meaning is coupled with a frank unwillingness on Kripke's part to offer the same analysis in the case of human "malfunction." Why? Because it suggests that our own meaning would be as derivative, as inaccessible to us directly, as to any artifact:

The idea that we lack "direct" access to the facts whether we mean plus or quus [Q or QB, in the two-bitser's case] is bizarre in any case. Do I not know, directly, and with a fair degree of certainty, that I mean plus? ... There may be some facts about me to which my access is indirect, and about which I must form tentative hypotheses: but surely the fact as to what I mean by "plus" is not one of them!

(p. 40)

This declaration is not necessarily Kripke speaking *in propria persona,* for it occurs in the midst of a dialectical response Kripke thinks Wittgenstein would make to a particular skeptical challenge, but he neglects to put any rebuttal in the mouth of the skeptic and is willing to acknowledge his sympathy for the position expressed.

And why not? Here, I think, we find as powerful and direct an expression as could be of the intuition that lies behind the belief in original intentionality. This is the doctrine Ruth Millikan calls *meaning rationalism,* and it is one of the central burdens of her important book, *Language, Thought, and Other Biological Categories,* to topple it from its traditional pedestal (Millikan 1984; see also Millikan, unpublished). Something has to give. Either you must abandon meaning rationalism – the idea that you are unlike the fledgling cuckoo not only in having access, but also in having privileged access to your meanings – or you must abandon the naturalism that insists that you are, after all, just a product of natural selection, whose intentionality is thus derivative and hence potentially indeterminate.

IS FUNCTION IN THE EYE OF THE BEHOLDER?

Attributions of intentional states to us cannot be sustained, I have claimed, without appeal to assumptions about "what Mother Nature had in mind," and now that we can see just how much weight that appeal must bear, it is high time to cash out the metaphor carefully.

Some have seen contradiction or at least an irresolvable tension, a symptom of deep theoretical incoherence, in my apparently willful use of anthropomorphic – more specifically, intentional – idioms to describe a process which I insist in the same breath to be mechanical, goalless, and lacking in foresight. Intentionality, according to Brentano, is supposed to be the "mark of the mental" and yet the chief beauty of the Darwinian theory is its elimination of Mind from the account of biological origins. What serious purpose could be served, then, by such a flagrantly deceptive metaphor? The same challenge could be put to Dawkins: How can it be wise to encourage people to think of natural selection as a watchmaker, while adding that this watchmaker is not only blind, but not even *trying* to make watches?

We can see more clearly the utility – in fact the inescapable utility – of the intentional stance in biology by looking at some other instances of its application. Genes are not the only micro-agents granted apparently mindful powers by sober biologists. Consider the following passages from L. Stryer's *Biochemistry* (1981) quoted by Alexander Rosenberg in "Intention and action among the macromolecules" (1986):

> A much more demanding *task* for these enzymes is to *discriminate* between similar amino acids .... However, the observed *error* frequency in vivo is only 1 in 3000, indicating that there must be subsequent *editing* steps to enhance fidelity. In fact the synthetase *corrects* its own *errors* .... How does the synthetase *avoid* hydrolyzing isoleucine-AMP, the *desired* intermediate?
>
> (pp. 664–5; Rosenberg's emphases)

It seems obvious that this is mere *as if* intentionality, a theorist's fiction, useful no doubt, but not to be taken seriously and literally. Macromolecules do not literally avoid anything or desire anything or discriminate anything. We, the interpreters or theorists, *make sense* of these processes by endowing them with mentalistic interpretations, but (one wants to say) the intentionality we attribute in these instances is neither real intrinsic intentionality, nor real derived intentionality, but mere *as if* intentionality.

The "cash value" of these metaphors, like the cash value of the metaphors about selfishness in genes that Dawkins scrupulously provides, is relatively close at hand. According to Rosenberg, "every state of a macromolecule which can be described in cognitive terms has both a unique, manageably long, purely physical characterization, and a unique, manageably describable disjunction of consequences" (p. 72), but this may be more an expression of an ideal that microbiologists firmly believe to be within their reach than an uncontroversial *fait accompli*. In similar fashion we could assure each other that for every vending machine known to exist, there is a unique, manageably long, manageably describable account of how it works, what would trick it, and why. That is, there are no mysteriously powerful coin detectors. Still, we can identify coin detectors as such – we can figure out that this is the competence that explains their existence – long before we know how to explain, mechanically, how that competence is achieved (or better: approximated).

Pending completion of our mechanical knowledge, we need the intentional characterizations of biology to keep track of what we are trying to explain, and even after we have all our mechanical explanations in place, we will continue to need the intentional level against which to measure the bargains Mother Nature has struck (see Dennett, forthcoming b).

This might be held sufficient methodological justification for the strategy of attributing intentional states to simple biological systems, but there is a further challenge to be considered. Rosenberg endorses the view – developed by many, but especially argued for in Dennett (1969 and 1983) – that a defining mark of intentionality is failure of substitution ("intensionality") in the idioms that must be used to characterize the phenomena. He then notes that the biologists' attributions to macromolecules, selfish genes, and the like do not meet this condition; one can substitute ad lib without worry about a change in truth value, so long as the "subject" (the believer or desirer) is a gene or a macromolecule or some such simple mechanism. For instance, the proofreading enzyme does not recognize the error it corrects *qua* error. And it is not that the synthetase itself *desires* that isoleucine-AMP be the intermediate amino acid; it has no conception of isoleucine *qua* intermediate.

The disappearance of intensionality at the macromolecular level at first seems a telling objection to the persistent use of intentional idioms to characterize that level, but if we leave it at that we miss a still deeper level at which the missing intentionality reappears. The synthetase may not desire that isoleucine-AMP be the intermediate amino acid, but it is only *qua* intermediate that the isoleucine is "desired" at all – as an unsubstitutable part in a design whose rationale is "appreciated" by the process of natural selection itself. And while the proofreading enzyme has no inkling that it is correcting errors *qua* errors, Mother Nature does! That is, it is only *qua* error that the items thus eliminated provoked the creation of the "proofreading" competence of the enzymes in the first place. The enzyme itself is just one of Nature's lowly soldiers, "theirs not to reason why, theirs but to do or die," but *there is* a reason why they do what they do, a reason "recognized" by natural selection itself.

Is there a reason, really, why these enzymes do what they do? Some biologists, peering into the abyss that has just opened, are tempted to renounce *all* talk of function and purpose, and they are right about one thing: there is no stable intermediate position.[5] If you are prepared to make any claims about the function of biological entities – for instance, if you want to maintain that it is perfectly respectable to say that eyes are for seeing and the eagle's wings for flying – then you take on a commitment to the principle that natural *selection* is well named. In Sober's (1984) terms, there is not just selection *of* features but selection *for* features. If you proceed to assert such claims, you find that they resist substitution in the classical manner of intentional contexts. Just as George IV wondered whether Scott was the author of *Waverley* without wondering whether Scott was Scott, so natural selection "desired" that isoleucine be the intermediate without desiring that isoleucine be isoleucine. And without this "discriminating" prowess of natural selection, we would not be able to sustain functional interpretations at all.

Certainly we can describe all processes of natural selection without appeal to such intentional language, but at enormous cost of cumbersomeness, lack of generality, and unwanted detail. We would miss the pattern

that was there, the pattern that permits prediction and supports counterfactuals. The "why" questions we can ask about the engineering of our
robot, which have answers that allude to the conscious, deliberate, explicit
reasonings of the engineers (in most cases) have their parallels when the
topic is organisms and their "engineering." If we work out the rationales of
these bits of organic genius, we will be left having to attribute – but not in
any mysterious way – an emergent appreciation or recognition of those
rationales to natural selection itself.

How can natural selection do this without intelligence? It does not
consciously seek out these rationales, but when it stumbles on them, the
brute requirements of replication ensure that it "recognizes" their value.
The illusion of intelligence is created because of our limited perspective on
the process; evolution may well have tried all the "stupid moves" in addition
to the "smart moves," but the stupid moves, being failures, disappeared
from view. All we see is the unbroken string of triumphs.[6] When we set
ourselves the task of explaining why *those* were the triumphs, we uncover the
reasons for things – the reasons already "acknowledged" by the relative
success of organisms endowed with those things.

The original reasons, and the original responses that "tracked" them,
were not ours, or our mammalian ancestors', but Nature's. Nature
appreciated these reasons without representing them.[7] And the design
process itself is the source of our own intentionality. We, the reason-
representers, the self-representers, are a late and specialized product. What
this representation of our reasons gives us is foresight: the real-time
anticipatory power that Mother Nature wholly lacks. As a late and
specialized product, a triumph of Mother Nature's high tech, our intentionality is highly derived, and in just the same way that the intentionality of our
robots (and even our books and maps) is derived. A shopping list in the
head has no more intrinsic intentionality than a shopping list on a piece of
paper. What the items on the list mean (if anything) is fixed by the role they
play in the larger scheme of purposes. We may call our own intentionality
real, but we must recognize that it is derived from the intentionality of
natural selection, which is just as real – but just less easily discerned because
of the vast difference in time scale and size.

So if there is to be any original intentionality – original just in the sense
of being derived from no other, ulterior source – the intentionality of
natural selection deserves the honor. What is particularly satisfying about
this is that we end the threatened regress of derivation with something of
the right metaphysical sort: a *blind* and *unrepresenting* source of our own
sightful and insightful powers of representation. As Millikan (unpublished,
ms. p. 8) says, "The *root* purposing here must be unexpressed purposing."

This solves the regress problem only by raising what will still seem to be
a problem to anyone who still believes in intrinsic, determinate intentionality. Since in the beginning was *not* the Word, there is no text which one
might consult to resolve unsettled questions about function, and hence
about meaning. But remember: the idea that a word – even a Word – *could*
so wear its meaning on its sleeve that it could settle such a question is itself
a dead end.

There is one more powerful illusion to scout. We think we have a good model of *determinate*, incontrovertible function because we have cases of conscious, deliberate design of which we know, in as much detail as you like, the history. We *know* the *raison d'être* of a pocket watch, or of a laying hen, because the people who designed (or redesigned) them have told us, in words we understand, exactly what they had in mind. It is important to recognize, however, that however incontrovertible these historical facts may be, their projections into the future have no guaranteed significance. Someone might set out with the most fervent, articulate and clear-sighted goal of making a pocket watch and succeed in making something that was either a terrible, useless pocket watch or a serendipitously superb paper-weight. Which is it? One can always insist that a thing is, essentially, what its creator set out for it to be, and then when the historical facts leave scant doubt about that psychological fact, the identity of the thing is beyond question. In literary criticism, such insistence is known, tendentiously but traditionally, as the Intentional Fallacy. It has long been argued in such circles that one does not *settle* any questions of the meaning of a text (or other artistic creation) by "asking the author." If one sets aside the author, the original creator, as a definitive and privileged guide to meaning, one can suppose that subsequent readers (users, selecters) are just as important signposts to "the" meaning of something, but of course they are just as fallible – if their endorsements are taken as predictors of *future* significance – and otherwise their endorsements are just more inert historical facts. So even the role of the Pepsi-Cola franchise holder in selecting the two-bitser *as* a q-balber is only one more event in the life history of the device in as much need of interpretation as any other – for this entrepreneur may be a fool. Curiously, then, we get *better* grounds for making reliable functional attributions (functional attributions that are likely to continue to be valuable aids to interpretation in the future) when we ignore "what people say" and read what function we can off the discernible prowesses of the objects in question, rather than off the history of design development.

We cannot begin to make sense of functional attributions until we abandon the idea that there has to be one, determinate, *right* answer to the question: What is it for? And if there is no deeper fact that could settle that question, there can be no deeper fact to settle its twin: What does it mean?[8]

Philosophers are not alone in their uneasiness with appeals to optimality of design and to what Mother Nature must have had in mind. The debate in biology between the adaptationists and their critics is a different front in the same edgy war. The kinship of the issues comes out most clearly, perhaps, in Stephen Jay Gould's reflections on the panda's thumb. A central theme in evolutionary theory, from Darwin to the present (especially in the writings of François Jacob (1977) on the *bricolage* or "tinkering" of evolutionary design processes, and in those of Gould himself) is that Mother Nature is a satisficer, an opportunistic maker-do, not "an ideal engineer" (Gould 1980, p. 20). The panda's celebrated thumb "is not, anatomically, a finger at all" (p. 22), but a sesamoid bone of the wrist, wrest from its earlier role and pressed into service (via some redesigning) *as* a thumb. "The sesamoid thumb wins no prize in an engineer's derby ... But it does its job" (p. 24). That is to say, it does its job *excellently* – and that is how we can be so sure what its job is; it is obvious what this appendage is *for*. So is it just like the q-balber that began life as a two-bitser? Gould (1980) quotes Darwin himself:

> Although an organ may not have been originally formed for some special purpose, if it now serves for this end we are justified in saying that it is specially contrived for it. On the same principle, if a man were to make a machine for some special purpose, but were to use old wheels, springs, and pulleys, only slightly altered, the whole machine, with all its parts, might be said to be specially contrived for that purpose. Thus throughout nature almost every part of each living being has probably served, in a slightly modified condition, for diverse purposes, and has acted in the living machinery of many ancient and distinct specific forms.

"We may not be flattered," Gould goes on to say, "by the metaphor of refurbished wheels and pulleys, but consider how well we work" (p. 26). From this passage it would seem that Gould was an unproblematic supporter of the methodology of reading function off prowess – which is certainly what Darwin is endorsing. But in fact, Gould is a well-known critic of adaptationist thinking, who finds a "paradox" (p. 20) in this mixture of tinkering and teleology. There is no paradox; there is only the "functional indeterminacy" that Dretske and Fodor see and shun. Mother Nature doesn't commit herself explicitly and objectively to *any* functional attributions; all such attributions depend on the mind-set of the intentional stance, in which we assume optimality in order to interpret what we find. The panda's thumb was no more *really* a wrist bone than it is a thumb. We will not likely be discomfited, in our interpretation, if we consider it *as* a thumb, but that is the best we can say, here or anywhere.[9]

After all these years we are still just coming to terms with this unsettling implication of Darwin's destruction of the Argument from Design: there is no ultimate User's Manual in which the *real* functions, and *real* meanings, of biological artifacts are officially represented. There is no more bedrock for what we might call original functionality than there is for its cognitivistic scion, original intentionality. You can't have realism about meanings without realism about functions. As Gould notes, "we may not be flattered" – especially when we apply the moral to our sense of our own authority about meanings – but we have no other reason to disbelieve it.

NOTES

All but the last section of this chapter appears under the same title, in Y. Wilks and D. Partridge (eds) *Source Book on the Foundations of Artificial Intelligence* (Cambridge: Cambridge University Press, 1987).

1   This tactic is hardly novel. Among earlier discussions of intentionality drawing on such examples of simple discriminating mechanisms are MacKenzie, unpublished (1978), Ackermann (1972), and Enc (1982).

2   For more on control and self-control, see my *Elbow Room: The Varieties of Free Will*

Worth Wanting (1984d), chapter 3, "Control and self-control"; and forthcoming a.

3   "There must, after all, be a finite number of general principles that govern the activities of our various cognitive-state-making and cognitive-state-using mechanisms and there must be explanations of why these principles have historically worked to aid our survival. To suppose otherwise is to suppose that our cognitive life is an accidental epiphenomenal cloud hovering over mechanisms that *evolution devised with other things in mind.*" (Millikan 1986, p. 55; my emphasis.)

4   Dretske happens to discuss the problem of predator detection in a passage that brings out this problem with his view:

> If (certain) bacteria did not have something inside that meant that *that* was the direction of magnetic north, they could not orient themselves so as to avoid toxic surface water. They would perish. If, in other words, an animal's internal sensory states were not rich in information, intrinsic natural meaning, about the presence of prey, predators, cliffs, obstacles, water and heat, it could not survive." (1985, p. 29.)

The trouble is that, given Dretske's conservative demands on information, the symmetry-detector wouldn't count as sending a signal with information (intrinsic natural meaning) about predators but only about patterns of vertical symmetry on the retina, and while no doubt it could be, and normally would be, supplemented by further transducers designed to make finer-grained distinctions between predators, prey, mates, rivals, and members of ignorable species, these could be similarly crude in their actual discriminatory powers. If, as Dretske suggests, some bacteria can survive with only north-detectors (they don't need toxic-water-detectors, as it happens), other creatures can get by with mere symmetry-detectors, so the last sentence quoted above is just false: most animals survive and reproduce just fine without the benefit of states that are rich enough in (Dretskean) information to inform their owners about prey, predators, cliffs, and the like.

5   Rosenberg (1986):

> Among evolutionary biologists, there are those who condemn the identification of anatomical structures as having specific adaptational significance, on the ground that such structures do not face selection individually, but only in the company of the rest of the organism. This makes ascriptions of adaptational "content" to a part of the organism indeterminate, since a different ascription together with other adjustments in our adaptational identifications can result in the same level of fitness for the whole organism. In the philosophy of psychology, the dual of this thesis is reflected in the indeterminacy of interpretation.

6   This illusion has the same explanation as the illusion exploited by con artists in "the touting pyramid" (Dennett 1984d, pp. 92ff). Schull (forthcoming) argues that the process of natural selection need not always be *perfectly* stupid, brute force trial and error of all possibilities. Thanks to the Baldwin effect, for instance, species themselves can be said to pretest some of the possibilities in phenotypic space, permitting a more efficient exploration by the genome of the full space of the adaptive landscape. Just as creatures who can "try out options in their heads" before committing themselves to action are smarter than those merely Skinnerian creatures that can only learn by real-world trial and error (Dennett 1974a), so species that "try out options in their phenotypic plasticity" can – without any Lamarckian magic – give Mother Nature a helping hand in their own redesign.

272   **Daniel C. Dennett**

7   Pursuing Schull's (forthcoming) extension of the application of the inten-
     tional stance to species, we can see that in one sense there is representation in
     the process of natural selection after all, in the history of variable proliferation
     of phenotypic "expressions" of genotypic ideas. For instance, we could say of a
     particular species that various of its subpopulations had "evaluated" particular
     design options and returned to the species' gene pool with their verdicts, some
     of which were accepted by the species.

8   Quine's thesis of the indeterminacy of radical translation is thus of a piece with
     his attack on essentialism; if things had real, intrinsic essences, they could have
     real, intrinsic meanings. Philosophers have tended to find Quine's skepticism
     about ultimate meanings much less credible than his animadversions against
     ultimate essences, but that just shows the insidious grip of meaning rationalism
     on philosophers.

9   We can complete our tour of two-bitser examples in the literature by
     considering Sober's (1984) discussion of the vexing problem of whether to call
     the *very first* dorsal fins to appear on a Stegosaurus an adaptation *for cooling*:

> Suppose the animal had the trait because of a mutation, rather than by
> selection. Can we say that the trait was an adaptation *in the case of that single
> organism?* Here are some options: (1) apply the concept of adaptation to
> historically persisting populations, not single organisms; (2) allow that
> dorsal fins were an adaptation for the original organism because of what
> happened later; (3) deny that dorsal fins are adaptations for the initial
> organism but are adaptations when they occur in subsequent organisms. My
> inclination is to prefer choice 3.
>
> (p. 197)

> See also his discussion of the functional significance of the skin-thickness of
> *Drosophila* moved to different environments (1984, pp. 209–10), and his
> discussion (p. 306) of how one might figure out which properties are being
> selected *for* by Mother Nature (now in the guise of Dawkins's crew coach):
> "Was the coach selecting for combinations of rowers? Was he selecting for
> particular rowers? We need not psychoanalyze the coach to find out." Not
> psychoanalysis, but at least the adoption of the intentional stance will help
> us do the reverse engineering we need to do to get any answers to this
> question.

REFERENCES

Ackermann, R. (1972) "Opacity in belief structures," *Journal of Philosophy*, LXIX,
     55–67.
Akins, K. (unpublished) "Information and organisms: or why nature doesn't build
     epistemic engines," doctoral dissertation, University of Michigan, Ann Arbor,
     1987.
Braitenberg, V. (1984) *Vehicles: Experiments in Synthetic Psychology*, Cambridge, MA:
     MIT Press/A Bradford Book.
Burge, T. (1986) "Individualism and psychology," *The Philosophical Review*, XCV, no.
     1, 3–46.
Chisholm, R. (1956) "Sentences about believing," *Aristotelian Society Proceedings*, 56,
     125–48.
—— (1957) *Perceiving: A Philosophical Study*, Ithaca: Cornell University Press.
Chomsky, N. (1980) "Rules and representations", *Behavioral and Brain Sciences*, 3,
     1–61.

Churchland, P. S. and Churchland, P. M. (1981) "Stalking the wild epistemic engine," *Nous*, 5–18.

Dawkins, R. (1976) *The Selfish Gene*, Oxford: Oxford University Press.

Dennett, D. C. (1969) *Content and Consciousness*, London: Routledge & Kegan Paul.

——(1974) "Why the law of effect will not go away," *Journal of the Theory of Social Behavior*, 5, 169–87.

——(1980a) "Passing the buck to biology" (commentary on Chomsky 1980), *Behavioral and Brain Sciences*, 3, 19.

——(1980b) "The milk of human intentionality" (commentary on Searle 1980b), *Behavioral and Brain Sciences*, 3, 428–30.

——(1982) "The myth of the computer: an exchange," *The New York Review of Books*, June 24, 56–7.

——(1983) "Intentional systems in cognitive ethology: the 'Panglossian paradigm' defended," *Behavioral and Brain Sciences*, 6, 343–90.

——(1984) "Computer models and the mind – a view from the east pole," *Times Literary Supplement*, December 14, 1984, 1453–4. (This is an earlier and truncated draft of Dennett 1986).

——(1984d) *Elbow Room: The Varieties of Free Will Worth Wanting*, Cambridge, MA: MIT Press/A Bradford Book.

——(1985) "Can machines think?" in M. Shafto (ed.) *How We Know*, San Francisco: Harper and Row.

——(1986) "The logical geography of computational approaches: a view from the East Pole," in R. Harnish and M. Brand (eds) *The Representation of Knowledge and Belief*. Tucson: University of Arizona Press.

——(forthcoming a) "A route to intelligence: oversimplify and self-monitor", in J. Khalfa (ed.) *Can Intelligence be Explained?* Oxford: Oxford University Press.

——(forthcoming b) "The moral first aid manual," 1986 Tanner Lecture, University of Michigan.

——(forthcoming c) "The myth of original intentionality," in W. Newton Smith and R. Viale (eds) *Modelling the Mind*, Oxford: Oxford University Press.

Dretske, F. (1981) *Knowledge and the Flow of Information*, Cambridge, MA: MIT Press/A Bradford Book.

——(1985) "Machines and the mental," Western Division APA Presidential Address, April 26, 1985 (printed in *Proceedings and Addresses of the APA* (1985) 59, 23–33).

——(1986) "Misrepresentation," in R. Bogdan (ed.) *Belief*, Oxford: Oxford University Press.

Enc, B. (1982) "Intentional states and mechanical devices," *Mind*, XCI, 161–82.

Fodor, J. (1981) *Representations*, Cambridge, MA: MIT Press/A Bradford Book.

——(1983) *The Modularity of Mind*, Cambridge, MA: MIT Press/A Bradford Book.

——(1987) *Psychosemantics*, Cambridge, MA: MIT Press/A Bradford Book.

Gould, S. J. (1980) *The Panda's Thumb*, New York: W. W. Norton & Co.

Haugeland, J. (1981) *Mind Design*, Cambridge, MA: MIT Press/A Bradford Book.

Hofstadter, D. and Dennett, D. C. (1981) *The Mind's I: Fantasies and Reflections on Mind and Soul*, New York: Basic Books.

Jacob, F. (1977) "Evolution and tinkering," *Science*, 196, 1,161–6.

Kripke, S. (1982) *Wittgenstein on Rules and Private Language*, Cambridge, MA: Harvard University Press.

Lettvin, J. Y., et al. (1959) 'What the frog's eye tells the frog's brain," *Proceedings of the Institute of Radio Engineers*, 1959, 1,940–51.

MacKenzie (unpublished) "Intentionality-One: Intentionality-Two," presented at the Canadian Philosophical Association Meetings, 1978.

Marr, D. (1982) *Vision*, Cambridge, MA: MIT Press.

Millikan, R. (1984) *Language, Thought and Other Biological Categories*, Cambridge, MA: MIT Press/A Bradford Book.

——(1986) "Thoughts without laws: cognitive science without content," *Philosophical Review*, XCV, 47–80.

——(unpublished) "Truth rules, hoverflies, and the Kripke–Wittgenstein paradox."

Nagel, T. (1979) *Mortal Questions*, Cambridge: Cambridge University Press.

——(1986) *The View From Nowhere*, Oxford: Oxford University Press.

Popper, K. and Eccles, J. (1977) *The Self and its Brain*, Berlin: Springer-International.

Putnam, H. (1975) "The meaning of 'meaning'," in Putnam, *Mind, Language, and Reality*, Cambridge: Cambridge University Press.

Ramachandran, V. S. (1985a) "Apparent motion of subjective surfaces," *Perception*, 14, 127–34.

——(1985b) Guest editorial in *Perception*, 14, 97–103.

Rosenberg, A. (1986) "Intentional psychology and evolutionary biology (part I: the uneasy analogy)," *Behaviorism*, 14, 15–27.

Schull, J. (forthcoming) "Evolution and learning: analogies and interactions," in E. Laszlo (ed.) *The Evolutionary Paradigm: Transdisciplinary Studies*. Durham: Duke University Press.

Searle, J. (1980a) *Expression and Meaning*, Cambridge: Cambridge University Press.

——(1980b) "Minds, brains, and programs," *Behavioral and Brain Sciences*, 3, 417–58.

——(1982) "The myth of the computer: an exchange," *The New York Review of Books*, June 24, 56–7.

——(1984) "Panel discussion: has artificial intelligence research illuminated human thinking?" in H. Pagels (ed.) *Computer Culture: The Scientific, Intellectual, and Social Impact of the Computer*. Annals of the New York Academy of Sciences, vol. 426.

——(1985) *Minds, Brains and Science*, Cambridge, MA: Harvard University Press.

Sober, E. (1984) *The Nature of Selection*, Cambridge, MA: MIT Press/A Bradford Book.

Stryer, L. (1981) *Biochemistry*, San Francisco: Freeman.

Wimsatt, W. (1974) "Complexity and organization," in K. Schaffner and R. S. Cohen (eds.) *PSA 1972* (Philosophy of Science Association). Dordrecht: Reidel, 67–86.

POSTSCRIPT

One puzzling feature of the response to "Evolution, error, and intentionality" has contributed to the direction of my current research on evolution. I was initially dumbfounded by the willingness of philosophers simply to dismiss or ignore – as too radical to be taken seriously, apparently – my suggestion that we are survival machines for our genes, as Dawkins has put it. This surprised me, for in point of fact the biology on which I based my philosophical extrapolations is not even controversial. It is uncontested that human bodies, like the bodies of all other creatures, are products of a design process that tracks, in the first instance, the "interests" of the genes whose phenotypic expressions those bodies are. There are substantive controversies about the importance of this fact, but not the fact itself.

I have come to see this reaction by philosophers as an example of a much broader naive anti-Darwinism that has flourished in the humanities, fed by misinformation from some of Darwin's popularizers. I decided to write a book (*Darwin's Dangerous Idea*, forthcoming) laying out the fundamental philosophical implications of the Darwinian revolution, to correct these ubiquitous flaws in the background assumptions of philosophers. There is great value to philosophy in well-informed Darwinian thinking, not the least of which is a proper theory of the origin of intentionality, of which I take "Evolution, error, and intentionality" to provide a sound sketch.

My claims about "reading Mother Nature's mind" have been expanded and further defended in "The interpretation of texts, people, and other artifacts," *Philosophy and Phenomenological Research*, 50, Supplement, 177–94, Fall 1990, and a different aspect of my defense of Dawkins's evolutionary perspective is found in "Memes and the exploitation of imagination," *Journal of Aesthetics and Art Criticism*, **48**, 127–35, Spring 1990, and some of the ideas in these essays were also presented in my 1991 book, *Consciousness Explained* (Boston: Little Brown).

I have also written several essays pursuing my disagreements with Dretske first adumbrated in this essay. "Ways of establishing harmony," first appeared in B. McLaughlin (ed.) *Dretske and His Critics* (Oxford: Blackwell, 1990), and was reprinted (slightly revised), in E. Villanueva (ed.) *Information, Semantics, and Epistemology* (Oxford: Blackwell, 1990). A follow-up article, incorporating material from these but adding further arguments and reflections is "La Compréhension Artisanale," (a French translation of "Do-it-yourself understanding"), in D. Fisette (ed.) *Daniel C. Dennett et les Stratégies Intentionnelles, Lekton*, 11, Winter (Université de Québec à Montréal, Montréal, 1992). The English version is available from the Center for Cognitive Studies at Tufts as a preprint (1990–94).

Part IV

Materialism and Value

14 The Scientific and the Ethical[1]

Bernard Williams

Discussions of objectivity often start from considerations about disagreement. We might ask why this should be so. It makes it seem as though disagreement were surprising, but there is no reason why that should be so (the earliest thinkers in the Western tradition found conflict at least as obvious a feature of the world as concord). The interest in disagreement comes about, rather, because neither agreement nor disagreement is universal. It is not that disagreement needs explanation and agreement does not, but that in different contexts disagreement requires different sorts of explanation, and so does agreement.

The way in which one understands a given kind of disagreement, and explains it, has important practical effects. It can modify one's attitude to others and one's understanding of one's own outlook. In relation to other people, one needs a view of what is to be opposed, rejected, and so forth, and in what spirit; for oneself, disagreement can raise a warning that one may be wrong, and if truth or correctness is what one is after, one may need to reform one's strategies.

Disagreement does not necessarily have to be overcome. It may remain an important and constitutive feature of one's relations to others, and also be seen as something that is merely to be expected in the light of the best explanations that we have of how such disagreement arises. There can be tension involved here, if one at once feels that the disagreement is about very important matters, and that there is a good explanation of why the disagreement is only to be expected. The tension is specially acute when the disagreement is not only important, but expresses itself in judgments that seem to demand assent from others.

Among types of disagreement, and the lessons that can be learned from them, there is a well-known polarity. At one extreme there is the situation of two children wanting one bun, or two heroes wanting one slave girl. The disagreement is practical and it is entirely explicable, and the explanation of it is not going to cast much doubt on the cognitive powers of the people involved. It may be said that this kind of case is so primitively practical that it hardly even introduces any judgment over which there is disagreement. Even at the most primitive level, of course, there is disagreement about *what is to be done*, but this is so near to desire and action that no one is going to think that the disagreement shows any failure of knowledge or understanding on anyone's part. It is simply that two people want incompatible things. But the conflict may well not remain as blank as that, and if the parties want to settle it by ordered speech rather than by violence, they will invoke more substantive judgments, usually of justice, and the children will talk about fairness, or the heroes about precedence.

In their most basic form, at least, these disagreements need not make anyone think that someone has failed to recognize or understand something, or that they cannot speak the language. At the opposite pole of the traditional contrast are disagreements that do make one think that. What these typically are depends on the theory of knowledge favoured by the commentator, but they often involve the observation under standard conditions of what J. L. Austin used to call 'middle-sized dry goods'. A feature of these examples that will be important later in the discussion is that the parties are assumed to share the same concepts, and to be trained in the recognition of furniture, pens, pennies or whatever it may be.

Around these paradigms there have been formed various oppositions: between practical and theoretical, or value and fact, or *ought* and *is*. Each of these has been thought to represent a fundamental difference in what disagreement means, and they are often taken to suggest contrasting hopes for resolving it. However, it is a mistake to suppose that these oppositions are different ways of representing just one distinction. Indeed, the two paradigm examples that I have mentioned significantly fail to correspond to the two ends of any one of these contrasts. The quarrel about the allocation of a good is certainly an example of the practical, but until one gets to the stage of taking seriously the claims of justice, it is not yet a disagreement about value. A disagreement in the perception of furniture is without doubt a disagreement about a matter of fact, but is not yet a disagreement about what is most often contrasted with the practical, namely the theoretical. To assemble these kinds of example into some one contrast requires more work to be done. It has been done, characteristically, by reducing the evaluative to the practical, and extending the factual to the theoretical. Both these manoeuvres are of positivist inspiration, and they are both suspect. It is not surprising that some philosophers now doubt whether there is any basic distinction at all that can be constructed to the traditional pattern.

I accept that there is no one distinction that is in question here. I also accept that the more positivistic formulations that have gone into defining each side of such a distinction are misguided. However, I believe that in relation to ethics there is a genuine and profound difference to be found, and also – it is a further point – that the difference is enough to motivate some version of the feeling (itself recurrent, if not exactly traditional) that science has some chance of being more or less what it seems, a systematized theoretical account of how the world really is, while ethical thought has no chance of being everything that it seems. The tradition is right, moreover, not only in thinking that there is such a distinction, but also in thinking that we can come to understand what it is through understanding disagreement. However, it is not a question of how much disagreement there is, nor even of what methods we have to settle disagreement, though that of course provides many relevant considerations. The basic difference lies rather in our reflective understanding of the best hopes that we could coherently entertain for eliminating disagreement in the two areas. It is a matter of what, under the most favourable conditions, would be the best explanation of disagreement being removed: the explanation – as I shall say from now on – of convergence.

The two "areas", as I have called them, are the *scientific* and the *ethical*. I hope to explain why one end should be labelled the "scientific", rather than, say, the "factual". It can be explained quite briefly why the other end, the ethical, is not called by any of several other familiar names. It is not called "the evaluative", because that additionally covers at least the area of aesthetic judgment, and that raises many questions of its own. It is not called "the normative", which covers only part of the interest of the ethical (roughly, the part concerned with rules), and also naturally extends to such things as the law, which again raise different questions. Last, it is not called "the practical", because that would displace a large part of the problem. It is not hard to concede that there is a distinction between the practical and (let us say) the non-practical. There is clearly such a thing as practical reasoning or deliberation, and that is not the same as thinking about how things are. It is *obviously* not the same, and that is why positivism thought that it had validated the traditional distinction by reducing the evaluative to the practical. But that reduction is mistaken, and it makes the whole problem look easier than it is.[2]

The basic idea behind the distinction between the scientific and the ethical, expressed in terms of convergence, is very simple. In a scientific enquiry there should ideally be convergence on an answer, where the best explanation of that convergence involves the idea that the answer represents how things are, whereas in the area of the ethical, at least at a high level of generality (the issue of generality is one that we shall come back to), there is no such coherent hope. The distinction does not turn on any difference in whether convergence will actually occur, and it is important that this is not what the argument is about. It might well turn out that there will be convergence in ethical outlook, at least among human beings. The point of the contrast is that even if that happens, it will not be correct to think that it has come about because convergence has been guided by how things actually are, whereas convergence in the sciences might be explained in that way if it does happen. This means, among other things, that we understand differently in the two cases the existence of convergence or, alternatively, its failure to come about.

I shall come back to ways in which we might understand ethical convergence. First, however, we must face certain arguments which suggest that there is really nothing at all in the distinction, expressed in these terms. There are two different directions from which that objection can come. In one version, it says that the notion of a convergence that comes about because of how things are is an empty notion. In the other, it says that the notion of such a convergence is not empty, but that it is available as much in ethical cases as in scientific – that is to say, the notion has some content, but it does nothing to help the distinction.

I have already said that the point of the distinction and of its explanation in terms of convergence does not turn on the question whether convergence as a matter of fact occurs. On the scientific side, however, it would be unrealistic to disconnect these ideas totally from the ways in which the history of Western science since the seventeenth century is to be understood. For one thing, any aspiration for the convergence of science that conceded at the same time that it had not occurred up to now might well seem merely Utopian and only fit to obscure the real issues, like the once fashionable hopes for a Galileo of the social sciences. More importantly, the conception of scientific progress in terms of convergence cannot be divorced from the history of Western science because it is the history of Western science that has done most to encourage it.

It is quite hard to deny that that history displays a considerable degree of convergence. What has been claimed is that this appearance has no real significance, because it is a cultural artefact, a product of the way in which we choose to narrate the history of science. Richard Rorty has written:[3]

> It is less paradoxical ... to stick to the classical notion of "better describing what was already there" for physics. This is not because of deep epistemological or metaphysical considerations, but simply because, when we tell our Whiggish stories about how our ancestors gradually crawled up the mountain on whose (possibly false) summit we stand, we need to keep some things constant throughout the story ... Physics is the paradigm of "finding" simply because it is hard (at least in the West) to tell a story of changing universes against the background of an unchanging moral law or poetic canon, but very easy to tell the reverse sort of story.

There are two notable faults in such a description of scientific success and what that success means. One is its attitude to the fact that it is easy to tell one kind of story and hard to tell the other. *Why* is the picture of "the world already there", helping to control our descriptions of it, so compelling? This seems to require some explanation on Rorty's account, but it does not get one. If the reference to "the West" implies a cultural or anthropological explanation, it is totally unclear what it would be: totally unclear, indeed, what it could be, if it is not going itself to assume an already existing physical world in which human beings come into existence and develop their cultures, and by which they are affected in various ways.

The point that an assumption of that kind is going to lie behind any explanations of what we do leads directly to the second fault in Rorty's account, that it is self-defeating. If the story that he tells were true, then there would be no perspective from which he could express it in this way. If it is overwhelmingly convenient to say that science describes what is already there, and if there are no deep metaphysical or epistemological issues here, but only a question of what is convenient (it is "simply because" of that that we speak as we do), then what everyone should be saying, including Rorty, is that science describes a world that is already there. But Rorty urges us not to say that, and in doing so, and in insisting, *as opposed to that*, on our talking of what it is convenient to say, he is trying to reoccupy the transcendental standpoint outside human speech and activity which is precisely what he wants us to renounce.[4]

A more effective level of objection lies in a negative claim that Rorty and others make, that no convergence of science, past or future, could possibly be explained in any contentful way by reference to the way that the world is, because there is an insoluble difficulty with the notion of "the world" as determining belief. It comes out as a dilemma. On the one hand, "the world" may be characterized in terms of our current beliefs about what it contains; it is a world of stars, people, grass, tables and so forth. When "the world" is taken in this way, we can of course say that our beliefs about the world are affected by the world, in the sense that for instance our beliefs about grass are affected by grass, but there is nothing illuminating or contentful in this – our conception of the world as the object of our beliefs can do no better than repeat the beliefs that we take to represent it. If, on the other hand, we try to form some idea of a world that is prior to any description of it, the world that all systems of belief and representation are trying to represent, then we have a quite empty notion of something completely unspecified and unspecifiable.[5] So either way we fail to have a notion of "the world" that will do what is required of it.

Each side of this dilemma takes all our representations of the world together, in the one case putting them all in, and in the other leaving them all out. But there is a third and more helpful possibility, that we should form a conception of the world that is "already there" in terms of some but not all of our representations, our beliefs and theories. In reflecting on the world that is there *anyway*, independent of our experience, we must concentrate not in the first instance on what our beliefs are about, but on how they represent what they are about. We can select among our beliefs and features of our world-picture some which we can reasonably claim to represent the world in a way that is to the maximum degree independent of our perspective and its peculiarities. The resultant picture of things, if we can carry through this task, can be called the "absolute conception" of the world.[6] In terms of that conception, we may hope to explain the possibility of our attaining that conception itself, and also the possibility of other, more perspectival, representations.

This notion of an absolute conception can serve to *make effective* a distinction between "the world as it is independently of our experience" and "the world as it seems to us". It does that by understanding "the world as it seems to us" as "the world as it seems peculiarly to us"; the absolute conception will, correspondingly, be that conception of the world that might be arrived at by any investigators, even if they were very different from us. What counts as a relevant difference from us, and indeed what for various levels of description will count as "us", will itself be explained on the basis of that conception itself; we shall be able to explain, for instance, why one kind of observer can make observations that another kind cannot make. It is centrally important that these ideas relate to science, not to all kinds of knowledge. We can *know* things, the content of which is perspectival: we can know that grass is green, for instance, though *green*, for certain, and probably *grass*, are concepts that would not be available to every competent observer of the world, and would not figure in the absolute conception. (As we shall see very soon, people can know things even more locally perspectival than that.) The point is not to give an account of knowledge, and the opposition that we are discussing is not to be expressed in terms of knowledge, but of science. The aim is to outline the possibility of a convergence characteristic of science, one that could contentfully be said to be a convergence on how things (anyway) are.

That possibility, as I have explained it, depends heavily on notions of explanation. The substance of the absolute conception (as opposed to those vacuous or vanishing ideas of "the world" that were offered before) lies in the idea that it could non-vacuously explain how it itself, and the various perspectival views of the world, should be possible. It is an important feature of modern science that it contributes to explaining how creatures who have the origins and characteristics that we have can understand a world which has the properties that this same science ascribes to the world. The achievements of evolutionary biology and the neuro-logical sciences are substantive in these respects, and the notions of explanation involved are not vacuous. It is true, however, that such explanations cannot themselves operate entirely at the level of the absolute conception, because what they have to explain are psychological and social phenomena, such as beliefs and theories and conceptions of the world, and there may be little reason to suppose that they, in turn, could be adequately characterized in non-perspectival terms. How far this may be so is a central philosophical question. But even if we allow that the explanations of such things must remain to some degree perspectival, this does not mean that we cannot operate the notion of the absolute conception. It will be a conception consisting of non-perspectival materials which will be available to any adequate investigator, of whatever constitution, and it will also help to explain to us, though not necessarily to those alien investigators, such things as our capacity to grasp that conception. Perhaps more than that will turn out to be available, but no more is necessary, in order to give substance to the idea of "the world" and to defeat the first line of objection to the distinction, in terms of possible convergence, between the scientific and the ethical.

The opposite line of objection urges that the idea of "converging on how things are" is available, to some adequate degree, in the ethical case as well. The place where this is to be seen is above all with those "thick" ethical concepts that possess a lot of substantive content. Many exotic examples of these can be drawn from other cultures, but there are enough left in our own: *coward, lie, brutality, gratitude*, and so forth. They are characteristically related to reasons for action. If a concept of this kind applies, this often provides someone with a reason for action, though that reason need not be a decisive one, and may be outweighed by other reasons. Of course, exactly what reason for action is provided, and to whom, depends on the situation, in ways that may well be governed by this and by other ethical concepts, but the general connection with action is clear enough. We may say, summarily, that such concepts are "action-guiding".

At the same time, their application is guided by the world. A concept of this sort may be rightly or wrongly applied, and people who have acquired it can agree that it applies or fails to apply to some new situation. In many cases that agreement will be spontaneous, while in other cases there is room for judgment and comparison. Some disagreement at the margin may be irresoluble, but that does not mean that the use of the concept is not controlled by the facts or by the users' perception of the world. (As with other concepts that are not totally precise, marginal disagreements can indeed help to show how their use *is* controlled by the facts.) We can say, then, that the application of these concepts is at the same time world-guided and action-guiding. How can it be both of these at once?

Prescriptivism gave a very simple answer to that question. According to prescriptivism, any such concept can be analysed into a descriptive and a prescriptive element: it is guided round the world by its descriptive content, but has a prescriptive flag attached to it. It is the first feature that allows it to be world-guided, while the second makes it action-guiding. Some of the difficulties with this picture concern the prescriptive element, and how that is supposed to guide action in the relevant sense (telling yourself to do something is not an obvious model for recognizing that one has a reason to do it). But the most significant objection, for this discussion, applies to the other half of the analysis. Prescriptivism claims that what governs the application of the concept to the world is the descriptive element, and that the evaluative interest of the concept plays no part in this. All the input into its use is descriptive, just as all the evaluative aspect is output. It follows that for any concept of this sort, one could produce another which picked out just the same features of the world, but which worked simply as a descriptive concept, lacking any prescriptive or evaluative force.

Against this, critics[7] have made the effective point that there is no reason to believe that a descriptive equivalent will necessarily be available. How we "go on" from one application of a concept to another is a function of the kind of interest that the concept represents, and one should not assume that one could see how people "go on" in their use of a concept of this sort, if one did not share the evaluative perspective in which the concept has its point. An insightful observer can indeed come to understand and anticipate the use of the concept without actually sharing the values of the people who use it: that is an important point, and we shall come back to it. But in imaginatively anticipating the use of the concept, he also has to grasp imaginatively its evaluative point. He cannot stand quite outside the evaluative interests of the community he is observing, and pick up the concept simply as a device for dividing up in a rather strange way certain neutral features of the world.

This seems a very plausible account, and certainly a possible one, of what is involved in mastering concepts of this kind and understanding their use. It needs, in fact, to be not much more than possible to play an important part in this argument, by reminding moral philosophy of what the demands made by an adequate philosophy of language or by the philosophy of social explanation may turn out to be. If it is not only possible but plausible, moral philosophy will be well advised to consider what needs to be said if it is true.

The sympathetic observer can follow the practice of the people he is observing; he can report, anticipate, and even take part in discussions of the use that they make of their concept. But, as with some other concepts of theirs, relating to religion, for instance, or to witchcraft, he is not ultimately identified with the use of this concept: it is not really his.[8] This possibility, of the insightful but not totally identified observer, bears on an important question, whether those who use ethical concepts of this kind can have ethical knowledge in virtue of properly applying those concepts. Let us assume, artificially, that we are dealing with a society that is maximally homogeneous and minimally given to general reflection; its members simply, all of them, use certain ethical concepts of this sort. (We may call it the "hypertraditional" society.) What would be involved in their having ethical knowledge? According to the best available accounts of propositional knowledge,[9] they would have to believe the judgments which they made; those judgments would have to be true; and their judgments would have to satisfy a further condition, which has been extensively discussed in the philosophy of knowledge, but which can be summarized by saying that those first two conditions must be non-accidentally linked: granted the way that the people have gone about their enquiries, it must be no accident that the belief they have acquired is a true one, and if the truth on the subject had been otherwise, they would have acquired a different belief, true in those different circumstances. Thus I may know, by looking at it, that the dice has come up 6, and that (roughly[10]) involves the claim that if it had come up 4, I would have come to believe, by looking at it, that it had come up 4 (the alternative situations to be considered have to be restricted to those moderately like the actual one). Taking a phrase from Robert Nozick, we can say that the third requirement – it involves a good deal more elaboration than I have suggested – is that one's belief should "track the truth".

The members of the hypertraditional society apply their "thick" concepts, and in doing so they make various judgments. If any of those judgments can ever properly be said to be true, then their beliefs, in those respects, can track the truth, since they can withdraw judgments of this sort if the circumstances turn out not to be what was supposed, can make an alternative judgment if it would be more appropriate, and so on. They have, each, mastered these concepts, and they can perceive the personal and social happenings to which the concepts apply. If there is truth here, their beliefs can track it. The question left is whether any of these judgments can be true.

An objection can be made to saying that they are. If they are true, then the observer can correctly say that they are; letting "F" stand in for one of their concepts, he can say for instance, "The headman's statement, *That is F*, is true". But then (the objection goes) he should be able to invoke a very basic principle about truth, the *disquotation principle*,[11] and say, in his own person, *that is F*. But he is not prepared to do that, since F is not one of his concepts.

How strong is this objection? It relies on the following principle: A cannot correctly say that B speaks truly in uttering S unless A could say something tantamount to S himself. (A lot of work has to be done to spell out what counts as something "tantamount" to S, if this is not going to run into merely technical difficulties, but let us suppose all such problems solved.) Imagine then a certain school slang, which uses special names for various objects, places and institutions in the school. It is a rule that these words are appropriately used only by someone who is a member of the school, and this rule is accepted and understood by a group wider than the members of the school themselves (it would have to be, if it is to be *that* rule at all). People know that if they use these terms in their own person they will be taken for members of the school, or else criticized, and so forth. This provides an exception to the principle, since observers cannot use these terms, but they can correctly say that members of the school, on various occasions, have spoken truly in using them.

In this simple case, it is of course true that the observers have other terms that refer to just the same things as the slang-terms, and that is not so, we are supposing, with the local ethical terms. That makes a difference, since in the school case the observer can clearly factor out what makes a given slang statement true, and what, as contrasted with that, makes it appropriate for a particular person to make it. But we can see the use of the ethical concept as a deeper example of the same thing. In both cases, there is a condition that has to be satisfied if one is to speak in that way, a condition that is satisfied by the local and not by the observer. In both cases, it is a matter of belonging to a certain culture. In the school case it is, so far as the example goes, only a variance of speech, while in the ethical case there is a deeper variance which means that the observer has no term which picks out exactly the same things as their term picks out, and is independent of theirs. He has, of course, an expression such as "what they call 'F'", and the fact that he can use that, although it is not independent of their term, is important: his intelligent use of it shows that he can indeed understand their use of their term, although he cannot use it himself.

We can understand in these circumstances why disquotation is not possible, and the fact that it is not gives us no more reason, it seems to me, than it does in the school case to deny that the locals can speak truly in using their own language. However, there is a different, and stronger, objection to saying, in the ethical case, that that is what they do. In the school case, the observer did not think that the locals' use of their terms implied anything that he actually believed to be false. In other cases, however, an observer may see local statements as false in this way. I am not referring to statements which the locals might equally have seen as false, those that are mistaken even in local terms. I mean the case in which the observer sees some whole segment of their discourse as involving a mistake. It is a complex question in social theory, in what cases that might be so. Social anthropologists have discussed whether ritual and magical conceptions should be seen as mistaken in our terms, or rather as operating at a different level, not commensurable with our scientific ideas. Whatever may be said more generally, it is quite hard to deny that magic, at least, is a causal conception, with implications that overlap with scientific conceptions of causality.[12] To the extent that that is so, magical conceptions can be seen from the outside as false, and then no one will have known to be true any statements claiming magical influence, even though they may have correctly used all the local criteria for claiming a given piece of magical influence. Those criteria do not reach to everything that, on this view of the matter, is involved in such claims. In cases of this sort, the problem with conceding truth to the locals' claims is the opposite of the one just discussed. It is not that their notions are different from the observer's, so that he cannot assert what they assert. The problem is that their statements imply notions that are similar enough to some of his, for him to deny what they assert.

One may see the local ethical statements in a way that raises that difficulty. On this reading, the locals' statements imply something that can be put in the observer's terms, and which he rejects: that it is *right*, or *all right*, to do things that he thinks it is not right, or all right, to do. Prescriptivism sees things in this way. The local statements entail, together with their descriptive content, an all-purpose *ought*. We have rejected the descriptive half of that analysis; is there any reason to accept the other half?

Of course, there is a quite minimal sense in which the locals think it "all right" to act as they do, and they do not merely imply this, but reveal it, in the practice under which they use these concepts and live accordingly. To say that they "think it all right" merely at this level is not to mention any further and disputable judgment of theirs, but merely to record their practice. Must we agree that there is a judgment, to be expressed by using some universal moral notion, which they accept and the observer may, very well, reject?

I do not think that we have to accept that idea. More precisely, I do not think that we can decide whether to accept it until we have a more general picture of the whole question: this is not an issue that by itself can force more general conclusions on us. The basic question is how we are to understand the relations between practice and reflection. The very general kind of judgment that is in question here – a judgment, that is to say, using a very general concept – is essentially a product of reflection, and it comes into question when someone stands back from the practices of the society and its use of these concepts and asks whether this is the right way to go on, whether these are good ways in which to assess actions, whether the kinds of character that are admired are good kinds of character to admire. Of course, in many traditional societies some degree of reflective questioning and criticism exists, and that itself is an important fact. It is for the sake of the argument, to separate the issues, that I have been using the idea of the hypertraditional society, where there is no reflection.

In relation to that society, the question now is this: does the practice of that society, in particular the judgments that members of the society make, imply answers to reflective questions about that practice, questions which they have never raised? Some judgments made by members of a society do have implications at a more general or theoretical level which they have never considered. That may be true of their magical judgments, if those are taken as causal claims, and it is true of their mathematical judgments, and of their judgments about the stars. We may be at some liberty whether to construe what they were saying as expressing mathematical judgments or opinions about the stars, but if we do interpret them as making those judgments and expressing those opinions, they will have those implications. If what a statement expresses is an opinion about the stars, one thing that follows is that it can be contradicted by another opinion about the stars.

There are two different ways in which we can see the activities of the hypertraditional society, which depend on different models of ethical practice. (They are in fact mere sketches or shells, rather than models: they still need their content to be supplied, but they can already have an effect.) One of them can be called an "objectivist" model. According to this, we shall see the members of the society as trying, in their local and limited way, to find out the truth about values, an activity in which we and other human beings, and perhaps creatures who are not human beings, are all engaged. We shall then see their judgments as having these implications, rather as we see primitive statements about the stars as having implications which can be contradicted by more sophisticated statements about the stars. On the other, contrasted, model we shall see their judgments rather as part of their way of living, a cultural artefact that they have come to inhabit (though they have not consciously built it). On this, non-objectivist, model, we shall take a different view of the relations between that practice and critical reflection. We shall not be disposed to see the level of reflection as, implicitly, already there, and we shall not want to say that their judgments have, just as they stand, these implications.

The choice between these two different ways of looking at their activities will determine whether we say that the people in the hypertraditional society have ethical knowledge or not. It is important to be quite clear what ethical knowledge is in question. It is knowledge involved in their making judgments in which they use their "thick" concepts. We are not considering whether they display knowledge *in using those concepts rather than some others*: that would be an issue at the reflective level. The question "does that society possess ethical knowledge?" is seriously ambiguous in that way. The collective reference to the society invites one to take the perspective in which their ethical representations are compared with other societies' ethical representations, and that is the reflective level, at which they certainly do not possess knowledge. There is another sense of the question in which it asks whether members of the society could, in exercising their concepts, express knowledge about the world to which they apply them, and the answer to that might be "yes".

The interesting result of this discussion is that the answer will be "yes" if we take the non-objectivist view of their ethical activities: on that view, various members of the society will have knowledge, when they deploy their concepts carefully, use the appropriate criteria, and so on. But on the objectivist view, they do not have knowledge, or at least, it is immensely unlikely that they do, since their judgments have (on that view) extensive implications at the reflective level which they have never considered, and we have every reason to believe that when those implications are con-sidered, the traditional use of ethical concepts will be seriously affected.

The objectivist view, while it denies knowledge to the unreflective society, may seem to promise knowledge at the reflective level. Indeed, it is characteristic of it to expect that it would be at that level that the demands of knowledge would for the first time be properly met. But there is no reason to think that, at least as things are, there is knowledge at the reflective level which is not either common to all ethical systems and has not much content ("one has to have a special reason to kill someone"), or else has simply survived from the unreflective level. The objectivist view sees the practice of the hypertraditional society, and the conclusions that we might reach at the reflective level, equally in terms of beliefs, and its idea is that we shall have a better hold on the truth about the ethical, and will be in a position to replace belief with knowledge, precisely in virtue of the processes of reflection. I see no reason to think that the demands of knowledge at this level, at least as things are, have been met. At the end of this paper I shall suggest that, so far as propositional knowledge of ethical truths is concerned, this is not simply a matter of how things now are. Rather, at a high level of reflective generality there could not be any ethical knowledge of this sort – or, at most, just one piece.

If we accept that there can be knowledge at the hypertraditional or unreflective level; and if we accept the obvious truth that reflection characteristically disturbs, unseats or replaces those traditional concepts; and if we agree that, at least as things are, the reflective level is not in a position to give us knowledge that we did not have before; then we reach the notably unSocratic conclusion that in ethics, *reflection can destroy knowledge.*

Another consequence, if we allow knowledge at the unreflective level, will be that not all propositional knowledge is additive. Not all pieces of knowledge can be combined into a larger body of knowledge. We may well have to accept that conclusion anyway from other contexts that involve perspectival views of the world. A part of the physical world may present itself as one colour to one kind of observer, and another to another; to another, it may not exactly be a colour that is presented at all. Call those qualities perceived by each kind of observer "A", "B", "C". Then a skilled observer of one kind can know that the surface is A, of another kind that it is B, and so on, but there is no knowledge that it is A and B and C. This result would disappear if what "A", "B", etc., meant were something relational; if, when observers said "that is A", they meant "A to observers like us". It is very doubtful that this is the correct account.[13] If it is not, the coherence of those pieces of knowledge is secured at a different level, when those various perceived qualities are related to the absolute conception. Their relation to that conception is also what makes it clear that the capacities that produce these various pieces of knowledge are all forms of *perception.* Of course, we have good reason to believe this before we possess any such theoretical conception, and certainly before we possess its details, as we still do not. That is because our everyday experience, unsurprisingly, reveals a good deal of what we are and how we are related to the world, and in that way itself leads us towards that theoretical conception.[14]

Some think of the knowledge given by applying ethical concepts as something like perception; but we can now see a vital asymmetry between the case of the ethical concepts, and the perspectival experience of secondary qualities. It lies in the fact that in the case of secondary qualities, what explains also justifies, but in the ethical case, this is not so. The psychological capacities that underly our perceiving the world in terms of certain secondary qualities have evolved so that the physical world will present itself to us in reliable and useful ways. Coming to know that these qualities constitute our form of perceptual engagement with the world, and how this mode of presentation works, will not unsettle the system.[15] In the ethical case, we have an analogy to the perceptual just to this extent, that there is local convergence under these concepts – the judgements of those who use them are indeed, as I put it before, world-guided. That is certainly enough to refute the simplest oppositions of fact and value. But if this is to mean anything for a wider objectivity, everything depends on what is to be said *next*. With secondary qualities, it is the explanation of the perspectival perceptions that enables us, when we come to reflect on them, to place them in relation to the perceptions of other people and other creatures; and, as we have just noticed, that leaves everything more or less where it was, so far as our perceptual judgments are concerned. The question is whether we can find an ethical analogy to that. Here we have to go outside the local, perspectival judgments, to a reflective or second-order account of them, and there the analogy gives out.

There is, first, a problem of what the second-order account is to be. An *explanation* of those local judgments and of the conceptual differences between societies will presumably have to come from the social sciences: cultural differences are what are in question. Perhaps no existing explanation of such things goes very deep, and we are not too clear how deep an explanation might go. But we do know that it will not look much like explanations of secondary quality perception. The capacities it will invoke will be those involved in finding our way around in a social world, not merely the physical world, and that, crucially, will mean *in some social world or other*, since it is certain both that human beings cannot live without some culture or other, and that there are many different cultures in which they can live, differing in their local perspectival concepts.

In any case, an explanatory theory is not enough to deal with the problems of objectivity raised by the local ethical concepts. In the case of secondary qualities, the explanation also justified, because it could show how the perceptions are related to physical reality, and how they can give knowledge of that reality, which is what they purport to do. The question with them is: is this a method of finding one's way around the physical world? The theoretical account explains how it is. In the ethical case, that is not the kind of question raised by reflection. If one asked the question "Is this a method of finding one's way around the social world?", one would have to be asking whether it was a method of finding one's way around some social world or other, and the answer to that must obviously be "Yes", unless the society were extremely disordered, which is not what we were supposing. The question raised is rather "Is this a good, acceptable, way of living compared with others?"; or, to put it another way, "Is this the best kind of social world?"

When these are seen to be the questions, the reflective account that we require turns out to involve reflective *ethical* considerations. Some believe that these considerations should take the form of an ethical theory. These reflective considerations will have to take up the job of justifying or unjustifying the local concepts once those have come to be questioned. If a wider objectivity were to come from all this, then the reflective ethical considerations would have themselves to be objective. This brings us back to the question that we touched on just now, whether the reflective level might generate its own ethical knowledge. If this is understood as our coming to have propositional knowledge of ethical truths, then we need some account of what "tracking the truth" will be. The idea that our beliefs can track the truth at this level must at least imply that a range of investigators could rationally, reasonably and unconstrainedly come to converge on a determinate set of ethical conclusions. What are the hopes for such a process? I do not mean of its actually happening, but rather of our forming a coherent picture of how it might happen. If it is construed as convergence on a body of ethical truths which is brought about and explained by the fact that they are truths – that would be the strict analogy to scientific objectivity – then I see no hope for it. In particular, there is no hope of extending to this level the kind of world-guidedness that we have been considering in the case of the "thick" ethical concepts. Discussions at the reflective level, if they are to have the ambition of considering all ethical experience and arriving at the truth about the ethical, will necessarily use the most general and abstract ethical concepts such as "right", and those concepts do not display that world-guidedness (which is why they were selected by prescriptivism in its attempt to find a pure evaluative element from which it could *detach* world-guidedness).

I cannot see any convincing theory of knowledge for the convergence of reflective ethical thought "on ethical reality" in even distant analogy to the scientific case. Nor is there a convincing analogy with mathematics, a case in which the notion of an independent reality is at least problematical. Every non-contradictory piece of mathematics is part of mathematics, though it may be left aside as too trivial or unilluminating or useless, but not every non-contradictory structure of ethical reflection can be part of one such subject, since they conflict with one another in ways that not only lack the kind of explanation that could form a credible theory of error, but have too many credible explanations of other kinds.

I do not believe, then, that we can understand the reflective level through a model in which we can come to know ethical propositions at that level, while in less reflective states we aim to possess that truth, but can at best arrive at beliefs. We must reject the objectivist view of ethical life as, in that way, a pursuit of ethical truth. But that does not rule out all forms of objectivism. There is a different project, of trying to give an objective grounding or foundation to ethical life, by showing that a certain kind of ethical life was the best for human beings, was most likely to meet their needs. The question asked by this approach is: granted that human beings need, in general, to share a social world, is there anything to be known about their needs and their most basic motivations that will show us what that world should best be?

I cannot argue the question here, but I doubt that there will turn out to be a very satisfying answer to that question. It is probable that any such considerations will radically under-determine the ethical options even in a given social situation (we must remember that what we take the situation to be is itself, in part, a function of what ethical options we can see). They may under-determine it in several different dimensions. Any ethical life is going to contain restraints on such things as killing, injury and lying, but those restraints can take very different forms. Again, with respect to the virtues, which is the most natural and promising field for this kind of enquiry, we only have to compare Aristotle's catalogue of the virtues with any that might be produced now to see how pictures of life that can be recognized as equally appropriate to human beings may differ very much in their spirit and in the actions and institutions that they would call for. We also have the idea that there are many and various forms of human excellence that will not all fit together into one harmonious whole. On that view, any determinate ethical outlook is going to represent some kind of special-ization of human possibilities. That idea is deeply entrenched in any naturalistic or, again, historical conception of human nature – that is to say, in any adequate conception of it – and I find it hard to believe that that will be overcome by an objective enquiry, or that human beings could turn out to have a much more determinate nature than is suggested by what we already know, one that timelessly demanded a life of a particular kind.

The project of giving to ethical life, in any very determinate form, an objective grounding in considerations about human nature is not, in my view, very likely to succeed. But it is at any rate a comprehensible project, and I believe that it represents the only form of ethical objectivity at the reflective level that is intelligible. For that reason, it is worth asking what would be involved in its succeeding. If it succeeded, that would not simply be a matter of agreement on a theory of human nature. The convergence itself would be partly on scientific matters, in a very broad social and psychological sense, but what would matter would be a convergence to which these scientific conclusions would provide only part of the means. Nor, on the other hand, would there be a convergence directly on to ethical truths, as in the other objectivist model. There would be one ethical belief which might perhaps be said to be in its own right an object of knowledge at the reflective level, to the effect that a certain kind of life was best for human beings. But that will not yield other ethical truths directly. The reason for this, to put it summarily, is that the excellence or satisfactoriness of a life does not stand to the beliefs involved in that life as premise to conclusion. Rather, an agent's (excellent or satisfactory) life is charac-terized by *having* those beliefs, and most of the beliefs will not be about that agent's dispositions or life, or about other people's dispositions, but about the social world. That life will involve, for instance, the agent's using some "thick" concepts rather than others. Reflection on the excellence of the life does not itself establish the truth of judgments using those concepts, or of the agent's other ethical judgments. It rather shows that there is good reason (granted a commitment to an ethical life at all) to live a life that involves those concepts and those beliefs.

The convergence that signalled the success of this project would be a convergence of practical reason, by which people came to lead the best kind of life and to have the desires that belonged to that; convergence in ethical belief would largely be a part and consequence of that process. One very general ethical belief would, indeed, be an object of knowledge at that level. Many particular ethical judgments, involving the favoured "thick" concepts, could be known to be true, but then judgments of that sort (I have argued) can very often be known to be true anyway, even when they occur, as they always have occurred, in a life that is not grounded at the objective level. The objective grounding would not bring it about that judgments using those concepts were true or could be known: that was so already. But it would enable us to recognize that certain of them were the best or most appropriate "thick" concepts to use. Between the two extremes of the one very general proposition, and the many quite concrete ones, other ethical beliefs would be true only in the oblique sense that they were the beliefs that would help us to find our way around in a social world which – on this optimistic programme – would have been shown to be the best social world for human beings.

That would be a structure very different from that of the objectivity of science. There is, then, a radical difference between ethics and science. Even if ethics were objective in the only way in which it could intelligibly be objective, its objectivity would be quite different from that of science. In addition, it is probably not objective in that way. However, that does not mean that there is a clear distinction between (any) fact and (any) value; nor does it mean that there is no ethical knowledge. There is some, and in the less reflective past there has been more.

NOTES

1 The lecture that I gave to the Royal Institute of Philosophy on this subject was subsequently much revised, and has become Chapter 8 ("Knowledge, science, convergence") of a book, *Ethics and the Limits of Philosophy*, published in the Fontana Masterguides Series early in 1985. It seemed more sensible not to go back to an earlier version of the text, and what appears here (with the agreement of Fontana Books) is a slightly abbreviated version of that chapter.

2 See David Wiggins, "Truth, invention and the meaning of life", *British Academy Lecture* (1976); and "Deliberation and practical reason', in *Essays on Aristotle's Ethics*, Amélie Rorty (ed.) (California, California University Press, 1980).

3 *Philosophy and the Mirror of Nature* (Princeton, Princeton University Press, 1980), 344–5. I have discussed Rorty's views in some detail in a review of his *Consequences of Pragmatism* (Minneapolis, 1982): *New York Review* **XXX**, No. 7 (28 April 1983).

4 There is a confusion between what might be called empirical and transcendental pragmatism. Some similar problems arise with the later work of Wittgenstein: see "Wittgenstein and idealism" in *Understanding Wittgenstein*, Royal Institute of Philosophy Lectures Volume 7 (London, Macmillan, 1974), and reprinted in *Moral Luck* (Cambridge, Cambridge University Press, 1981); and Jonathan Lear, "Leaving the world alone", *Journal of Philosophy* **79** (1982).

5 Rorty, "The world well lost" in *Consequences of Pragmatism*, 14. See also Donald Davidson, "The very idea of a conceptual scheme", *Proceedings and Addresses of*

the American Philosophical Association **67** (1973/4).

6 Cf. *Descartes: The Project of Pure Enquiry* (Harmondsworth, Penguin Books, 1978). See also N. Jardine, "The possibility of absolutism", in *Science, Belief, and Behaviour: Essays in Honour of R. B. Braithwaite*, D. H. Mellor (ed.) (Cambridge, Cambridge University Press, 1980); and Colin McGinn, *The Subjective View* (Oxford, Clarendon Press, 1983).

7 Notably John McDowell, "Are moral requirements hypothetical imperatives?", *Proceedings of the Aristotelian Society* Supplementary Volume 52 (1978); "Virtue and reason", *Monist* **62** (1979). McDowell is above all concerned with the state of mind and motivations of a virtuous person, but I understand his view to have the more general implications discussed in the text. The idea that it might be impossible to pick up an evaluative concept unless one shared its evaluative interest I take to be basically a Wittgensteinian idea. I first heard it expressed by Philippa Foot and Iris Murdoch in a seminar in the 1950s. For the application of ideas from Wittgenstein's later philosophy to ethics, see e.g. Hanna F. Pitkin, *Wittgenstein and Justice* (California, California University Press, 1972), and Sabina Lovibond, *Realism and Imagination in Ethics* (Oxford, Blackwell, 1983). McDowell himself draws important consequences in the philosophy of mind, rejecting the "belief and desire" model of rational action. I do not accept these consequences, but I shall not try to argue the question here. Some considerations later in this paper, about the differences between ethical belief and sense perception, bear closely on it.

8 McDowell ("Virtue and reason") allows for this possibility, but he draws no consequences from it, and ignores intercultural conflict altogether. He traces scepticism about objectivity in ethics, revealingly, to what he calls a "philistine scientism", on the one hand, and to a philosophical pathology on the other, of vertigo in the face of unsupported practices. Leaving aside his attitude to the sciences, McDowell seems rather unconcerned even about history, and says nothing about differences in outlook over time. It is significant that in a discussion of the virtues that mostly relates to Aristotle, he takes as an example kindness, which is not an Aristotelian virtue.

9 The most subtle and ingenious discussion of propositional knowledge I know is that of Robert Nozick in Chapter 3 of his *Philosophical Explanations* (Cambridge, Mass., Harvard University Press, 1981). Some central features of Nozick's account, notably its use of subjunctive conditionals, had been anticipated by Fred Dretske, as Nozick acknowledges in his note 53 to that chapter, which gives references.

10 How rough? Perhaps he cannot read four dots as 4, though he can read six dots as 6. What if he can only read six dots as 6, and everything else as not 6?

11 A. Tarski, "The concept of truth in formalized languages", in *Logic, Semantics, Meta-Mathematics* (Oxford, Oxford University Press, 1956). On the present issue, cf. David Wiggins, "What would be a substantial theory of truth?", in *Philosophical Subjects: Essays Presented to P. F. Strawson*, Z. van Straaten (ed.) (Oxford, Blackwell, 1980). Wiggins' discussion raises a further issue, whether the observer could even understand what the sentences mean, unless he could apply a disquotational truth formula to them. (In this he is influenced by Donald Davidson, "Truth and meaning", *Synthese* **17** (1967).) The fact that there can be a sympathetic but non-identified observer shows that it cannot be impossible to understand something although one is unwilling to assert it oneself.

12 See John Skorupski, *Symbol and Theory* (Cambridge, Cambridge University Press, 1976).

13 Cf. Wiggins, "Truth, invention and the meaning of life"; Colin McGinn, *The Subjective View* (Oxford, Oxford University Press, 1983), 9–10, 119–20.

14 A formulation of the distinction between primary and secondary qualities is very nearly as old in the Western tradition as the self-conscious use of a principle of sufficient reason.

15 I have taken two sentences here from an article, "Ethics and the fabric of the world", to appear in *Morality and Objectivity*, Ted Honderich (ed.) (London, Routledge, forthcoming), a volume of essays in memory of John Mackie; it discusses Mackie's views on these subjects, and in particular his idea that perceptual and moral experience each involve a comparable error. See also McGinn, *The Subjective View*, especially ch. 7.

15 How to be a Moral Realist

Richard N. Boyd

1 INTRODUCTION

1.1 Moral realism

Scientific realism is the doctrine that scientific theories should be understood as putative descriptions of real phenomena, that ordinary scientific
methods constitute a reliable procedure for obtaining and improving
(approximate) knowledge of the real phenomena which scientific theories
describe, and that the reality described by scientific theories is largely
independent of our theorizing. Scientific theories describe reality and
reality is "prior to thought" (see Boyd 1982).

By "moral realism" I intend the analogous doctrine about moral
judgments, moral statements, and moral theories. According to moral
realism:

1   Moral statements are the sorts of statements which are (or which
    express propositions which are) true or false (or approximately true,
    largely false, etc.);
2   The truth or falsity (approximate truth ...) of moral statements is
    largely independent of our moral opinions, theories, etc.;
3   Ordinary canons of moral reasoning – together with ordinary canons
    of scientific and everyday factual reasoning – constitute, under many
    circumstances at least, a reliable method for obtaining and improving
    (approximate) moral knowledge.

It follows from moral realism that such moral terms as "good", "fair", "just",
"obligatory" usually correspond to real properties or relations and that our
ordinary standards for moral reasoning and moral disputation – together
with reliable standards for scientific and everyday reasoning – constitute a
fairly reliable way of finding out which events, persons, policies, social
arrangements, etc. have these properties and enter into these relations. It
is *not* a consequence of moral realism that our ordinary procedures are
"best possible" for this purpose – just as it is not a consequence of scientific
realism that our existing scientific methods are best possible. In the
scientific case, improvements in knowledge can be expected to produce
improvements in method (Boyd 1980, 1982, 1983, 1985a, 1985b, 1985c),
and there is no reason to exclude this possibility in the moral case.

Scientific realism contrasts with instrumentalism and its variants and with views like that of Kuhn (1970) according to which the reality which scientists study is largely constituted by the theories they adopt. Moral realism contrasts with non-cognitivist metaethical theories like emotivism and with views according to which moral principles are largely a reflection of social constructs or conventions.

What I want to do in this essay is to explore the ways in which recent developments in realist philosophy of science, together with related "naturalistic" developments in epistemology and philosophy of language, can be employed in the articulation and defense of moral realism. It will not be my aim here to establish that moral realism is true. Indeed, if moral realism is to be defended along the lines I will indicate here then a thoroughgoing defense of moral realism would be beyond the scope of a single essay. Fortunately a number of extremely important defenses of moral realism have recently been published (see, e.g., Brink 1984, forthcoming; Gilbert 1981b, 1982, 1984b, 1986b, forthcoming; Miller 1984b; Railton 1986; Sturgeon 1984a, 1984b). What I hope to demonstrate in the present essay is that moral realism can be shown to be a more attractive and plausible philosophical position if recent developments in realist philosophy of science are brought to bear in its defense. I intend the general defense of moral realism offered here as a proposal regarding the metaphysical, epistemological, and semantic framework within which arguments for moral realism are best formulated and best understood.

In addition, I am concerned to make an indirect contribution to an important recent debate among Marxist philosophers and Marx scholars concerning the Marxist analysis of moral discourse (see, e.g., Gilbert 1981a, 1981b, 1982, 1984b, 1986a, 1986b; Miller 1979, 1981, 1982, 1983, 1984a, 1984b; Wood 1972, 1979). Two questions are central in this debate: the question of what metaethical views Marx and other Marxist figures actually held or practiced and the question of what metaethical views are appropriate to a Marxist analysis of history and in particular to a Marxist analysis of the role of class ideology in the determination of the content of moral conceptions. I have nothing to contribute to the efforts to answer the first question, which lies outside my competence. About the second, I am convinced that Marxists should be moral realists and that the admirably motivated decision by many antirevisionist Marxists to adopt a nonrealist relativist stance in metaethics represents a sectarian (if nonculpable) error. I intend the defense of moral realism presented here to be fully compatible with the recognition of the operation in the history of moral inquiry of just the sort of ideological forces which Marxist historians (among others) have emphasized. A thoroughgoing defense of this compatibility claim is not attempted in the present essay; I develop it in a forthcoming essay.

1.2 Scientific knowledge and moral skepticism

One of the characteristic motivations for anti-realistic metaethical positions – either for non-cognitivist views or for views according to which moral knowledge has a strong constructive or conventional component – lies in a presumed epistemological contrast between ethics, on the one hand, and the sciences, on the other. Scientific methods and theories appear to have properties – objectivity, value-neutrality, empirical testability, for example – which are either absent altogether or, at any rate, much less significant in the case of moral beliefs and the procedures by which we form and criticize them. These differences make the methods of science (and of everyday empirical knowledge) seem apt for the *discovery* of facts while the 'methods' of moral reasoning seem, at best, to be appropriate for the rationalization, articulation, and application of preexisting social conventions or individual preferences.

Many philosophers would like to explore the possibility that scientific beliefs and moral beliefs are not so differently situated as this presumed epistemological contrast suggests. We may think of this task as the search for a conception of "unified knowledge" which will bring scientific and moral knowledge together within the same analytical framework in much the same way as the positivists' conception of "unified science" sought to provide an integrated treatment of knowledge within the various special sciences. There are, roughly, two plausible general strategies for unifying scientific and moral knowledge and minimizing the apparent epistemological contrast between scientific and moral inquiry:

1   Show that our scientific beliefs and methods actually possess many of the features (e.g., dependence on nonobjective "values" or upon social conventions) which form the core of our current picture of moral beliefs and methods of moral reasoning.
2   Show that moral beliefs and methods are much more like our current conception of scientific beliefs and methods (more "objective", "external", "empirical", "intersubjective", for example) than we now think.

The first of these options has already been explored by philosophers who subscribe to a "constructivist" or neo-Kantian conception of scientific theorizing (see, e.g., Hanson 1958; Kuhn 1970). The aim of the present essay will be to articulate and defend the second alternative. In recent papers (Boyd 1979, 1982, 1983, 1985a, 1985b, 1985c) I have argued that scientific realism is correct, but that its adequate defense requires the systematic adoption of a distinctly naturalistic and realistic conception of knowledge, of natural kinds, and of reference. What I hope to show here is that once such a distinctly naturalistic and realistic conception is adopted, it is possible to offer a corresponding defense of moral realism which has considerable force and plausibility.

My argumentative strategy will be to offer a list of several challenges to moral realism which will, I hope, be representative of those considerations which make it plausible that there is the sort of epistemological contrast between science and ethics which we have been discussing. Next, I will present a summary of some recent work in realistic philosophy of science and related "naturalistic" theories in epistemology and the philosophy of language. Finally, I will indicate how the results of this recent realistic and naturalistic work can be applied to rebut the arguments against moral realism and to sketch the broad outlines of an alternative realistic conception of moral knowledge and of moral language.

2 SOME CHALLENGES TO MORAL REALISM

2.1 Moral intuitions and empirical observations

In the sciences, we decide between theories on the basis of observations, which have an important degree of objectivity. It appears that in moral reasoning, moral intuitions play the same role which observations do in science: we test general moral principles and moral theories by seeing how their consequences conform (or fail to conform) to our moral intuitions about particular cases. It appears that it is the foundational role of observations in science which makes scientific objectivity possible. How could moral intuitions possibly play the same sort of foundational role in ethics, especially given the known diversity of moral judgments between people? Even if moral intuitions do provide a "foundation" for moral inquiry, wouldn't the fact that moral "knowledge" is grounded in intuitions rather than in observation be exactly the sort of fundamental epistemological contrast which the received view postulates, especially since peoples' moral intuitions typically reflect the particular moral theories or traditions which they already accept, or their culture, or their upbringing? Doesn't the role of moral intuitions in moral reasoning call out for a "constructivist" metaethics? If moral intuitions don't play a foundational role in ethics and if morality is supposed to be epistemologically like science, *then what plays, in moral reasoning, the role played by observation in science?*

2.2 The role of "reflective equilibrium" in moral reasoning

We have already seen that moral intuitions play a role in moral reasoning which appears to threaten any attempt to assimilate moral reasoning to the model of objective empirical scientific methodology. Worse yet, as Rawls (1971) has reminded us, what we do with our moral intuitions, our general moral principles, and our moral theories, in order to achieve a coherent moral position, is to engage in "trading-off" between these various categories of moral belief in order to achieve a harmonious "equilibrium". Moral reasoning *begins* with moral *presuppositions*, general as well as particular, and proceeds by negotiating between conflicting *presuppositions*. It is easy to see how this could be a procedure for rationalization of individual or social norms or, to put it in more elevated terms, a procedure for the "construction" of moral or ethical systems. But if ethical beliefs and ethical reasoning are supposed to be like scientific beliefs and methods, then this procedure would have to be a procedure for *discovering* moral facts! How could any procedure so presupposition-dependent be a *discovery* procedure rather than a *construction procedure*? (See Dworkin 1973.)

2.3 Moral progress and cultural variability

If moral judgments are a species of factual judgment, then one would expect to see moral progress, analogous to progress in science. Moreover, one of the characteristics of factual inquiry in science is its relative independence from cultural distortions: scientists with quite different cultural backgrounds can typically agree in assessing scientific evidence. If moral reasoning is reasoning about objective moral *facts*, then what explains our lack of progress in ethics and the persistence of cultural variability in moral beliefs?

2.4 Hard cases

If goodness, fairness, etc. are real and objective properties, then what should one say about the sorts of hard cases in ethics which we can't seem *ever* to resolve? Our experience in science seems to be that hard scientific questions are only *temporarily* rather than permanently unanswerable. Permanent disagreement seems to be very rare indeed. Hard ethical questions seem often to be permanent rather than temporary.

In such hard ethical cases, is there a fact of the matter inaccessible to moral inquiry? If so, then doesn't the existence of such facts constitute a significant epistemological difference between science and ethics? If not, if there are not facts of the matter, then isn't moral realism simply refuted by such indeterminacy?

2.5 Naturalism and naturalistic definitions

If goodness, for example, is a real property, then wouldn't it be a *natural* property? If not, then isn't moral realism committed to some unscientific and superstitious belief in the existence of non-natural properties? If goodness would be a natural property, then isn't moral realism committed to the extremely implausible claim that moral terms like "good" possess naturalistic definitions?

2.6 Morality, motivation, and rationality

Ordinary factual judgments often provide us with reasons for action; they serve as constraints on rational choice. But they do so only because of our antecedent interests or desires. If moral judgments are merely factual judgments, as moral realism requires, then the relation of moral judgments to motivation and rationality must be the same. It would be possible in principle for someone, or some thinking thing, to be entirely rational while finding moral judgments motivationally neutral and irrelevant to choices of action.

If this consequence follows from moral realism, how can the moral realist account for the particularly close connection between moral judgments and judgments about what to do? What about the truism that moral judgments have commendatory force as a matter of their meaning or the plausible claim that the moral preferability of a course of action always provides a reason (even if not an overriding one) for choosing it?

2.7 The semantics of moral terms

Moral realism is an anti-subjectivist position. There is, for example, supposed to be a single objective property which we're all talking about when we use the term "good" in moral contexts. But people's moral concepts differ profoundly. How can it be maintained that our radically different concepts of "good" are really concepts of one and the same property? Why not a different property for each significantly different conception of the good? Don't the radical differences in our conceptions of the good suggest either a non-cognitivist or a constructivist conception of the semantics of ethical terms?

2.8 Verificationism and anti-realism in ethics

Anti-realism in ethics, like the rejection of theoretical realism in science, is a standard positivist position. In the case of science, there is a straightforward verificationist objection to realism about alleged "theoretical entities": they are unobservables; statements about them lie beyond the scope of empirical investigation and are thus unverifiable in principle. (See Boyd 1982 for a discussion of various formulations of this key verificationist argument.)

It is interesting to note that the challenges to moral realism rehearsed in 2.1–2.7 do not take the form of so direct an appeal to verificationism. Only in the case of the concern about non-natural moral properties (2.5) might the issue of verifiability be directly relevant, and then only if the objection to non-natural properties is that they would be unobservable. Instead, the arguments in 2.1–2.7 constitute an *indirect* argument against moral realism: they point to features of moral beliefs or of moral reasoning for which, it is suggested, the best explanation would be one which entailed the rejection of moral realism. Moreover, what is true of the challenges to moral realism rehearsed above is typical: by and large positivists, and philosophers influenced by positivism, did not argue directly for the unverifiability of moral statements; they did not make an appeal to the unobservability of alleged moral properties or deny that moral theories had observational consequences. Instead, they seemed to take a non-cognitivist view of ethics to be established by an "inductive inference to the best explanation" of the sort of facts cited in 2.1–2.7.

In this regard, then, the standard arguments against moral realism are more closely analogous to Kuhnian objections to scientific realism than they are to the standard verificationist arguments against the possibility of knowledge of "theoretical entities." Sections 2.1, 2.2, 2.3, and 2.7 rehearse arguments which are importantly similar to Kuhn's arguments from the paradigm dependence of scientific concepts and methods to a constructivist and anti-realistic conception of science. I have argued elsewhere (Boyd 1979, 1982, 1983, 1985a) that a systematic rebuttal to the verificationist epistemology and philosophy of language which form the foundations of logical positivism can in fact be extended to a defense of scientific realism against the more constructivist and neo-Kantian considerations represented by Kuhn's work. If the arguments of the present essay are successful, then this conclusion can be generalized: a realist and anti-empiricist account in the philosophy of science can be extended to a defense of moral *realism* as well, even though the challenges to moral realism are apparently only indirectly verificationist.

3 REALIST PHILOSOPHY OF SCIENCE

3.1 The primacy of reality

By "scientific realism" philosophers mean the doctrine that the methods of science are capable of providing (partial or approximate) knowledge of unobservable ("theoretical") entities, such as atoms or electromagnetic fields, in addition to knowledge about the behavior of observable phenomena (and of course, that the properties of these and other entities studied by scientists are largely theory-independent).

Over the past three decades or so, philosophers of science within the empiricist tradition have been increasingly sympathetic toward scientific realism and increasingly inclined to alter their views of science in a realist direction. The reasons for this realist tendency lie largely in the recognition of the extraordinary role which theoretical considerations play in actual (and patently successful) scientific practice. To take the most striking example, scientists routinely modify or extend operational "measurement" or "detection" procedures for "theoretical" magnitudes or entities on the basis of new theoretical developments. This sort of methodology is perfectly explicable on the realist assumption that the operational procedures in question really are procedures for the measurement or detection of unobservable entities and that the relevant theoretical developments reflect increasingly accurate knowledge of such "theoretical" entities. Accounts of the revisability of operational procedures which are compatible with a non-realist position appear inadequate to explain the way in which theory-dependent revisions of "measurement" and "detection" procedures make a positive methodological contribution to the progress of science.

This pattern is quite typical: The methodological contribution made by theoretical considerations in scientific methodology is inexplicable on a non-realist conception but easily explicable on the realist assumption that such considerations are a reflection of the growth of *theoretical* knowledge. (For a discussion of this point see Boyd 1982, 1983, 1985a, 1985b.) Systematic development of this realist theme has produced developments in epistemology, metaphysics, and the philosophy of language which go far beyond the mere rejection of verificationism and which point the way toward a distinctly realist conception of the central issues in the philosophy of science. These developments include the articulation of causal or naturalistic theories of reference (Kripke 1971, 1972; Putnam 1975a; Boyd 1979, 1982), of measurement (Byerly and Lazara 1973), of "natural kinds" and scientific categories (Quine 1969a; Putnam 1975a; Boyd 1979, 1982, 1983, 1985b), of scientific epistemology generally (Boyd 1972, 1979, 1982,

1983, 1985a, 1985b, 1985c), and of causation (Mackie 1974; Shoemaker 1980; Boyd 1982, 1985b).

Closely related to these developments has been the articulation of causal or naturalistic theories of knowledge (see, e.g., Armstrong 1973; Goldman 1967, 1976; Quine 1969b). Such theories represent generalizations of causal theories of perception and reflect a quite distinctly realist stance with respect to the issue of our knowledge of the external world. What all these developments – both within the philosophy of science and in epistemology generally – have in common is that they portray as a posteriori and contingent various matters (such as the operational "definitions" of theoretical terms, the "definitions" of natural kinds, or the reliability of the senses) which philosophers in the modern tradition have typically sought to portray as a priori. In an important sense, these developments represent the fuller working out of the philosophical implications of the realist doctrine that reality is prior to thought. (For a further development of this theme see Boyd 1982, 1983, 1985a, 1985b.) It is just this a posteriority and contingency in philosophical matters, I shall argue, which will make possible a plausible defense of moral realism against the challenges outlined in part 2.

In the remaining sections of part 3 I will describe some of the relevant features of these naturalistic and realistic developments. These "results" in recent realistic philosophy are not, of course, uncontroversial, and it is beyond the scope of this essay to defend them. But however much controversy they may occasion, unlike moral realism, they do not occasion incredulity: they represent a plausible and defensible philosophical position. The aim of this essay is to indicate that, if we understand the relevance of these recent developments to issues in moral philosophy, then moral realism should, though controversial, be equally credible.

3.2 Objective knowledge from theory-dependent methods

I suggested in the preceding section that the explanation for the movement toward realism in the philosophy of science during the past two or three decades lies in the recognition of the extraordinarily theory-dependent character of scientific methodology and in the inability of any but a realist conception of science to explain why so theory-dependent a methodology should be reliable. The theoretical revisability of measurement and detection procedures, I claimed, played a crucial role in establishing the plausibility of a realist philosophy of science.

If we look more closely at this example, we can recognize two features of scientific methodology which are, in fact, quite general. In the first place, the realist's account of the theoretical revisability of measurement and detection procedures rests upon a conception of scientific research as *cumulative by successive approximations to the truth.*

Second, this cumulative development is possible because *there is a dialectical relationship between current theory and the methodology for its improvement.* The approximate truth of current theories explains why our existing measurement procedures are (approximately) reliable. That reliability, in turn, helps to explain why our experimental or observational investigations are successful in uncovering new theoretical knowledge, which, in turn, may produce improvements in experimental techniques, etc.

These features of scientific methodology are *entirely* general. Not only measurement and detection procedures but all aspects of scientific methodology – principles of experimental design, choices of research problems, standards for the assessment of experimental evidence, principles governing theory choice, and rules for the use of theoretical language – are highly dependent upon current theoretical commitments (Boyd 1972, 1973, 1979, 1980, 1982, 1983, 1985a, 1985b; Kuhn 1970; van Fraassen 1980). No aspect of scientific method involves the "presupposition-free" testing of individual laws or theories. Moreover, the theory dependence of scientific methodology *contributes* to its reliability rather than detracting from it.

The only scientifically plausible explanation for the reliability of a scientific methodology which is so theory-dependent is a thoroughgoingly realistic explanation: Scientific methodology, dictated by currently accepted theories, is reliable at producing further knowledge precisely *because, and to the extent that, currently accepted theories are relevantly approximately true.* For example, it is because our current theories are approximately true that the canons of experimental design which they dictate are appropriate for the rigorous testing of new (and potentially more accurate) theories. What the scientific method provides is a paradigm-dependent paradigm-modification strategy: a strategy for modifying or amending our existing theories in the light of further research, which is such that its methodological principles at any given time will themselves depend upon the theoretical picture provided by the currently accepted theories. If the body of accepted theories is itself relevantly sufficiently approximately true, then this methodology operates to produce a subsequent dialectical improvement both in our knowledge of the world and in our methodology itself. Both our new theories and the methodology by which we develop and test them depend upon previously acquired theoretical knowledge. It is not possible to explain even the instrumental reliability of actual scientific practice without invoking this explanation and without adopting a realistic conception of scientific knowledge (Boyd 1972, 1973, 1979, 1982, 1983, 1985a, 1985b, 1985c).

The way in which scientific methodology is theory-dependent dictates that we have a strong methodological preference for new theories which are plausible in the light of our existing theoretical commitments; this means that we prefer new theories which relevantly resemble our existing theories (where the determination of the relevant respects of resemblance is itself a theoretical issue). The reliability of such a methodology is explained by the approximate truth of existing theories, and one consequence of this explanation is that *judgments of theoretical plausibility are evidential.* The fact that a proposed theory is itself plausible in the light of previously confirmed theories is evidence for its (approximate) truth (Boyd 1972, 1973, 1979, 1982, 1983, 1985a, 1985b, 1985c). A purely conventionalistic account of the methodological role of considerations of theoretical plausibility cannot be adequate because it cannot explain the contribution which such considerations make to the instrumental reliability of scientific methodology (Boyd 1979, 1982, 1983).

The upshot is this: The theory-dependent conservatism of scientific methodology is *essential* to the rigorous and reliable testing and development of new scientific theories; on balance, theoretical "presuppositions" play neither a destructive nor a conventionalistic role in scientific methodology. They are essential to its reliability. If by the "objectivity" of scientific methodology we mean its capacity to lead to the discovery of *theory-independent reality*, then scientific methodology is objective precisely because it *is theory-dependent* (Boyd 1979, 1982, 1983, 1985a, 1985b, 1985c).

3.3 Naturalism and radical contingency in epistemology

Modern epistemology has been largely dominated by positions which can be characterized as "foundationalist": all knowledge is seen as ultimately grounded in certain foundational beliefs which have an epistemically privileged position – they are a priori or self-warranting, incorrigible, or something of the sort. Other true beliefs are instances of knowledge only if they can be justified by appeals to foundational knowledge. Whatever the nature of the foundational beliefs, or whatever their epistemic privilege is supposed to consist in, it is an a priori question which beliefs fall in the privileged class. Similarly, the basic inferential principles which are legitimate for justifying non-foundational knowledge claims, given foundational premises, are such that they can be identified a priori and it can be shown a priori that they are rational principles of inference. We may fruitfully think of foundationalism as consisting of two parts, *premise foundationalism*, which holds that all knowledge is justifiable from an a priori specifiable core of foundational beliefs, and *inference foundationalism*, which holds that the principles of justifiable inference are ultimately reducible to inferential principles which can be shown a priori to be rational.

Recent work in "naturalistic epistemology" or "causal theories of knowing" (see, e.g., Armstrong 1973; Goldman 1967, 1976; Quine 1969b) strongly suggest that the foundationalist conception of knowledge is fundamentally mistaken. For the crucial case of perceptual knowledge, there seem to be (in typical cases at least) neither premises (foundational or otherwise) nor inferences; instead, perceptual knowledge obtains when perceptual beliefs are produced by epistemically reliable mechanisms. For a variety of other cases, even where premises and inferences occur, it seems to be the reliable production of belief that distinguishes cases of knowledge from other cases of true belief. A variety of naturalistic considerations suggests that there are no beliefs which are epistemically privileged in the way foundationalism seems to require.

I have argued (see Boyd 1982, 1983, 1985a, 1985b, 1985c) that the defense of scientific realism requires an even more thoroughgoing naturalism in epistemology and, consequently, an even more thoroughgoing rejection of foundationalism. In the first place, the fact that scientific knowledge grows cumulatively by successive approximation and the fact that the evaluation of theories is an ongoing social phenomenon require that we take the crucial causal notion in epistemology to be reliable *regulation* of belief rather than reliable belief *production*. The relevant conception of belief regulation must reflect the approximate social and dialectical character of the growth of scientific knowledge. It will thus be true that the causal mechanisms relevant to knowledge will include mechanisms, social and technical as well as psychological, for the criticism, testing, acceptance, modification, and transmission of scientific theories and doctrines. For that reason, an understanding of the role of social factors in science may be relevant not only for the sociology and history of science but for the epistemology of science as well. The epistemology of science is in this respect dependent upon empirical knowledge.

There is an even more dramatic respect in which the epistemology of science rests upon empirical foundations. All the significant methodological principles of scientific inquiry (except, perhaps, the rules of deductive logic, but see Boyd 1985c) are profoundly theory-dependent. They are a reliable guide to the truth *only* because, and to the extent that, the body of background theories which determines their application is relevantly approximately true. The rules of rational scientific inference are not reducible to some more basic rules whose reliability as a guide to the truth is independent of the truth of background theories. Since it is a contingent empirical matter which background theories are approximately true, the rationality of scientific principles of inference ultimately rests on a contingent matter of empirical fact, just as the epistemic role of the senses rests upon the contingent empirical fact that the senses are reliable detectors of external phenomena. Thus inference foundationalism is radically false; there are no a priori justifiable rules of nondeductive inference. The epistemology of empirical science is an empirical science. (Boyd 1982, 1983, 1985a, 1985b, 1985c.)

One consequence of this radical contingency of scientific methods is that the emergence of scientific rationality as we know it depended upon the logically, epistemically, and historically contingent emergence of a relevantly approximately true theoretical tradition. It is not possible to understand the initial emergence of such a tradition as the consequence of some more abstractly conceived scientific or rational methodology which itself is theory-independent. There is no such methodology. We must think of the establishment of the corpuscular theory of matter in the seventeenth century as the beginning of rational methodology in chemistry, not as a consequence of it (for a further discussion see Boyd 1982).

3.4 Scientific intuitions and trained judgment

Both noninferential perceptual judgments and elaborately argued explicit inferential judgments in theoretical science have a purely contingent a posteriori foundation. Once this is recognized, it is easy to see that there are methodologically important features of scientific practice which are intermediate between noninferential perception and explicit inference. One example is provided by what science textbook authors often refer to as "physical intuition", "scientific maturity", or the like. One of the intended consequences of professional training in a scientific discipline (and other disciplines as well) is that the student acquire a "feel" for the issues and the actual physical materials which the science studies. As Kuhn (1970) points out, part of the role of experimental work in the training of professional scientists is to provide such a feel for the paradigms or "worked examples" of good scientific practice. There is very good reason to believe that having good physical (or biological or psychological) intuitions is important to epistemically reliable scientific practice. It is also quite clear both that the acquisition of good scientific intuitions depends on learning explicit theory, as well as on other sorts of training and practice, *and* that scientists are almost never able to make fully explicit the considerations which play a role in their intuitive judgments. The legitimate role of such "tacit" factors in science has often been taken (especially by philosophically inclined scientists) to be an especially puzzling feature of scientific methodology.

From the perspective of the naturalistic epistemology of science, there need be no puzzle. It is, of course, a question of the very greatest psychological interest just how intuitive judgments in science work and how they are related to explicit theory, on the one hand, and to experimental practice, on the other. But it seems overwhelmingly likely that scientific intuitions should be thought of as trained judgments which resemble perceptual judgments in not involving (or at least not being fully accounted for by) explicit inferences, but which resemble explicit inferences in science in depending for their reliability upon the relevant approximate truth of the explicit theories which help to determine them. This dependence upon the approximate truth of the relevant background theories will obtain even in those cases (which may be typical) in which the tacit judgments reflect a deeper understanding than that currently captured in explicit theory. It is an important and exciting fact that some scientific knowledge can be represented tacitly before it can be represented explicitly, but this fact poses no difficulty for a naturalistic treatment of scientific knowledge. Tacit or intuitive judgments in science are reliable because they are grounded in a theoretical tradition (itself partly tacit) which is, as a matter of contingent empirical fact, relevantly approximately true.

3.5 Non-Humean conceptions of causation and reduction

The Humean conception of causal relations according to which they are analyzable in terms of regularity, correlation, or deductive subsumability under laws is defensible only from a verificationist position. If verificationist criticisms of talk about unobservables are rejected – as they should be – then there is nothing more problematical about talk of causal powers than there is about talk of electrons or electromagnetic fields. There is no reason to believe that causal terms have definitions (analytic or natural) in noncausal terms. Instead, "cause" and its cognates refer to natural phenomena whose analysis is a matter for physicists, chemists, psychologists, historians, etc., rather than a matter of conceptual analysis. In particular, it is perfectly legitimate – as a naturalistic conception of epistemology requires – to employ unreduced causal notions in philosophical analysis. (Boyd, 1982, 1985b; Shoemaker 1980).

One crucial example of the philosophical application of such notions lies in the analysis of "reductionism". If a materialist perspective is sound, then *in some sense* all natural phenomena are "reducible" to basic physical phenomena. The (prephilosophically) natural way of expressing the relevant sort of reduction is to say that all substances are composed of purely physical substances, all forces are composed of physical forces, all causal powers or potentialities are realized in physical substances and their causal powers, etc. This sort of analysis freely employs unreduced causal notions. If it is "rationally reconstructed" according to the Humean analysis of such notions, we get the classic analysis of reduction in terms of the syntactic reducibility of the theories in the special sciences to the laws of physics, which in turn dictates the conclusion that all natural properties must be definable in the vocabulary of physics. Such an analysis is entirely without justification from the realistic and naturalistic perspective we are considering. Unreduced causal notions are philosophically acceptable, and the Humean reduction of them mistaken. The prephilosophically natural analysis of reduction is also the philosophically appropriate one. In particular, purely physical objects, states, properties, etc. need not have definitions in "the vocabulary of physics" or in any other reductive vocabulary (see Boyd 1982).

3.6 Natural definitions

Locke speculates at several places in Book IV of the *Essay* (see, e.g., IV, iii, 25) that when kinds of substances are defined by "nominal essences", as he thinks they must be, it will be impossible to have a general science of, say, chemistry. The reason is this: nominal essences define kinds of substance in terms of sensible properties, but the factors which govern the behavior (even the observable behavior) of substances are insensible corpuscular real essences. Since there is no reason to suppose that our nominal essences will correspond to categories which reflect uniformities in microstructure, there is no reason to believe that kinds defined by nominal essences provide a basis for obtaining general knowledge of substances. Only if we could sort substances according to their hidden real essences would systematic general knowledge of substances be possible.

Locke was right. Only when kinds are defined by natural rather than conventional definitions is it possible to obtain sound scientific explanations (Putnam 1975a; Boyd 1985b) or sound solutions to the problem of "projectibility" in inductive inference in science (Quine 1969a; Boyd 1979, 1982, 1983, 1985a, 1985b, 1985c). Indeed this is true not only for the definitions of natural kinds but also for the definitions of the properties, relations, magnitudes, etc. to which we must refer in sound scientific reasoning. In particular, a wide variety of terms do not possess analytic or stipulative definitions and are instead defined in terms of properties, relations, etc. which render them appropriate to particular sorts of scientific or practical reasoning. In the case of such terms, proposed definitions are always in principle revisable in the light of new evidence or new theoretical developments. Similarly, the fact that two people or two linguistic communities apply different definitions in using a term is not, by itself, sufficient to show that they are using the term to refer to different kinds, properties, etc.

3.7 Reference and epistemic access

If the traditional empiricist account of definition by nominal essences (or "operational definitions" or "criterial attributes") is to be abandoned in favor of a naturalistic account of definitions (at least for some terms) then a naturalistic conception of reference is required for those cases in which the traditional empiricist semantics has been abandoned. Such a naturalist account is provided by recent casual theories of reference (see, e.g., Feigl 1956; Kripke 1972; Putnam 1975a). The reference of a term is established by causal connections of the right sort between the use of the term and (instances of) its referent.

The connection between causal theories of reference and naturalistic theories of knowledge and of definitions is quite intimate: reference is itself an epistemic notion and the sorts of causal connections which are relevant to reference are just those which are involved in the reliable regulation of belief (Boyd 1979, 1982). *Roughly*, and for nondegenerate cases, a term t refers to a kind (property, relation, etc.) k just in case there exist causal mechanisms whose tendency is to bring it about, over time, that what is predicated of the term t will be approximately true of k (excuse the blurring of the use–mention distinction). Such mechanisms will typically include the existence of procedures which are approximately accurate for recognizing members or instances of k (at least for easy cases) and which relevantly govern the use of t, the social transmission of certain relevantly approximately true beliefs regarding k, formulated as claims about t (again excuse the slight to the use–mention distinction), a pattern of deference to experts on k with respect to the use of t, etc. (for a fuller discussion see Boyd 1979, 1982). When relations of this sort obtain, we may think of the properties of k as regulating the use of t (via such causal relations), and we may think of what is said using t as providing us with socially coordinated *epistemic access* to k; t refers to k (in nondegenerate cases) just in case the socially coordinated use of t provides significant epistemic access to k, and not to other kinds (properties, etc.) (Boyd 1979, 1982).

3.8 Homeostatic property-cluster definitions

The sort of natural definition[1] in terms of corpuscular real essences anticipated by Locke is reflected in the natural definitions of chemical kinds by molecular formulas; "water H_2O" is by now the standard example (Putnam 1975a). Natural definitions of this sort specify necessary and sufficient conditions for membership in the kind in question. Recent *non*-naturalistic semantic theories in the ordinary language tradition have examined the possibility of definitions which do not provide necessary and sufficient conditions in this way. According to various property-cluster or criterial attribute theories, some terms have definitions which are provided by a collection of properties such that the possession of an adequate number of these properties is sufficient for falling within the extension of the term. It is supposed to be a conceptual (and thus an a priori) matter what properties belong in the cluster and which combinations of them are sufficient for falling under the term. Insofar as different properties in the cluster are differently "weighted" in such judgments, the weighting is determined by our concept of the kind or property being defined. It is characteristically insisted, however, that our concepts of such kinds are "open textured" so that there is some indeterminacy in extension *legitimately* associated with property-cluster or criterial attribute definitions. The "imprecision" or "vagueness" of such definitions is seen as a perfectly appropriate feature of ordinary linguistic usage, in contrast to the artificial precision suggested by rigidly formalistic positivist conceptions of proper language use.

I shall argue (briefly) that – despite the philistine antiscientism often associated with "ordinary language" philosophy – the property-cluster conception of definitions provides an extremely deep insight into the possible form of *natural* definitions. I shall argue that there are a number of scientifically important kinds, properties, etc. whose natural definitions are very much like the property-cluster definitions postulated by ordinary-language philosophers (for the record, I doubt that there are any terms whose definitions actually fit the ordinary-language model, because I doubt that there are any significant "conceptual truths" at all). There are natural kinds, properties, etc. whose natural definitions involve a kind of property cluster *together with* an associated indeterminacy in extension. Both the property-cluster form of such definitions and the associated indeterminacy are dictated by the scientific task of employing categories which correspond to inductively and explanatorily relevant causal structures. In particular, the indeterminacy in extension of such natural definitions could not be remedied without rendering the definitions *un*natural in the sense of being scientifically misleading. What I believe is that the following sort of situation is commonplace in the special sciences which study complex structurally or functionally characterized phenomena:

1 There is a family *F* of properties which are "contingently clustered" in nature in the sense that they co-occur in an important number of cases.
2 Their co-occurrence is not, at least typically, a statistical artifact, but rather the result of what may be metaphorically (sometimes literally) described as a sort of *homeostasis*. Either the presence of some of the properties in *F* tends (under appropriate conditions) to favor the presence of the others, or there are underlying mechanisms or processes which tend to maintain the presence of the properties in *F*, or both.
3 The homeostatic clustering of the properties in *F* is causally important: there are (theoretically or practically) important effects which are produced by a conjoint occurrence of (many of) the properties in *F*

       together with (some or all of) the underlying mechanisms in question.

4 There is a kind term t which is applied to things in which the homeostatic clustering of most of the properties in F occurs.

5 This t has no analytic definition; rather all or part of the homeostatic cluster F together with some or all of the mechanisms which underlie it provides the natural definition of t. The question of just which properties and mechanisms belong in the definition of t is an a posteriori question – often a difficult theoretical one.

6 Imperfect homeostasis is nomologically possible or actual: some thing may display some but not all of the properties in F; some but not all of the relevant underlying homeostatic mechanisms may be present.

7 In such cases, the relative importance of the various properties in F and of the various mechanisms in determining whether the thing falls under t – if it can be determined at all – is a theoretical rather than a conceptual issue.

8 In cases in which such a determination is possible, the outcome will typically depend upon quite particular facts about the actual operation of the relevant homeostatic mechanisms, about the relevant background conditions, and about the causal efficacy of the partial cluster of properties from F. For this reason the outcome, if any, will typically be different in different possible worlds, even when the partial property cluster is the same and even when it is unproblematical that the kind referred to by t in the actual world exists.

9 Moreover, there will be many cases of extensional vagueness which are such that they are not resolvable, even given all the relevant facts and all the true theories. There will be things which display some but not all of the properties in F (and/or in which some but not all of the relevant homeostatic mechanisms operate) such that no rational considerations dictate whether or not they are to be classed under t, assuming that a dichotomous choice is to be made.

10 The causal importance of the homeostatic property cluster F together with the relevant underlying homeostatic mechanisms is such that the kind or property denoted by t is a natural kind in the sense discussed earlier.

11 No refinement of usage which replaces t by a significantly less extensionally vague term will preserve the naturalness of the kind referred to. Any such refinement would either require that we treat as important distinctions which are irrelevant to causal explanation or to induction, or that we ignore similarities which are important in just these ways.

    The reader is invited to assure herself that 1–11 hold, for example, for the terms "healthy" and "is healthier than." Whether these are taken to be full-blown cases of natural property (relation) terms is not crucial here. They do illustrate almost perfectly the notion of a homeostatic property cluster and the correlative notion of a homeostatic cluster term. It is especially important to see *both* that a posteriori theoretical considerations in medicine can sometimes decide problematical cases of healthiness or of relative healthiness, often in initially counterintuitive ways *and* that nevertheless only highly artificial modifications of the notions of health and relative health could eliminate most or all of the extensional vagueness which they possess. One way to see the latter point is to consider what we would do if, for some statistical study of various medical practices, we were obliged to eliminate most of the vagueness in the notion of relative healthiness even where medical theory was silent. What we would strive to do would be to resolve the vagueness in such a way as not to bias the results of the study – not to favor one finding about the efficacy of medical practices over another. The role of natural kinds is, by contrast, precisely *to bias* (in the pejoratively neutral sense of the term) inductive generalization (Quine 1969a; Boyd 1979, 1981, 1983, 1985a, 1985b). Our concern not to bias the findings reflects our recognition that the resolution of vagueness in question would be *un*natural in the sense relevant to this inquiry.

The paradigm cases of natural kinds – biological species – are examples of homeostatic cluster kinds in this sense. The appropriateness of any particular biological species for induction and explanation in biology depends upon the *imperfectly* shared and homeostatically related morphological, physiological, and behavioral features which characterize its members. The definitional role of mechanisms of homeostasis is reflected in the role of interbreeding in the modern species concept; for sexually reproducing species, the exchange of genetic material between populations is thought by some evolutionary biologists to be essential to the homeostatic unity of the other properties characteristic of the species and it is thus reflected in the species definition which they propose (see Mayr 1970). The *necessary* indeterminacy in extension of species terms is a consequence of evolutionary theory, as Darwin observed: speciation depends on the existence of populations which are intermediate between the parent species and the emerging one. Any "refinement" of classification which artificially eliminated the resulting indeterminacy in classification would obscure the central fact about heritable variations in phenotype upon which biological evolution depends. More determinate species categories would be scientifically inappropriate and misleading.

It follows that a consistently developed scientific realism *predicts* indeterminacy for those natural kind or property terms which refer to complex phenomena; such indeterminacy is a necessary consequence of "cutting the world at its (largely theory-independent) joints." Thus consistently developed scientific realism *predicts* that there will be some failures of bivalence for statements which refer to complex homeostatic phenomena (contrast, e.g., Putnam 1983 on "metaphysical realism" and vagueness). Precision in describing indeterminate or "borderline" cases of homeostatic cluster kinds (properties, etc.) consists not in the introduction of artificial precision in the definitions of such kinds but rather in a detailed description of the ways in which the indeterminate cases are like and unlike typical members of the kind (see Boyd 1982 on borderline cases of knowledge, which are themselves homeostatic cluster phenomena).

4 HOW TO BE A MORAL REALIST

4.1 Moral semantics, intuitions, reflective equilibrium, and hard cases

Some philosophical opportunities are too good to pass up. For many of the more abstract challenges to moral realism, recent realistic and naturalistic work in the philosophy of science is suggestive of possible responses in its defense. Thus for example, it has occurred to many philosophers (see, e.g., Putnam 1975b) that naturalistic theories of reference and of definitions might be extended to the analysis of moral language. *If* this could be done successfully *and if* the results were favorable to a realist conception of morals, then it would be possible to reply to several anti-realist arguments. For example, against the objection that wide divergence of moral concepts or opinions between traditions or cultures indicates that, at best, a constructivist analysis of morals is possible, the moral realist might reply that differences in conception or in working definitions need not indicate the absence of shared causally fixed referents for moral terms.

Similarly, consider the objection that a moral realist must hold that goodness is a natural property, and thus commit the "naturalistic fallacy" of maintaining that moral terms possess analytic definitions in, say, physical terms. The moral realist may choose to agree that goodness is probably a physical property but deny that it has any analytic definition whatsoever. If the realist's critique of the syntactic analysis of reductionism in science is also accepted, then the moral realist can deny that it follows from the premise that goodness is a physical property or that goodness has any physical definition, analytic or otherwise.

If the moral realist takes advantage of naturalistic and realistic conceptions in epistemology as well as in semantic theory, other rebuttals to anti-realist challenges are suggested. The extent of the potential for rebuttals of this sort can best be recognized if we consider the objection that the role of reflective equilibrium in moral reasoning dictates a constructivist rather than a realist conception of morals. The moral realist might reply that the dialectical interplay of observations, theory, and methodology which, according to the realist, constitutes the *discovery* procedure for scientific inquiry *just* is the method of reflective equilibrium, so that the prevalence of that method in moral reasoning cannot *by itself* dictate a non-realist conception of morals.

If the response just envisioned to the concern over reflective equilibrium is successful, then the defender of moral realism will have established that – in moral reasoning as in scientific reasoning – the role of culturally transmitted presuppositions in reasoning does not necessitate a constructivist (or non-cognitivist) rather than a realist analysis of the subject matter. *If* that is established, then the moral realist might defend the epistemic role of culturally determined intuitions in ethics by treating ethical intuitions on the model of theory-determined intuitions in science, which the scientific realist takes to be examples of epistemically reliable trained judgments.

Finally, if the moral realist is inclined to accept the anti-realist's claim that the existence of hard cases in ethics provides a reason to doubt that there is a moral fact of the matter which determines the answer in such cases (more on this later), then the scientific realist's conclusion that bivalence fails for some statements involving homeostatic cluster kind terms *might* permit the moral realist to reason that similar failures of bivalence for some ethical statements need not be fatal to moral realism.

In fact, I propose to employ just these rebuttals to the various challenges to moral realism I have been discussing. They represent the application of a coherent naturalistic conception of semantics and of knowledge against the challenges raised by the critic of moral realism. But they do not stand any chance of rebutting moral anti-realism unless they are incorporated into a broader conception of morals and of moral knowledge which meets certain very strong constraints. These constraints are the subject of the next section.

4.2 Constraints on a realist conception of moral knowledge

Suppose that a defense of moral realism is to be undertaken along the lines just indicated. What constraints does that particular defensive strategy place on a moral realist's conception of morals and of moral knowledge? Several important constraints are suggested by a careful examination of the realist doctrines in the philosophy of science whose extension to moral philosophy is contemplated.

In the first place, the scientific realist is able to argue that "reflective equilibrium" in science and a reliance on theory-dependent scientific intuitions are epistemically reliable *only* on the assumption that the theoretical tradition which governs these methodological practices contains theories which are relevantly approximately true. Indeed, the most striking feature of the consistently realistic epistemology of science is the insistence that the epistemic reliability of scientific methodology is contingent upon the establishment of such a theoretical tradition. Moreover, the possibility of offering a realist rather than a constructivist interpretation of reflective equilibrium and of intuition in science rests upon the realist's claim that observations and theory-mediated measurement and detection of "unobservables" in science represent epistemically relevant causal interactions between scientists and a theory-independent reality. Were the realist unable to treat observation and measurement as providing "epistemic access" to reality in this way, a constructivist treatment of scientific knowledge would be almost unavoidable.

Similarly, the scientific realist is able to employ a naturalistic conception of definitions and of reference only because (1) it is arguable that the nature of the subject matter of science dictates that kinds, properties, etc. be defined by nonconventional definitions, and (2) it is arguable that actual scientific practices result in the establishment of "epistemic access" to the various "theoretical entities" which, the realist maintains, are (part of) the subject matter of scientific inquiry.

Finally, the realist can insist that realism not only can tolerate but implies certain failures of bivalence only because it can be argued that homeostatic cluster kinds (properties, etc.) must have indeterminacy in extension in order for reference to them to be scientifically fruitful. These considerations suggest that the following constraints must be satisfied by an account of moral knowledge if it is to be the basis for the proposed defense of moral realism:

1   It must be possible to explain how our moral reasoning *started out* with a stock of relevantly approximately true moral beliefs so that reflective equilibrium in moral reasoning can be treated in a fashion analogous to the scientific realist's treatment of reflective equilibrium in scientific reasoning. Note that this constraint does not require that it be possible to argue that we started out with close approximations to the truth (seventeenth-century corpuscular theory was quite far from the truth). What is required is that the respects of approximation be such that it is possible to see how continued approximations would be forthcoming as a result of subsequent moral and nonmoral reasoning.

2   There must be an answer to the question "What plays, in moral reasoning, the role played by observation in science?" which can form the basis for a realist rather than a constructivist conception of the foundations of reflective equilibrium in moral reasoning.

3   It must be possible to explain why moral properties, say goodness, would require natural rather than conventional definitions.

4   It must be possible to show that our ordinary use of moral terms provides us with epistemic access to moral properties. Moral goodness must, to some extent, regulate the use of the word "good" in moral reasoning. Here again examination of the corresponding constraint in the philosophy of science indicates that the regulation need not be nearly perfect, but it must be possible to show that sufficient epistemic access is provided to form the basis for the growth of moral knowledge.

5   It must be possible to portray occasional indeterminacy in the extension of moral terms as rationally dictated by the nature of the subject matter in a way analogous to the scientific realist's treatment of such indeterminacy in the case of homeostatic cluster terms.

In the work of scientific realists, the case that the analogous constraints are satisfied has depended upon examination of the substantive findings of various of the sciences (such as, e.g., the atomic theory of matter or the Darwinian conception of speciation). It is very unlikely that an argument could be mounted in favor of the view that moral knowledge meets the constraints we are considering which does not rely in a similar way on substantive doctrines about the foundations of morals. What I propose to do instead is to *describe* one account of the nature of morals which almost ideally satisfies the constraints in question and to indicate how a defense of moral realism would proceed on the basis of this account.

It will not be my aim here to defend this account of morals against morally plausible rivals. In fact, I am inclined to think – *partly* because of the way in which it allows the constraints we are considering to be satisfied – that *if* there is a truth of the matter about morals (that is, if moral realism is true), then the account I will be offering is close to the truth. But my aim in this paper is merely to establish that moral realism is plausible and defensible. The substantive moral position I will consider is a plausible version of nonutilitarian consequentialism, one which – I believe – captures many of the features which make consequentialism *one* of the standard and plausible positions in moral philosophy. If moral realism is defensible on the basis of a plausible version of consequentialism, then it is a philosophically defensible position which must be taken seriously in metaethics; and that's all I'm trying to establish here.

It is, moreover, pretty clear that a variety of plausible alternative conceptions of the foundations of morals satisfy the constraints we are discussing. If I am successful here in mounting a plausible defense of moral realism, given the substantive conception I will propose, then it is quite likely that the very powerful semantic and epistemic resources of recent realist philosophy of science could be effectively employed to defend moral realism on the basis of many of the alternative conceptions. I leave it to the defenders of alternative conceptions to explore these possibilities. The defense of moral realism offered here is to be thought of as (the outline of) a "worked example" of the application of the general strategy proposed in 4.1.

One more thing should be said about the substantive conception of morals offered here. Like any naturalistic account, it rests upon potentially controversial empirical claims about human psychology and about social theory. It is a commonplace, I think, that moral realism is an optimistic position (or, perhaps, that it is typically an optimist's position). One nice feature of the substantive analysis of morals upon which my defense of moral realism will be based is that it quite obviously rests upon optimistic claims about human potential. Perhaps in that respect it is well suited to serve as a representative example of the variety of substantive moral views which would satisfy the constraints in question. (For a further discussion of the methodological implications of the moral realist's reliance on particular substantive moral theories see section 5.3.)

4.3 Homeostatic consequentialism

In broad outline, the conception of morals upon which the sample defense of moral realism will rest goes like this:

1   There are a number of important human goods, things which satisfy important human needs. Some of these needs are physical or medical. Others are psychological or social; these (probably) include the need for love and friendship, the need to engage in cooperative efforts, the need to exercise control over one's own life, the need for intellectual and artistic appreciation and expression, the need for physical recreation, etc. The question of just which important human needs there are is a potentially difficult and complex empirical question.

2   Under a wide variety of (actual and possible) circumstances these human goods (or rather instances of the satisfaction of them) are homeostatically clustered. In part they are clustered because these goods themselves are – when present in balance or moderation – mutually supporting. There are in addition psychological and social mechanisms which when, and to the extent to which, they are present

contribute to the homeostasis. They probably include cultivated attitudes of mutual respect, political democracy, egalitarian social relations, various rituals, customs, and rules of courtesy, ready access to education and information, etc. It is a complex and difficult question in psychology and social theory just what these mechanisms are and how they work.

3   Moral goodness is defined by this cluster of goods and the homeostatic mechanisms which unify them. Actions, policies, character traits, etc. are morally good to the extent to which they tend to foster the realization of these goods or to develop and sustain the homeostatic mechanisms upon which their unity depends.

4   In actual practice, a concern for moral goodness can be a guide to action for the morally concerned because the homeostatic unity of moral goodness tends to mitigate possible conflicts between various individual goods. In part, the possible conflicts are mitigated just because various of the important human goods are mutually reinforcing. Moreover, since the existence of effective homeostatic unity among important human goods is part of the moral good, morally concerned choice is constrained by the imperative to balance potentially competing goods in such a way that homeostasis is maintained or strengthened. Finally, the improvement of the psychological and social mechanisms of homeostasis themselves is a moral good whose successful pursuit tends to further mitigate conflicts of the sort in question. In this regard, moral practice resembles good engineering practice in product design. In designing, say, automobiles there are a number of different desiderata (economy, performance, handling, comfort, durability ...) which are potentially conflicting but which enjoy a kind of homeostatic unity if developed in moderation. One feature of good automotive design is that it promotes these desiderata within the limits of homeostasis. The other feature of good automotive design (or, perhaps, of good automotive engineering) is that it produces technological advances which permit that homeostatic unity to be preserved at higher levels of the various individual desiderata. So it is with good moral practice as well.[2]

I should say something about how the claim that the nature of the constituents of moral goodness is an empirical matter should be understood. I mean the analogy between moral inquiry and scientific inquiry to be taken *very* seriously. It is a commonplace in the history of science that major advances often depend on appropriate social conditions, technological advances, and prior scientific discoveries. Thus, for example, much of eighteenth-century physics and chemistry was possible only because there had developed (a) the social conditions in which work in the physical sciences was economically supported, (b) a technology sufficiently advanced to make the relevant instrumentation possible, and (c) the theoretical social potential. Much of this knowledge is genuinely *experimental* knowledge and the relevant experiments are ("naturally" occurring) political and social experiments whose occurrence and whose interpretation depends both on "external" factors and upon the current state of our moral understanding. Thus, for example, we would not have been able to explore the dimensions of our needs for artistic expression and appreciation had not social and technological developments made possible cultures in which, for some classes at least, there was the leisure to produce and consume art. We would not have understood the role of political democracy in the homeostasis of the good had the conditions not arisen in which the first limited democracies developed. Only after the moral insights gained from the first democratic experiments were in hand, were we equipped to see the depth of the moral peculiarity of slavery. Only since the establishment of the first socialist societies are we even beginning to obtain the data necessary to assess the role of egalitarian social practices in fostering the good.

It is also true of moral knowledge, as it is in case of knowledge in other "special sciences", that the improvement of knowledge may depend upon theoretical advances in related disciplines. It is hard, for example, to see how deeper understanding in history or economic theory could fail to add to our understanding of human potential and of the mechanisms underlying the homeostatic unity of the good.

Let us now consider the application of the particular theory of the good presented here as a part of the strategy for the defense of moral realism indicated in the preceding section. I shall be primarily concerned to defend the realist position that moral goodness is a real property of actions, policies, states of affairs, etc. and that our moral judgments are, often enough, reflections of truths about the good. A complete realist treatment of the semantics of moral terms would of course require examining notions like obligation and justice as well. I will not attempt this examination here, in part because the aim of this essay is merely to indicate briefly how a plausible defense of moral realism might be carried out rather than to carry out the defense in detail. Moreover, on a consequentialist conception of morals such notions as obligation and justice are derivative ones, and it is doubtful if the details of the derivations are relevant to the defense of moral realism in the way that the defense of a realist conception of the good is.

In the remaining sections of the essay I shall offer a defense of homeostatic consequentialist moral realism against the representative anti-realist challenges discussed in part 2. The claim that the term "good" in its moral uses refers to the homeostatic cluster property just described (or even the claim that there is such a property) represents a complex and controversial philosophical and empirical hypothesis. For each of the responses to anti-realist challenges which I will present; there are a variety of possible anti-realist rebuttals, both empirical and philosophical. It is beyond the scope of this essay to explore these rebuttals and possible moral realist responses to them in any detail. Instead, I shall merely indicate how plausible realist rebuttals to the relevant challenges can be defended. Once again, the aim of the present paper is not to establish moral realism but merely to establish its plausibility and to offer a general framework within which further defenses of moral realism might be understood.

4.4 Observations, intuitions, and reflective equilibrium

Of the challenges to moral realism we are considering, two are straight-forwardly epistemological. They suggest that the role of moral intuitions and of reflective equilibrium in moral reasoning dictate (at best) a constructivist interpretation of morals. As we saw in section 4.2, it would be possible for the moral realist to respond by assimilating the role of moral intuitions and reflective equilibrium to the role of scientific intuitions and theory-dependent methodological factors in the realist account of scientific knowledge, but this response is viable only if it is possible to portray many of our background moral beliefs and judgments as relevantly approximately true and only if there is a satisfactory answer to the question: "What plays, in moral reasoning, the role played in science by observation?" Let us turn first to the latter question.

I propose the answer: "Observation".

According to the homeostatic consequentialist conception of morals (indeed, according to any naturalistic conception) goodness is an ordinary natural property, and it would be odd indeed if observations didn't play the same role in the study of this property that they play in the study of all the others. According to the homeostatic consequentialist conception, good-ness is a property quite similar to the other properties studied by psychologists, historians, and social scientists, and observations will play the same role in moral inquiry that they play in the other kinds of empirical inquiry about people.

It is worth remarking that in the case of any of the human sciences *some* of what must count as observation is observation of oneself, and *some* is the sort of self-observation involved in introspection. Moreover, *some* of our observations of other people will involve trained judgment and the operation of sympathy. No reasonable naturalistic account of the founda-tions of psychological or social knowledge *or* of our technical knowledge in psychology or the social sciences will fail to treat such sources of belief – when they are generally reliable – as cases of observation in the relevant sense.

It is true, of course, that both the content and the evidential assessment of observations of this sort will be influenced by theoretical considerations, but this does not distinguish observations in the human sciences from those in other branches of empirical inquiry. The theory dependence of observations and their interpretation is simply one aspect of the pervasive theory dependence of methodology in science which the scientific realist cheerfully acknowledges (since it plays a crucial role in arguments for scientific realism). It is possible to defend a realist interpretation of the human sciences because it is possible to argue that actual features in the world constrain the findings in those sciences sufficiently that the relevant background theories will be approximately true enough for theory-dependent observations to play a reliable epistemic role.

In the case of moral reasoning, observations and their interpretation will be subject to just the same sort of theory-dependent influences. This theory dependence is one aspect of the general phenomenon of theory dependence of methodology in moral reasoning which we, following Rawls, have been describing as reflective equilibrium. We will be able to follow the example of scientific realists and to treat the observations which play a role in moral reasoning as sufficiently reliable for the defense of moral realism just in case we are able to portray the theories upon which they and their interpretation depend as relevantly approximately true – that is, just in case we are able to carry out the other part of the moral realist's response to epistemic challenges and to argue that our background moral beliefs are sufficiently near the truth to form the foundations for a reliable empirical investigation of moral matters. Let us turn now to that issue.

What we need to know is whether it is reasonable to suppose that, for quite some time, we have had background moral beliefs sufficiently near the truth that they could form the basis for subsequent improvement of moral knowledge in the light of further experience and further historical developments. Assuming, as we shall, a homeostatic consequentialist conception of morals, this amounts to the question whether our background beliefs about human goods and the psychological and social mechanisms which unite them had been good enough to guide the gradual process of expansion of moral knowledge envisioned in that conception. Have our beliefs about our own needs and capacities been good enough – since, say the emergence of moral and political philosophy in ancient Greece – that we have been able to respond to new evidence and to the results of new social developments by expanding and improving our understanding of those needs and capacities even when doing so required rejecting some of our earlier views in favor of new ones? It is hard to escape the conclusion that this is simply the question "Has the rational empirical study of human kind proven to be possible?" Pretty plainly the answer is that such study has proven to be possible, though difficult. In particular we have improved our understanding of our own needs and our individual and social capacities by just the sort of historically complex process envisioned in the homeostatic consequentialist conception. I conclude therefore that there is no reason to think that reflective equilibrium – which is just the standard methodology of any empirical inquiry, social or otherwise – raises any epistemological problems for the defense of moral realism.

Similarly, we may now treat moral intuitions exactly on a par with scientific intuitions, as a species of trained judgment. Such intuitions are *not* assigned a foundational role in moral inquiry; in particular they do not substitute for observations. Moral intuitions are simply one cognitive manifestation of our moral understanding, just as physical intuitions, say, are a cognitive manifestation of 'physicists' understanding of their subject matter. Moral intuitions, like physical intuitions, play a limited but legitimate role in empirical inquiry *precisely because* they are linked to theory *and* to observations in a generally reliable process of reflective equilibrium.

It may be useful by way of explaining the epistemic points made here to consider very briefly how the moral realist might respond to one of the many possible anti-realist rebuttals to what has just been said. Consider the following objection: The realist treatment of reflective equilibrium requires that our background moral beliefs have been for some time relevantly approximately true. As a matter of fact, the overwhelming majority of people have probably always believed in some sort of theistic foundation of morals: moral laws are God's laws; the psychological capacities which underlie moral practice are a reflection of God's design; etc. According to the homeostatic consequentialism which we are supposed to accept for the sake of argument, moral facts are mere natural facts. Therefore, according to homeostatic consequentialism, most people have always had profoundly mistaken moral beliefs. How then can it be claimed that our background beliefs have been relevantly approximately true?

I reply that – assuming that people have typically held theistic beliefs of the sort in question – it does follow from homeostatic consequentialism that they have been *in that respect* very wrong indeed. But being wrong in that respect does not preclude their moral judgments having been relatively reliable reflections of facts about the homeostatic cluster of fundamental human goods, according to the model of the development of moral knowledge discussed earlier. Until Darwin, essentially all biologists attributed the organization and the adaptive features of the physiology, anatomy, and behavior of plants and animals to God's direct planning. That attribution did not prevent biologists from accumulating the truly astonishing body of knowledge about anatomy, physiology, and animal behavior upon which Darwin's discovery of evolution by natural selection depended; nor did it prevent their recognizing the profound biological insights of Darwin's theory. Similarly, seventeenth-century corpuscular chemistry did provide the basis for the development of modern chemistry in a way that earlier quasi-animistic "renaissance naturalism" in chemistry could not. Early corpuscular theory was right that the chemical properties of substances are determined by the fundamental properties of stable "corpuscles"; it was wrong about almost everything else, but what it got right was enough to point chemistry in a fruitful direction. I understand the analogy between the development of scientific knowledge and the development of moral knowledge to be very nearly exact.

There may indeed be one important respect in which the analogy between the development of scientific knowledge and the development of moral knowledge is *in*exact, but oddly, this respect of disanalogy makes the case for moral realism stronger. One of the striking consequences of a full-blown naturalistic and realistic conception of knowledge is that our knowledge, even our most basic knowledge, rests upon logically contingent "foundations". Our perceptual knowledge, for example, rests upon the logically contingent a posteriori fact that our senses are reliable detectors of certain sorts of external objects. In the case of perceptual knowledge, however, there is a sense in which it is nonaccidental, noncontingent, that our senses are reliable detectors. The approximate reliability of our senses (with respect to some applications) is explained by evolutionary theory in a quite fundamental way (Quine 1969a). By contrast, the reliability of our methodology in chemistry is much more dramatically contingent. As a matter of fact, early thinkers tried to explain features of the natural world by analogy to sorts of order they already partly understood: mathematical, psychological, and mechanical. The atomic theory of matter represents one such attempt to assimilate chemical order to the better-understood mechanical order. In several important senses it was highly contingent that the microstructure of matter turned out to be particulate and mechanical enough that the atomic (or "corpuscular") *guess* could provide the foundation for epistemically reliable research in chemistry. The accuracy of our guess in this regard is not, for example, explained by either evolutionary necessity or by deep facts about our psychology. In an important sense, the seventeenth-century belief in the corpuscular theory of matter was not reliably produced. It was not produced by an antecedent generally reliable methodology: reasoning by analogy is *not* generally reliable except in contexts where a rich and approximately accurate body of theory *already* exists to guide us in finding the right respects of analogy (see Boyd 1982).

By contrast, the emergence of relevantly approximately true beliefs about the homeostatic cluster of fundamental human goods – although logically contingent – was much less strikingly "accidental". From the point of view either of evolutionary theory or of basic human psychology it is hardly accidental that we are able to recognize many of our own and others' fundamental needs. Moreover, it is probably not accidental from an evolutionary point of view that we were able to recognize some features of the homeostasis of these needs. Our initial relevantly approximately accurate beliefs about the good may well have been produced by generally reliable psychological and perceptual mechanisms and thus may have been clear instances of knowledge in a way in which our initial corpuscular beliefs were not (for a discussion of the latter point see Boyd 1982). It is *easier*, not *harder*, to explain how moral knowledge is possible than it is to explain how scientific knowledge is possible. Locke was right that we are fitted by nature for moral knowledge (in both the seventeenth- and the twentieth-century senses of the term) in a way that we are not so fitted for scientific knowledge of other sorts.

4.5 Moral semantics

We have earlier considered two objections to the moral realist's account of the semantics of moral terms. According to the first, the observed diversity of moral concepts – between cultures as well as between individuals and groups within a culture – suggests that it will not be possible to assign a single objective subject matter to their moral disputes. The divergence of concepts suggests divergence of reference of a sort which constructivist relativism is best suited to explain. According to the second objection, moral realism is committed to the absurd position that moral terms possess definitions in the vocabulary of the natural sciences. We have seen that a moral realist rebuttal to these challenges is possible which assimilates moral terms to naturalistically and nonreductively definable terms in the sciences. Such a response can be successful only if (1) there are good reasons to think that moral terms must possess natural rather than stipulative definitions and (2) there are good reasons to think that ordinary uses of moral terms provide us with epistemic access to moral properties, so that, for example, moral goodness to some extent regulates our use of the word "good" in moral contexts.

The homeostatic consequentialist conception of morals provides a justification for the first of these claims. If the good is defined by a homeostatic phenomenon the details of which we still do not entirely know, then it is a paradigm case of a property whose "essence" is given by a natural rather than a stipulative definition.

Is it plausible that the homeostatic cluster of fundamental human goods has, to a significant extent, regulated the use of the term "good" so that there is a general tendency, of the sort indicated by the homeostatic consequentialist conception of the growth of moral knowledge, for what we say about the good to be true of that cluster? If what I have already said about the possibility of defending a realist conception of reflective equilibrium in moral reasoning is right, the answer must be "yes." Such a tendency is guaranteed by basic evolutionary and psychological facts, and it is just such a tendency which we can observe in the ways in which our conception of the good has changed in the light of new evidence concerning human needs and potential. Indeed, the way we ("pre-analytically") recognize moral uses of the term "good" and the way we identify moral terms in other languages are precisely by recourse to the idea that moral terms are those involved in discussions of human goods and harms. We tacitly assume *something like* the proposed natural definition of "good" in the practice of translation of moral discourse. I think it will help to clarify this realist response if we consider two possible objections to it. The first objection reflects the same concern about the relation between moral and theological reasoning that we examined in the preceding section. It goes like this: How is it possible for the moral realist who adopts homeostatic consequentialism to hold that there is a general tendency for our beliefs about the good to get truer? After all, the error of thinking of the good as being defined by God's will persists unabated and is – according to the homeostatic consequentialist's conception – a very important falsehood.

I reply, first, that the sort of tendency to the truth required by the epistemic access account of reference is not such that it must preclude serious errors. Newtonians were talking about mass, energy, momentum, etc. all along, even though they were massively wrong about the structure of space-time. We might be irretrievably wrong about some other issue in physics and still use the terms of physical theory to refer to real entities, magnitudes, etc. All that is required is a significant epistemically relevant causal connection between the use of a term and its referent.

Moreover, as I suggested earlier, it is characteristic of what we recognize as moral discourse (whether in English or in some other language) that considerations of human well-being play a significant role in determining what is said to be "good". The moral realist need not deny that other considerations – perhaps profoundly false ones – also influence what we say is good. After all, the historian of biology need not deny that the term "species" has relatively constant reference throughout the nineteenth century, even though, prior to Darwin, religious considerations injected profound errors into biologists' conception of species. Remember that we do not ordinarily treat a theological theory as a theory *of* moral goodness at all unless it says something about what we independently recognize as human well-being. The role of religious considerations in moral reasoning provides a challenge for moral realists, but exactly the same challenge faces a realist interpretation of biological or psychological theorizing before the twentieth century, and it can surely be met.

The second objection I want to consider represents a criticism of moral realism often attributed to Marx (see, e.g., Wood 1972; for the record I believe that Marx's position on this matter was confused and that he vacillated between an explicit commitment to the relativist position, which Wood discusses, and a tacit commitment to a position whose reconstruction would look something like the position defended here). The objection goes like this: The moral realist – in the guise of the homeostatic con-sequentialist, say – holds that what regulate the use of moral terms are facts about human well-being. But this is simply not so. Consider, for example, sixteenth-century discussions of rights. One widely acknowledged "right" was the divine right of kings. Something surely regulated the use of the language of rights in the sixteenth century, but it clearly wasn't human well-being construed in the way the moral realist intends. Instead, it was the well-being of kings and of the aristocratic class of which they were a part.

I agree with the analysis of the origin of the doctrine of the divine right of kings; indeed, I believe that such class determination of moral beliefs is a commonplace phenomenon. But I do not believe that this analysis under-mines the claim that moral terms refer to aspects of human well-being. Consider, for example, the psychology of thinking and intelligence. It is extremely well documented (see, e.g., Gould 1981; Kamin 1974) that the content of much of the literature in this area is determined by class interests rather than by the facts. Nevertheless, the psychological terms occurring in the most egregiously prejudiced papers refer to real features of human psychology; this is so because, in other contexts, their use is relevantly regulated by such features. Indeed – and this is the important point – if there were not such an epistemic (and thus referential) connection to real psychological phenomena, the ideological rationalization of class structures represented by the class-distorted literature would be ineffective. It's only when people come to believe, for example, that Blacks lack a trait, *familiar in other contexts as "intelligence"*, that racist theories can serve to rationalize the socioeconomic role to which Blacks are largely confined.

Similarly, I argue, in order for the doctrine of the divine right of kings to serve a class function, it had to be the case that moral language was often enough connected to issues regarding the satisfaction of real human needs. Otherwise, an appeal to such a supposed right would be ideologically ineffective. Only when rights-talk has *some* real connection to the satisfac-tion of the needs of non-aristocrats could this instance of rights-talk be useful to kings and their allies.

Once again, when the analogy between moral inquiry and scientific inquiry is fully exploited, it becomes possible to defend the doctrines upon which moral realism rests.

4.6 Hard cases and divergent views

Two of the challenges to moral realism we are considering are grounded in
the recognition that some moral issues seem very hard to resolve. On the
one hand, there seem to be moral dilemmas which resist resolution even for
people who share a common moral culture. Especially with respect to the
sort of possible cases often considered by moral philosophers, there often
seems to be no rational way of deciding between morally quite distinct
courses of action. Our difficulty in resolving moral issues appears even
greater when we consider the divergence in moral views that exists between
people from different backgrounds or cultures. The anti-realist proposes to
explain the difficulties involved by denying that there is a common
objective subject matter which determines answers to moral questions.

We have seen that – to the extent that she chooses to take the difficulties
in resolving moral issues as evidence for the existence of moral statements
for which bivalence fails – the moral realist can try to assimilate such
failures to the failures of bivalence which realist philosophy *predicts* in the
case, for example, of some statements involving homeostatic cluster terms.
Such a response will work only to the extent that moral terms can be shown
to possess natural definitions relevantly like homeostatic cluster definitions.
Of course, according to homeostatic consequentialism, moral terms (or
"good" at any rate) just are homeostatic cluster terms, so this constraint is
satisfied. What I want to emphasize is that a moral realist *need not* invoke
failures of bivalence in every case in which difficulties arise in resolving
moral disputes.

Recall that on the conception we are considering moral inquiry is about
a complex and difficult subject matter, proceeds often by the analysis of
complex and "messy" naturally occurring social experiments, and is subject
to a very high level of social distortion by the influence of class interests and
other cultural factors. In this regard moral inquiry resembles inquiry in any
of the complex and politically controversial social sciences. In such cases,
even when there is no reason to expect failures of bivalence, one would
predict that the resolution of some issues will prove difficult or, in some
particular social setting, impossible. Thus the moral realist can point to the
fact that moral inquiry is a species of social inquiry to explain much of the
observed divergence in moral views and the apparent intractability of many
moral issues.

Similarly, the complexity and controversiality of moral issues can be
invoked to explain the especially sharp divergence of moral views often
taken to obtain between different cultures. For the homeostatic consequentialist version of moral realism to be true it must be the case that in
each culture in which moral inquiry takes place the homeostatically
clustered human goods epistemically regulate moral discourse to an
appreciable extent. On the realistic and naturalistic conception of the
growth of knowledge, this will in turn require that the moral tradition of the
culture in question embody some significant approximations to the truth
about moral matters. It is, however, by no means required that two such
cultural traditions have started with initial views which approximated the

truth to the same extent or along the same dimensions, nor is it required that they have been subjected to the same sorts of social distortion, nor that they have embodied the same sorts of naturally occurring social experimentation. It would thus be entirely unsurprising if two such traditions of moral inquiry should have, about some important moral questions, reached conclusions so divergent that no resolution of their disagreement will be possible within the theoretical and methodological framework which the two traditions *currently* have in common, even though these issues may possess objective answers eventually discoverable from within either tradition or from within a broader tradition which incorporates insights from both.

In this regard it is useful to remember the plausibility with which it can be argued that, if there were agreement on all the nonmoral issues (including theological ones), then there would be no moral disagreements. I'm not sure that this is exactly right. For one thing, the sort of moral agreement which philosophers typically have in mind when they say this sort of thing probably does not include agreement that some question has an indeterminate answer, which is something predicted by homeostatic consequentialism. Nevertheless, careful philosophical examination will reveal, I believe, that agreement on nonmoral issues would eliminate *almost all* disagreement about the sorts of moral issues which arise in ordinary moral practice. Moral realism of the homeostatic consequentialist variety provides a quite plausible explanation for this phenomenon.

It is nevertheless true that, for some few real-world cases and for *lots* of the contrived cases so prevalent in the philosophical literature, there does appear to be serious difficulty in finding rational resolutions – assuming as we typically do that an appeal to indeterminacy of the extension of "good" doesn't count as a resolution. In such cases the strategy available to the moral realist *is* to insist that failures of bivalence do occur just as a homeostatic consequentialist moral realist predicts.

Philosophers often suggest that the major normative ethical theories will yield the same evaluations in almost all actual cases. Often it is suggested that this fact supports the claim that there is some sort of objectivity in ethics, but it is very difficult to see just why this should be so. Homeostatic consequentialist moral realism provides the basis for a satisfactory treatment of this question. Major theories in normative ethics have almost always sought to provide definitions for moral terms with almost completely definite extensions. This is, of course, in fact a mistake; moral terms possess homeostatic cluster definitions instead. The appearance of sharp divergence between major normative theories, with respect to the variety of possible cases considered by philosophers, arises from the fact that they offer different putative resolutions to issues which lack any resolution *at all* of the sort anticipated in those theories. The general agreement of major normative theories on almost all actual cases is explained both by the fact that the actual features of the good regulate the use of the term "good" in philosophical discourse *and* by the homeostatic character of the good: when different normative theories put different weight on different components of the good, the fact that such components are – in actual cases – linked by reliable homeostatic mechanisms tends to mitigate, in real-world cases, the effects of the differences in the weights assigned. Homeostatic consequentialism represents the common grain of truth in other normative theories. (For further discussion of the resulting case for moral realism see section 5.4.)

4.7 Morality, motivation, and rationality

There remains but one of the challenges to moral realism which we are here considering. It has often been objected against moral realism that there is some sort of logical connection between moral judgments and reasons for action which a moral realist cannot account for. It might be held, for example, that the recognition that one course of action is morally preferable to another *necessarily* provides a reason (even if not a decisive one) to prefer the morally better course of action. Mere facts (especially mere *natural* facts) cannot have this sort of logical connection to rational choice or reasons for action. Therefore, so the objection goes, there cannot be moral facts; moral realism (or at least naturalistic moral realism) is impossible.

It is of course true that the naturalistic moral realist must deny that moral judgments necessarily provide reasons for action; surely, for example, there could be nonhuman cognizing systems which could understand the natural facts about moral goodness but be entirely indifferent to them in choosing how to act. Moral judgments might provide for them no reasons for action whatsoever. Moreover, it is hard to see how the naturalistic moral realist can escape the conclusion that it would be *logically possible* for there to be a human being for whom moral judgments provided no reasons for action. The moral realist must therefore deny that the connection between morality and reasons for action is so strong as the objection we are considering maintains. The appearance of an especially intimate connection must be explained in some other way.

The standard naturalist response is to explain the apparent intimacy of the connection by arguing that the natural property moral goodness is one such that for psychologically normal humans, the fact that one of two choices is morally preferable will in fact provide some reason for preferring it. The homeostatic consequentialist conception of the good is especially well suited to this response since it defines the good in terms of the homeostatic unity of fundamental human needs. It seems to me that this explanation of the close connection between moral judgments and reasons for action is basically right, but it ignores – it seems to me – one important source of the anti-realist's intuition that the connection between moral judgments and rational choice must be a necessary one. What I have in mind is the very strong intuition which many philosophers share that the person for whom moral judgments are motivationally indifferent would not only be psychologically atypical but would have some sort of *cognitive* deficit with respect to moral reasoning as well. The anti-realist diagnoses this deficit as a failure to recognize a definitional or otherwise necessary connection between moral goodness and reasons for action.

I think that there is a deep insight in the view that people for whom questions of moral goodness are irrelevant to how they would choose to act suffer a cognitive deficit. I propose that the deficit is not – as the anti-realist would have it – a failure to recognize a necessary connection between moral judgments and reasons for action. Instead, I suggest, if we adopt a naturalistic conception of moral knowledge we can diagnose in such people a deficit in the capacity to make moral judgments somewhat akin to a perceptual deficit. What I have in mind is the application of a causal theory of moral knowledge to the examination of a feature of moral reasoning which has been well understood in the empiricist tradition since Hume, that is, the role of sympathy in moral understanding.

It is extremely plausible that for normal human beings the capacity to access human goods and harms – the capacity to *recognize* the extent to which others are well or poorly off with respect to the homeostatic cluster of moral goods and the capacity to *anticipate correctly* the probable effect on others' well-being of various counterfactual circumstances – depends upon their capacity for sympathy, their capacity to imagine themselves in the situation of others or even to find themselves involuntarily doing so in cases in which others are especially well or badly off. The idea that sympathy plays this sort of cognitive role is a truism of nineteenth-century faculty psychology, and it is very probably right.

It is also very probably right, as Hume insists, that the operation of sympathy is *motivationally* important: as a matter of contingent psycho-logical fact, when we put ourselves in the place of others in imagination, the effects of our doing so include our taking pleasure in others' pleasures and our feeling distress at their misfortune, and we are thus motivated to care for the well-being of others. The psychological mechanisms by which all this takes place may be more complicated than Hume imagined, but the fact remains that one and the same psychological mechanism – sympathy – plays *both* a cognitive *and* a motivational role in normal human beings. We are now in a position to see why the morally unconcerned person, the person for whom moral facts are motivationally irrelevant, probably suffers a *cognitive* deficit with respect to moral reasoning. Such a person would have to be deficient in sympathy, because the motivational role of sympathy is precisely to make moral facts motivationally relevant. In consequence, she or he would be deficient with respect to a cognitive capacity (sympathy) which is ordinarily important for the correct assessment of moral facts. The motivational deficiency would, as a matter of contingent fact about human psychology, be a cognitive deficiency as well.

Of course it does not follow that there could not be cognizing systems which are quite capable of assessing moral facts without recourse to anything like sympathy; they might, for example, rely on the application of a powerful tacit or explicit theory of human psychology instead. Indeed it does not follow that there are not actual people – some sociopaths and con artists, for example – who rely on such theories instead of sympathy. But it is true, just as the critic of moral realism insists, that there is generally a cognitive deficit associated with moral indifference. The full resources of naturalistic epistemology permit the moral realist to acknowledge and explain this important insight of moral anti-realists.

4.8 Conclusion

I have argued that if the full resources of naturalistic and realistic conceptions of scientific knowledge and scientific language are deployed and if the right sort of positive theory of the good is advanced, then it is possible to make a plausible case for moral realism in response to typical anti-realist challenges. Two methodological remarks about the arguments I have offered may be useful. In the first place, the rebuttals I have offered to challenges to moral realism really do depend strongly upon the naturalistic and nonfoundational aspects of current (scientific) realist philosophy of science. They depend, roughly, upon the aspects of the scientific realist's program which make it plausible for the scientific realist to claim that philosophy is an empirical inquiry continuous with the sciences and with, e.g., history and empirical social theory. I have argued elsewhere (Boyd 1981, 1982, 1983, 1985a, 1985b, 1985c) that these aspects of scientific realism are essential to the defense of scientific realism against powerful empiricist and constructivist arguments.

If we now ask how one should decide between scientific realism and its rivals, I am inclined to think that the answer is that the details of particular technical arguments will not be sufficient to decide the question rationally; instead, one must assess the overall conceptions of knowledge, language, and understanding which go with the rival conceptions of science (I argue for this claim in Boyd 1983). *One* important constraint on an acceptable philosophical conception in these areas is that it permit us to understand the obvious fact that moral reasoning is not nearly so different from scientific or other factual reasoning as logical positivists have led us to believe. It is initially plausible, I think, that a constructivist conception of science is favored over both empiricist and realist conceptions insofar as we confine our attention to this constraint. If what I have said here is correct, this may well not be so. Thus the successful development of the arguments presented here may be relevant not only to our assessment of moral realism but to our assessment of scientific realism as well. Here is a kind of methodological unity of philosophy analogous to (whatever it was which positivists called) "unity of science".

My second methodological point is that the arguments for moral realism presented here depend upon optimistic empirical claims both about the organic unity of human goods and about the possibility of reliable knowledge in the "human sciences" generally. Although I have not argued for this claim here, I believe strongly that any plausible defense of naturalistic moral realism would require similarly optimistic empirical assumptions. I am also inclined to believe that insofar as moral anti-realism is plausible its plausibility rests not only upon technical philosophical arguments but also upon relatively pessimistic empirical beliefs about the same issues. I suggest, therefore, that our philosophical examination of the issues of moral realism should include, in addition to the examination of technical arguments on both sides, the careful examination of empirical claims about the unity and diversity of human goods and about our capacity for knowledge of ourselves. That much of philosophy ought surely to be at least partly empirical.

5 ADDENDUM

5.1 History

This paper, in the form in which it appears here, was written in 1982. Since that time it has undergone a transformation into a work, *Realism and the Moral Sciences* (Boyd, forthcoming, henceforth *RMS*) much too long to publish or excerpt for the present volume. I do however want to indicate briefly the direction in which the line of argument presented here has been developed in that later work. I shall briefly summarize three ways in which *RMS* goes beyond the argumentative strategy of this essay: a further characterization of homeostatic property-cluster definitions, a response to an apparent circularity resulting from the employment of a sample substantive moral theory, and an indication of the most general evidence favoring moral realism.

5.2 Homeostatic property clusters again

In *RMS* I add an additional clause to the account of homeostatic property-cluster definitions as follows:

12   The homeostatic property cluster which serves to define *t* is not individuated extensionally. Instead, property clusters are individuated like (type or token) historical objects or processes: certain changes over time (or in space) in the property cluster or in the underlying homeostatic mechanisms preserve the identity of the defining cluster. In consequence, the properties which determine the conditions for falling under *t* may vary over time (or space), *while t continues to have the same definition.* (To fall under *t* is to participate in the (current temporal and spatial stage of) the relevant property clustering. The historicity of the individuation criteria for definitional property clusters of this sort reflects the explanatory or inductive significance (for the relevant branches of theoretical or practical inquiry) of the historical development of the property cluster and of the causal factors which produce it, and considerations of explanatory and inductive significance determine the appropriate standards of individuation for the property cluster itself. The historicity of the individuation conditions for the property cluster is thus essential for the naturalness of the kind to which *t* refers.

This modification is suggested by the example of biological species definitions. The property cluster and homeostatic mechanisms which define a species must in general be individuated nonextensionally as a process-like historical entity. This is so because the mechanisms of reproductive isolation which are fundamentally definitional for many sexually reproducing species may vary significantly over the life of a species. Indeed, it is universally recognized that selection for characters which enhance reproductive isolation from related species is a significant factor in phyletic evolution, and it is one which necessarily alters over time a species' defining property cluster and homeostatic mechanisms (Mayr 1970).

I propose in *RMS* that the homeostatic property-cluster definition of moral goodness exhibits this sort of historicality. This additional factor increases the complexity of that definition considerably. Moreover there are failures of bivalence in the individuation of homeostatic property-cluster definitions, especially across possible worlds, just as there are for other sorts of historically individuated entities. These bivalence failures with respect to the individuation of the definition of moral goodness increase the range of counterfactual cases for which there will be failures of bivalence in the application of the term "good". The resources available to the moral realist for explaining divergent moral opinions, especially with respect to counterfactual cases, are thus enhanced.

5.3 Hard cases, cultural variability, and an apparent circularity of argumentation

In part 4 of the present essay, I defend moral realism from the perspective of a sample substantive moral theory, homeostatic consequentialism. I argue that since this substantive theory is defensible and since it affords the basis for a reasonable defense of a moral realism, moral realism is itself philosophically defensible. In *RMS* I consider a possible objection to this argumentative strategy. According to the objection, the defense of moral realism offered here requires a realistic understanding of homeostatic consequentialism, since otherwise, for example, the moral properties to which epistemic access is demonstrated might be purely socially constructed or conventional, as constructivist anti-realists in ethics maintain. The realist understanding of homeostatic consequentialism, so the objection goes, begs the question against the anti-realist so that the defense of moral realism is not even prima facie successful.

I examine this objection in the light of the corresponding objection to arguments for scientific realism. I argue that a defense of scientific realism requires that the realist articulate and defend a *theory of epistemic contact* and a *theory of error* for those traditions of inquiry for which she offers a realist account. Each of these theories must necessarily rest upon the best available theories of the relevant subject matter, realistically understood. In order to see why the question is not necessarily begged against the anti-realist we need to distinguish two sorts of anti-realist arguments from the diversity of opinions or intractability of issues within the relevant area of inquiry.

The first sort of argument, which I call the *external argument from theoretical diversity*, challenges the realist to explain the diversity of theoretical conceptions and the difficulty of their resolution within the relevant tradition of inquiry. An adequate realist response to this challenge will consist of an account of the epistemically significant causal relations between inquirers and the supposed theory-independent subject matter of that tradition, together with a theory of the sources of error within the tradition which account for the observed diversity of theoretical conceptions and for whatever difficulty exists in resolving the resulting theoretical disputes. These theories of epistemic contact and of error will necessarily and properly reflect the best available current theories of the subject matter in question realistically understood. No question is begged against the anti-realist because the realistically understood theories of epistemic contact and of error do not *by themselves* constitute the argument for realism. Instead, the philosophical contest is between larger-scale *philosophical packages*: a realist package which incorporates the realistically understood theories of epistemic contact and of error into a larger account of the metaphysics, epistemology, semantics, methodology, and historical development of the relevant areas of inquiry and various competing anti-realist packages of comparable scope.

Indeed, I argue, an understanding of scientific realism according to which it is grounded in realistically understood theories of epistemic contact and of error is essential not only for a fair presentation of the case *for* realism but also for a fair presentation of the various cases *against* it. I conclude, by analogy, that no questions are begged with respect to the external argument from theoretical diversity in the moral realist's reliance upon realistically understood theories of epistemic contact and of error.

I also identify a fundamentally different anti-realist argument from theoretical diversity, which I call the *internal argument from theoretical diversity* and which represents, I suggest, an important but largely inexplicit consideration in arguments against realism, whether scientific or moral. The internal argument is directed against the evidential acceptability of the realist's philosophical package even by its own standards. The argument proceeds by identifying a widely accepted and (so far as I can see) unobjectionable methodological principle according to which the prevalence of a variety of competing theoretical conceptions within a subject area would reduce one's confidence in the truth (or approximate truth) of any one of them. This principle is then applied against the realist's theories of epistemic contact and of error. It is argued that the existence of a diversity of competing theories in the relevant area(s) of inquiry renders epistemically illegitimate the particular theoretical commitments which underlie whichever theories of epistemic contact and of error the realist chooses to adopt.

The problem raised by this criticism of the realist's philosophical package is not that it does a poorer job than that of some anti-realist competitors in explaining theoretical diversity; rather the objection is that the realist must, by her own standards of evidence, hold that there is little evidence favoring the theoretical conceptions which underlie her own philosophical position.

It is important to recognize that because it appeals to standards of evidence which are prephilosophically generally accepted and are presumed to be internal to the relevant discipline(s), the internal argument from theoretical diversity is cogent only with respect to the theoretical diversity represented by those competing theories which are plausible candidates given the best current methodological standards in the relevant disciplines. It thus contrasts sharply with the external argument. To respond appropriately to the latter, the realist must be in a position to adequately explain *all* of the diverse opinions (however implausible by current standards) within the history of the tradition of inquiry regarding which she defends a realist conception. In responding to the internal argument, by contrast, she need only respond to the challenge to her theoretical commitments which is raised by the diversity within currently plausible theoretical conceptions, where plausibility is assessed by the best available contemporary standards.

I suggest in *RMS* that the way in which scientific realists have tacitly met this (itself inexplicit) objection can be reconstructed as follows: Instead of offering, for the discipline(s) in question, a single theory of epistemic contact and a single theory of error derived from one of the plausible alternative theoretical conceptions, the realist should be thought of as offering a family of such pairs of theories, one pair grounded in each of the alternative conceptions. She then should be thought of as arguing that these alternative theories of epistemic contact and of error participate sufficiently in a relationship of (*partial*) *mutual ratification* sufficiently deep that an adequate realist philosophical package can be grounded in their disjunction. By their partial mutual ratification I intend the relationship which obtains if the rival theories of epistemic contact and of error agree about a large number of particular cases of epistemic success and of error and if they give similar accounts about the nature of evidential relationships between data and doctrines within the relevant field(s) without, of course, agreeing in all of the theoretical details of their accounts of those relationships.

The levels of mutual ratification between competing theories of epistemic contact and of error which are required for the defense of realism will depend on the broader dialectical interactions of the competing philosophical packages, realist and anti-realist. It is nevertheless possible to identify an extremely strong pattern of mutual ratification which seems to characterize the methodological situation of those mature sciences regarding which realism is agreed to be an especially plausible position.

For any particular body of inquiry we may construct a conditionalized theory of epistemic contact and of error as follows. First, we form each of the propositions of the form "If T then $(C$ and $E)$", where T is one of the currently plausible theoretical conceptions in the relevant field and C and E are the theories of epistemic contact and of error for the history of the relevant body of inquiry which are best suited to a defense of a realist conception of that body of inquiry, on the assumption that T is the (largely) correct choice from among the competing plausible alternatives. We then form the conditionalized theory of epistemic contact and of error by taking the conjunction of each of these propositions. Let us say that a situation of mutual conditional ratification obtains if (a) the individual theories of epistemic contact and of error obtained from the various plausible theories agree on many actual cases of evidential judgments and (b) the conditionalized theory of epistemic contact is rationally acceptable given the standards of evidence common to *all* the competing theoretical conceptions. It is this strong pattern of *conditional mutual ratification* which seems to characterize those areas of inquiry about which realism seems especially plausible.

Having characterized mutual conditional ratification in *RMS*, I then develop the claim of the present essay that a defense of moral realism along roughly the lines developed in part 4 is possible on the basis of any of the genuinely plausible general moral theories. I consider the theories of epistemic contact and of error which would be appropriate to such theories, and I conclude that to a *very* good first approximation conditional mutual ratification obtains with respect to the spectrum of general moral theories which are genuinely plausible by the best current standards. Indeed, I argue, an especially strong form of conditional mutual ratification obtains which is characterized by three additional features:

1   To an extremely good first approximation, moral judgments regarding actual cases of actions, policies, character traits, etc. are – given prevailing standards of moral argument – dictated by judgments regarding nonmoral factual questions (including, for example, questions about human nature, about the nature of social, political, and economic processes, about whether or not there are any gods, and about their natures if there are any ...). In consequence, moral disagreements regarding such actual cases can be seen (on a philosophically appropriate rational reconstruction) as stemming from disagreements over nonmoral factual matters. (I call this relationship the *rational supervenience* of the relevant moral judgments on nonmoral factual judgments.)

2   Rational supervenience appears to fail for a few actual cases and for many counterfactual ones. For almost all of these it is plausible to argue that the cases in question are ones in which there is unrecognized failure of bivalence. For the few remaining cases of apparent failures of rational supervenience realist explanations in terms of nonculpable inadequacies in methodology or theoretical understanding are readily available. This conception of the sources of failures of rational supervenience is itself ratified by all of the genuinely plausible competing general moral theories.

3   The conditionalized theory of epistemic contact and of error upon which the plausible competing general moral theories agree is such that it attributes differences in judgments regarding *general* moral theories to differences over nonmoral factual matters. Thus, rational supervenience upon nonmoral factual judgments obtains for general moral theories as well as for particular moral judgments.

It is upon this quite striking form of conditional mutual ratification that, in my view, the moral realist's response to the internal argument from theoretical diversity properly rests.

5.4 The evidence for moral realism

In the present essay I argue that moral realism can be defended on the basis of a particular substantive moral theory (homeostatic consequentialism) which is itself defensible. I conclude that moral realism is itself a defensible position worthy of further development, and of criticisms appropriate to the epistemological, semantic, and metaphysical arguments in its favor which the analogy with scientific realism suggests. I suggest here (and argue in *RMS*) that the same sort of defense can be formulated on the basis of any of the other plausible competing moral theories. Thus, if the arguments I offer are correct, there is reason to believe that the defender of any of the currently plausible general moral theories should defend her theory on a realist understanding of its content and should herself be a moral realist. The question remains what the attitude toward moral realism should be of the philosopher who is, as yet, not committed to any particular general moral theory.

I address this question in *RMS*. I maintain that the best argument for moral realism in the present philosophical context probably would consist of a more thoroughgoing defense of a particular naturalistic and realistic substantive moral theory much like homeostatic consequentialism. I also conclude, however, that there is powerful evidence favoring moral realism whose persuasive force does not depend upon establishing the case for any particular moral theory. Indeed, I suggest that the strongest such evidence is provided by the phenomenon of conditional mutual ratification just discussed and especially by the apparent rational supervenience of moral opinion upon nonmoral factual opinion which it reveals.

Three considerations suggest that the phenomenon in question provides especially good prima facie evidence for moral realism. In the first place, the current philosophical setting is one in which answers are seen to be readily available to the more abstract epistemological and semantic objections to moral realism (those raised by the issues of the nature of the analog in moral inquiry of observations in science, of the epistemic roles of moral intuitions and of reflective equilibrium, of the nature of the definitional and referential semantics of moral terms). In such a setting the arguments from the diversity of moral theories and from the corresponding intractability of moral disputes – just the arguments addressed by the articulation of a family of conditionally mutually ratifying theories of epistemic contact and of error – emerge as the strongest arguments against moral realism.

Second, the anti-realist arguments from diversity and intractability are especially persuasive because they appear to establish that even the philosopher with substantial initial moral commitments will be forced to the conclusion that the non-reality (or the purely socially constructed nature) of her subject matter provides the only plausible explanation for the diversity of moral opinions and the intractability of moral disputes. What the finding of conditional mutual ratification of theories of epistemic contact and of error and the associated rational supervenience of moral opinions upon nonmoral factual opinions indicates is that, by contrast, there is an alternative realist explanation for divergence and intractability which is ratified by all the currently plausible moral theories.

Finally, the most convincing evidence against moral realism stemming from divergence and intractability seems (at least for many professional philosophers) to come from an examination of the many counterfactual cases regarding which "moral intuitions" sharply diverge. The foundational role which many philosophers assign (if only tacitly) to philosophical intuitions and especially to moral intuitions makes this evidence against moral realism seem especially strong. It is precisely with respect to such cases that the treatment of the epistemic role of moral intuitions and the identification of sources of bivalence failures for counterfactual cases which are incorporated in the various conditionally mutually ratifying theories of epistemic contact and of error are most effective. Thus, the realist resources for explaining divergence and intractability reflected in those theories seem especially well suited to rebut the most convincing of the anti-realist arguments in question.

I should add that in *RMS* I examine in detail a related objection to moral realism: that the moral realist is (in contrast to the constructivist moral irrealist) compelled to adopt an implausible and objectionable chauvinist attitude toward moral communities (especially prescientific communities) whose moral views depart sharply from her own. A tendency toward such chauvinism was certainly a feature of logical positivist treatments of scientific objectivity and it is initially plausible to conclude that it will mark the moral realist's conception as well.

By way of examining the question of chauvinism, I define three relations of commensurability which might obtain within a tradition of inquiry. *Semantic commensurability* obtains just in case there is a common subject matter for all the temporal stages of the tradition and its various subtraditions. *Global methodological commensurability* obtains just in case the differences between the prevailing theoretical conceptions between any two tradition (or subtradition) stages are always resolvable by the appropriate application of research methods endorsed by each. *Local methodological commensurability* obtains just in case this sort of resolution is always possible for the differences between consecutive tradition stages or between contemporaneous stages of different subtraditions within the tradition of inquiry in question.

I argue that the tendency toward chauvinism within positivist philosophy of science – insofar as its origins were internal to technical philosophy rather than more broadly social – stemmed from a tendency for positivists to hold that semantic commensurability entails (or at any rate strongly suggests) global methodological commensurability and from a consequent tendency to apply contemporary standards of scientific methodology when assessing the rationality of members of different earlier communities of inquirers. By contrast, I argue, scientific realism predicts wholesale failures of global methodological commensurability and makes only highly qualified predictions of local methodological commensurability, even where global semantic commensurability obtains. Thus, the chauvinist tendencies internal to the positivist tradition are not only absent from the realist tradition but corrected within it.

I conclude, by analogy, that contemporary moral realism likewise embodies an appropriate antichauvinist conception of methodology, which is not to say that it is proof against chauvinism deriving from external social influences. Finally, I argue that the alternative constructivist relativist approach is in important respects chauvinist and uncritical. It holds the current stages in the relevant research traditions just as much immune from criticism as it does earlier and prescientific stages and it precludes the diagnosis of culpable methodological errors (culturally chauvinist errors among them) when these do occur, whether in the current stages of the relevant tradition or in its earlier stages. If it is otherwise defensible, realism then represents the preferred antidote to cultural chauvinism.

Finally, I further develop the theme suggested in the present essay that moral realism is an optimistic position. I argue that, given available evidence, the most plausible way in which the doctrine here identified as moral realism could prove to be wrong would be for the broad family of basic human goods to be incapable of a suitably strong homeostatic unity. The non-realist alternative I envision as most plausible would have "relativist" features and would entail the dependence of (some) moral truths upon the moral beliefs actually held in the relevant moral communities. What I have in mind is a situation in which the following are both true:

1   (The relativist component.) The sorts of fundamental human goods typically recognized as relevant in moral reasoning lack the sort of homeostatic unity tacitly presupposed in moral discourse: there is no psychologically and socially stable way of ameliorating the conflicts between them and adjudicating those which remain which are satisfactory by reasonable prevailing moral standards. Instead, there are two (or more) stable ways of achieving homeostasis between those goods, each capable of sustaining a morality (and moral progress) of sorts, but in each (all) of them certain human goods are necessarily slighted with respect to the others in a way certainly unacceptable by contemporary moral standards. This plurality of morally compromised forms of moral homeostasis is not remediable by future moral, economic, or political developments: it reflects nonmaleable features of human nature. Most difficult disagreements in substantive moral philosophy reflect the tacit adherence of the disputants to one or the other of these stable "moralities" or their unsuccessful attempts to formulate viable alternatives comprising the best features of both (several), or both. Resolution of those disagreements requires that we recognize the conflation of moral standards that caused them and that we (relativistically) disambiguate our uses of moral terms.

2   (The belief dependence component.) Actually practiced stable moral arrangements will necessarily approximate one rather than the other(s) of the available stable forms of moral homeostasis. Insofar as we think of participants in such an arrangement as reasoning about the features of their own particular form of moral homeostasis when they engage in moral reasoning (as the first component suggests that we should), we will find that the truth of some of their important moral beliefs (so construed) will depend quite strongly on their having generally adopted the moral beliefs peculiarly appropriate to the tradition of moral practice in which they function. This will be so for two reasons. First, it will be generally true on their moral conception that the

goodness (justice, permissibility ...) of actions, practices, policies, character traits, etc. will depend upon the ways in which they contribute (or fail to contribute) to the satisfaction of fundamental human needs. Second, the nature of fundamental human needs (at least within the relevant moral communities) will be significantly determined by the moral beliefs held within the community: needs accorded a prominent role in the community's moral scheme will (in consequence of the effects of moral and social teaching on individual development) be more strongly felt than those needs assigned a less prominent role, even when, for those raised in (one of) the alternative sort(s) of moral community, the psychological importance of the needs might be reversed. Morally important human needs (and their relative importance) are thus significantly created by one's participation in one or the (an)other sort of moral community: such communities make among their members the moral psychology appropriate to their moral practices. Because of the limitation of homeostasis between human goods specified in (1), no more encompassing moral psychology is possible.

It is, I think, evident why the conception of our moral situation envisioned in (1) and (2) is properly described as pessimistic. What I argue in *RMS* is that it is nevertheless only in a relatively uninteresting sense *non-realistic.* The dependence of the truth of moral propositions upon moral beliefs envisioned in (2) would be, I argue, an ordinary case of causal dependence and not the sort of logical dependence required by a constructivist conception of morals analogous to a Kuhnian neo-Kantian conception of the dependence of scientific truth on the adoption of theories or paradigms. The subject matter of moral inquiry in each of the relevant communities would be theory-and-belief-independent in the sense relevant to the dispute between realist and social constructivists.

The relativism envisioned in (1) would then, I argue, properly be seen as an ordinary realist case of partial denotation (in the sense of Field 1973). Thus, although the situation envisioned in (1) and (2) would refute moral realism as that doctrine is ordinarily construed (and as it is construed in the present essay), it would not undermine a generally realistic conception of moral language in favor of a constructivist one. The case for the former conception, I suggest, is quite strong indeed.

NOTES

An early version of this paper, incorporating the naturalistic treatments of the roles of reflective equilibrium and moral intuitions in moral reasoning and a naturalistic conception of the semantics of moral terms (but not the homeostatic property cluster formulation of consequentialism), was presented to the Philosophy Colloquium at Case-Western Reserve University in 1977. I am grateful to the audience at that colloquium for helpful criticisms which greatly influenced my formulation of later versions.

In approximately the version published here, the paper was presented at the University of North Carolina, the University of Chicago, Cornell University, the

Universities of California at Berkeley and at Los Angeles, the University of Washington, Dartmouth College, and Tufts University. Papers defending the general homeostatic property-cluster account of natural definitions were presented at Oberlin, Cornell, and Stanford. Extremely valuable criticisms from the audiences at these universities helped me in developing the more elaborate defense of moral realism presented in *Realism and the Moral Sciences* and summarized in part 5 of the present essay.

My interest in the question of moral realism initially arose from my involvement in the anti-Vietnam War movement of the late 1960s and was sustained in significant measure by my participation in subsequent progressive movements. I have long been interested in whether or not moral relativism played a progressive or a reactionary role in such movements; the present essay begins an effort to defend the latter alternative. I wish to acknowledge the important influence on my views of the Students for a Democratic Society (especially its Worker–Student Alliance Caucus), the International Committee against Racism, and the Progressive Labor party. Their optimism about the possibility of social progress and about the rational capacity of ordinary people have played an important role in the development of my views.

I have benefited from discussions with many people about various of the views presented here. I want especially to thank David Brink, Norman Daniels, Philip Gasper, Paul Gomberg, Kristin Guyot, Terence Irwin, Barbara Koslowski, David Lyons, Christopher McMahon, Richard Miller, Milton Rosen, Sydney Shoemaker, Robert Stalnaker, Stephen Sullivan, Milton Wachsberg, Thomas Weston, and David Whitehouse. My thinking about homeostatic property-cluster definitions owes much to conversations with Philip Gasper, David Whitehouse, and especially Kristin Guyot. I am likewise indebted to Richard Miller for discussions about the foundations of non-utilitarian consequentialism. My greatest debt is to Alan Gilbert and Nicholas Sturgeon. I wish to thank the Society for the Humanities at Cornell University for supporting much of the work reflected in part 5.

1   This is the only section of part 3 which advances naturalistic and realistic positions not already presented in the published literature. It represents a summary of work in progress. For some further developments see section 5.2.

2   Two points of clarification about the proposed homeostatic consequentialist definition of the good are in order. In the first place, I understand the homeostatic cluster which defines moral goodness to be social rather than individual. The properties in homeostasis are to be thought of as instances of the satisfaction of particular human needs among people generally, rather than within the life of a single individual. Thus, the homeostatic consequentialist holds not (or at any rate not merely) that the satisfaction of each of the various human needs within the life of an individual contributes (given relevant homeostatic mechanisms) to the satisfaction of the others in the life of that same individual. Instead, she claims that, given the relevant homeostatic mechanisms, the satisfaction of those needs for one individual tends to be conducive to their satisfaction for others, and it is to the homeostatic unity of human need satisfaction in the society generally that she or he appeals in proposing a definition of the good.

Homeostatic consequentialism as I present it here is, thus, not a version of ethical egoism. I am inclined to think that individual well-being has a homeostatic property-cluster definition and thus that a homeostatic property-cluster conception of the definition of the good would be appropriate to the formulation of the most plausible versions of egoism, but I do not find even those versions very plausible and it is certainly not a version of egoism to which I mean to appeal in illustrating the proposed strategy for defending moral realism.

Second, I owe to Judith Jarvis Thomson the observation that, strictly speaking, the homeostatic consequentialist conception of the good does not conform to the more abstract account of homeostatic property-cluster definitions presented in section 3.8. According to that account, the homeostatically united properties and the definitionally relevant properties associated with the relevant mechanisms of homeostasis are all properties of the same kind of thing: organisms, let us say, in the case of the homeostatic property-cluster definition of a particular biological species.

By contrast, some of the properties which characterize human well-being and the mechanisms upon which its homeostatic unity depends are (on the homeostatic consequentialist conception) in the first instance properties of individuals, whereas others are properties of personal relations between individuals and still others are properties of large-scale social arrangements. Homeostatic unity is postulated between instances of the realization of the relevant properties in objects of different logical type.

It should be obvious that the additional logical complexity of the proposed homeostatic property cluster definition of the good does not vitiate the rebuttals offered here to anti-realist arguments. For the record, it seems to me that Professor Thomson's observation in fact applies to the actual case of species definitions as well: some of the homeostatically united properties and homeostatic mechanisms which define a species are in the first instance properties of individual organisms, some properties of small groups of organisms, some of larger populations (in the standard sense of that term), and some of the relations between such populations.

REFERENCES

Armstrong, D. M. (1973) *Belief, Truth and Knowledge*, Cambridge: Cambridge University Press.

Boyd, R. (1972) "Determinism, laws and predictability in principle," *Philosophy of Science* (39): 431–50.

—— (1973) "Realism, underdetermination and a causal theory of evidence," *Noûs* (7): 1–12.

—— (1979) "Metaphor and theory change," in A. Ortony (ed.) *Metaphor and Thought*. Cambridge: Cambridge University Press.

—— (1980) "Materialism without reductionism: what physicalism does not entail," in N. Block (ed.) *Readings in Philosophy of Psychology*, vol. 1. Cambridge, Mass.: Harvard University Press.

—— (1982) "Scientific realism and naturalistic epistemology," In P. D. Asquith and R. N. Giere (eds) *PSA* 1980, vol. 2. East Lansing: Philosophy of Science Association.

—— (1983) "On the current status of the issue of scientific realism," *Erkenntnis* (19): 45–90.

—— (1985a) "Lex orendi est lex credendi," in Paul Churchland and Clifford Hooker (eds) *Images of Science: Scientific Realism Versus Constructive Empiricism*. Chicago: University of Chicago Press.

—— (1985b) "Observations, explanatory power, and simplicity," in P. Achinstein and O. Hannaway (eds) *Observation, Experiment, and Hypothesis in Modern Physical Science*. Cambridge, Mass.: MIT Press.

—— (1985c) "The logician's dilemma: deductive logic, inductive inference and logical empiricism," *Erkenntnis* (22): 197–252.

Boyd, R. (forthcoming) *Realism and the Moral Sciences* (unpublished manuscript).

Brink, D. (1984) "Moral realism and the skeptical arguments from disagreement and queerness" *Australasian Journal of Philosophy* (62.2): 111–25.

—— (forthcoming) *Moral Realism and the Foundation of Ethics*, Cambridge: Cambridge University Press.

Byerly, H., and V. Lazara (1973) "Realist foundations of measurement," *Philosophy of Science* (40): 10–28.

Carnap, R. (1934) *The Unity of Science*, trans. M. Black, London: Kegan Paul.

Dworkin, R. (1973) "The original position," *University of Chicago Law Review* (40): 500–33.

Feigl, H. (1956) "Some major issues and developments in the philosophy of science of logical empiricism," in H. Feigl and M. Scriven (eds) *Minnesota Studies in the Philosophy of Science*, vol. 1. Minneapolis: University of Minnesota Press.

Field, H. (1973) "Theory change and the indeterminacy of reference," *Journal of Philosophy* (70): 462–81.

Gilbert, A. (1981a) *Marx's Politics: Communists and Citizens*, New Brunswick, NJ: Rutgers University Press.

—— (1981b) "Historical theory and the structure of moral argument in Marx," *Political Theory* (9): 173–205.

—— (1982) "An ambiguity in Marx's and Engels's account of justice and equality," *American Political Science Review* (76): 328–46.

—— (1984a) "The storming of heaven: capital and Marx's politics," in J. R. Pennock (ed.) *Marxism Today*, Nomos (26). New York: New York University Press.

—— (1984b) "Marx's moral realism: eudaimonism and moral progress," in J. Farr and T. Ball (eds) *After Marx*, Cambridge: Cambridge University Press.

—— (1986a) "Moral realism, individuality and justice in war," *Political Theory* (14): 105–35.

—— (1986b) "Democracy and individuality," *Social Philosophy and Policy* (3): 19–58.

—— (forthcoming) *Equality and Objectivity.*

Goldman, A. (1967) "A causal theory of knowing," *Journal of Philosophy* (64): 357–72.

—— (1976) "Discrimination and perceptual knowledge," *Journal of Philosophy* (73): 771–91.

Goodman, N. (1973) *Fact, Fiction, and Forecast*, 3rd edn, Indianapolis: Bobbs-Merrill.

Gould, S. J. (1981) *The Mismeasure of Man*, New York: W. W. Norton.

Hanson, N. R. (1958) *Patterns of Discovery*, Cambridge: Cambridge University Press.

Kamin, L. J. (1974) *The Science and Politics of I.Q.*, Potomac, Md.: Lawrence Erlbaum Associates.

Kripke, S. A. (1971) "Identity and necessity," in M. K. Munitz (ed.) *Identity and Individuation*. New York: New York University Press.

—— (1972) "Naming and necessity," in D. Davidson and G. Harman (eds) *The Semantics of Natural Language*. Dordrecht: D. Reidel.

Kuhn, T. (1970) *The Structure of Scientific Revolutions*, 2nd edn, Chicago: University of Chicago Press.

Mackie, J. I. (1974) *The Cement of the Universe*, Oxford: Oxford University Press.

Mayr, E. (1970) *Populations, Species and Evolution*, Cambridge, Mass.: Harvard University Press.

Miller, R. (1978) "Methodological individualism and social explanation," *Philosophy of Science* (45): 387–414.

—— (1979) "Reason and committment in the social sciences," *Philosophy and Public Affairs* (8): 241–66.

———— (1981) "Rights and reality," *Philosophical Review* (90): 383–407.

———— (1982) "Rights and consequences," *Midwest Studies in Philosophy* (7): 151–74.

———— (1983) "Marx and morality," *Nomos* (26): 3–32.

———— (1984a) *Analyzing Marx*, Princeton: Princeton University Press.

———— (1984b) "Ways of moral learning," *Philosophical Review* (94): 507–56.

Putnam, H. (1975a) "The meaning of 'meaning'," in H. Putnam, *Mind, Language and Reality*. Cambridge: Cambridge University Press.

———— (1975b) "Language and reality," in H. Putnam, *Mind, Language and Reality*. Cambridge: Cambridge University Press.

———— (1983) "Vagueness and alternative logic," in H. Putnam, *Realism and Reason*. Cambridge: Cambridge University Press.

Quine, W. V. O. (1969a) "Natural kinds," in W. V. O. Quine, *Ontological Relativity and Other Essays*. New York: Columbia University Press.

———— (1969b) "Epistemology naturalized," in W. V. O. Quine, *Ontological Relativity and Other Essays*. New York: Columbia University Press.

Railton, P. (1986) "Moral realism," *Philosophical Review* (95): 163–207.

Rawls, J. (1971) *A Theory of Justice*, Cambridge, Mass.: Harvard University Press.

Shoemaker, S. (1980) "Causality and properties," in P. van Inwagen (ed.) *Time and Cause*. Dordrecht: D. Reidel.

Sturgeon, N. (1984a) "Moral explanations," in D. Copp and D. Zimmerman, (eds) *Morality, Reason and Truth*. Totowa, NJ: Rowman and Allanheld.

———— (1984b) "Review of P. Foot, *Moral Relativism* and *Virtues and Vices*," *Journal of Philosophy* (81): 326–33.

Van Fraassen, B. (1980) *The Scientific Image*, Oxford: Oxford University Press.

Wood, A. (1972) "The Marxian critique of justice," *Philosophy and Public Affairs* (1): 244–82.

———— (1979) "Marx on right and justice: a reply to Husami," *Philosophy and Public Affairs* (8): 267–95.

———— (1984) "A Marxian approach to 'the problem of justice'," *Philosophica* (33): 9–32.

POSTSCRIPT: MATERIALISM AND REALISM IN METAETHICS

Materialist metaethics In a volume on materialism, it is important to ask what the connection is between the moral realism defended in "How to be a Moral Realist" (HMR) and materialism. The sample moral theory employed in HMR, homeostatic consequentialism, is a *naturalistic* conception of morality on the assumption that all of the components of human flourishing are features of the natural world; it is a *materialist* conception on the further assumption that all of the components of human flourishing (including the mental components) are physical (a dualist could be a homeostatic consequentialist naturalistic moral realist).

Many apparently anti-realist conceptions in ethics are best understood as parts of attempts to articulate a materialist understanding of moral practice. Both Mackie's (1977) argument from queerness and Harman's (1977) criticisms of standard versions of moral realism involve arguments to the effect that moral facts would not fit into the natural order as revealed by scientific reasoning. Similarly, many philosophers who adopt apparently anti-realist relativist conceptions in metaethics do so because they adopt a naturalistic outlook which, they believe, makes no room for non-relative moral facts. While, as we have seen, such naturalistic concerns do not entail a materialist outlook, most naturalistically inclined philosophers have in fact been materialists. So, materialist moral realism is just one materialist approach to metaethics; non-cognitivism, "error" theories, and various versions of moral relativism are also materialist options.[1]

Although there are lots of materialist options in metaethics, the fact that moral practices are involved does not seem to pose any special problems in saying what it is for a materialist metaethical position to be *materialist*: materialism in metaethics says about moral phenomena – if there are any – and about other phenomena implicated in moral practice just whatever it is that materialism says about phenomena generally. There are controversies about what that whatever-it-is is (between reductionist and anti-reductionist accounts for example), but there does not seem to be any additional problem in characterizing what it is for a meta*ethical* theory to be materialist. For the question of what makes a realist metaethical theory *realist* the situation is quite different.

Metaethical realism: some problems   Some versions of moral relativism seem plainly anti-realist. I suggested in section 5.4 of HMR that if moral realism, as I presented it in that paper, were false then the most likely alternative metaethical theory would be one which had a significant relativistic component, but that the relativism involved was congruent with a broadly realist approach to moral discourse. Thus I there suggested that some versions of moral relativism were best understood as variants of moral realism.

The question thus arises of how realism and anti-realism in metaethics are to be distinguished. Other examples also raise the same question. What about cognitivist positions with a Wittgensteinian flavor which follow in a tradition deriving from Foot (1959), in holding that some fundamental moral principles are conceptual truths reflecting a form of life? They share with obviously realist positions the view that moral statements can be true or false and that moral knowledge is possible, but they have a conventionalistic element which is reminiscent more of neo-Kantian social constructivism (à la Kuhn) in the philosophy of science than of scientific realism. Are these positions realist or anti-realist, or is the question ill motivated?

In recent papers (Boyd 1990a, 1990b, 1991, 1992) I explored the contrast between realist and non-realist conceptions in the philosophy of science. I propose to apply some of the results to clarifying the distinction between realist and anti-realist approaches to metaethics. Since most metaethical positions whose relation to moral realism is unclear more closely resemble social constructivism in the philosophy of science than they resemble empiricism, I'll focus my attention on the distinction between realist and constructivist conceptions of science and on corresponding distinctions in metaethics.

Realism and anti-realism in the philosophy of science: the metaphysics and epistemology of conventionality   In the papers cited I concluded that the key difference between realist and neo-Kantian social constructivist positions in the philosophy of science lies in their contrasting conceptions of the metaphysics of conventionality and the contrasting epistemological conceptions dictated by those metaphysical conceptions. The realist, I concluded, holds – in contrast to the neo-Kantian constructivist – that social conventions in science are *metaphysically innocent*: that scientific propositions which are true by convention have no ontological import.[2] Her commitment to this *metaphysical innocence thesis* leads to two closely related criticisms of neo-Kantian conceptions according to which (some) fundamental scientific laws or principles are true by convention:

1 Scientific principles which are true by convention cannot play the explanatory and methodological role which fundamental laws in fact play in science.
2 The constructivist's failure to accept this consequence of metaphysical innocence leads her to mistakenly treat fundamental scientific laws as knowable largely *a priori*.

An example will illustrate these points. Consider the methodology of a scientific study which employs a Geiger counter to detect atomic radiation. The justification for this procedure will – as the discussion of the philosophy of science in HMR indicates – be theory dependent: it will, for example, appeal to physical principles to explain why the interaction of the radiation to be detected with the gas in the Geiger–Müller tube causes ionization of the gas, why that ionization in turn makes the gas conductive, how the electrical components in the Geiger counter detect the resulting current flow, etc. Lots of fundamental physical principles would be required for spelling out this explanation and the resulting justification for using Geiger counters; one is the law of the conservation of charge. Let us suppose, for the sake of illustration, that a neo-Kantian constructivist holds that this law is made true by linguistic or social convention.

The explanation for the reliability of Geiger counters, and the physical principles crucial to it, have clear ontological implications: a causal story about the interaction of particles, fields, and their properties (including charge) is the core of the explanation. The explanation is, in particular, defective if the law of charge conservation does not have ontological import.

Consider now the constructivist proposal that the conservation law in question is true by convention. According to the scientific realist's *metaphysical innocence thesis*, scientific principles which are true by convention lack ontological import, whereas according to the social constructivist they need not. Therefore, the realist, but not the constructivist, must hold that the explanation for the reliability of the Geiger counter is compromised by the constructivist's conventionality claim.

Since that explanation provides the justification for the use of Geiger counters as radiation detectors, there is a difference between realists and constructivists on epistemological matters corresponding to their differences on matters ontological. According to the realist, but not according to the constructivist, a scientific law or principle is deprived of its epistemological or methodological import when it is established that the law or principle is true by convention. Thus, according to the realist, the constructivist who asserts that a scientific principle is true by convention cannot offer an adequate justification for those features of scientific methodology whose ordinary scientific justification depends on that principle.

A related point follows. If the conservation law is true by convention then we can have largely *a priori* knowledge of it. But, that would mean that we sometimes have *a priori* causal knowledge. The social constructivist, for whom truths by convention can have metaphysical import, can accept this conclusion. The realist cannot. On her view, the conservation law cannot be knowable *a priori* as constructivism requires.

Thus realists and constructivists differ over the weight which *a priori* conventional considerations can bear in accounting for the substantive and epistemological achievements of science. According to the realist when the constructivist treats a fundamental scientific principle as true by convention she underestimates how difficult it is to rationally establish it, and she cannot account for the ontological and epistemological achievement that the knowledge of that principle represents: the achievement scientists rely on when they deploy the principle in causal explanations or in justifying methodological procedures.

A criterion for realism in the philosophy of science   What I proposed in the papers cited is that the metaphysical innocence thesis and its epistemological corollaries provide a criterion for distinguishing realist from anti-realist treatments of conventionality in the philosophy of science.

An important point which will carry over to our discussion of metaethics is that applications of the metaphysical innocence criterion are sensitive to estimates of *context of achievement.* Suppose that some philosopher holds that a particular scientific principle is true by convention. If the issue between realists and anti-realists is over the role of truths by convention in accounting for ontological, explanatory, and epistemological achievements in science, then whether our philosopher's position is anti-realist will depend, in part, on what her particular conception is of the achievements in the relevant discipline. If in her scientific judgment the principle is without ontological, causal, or methodological import, then her overall position need not be anti-realist. So two philosophers who have different conceptions of the achievements in a discipline may agree that a particular proposition accepted within that discipline is true by convention but differ in whether or not they are thereby committed to anti-realism. (There are real cases like this in science; see Boyd 1990b, 1991, and especially Guyot 1987, on cladism.)

If we are to understand the metaphysical innocence criterion, and especially if we are to see how to extend it to metaethics, we need to understand that the basis of the criterion is the realist's insistence on applying a naturalistic standard of *supervenience relation reduction* to the constructivist's conventionality claims.

Let's return to the question of the reliability of Geiger counters. Roughly, the realist's complaint against the constructivist's analysis is that the reliability of Geiger counters cannot be causally explained by a principle whose truth consists in the fact that physics professors profess it.

According to the realist, the truth of the conservation law supervenes mainly on facts about the interactions of subatomic particles and fields and it is because of the causal powers of those physical factors that the law has explanatory force. Of course the social constructivist agrees that, in *some* (prephilosophical) sense, the truth of the conservation law supervenes on such physical facts but, on her conception, the deep metaphysical point is that *really* those facts *and* the truth of the conservation law supervene on curricular decisions in graduate programs in physics and the like. The realist insists that the truth of a scientific principle whose truth supervenes on social phenomena in this way cannot play the causal–explanatory role required by the theory-dependent justification of reliability of Geiger counters. Why not?

The realist's answer reflects elements of philosophical naturalism (Boyd 1992); she proposes to hold the constructivist's supervenience claims regarding the truth of scientific principles to the ordinary *scientific* standards to which we usually hold supervenience claims. She asks whether it makes scientific sense to suppose that the truth of the conservation law supervenes on facts about the social structure of professional physics while still assigning that law a role in causal explanations of, e.g., the reliability of Geiger counters, she proposes that the answer is "no," *and* (here's the naturalistic element) she proposes that this is a reason for rejecting the constructivist's supervenience claim.

The standards for assessing supervenience claims which the realist relies on embody a general constraint of *supervenience relation "reduction"* which will be familiar from considering how we assess supervenience claims in the course of ordinary scientific work. Consider the claim that genetic phenomena supervene on chemical phenomena in which DNA replication plays a crucial role. For that claim to have proven scientifically acceptable two sorts of "reduction" had to be established between the alleged supervenience base and the genetic phenomena about which scientists already knew:

1   (Content "reduction"): It had to be established that the content of (most of) earlier genetic findings remained scientifically explicable assuming the truth of the supervenience claims. Accepting the supervenience claim must, in general, not have rendered the substantive claims of earlier genetics unacceptable by ordinary scientific standards.

2   (Methodological "reduction"): It had to be established that the proposed supervenience relation did not undermine the justification for (most of) the previously well established genetic knowledge or genetic methodology. By ordinary scientific standards, the adoption of the proposed supervenience claim must, in general, not have undermined the logic of confirmation of previously established genetic findings (either by rendering them unconfirmed or by trivializing

their confirmation by treating them as *a priori*) and it must not, in general, have de-legitimated later methodological applications of those findings.

Had either of these conditions failed of satisfaction then the scientific case for the supervenience claim would have been seriously undermined. Of course each of these conditions is the special case for genetics of a condition which scientists ordinarily insist that scientific claims about supervenience must meet (just substitute "the discipline (or sub-discipline) in question" for "genetics"). What the realist maintains is that these conditions do fail in the case of the supervenience claims reflected in constructivist accounts of the role of conventionality in science *and* that this is a reason for rejecting those claims.

I propose that the supervenience relation reduction constraint constitutes the basis of realist critiques of social constructivism in the philosophy of science *and that a failure to satisfy supervenience relation reduction is what distinguishes anti-realist conceptions of conventionality in science from realist conceptions.*

One can make the naturalistic metaphysics behind the metaphysical innocence thesis explicit by seeing that the realist affirms and the neo-Kantian social constructivist denies the *no non-causal contribution thesis* (2N2C): the thesis that social practices (including the adoption of social conventions) make no *non-causal* contribution to the causal structures of natural phenomena. This thesis sets a limit on the causal–explanatory role of the truth of principles which are true by convention: if what makes a statement true is certain convention-constituting social practices and if (as 2N2C says) these practices make no non-causal contribution to causal relations, then the only things the truth of the statement can explain or justify are things which are explained or justified by the social phenomena on which its truth supervenes.

The reduction constraint requires that, in a certain sense of reduction, a supervenience thesis must allow for an appropriate reduction of the achievements of existing or previous scientific inquiry. It is important to see that nothing like syntactic or meaning reduction is required. In the case of genetics it is not required that there be a reduction of the vocabulary or laws of genetics to those of chemistry. What is required is that it be explicable by ordinary scientific standards how phenomena in the proposed supervenience base could causally explain (most of) the phenomena acknowledged by the best established earlier theories of the supervening phenomena, and that (most of) the methods by which those earlier theories were established and are currently being applied be ratifiable given the supervenience thesis.

Applications of the reduction constraint will be highly theory dependent. The constraint requires the "reduction" of the best established theories and methods regarding the supervenient phenomena, so judgments about *context of achievement* will determine the methodological force of the constraint. Moreover, in assessing the prospect for the sort of reduction required, someone who applies the constraint must rely on other background scientific theories both about the phenomena studied by the scientific discipline in question and about the causal relations which obtain between social practices and those phenomena.

Thus two philosophers could agree about the same scientific principle that it was true by convention, could agree about the details of the relevant convention-constituting social relations, *and* could agree about the achievement context, and yet one's position might be compatible with realism and the other's not because they accepted different scientific theories regarding the causal powers and relations of the phenomena at issue or of the relevant social practices. For this reason it is better to think of the supervenience relation reduction criterion as applying not to particular conceptions of conventionality but to broader *philosophical* (or *partly philosophical*) *packages*, in the sense of that term introduced in part 5 of HMR. One consequence of this theory dependence is that the narrower one's conception of the achievement context regarding a body of inquiry, the greater will be the level of conventionality one can accept while honoring the reduction constraint.

Realist and anti-realist conceptions of conventionality: a general proposal I propose that we may take the reduction constraint just discussed as the criterion which fixes the distinction between conceptions of conventionality which are compatible with realism and those which are not for any discipline, including ethics.

This *reduction criterion* is best thought of as applying not to conceptions of conventionality in isolation but to philosophical packages including, for example, substantive and methodological claims in the relevant discipline, together perhaps with similar claims in related disciplines. Packages embodying a conception of conventionality regarding a discipline exhibit anti-realist aspects to the extent that they involve claims of the supervenience of the truth of statements on social practices which fail to satisfy the reduction constraint with respect to the substantive and methodological achievements of that discipline, or of related disciplines.

Several points of clarification are in order. First, when the discipline at issue involves practical as well as theoretical reasoning I intend that its substantive and methodological achievements in the practical domain lie within the scope of the reduction constraint. When the results of inquiry or practice in a discipline go toward providing reasons or justifications for actions or policies, then I am proposing (1) that the relevant philosophical package should include the resources necessary to provide an understanding of why this should be so, and (2) that in applying the reduction constraint one must inquire whether, in the light of that understanding, the supervenience claims at issue compromise the justifications or reasons in question. Thus for two philosophers who offer the same account of conventionality in a domain involving practical reasoning, the import of the reduction criterion may be different if those philosophers differ either about the extent to which the achievements in that domain provide reason or justification for actions or policies, or about their understanding of the nature of the justifications provided.

Another important point concerns the standards by which one is to assess whether or not the supervenience proposal compromises the substantive and methodological achievements in question. Thinking back to the Geiger counter example, we can see that the answer should be, at least roughly, "by prevailing standards in the relevant disciplines." *Roughly*, in part because different philosophers who defend the same conception of what is conventional and what is not in a discipline may differ in their approach to controversies within the discipline, and may in consequence advance philosophical packages which incorporate different versions of the prevailing standards. I also want to leave open the possibility that philosophical packages should include novel critiques of some of the prevailing substantive doctrines or methodological practices within a discipline or should incorporate novel alternatives to them. Philosophical packages of the sort to which the reduction criterion should be applied must be thought of as providing a sufficiently rich conception of the "state of the art" substantively and methodologically in the target discipline and related disciplines that the compatibility of the proposed account of supervenience with that "state of the art" can be assessed.

What will not work, if the reduction criterion is to be adequate, is for the philosophical packages under consideration to include distinctly philosophical views about the epistemology or metaphysics of conventionality in the discipline in question. Back to Geiger counters. Consider a philosophical package which includes the standard bits of physics necessary to explain and justify the use of Geiger counters as radiation detectors, the thesis that the law of charge conservation is true by definition, *and* a philosophical defense of the claim that only a neo-Kantian conception of the epistemology and metaphysics of science can account for scientific knowledge. *That* philosophical package will satisfy the reduction constraint. By it's lights, treating the conservation law as true by convention will not compromise the findings and methods of the relevant sciences but instead ratify them. So, for the purposes at hand, we should think of philosophical packages as being innocent of any distinctly philosophical views of, e.g., the metaphysics of conventionality.

There are two characteristic ways in which a philosophical package embodying an account of conventionality within a discipline might fail to satisfy the reduction criterion.

1   There might be some finding, or methodological practice, or practical conclusion, which counts as an achievement by the standards of the philosophical package such that (a) by the ordinary standards of the relevant discipline (modified perhaps by special features of the philosophical package) the justification of this achievement requires premises some of which are treated as conventionally true by the account in question, and (b) when the supervenience claims regarding the truth of these premises are made explicit they compromise the justification in question.

2   There might be some proposition which the account in question treats as true by definition such that (a) by the ordinary standards of the discipline (modified perhaps by special features of the philosophical package) this

proposition is in need of justification, and (b) by those standards it would be an insufficient justification for the proposition in question to treat it as a truth by convention or to cite the social facts upon which – according to the account in question – its truth supervenes.

Let us turn now to applying the reduction criterion to doctrines in metaethics.

Error theories can be realist Error theories in metaethics hold that moral statements all have false presuppositions and that they are all either false or truth-valueless (depending on the error theorist's preferred semantics for statements with false presuppositions). Such theories are typically naturalistically, indeed materialistically, motivated. In this they have an affinity with many recent versions of moral realism.

There is an even deeper connection to moral realism. We may view error theories as extreme cases of conventionalistic conceptions in metaethics. If by conventions governing language use we mean regularities which are normative in the sense that we rely on them to make discourse possible, then on the error theorist's view there must be conventions for the use of moral language; without relying on such conventions the error theorist could not identify the false presuppositions of moral discourse. What the error theorist maintains is that neither these conventions nor any other semantic facts are sufficient to rescue moral statements from being uniformly false (or truth-valueless). All moral discourse has going for it cognitively is some conventions, and even they aren't enough.

Thus, on the error theorist's view, there are no substantive or methodological achievements in moral *theorizing*. The philosophical package which represents her view couples a bleak conventionality about moral language with an equally bleak conception of the achievements of moral theory. Thus the package acknowledges no *theoretical* achievements whose justification could be undermined by the conception of conventionality it embodies. If the package does not assign an inappropriate role to conventionality in justifying the *practical* achievements of moral practice (as it certainly will not if it is a debunking account which denied that there are such achievements) then it satisfies the reduction criterion.

It follows that debunking error theories, and probably some others, count as realist by the criterion I propose. It seems to me that this is independently plausible. Consider scientific atheism for example, which entails an error theory about theological discourse. Scientific atheists propose to hold god talk and electron talk to the same ontological standards; they differ from traditional theists in thinking that god talk fails to meet those standards. Note how different their position is from that of an empiricist who denies the possibility of (even atheist) knowledge of matters theological or the constructivists who might hold that the reality of god(s) consists in the acceptance of certain patterns of theological and liturgical practices. The atheist believes that the ontological questions raised by theology are real and answerable questions and that they cannot be answered by convention. In that respect her position is straightforwardly realist (see Boyd 1990b).

The debunking error theorist adopts an exactly analogous position. She holds that moral discourse has ontological or metaphysical commitments, that the question of whether these commitments are correct is a real and answerable question, that it cannot be answered by convention, and that the answer is "no."

I am not suggesting that it is altogether wrong to follow custom and to reserve the term "moral realism" for doctrines which (among other things) posit moral knowledge. What I do suggest is that the similarities between naturalistic error theories and more obvious cases of realist metaethical theories are far more important, from the point of view of the metaphysics and epistemology of morals, than the differences.

Sufficiently debunking conventionalistic relativism is also realist Some extremely conventionalistic metaethical positions take suitably idealized consistent versions of the prevailing moral practices within any community to conventionally define the extensions of its moral terms. These positions are profoundly relativistic, since they posit a different semantics for moral terms for every case in which there is any difference between community moral practices. They seem to be paradigmatically anti-realist. In fact, the most debunking conventionalistic relativist theories are realist.

Suppose that a philosopher agrees with debunking error theorists that moral discourse has deeply false presuppositions and that it has no theoretical or practical achievements. Suppose however that she treats moral terms as natural kind terms which lack a real referent and adopts for them the nominalist default semantics suggested by Putnam (1970). She will then have adopted the semantic conception of an extreme conventionalist moral relativist. Like the debunking error theorist's, her philosophical conception of morals will satisfy the reduction constraint and her position on moral discourse will likewise be a realist one. What makes a conception of conventionality realist or anti-realist is not how extensive it makes conventionality in a discipline but how much work it makes conventional truths do.

How to tell realist from anti-realist varieties of non-debunking relativism Non-debunking moral relativism, at least when it is morally plausible, is not as nominalistic as the relativism which arises from the employment of a Putnamesque default semantics. When philosophers advance non-debunking versions of relativism they ordinarily think of the extensions of the extensions of the moral terms used within a community as fixed by some idealization of the community's standards where there are moral as well as purely logical constraints on the idealization. Still, moral relativist positions posit a significant level of conventionality in moral discourse. The truth conditions for moral statements will depend significantly on the moral customs and practices prevailing in the particular moral communities in which they occur. The truth of a moral claim will thus supervene significantly on the customs and practices of the relevant community.

I suggest in HMR that some versions of moral relativism are varieties of moral realism. Some versions seem plainly anti-realist. How are the realist versions of relativism to be distinguished from the anti-realist? The answer has two parts. The first of these I made explicit in part 5 of HMR. On any morally reasonable conception, issues of human happiness, of human needs, and of human nature generally are morally relevant. Moreover it is plausible that what humans are like – what they need, what makes them happy, what their "nature" is – depends at least in part on what their beliefs are about these matters and about moral matters generally. The fact that these morally relevant features of humans depend thus on beliefs, and that such beliefs differ relevantly from community to community, may legitimately play a role in the articulation of a relativist philosophical package in metaethics. Whether or not such an appeal to the belief dependence of human nature renders the package anti-realist will depend, I suggest, entirely on whether the account of belief dependence in question honors 2N2C. If the dependence of human nature on moral and other beliefs can – given prevailing scientific standards and the peculiar resources of philosophical package in question – be treated as causal then no anti-realism is implied. If the package posits a non-causal "conceptual" dependence then, I suggest, it represents an anti-realist position in metaethics.

The second part concerns justified practical reasoning. On a non-debunking version of moral relativism, the fact that some moral judgment is true provides, at least ordinarily and for ordinary people, a rational (although not necessarily definitive) reason for action or choice. For an ordinary member of a moral community, then, the moral practices of *that* community will, according to the relativist, have this sort of rational claim with respect to her practical reason in a way which the practices of other moral communities do not (since it is the practices of *her* community which define the extensions of moral terms in her use of them). A philosophical package containing a non-debunking version of moral relativism must contain the resources for justifying this special claim of local moral practices on practical reason.

It is the nature of this justification which is crucial in determining whether or not the package satisfies the reduction constraint. By ordinary moral standards, the fact that a community other than one's own with a recognizable moral tradition makes moral judgments leading to different practical judgments provides a non-trivial challenge to the standards of one's own community: "Could it be that their practices are better in some respects than ours? Have we something to learn from them?" If a philosophical package treats local moral practices as *always* meeting such challenges, as it must if it says they are true by convention, then it must provide the resources to address these challenges on behalf of those local practices.

What I suggest is that – on any version of prevailing moral standards which does not incorporate a defense of metaethical relativism – it is *not* a sufficient rebuttal to this challenge to indicate that the local standards are the *local* convention, or to cite the details of the social practices upon which the establishment of those local moral practices supervenes. A philosophical package which offers a rebuttal of this form – one which treats the challenge as resting, for example, on a semantic confusion – will not satisfy the reduction criterion and will be anti-realist.

On the other hand, a version of moral relativism like the one discussed in HMR which provides entirely non-conventional reasons for believing that a fruitful "splitting of the differences" between local and exotic practices is impossible, can provide – by ordinary moral standards – a justification for an ordinary member of the local moral community ordinarily to assign a special role to local moral practices in practical reason. Metaethical relativist philosophical packages with resources of this sort are, in that respect at least, realist.

Realism and "conceptual analysis" in ethics   There is a venerable tradition in recent non-debunking moral philosophy of arguing that some general moral principle, or some general characterization of morality or of moral reasoning, is a conceptual truth: a truth by linguistic or social convention. Thus, for example, the claim that morality is concerned with human goods and harms, or that morality crucially involves considerations of duty, or that certain principles of universalizability are moral truths, might be offered as the result of conceptual analysis.

I deny that any such conceptual analysis is compatible with moral realism. For any highly general moral claim of the sort in question, I suggest, there will always be serious incompatible alternative claims such that (1) on any version of prevailing standards for moral argumentation which does not beg the question by incorporating a conventionalistic conception of the relevant issue, the claim in question cannot be rationally accepted without a rebuttal to those serious alternatives, and (2) by any such version of prevailing argumentative standards, the rebuttals cannot be conventionalistic.

I invite the reader to examine cases to see how often such serious alternatives can be found to moral principles which have been defended as results of conceptual analysis. My confidence that for any such principle at least one such serious alternative will be available rests on my conviction that, by any non-question-begging version of prevailing standards for moral argumentation, the debunking positions of anti-moralists like Thrasymachus or Marx are in need of non-conventionalistic rebuttal.

Realism, arbitrariness, and political critiques of morality   Contemporary philosophers, social theorists, literary theorists, and others, who join Thrasymachus and Marx in offering political critiques of morality generally, or of particular moral concepts and categories, hold that some or all parts of moral practice systematically serve a highly nonadmirable social function. Often they put the political and normative import of their claims by describing some feature of morality or of moral practice as "arbitrary." The same rhetorical device is often used to indicate the normative import of similar claims about medical, scientific, or social scientific categories like race, gender, sexual abnormality, and the like.

I think that these political critiques are often informative (see the brief discussion of morality and Marxism in HMR), and I agree that when they are correct they show that the relevant practices, concepts, or categories are *arbitrary* in a perfectly good normative sense of that term.

The joint cultural impact of empiricism and postmodernism is such that authors who have argued for this sort of arbitrariness in moral, scientific, or other categories often elaborate their claim of arbitrariness by denying "essentialism" about the relevant categories and affirming instead that these categories have conventional or nominal definitions, in the empiricist sense derived from Locke.

This can't be right. On any version of conventionalism even distantly related to Locke's, the extension of a general term is fixed by our concept of it in such a way that we could not be seriously wrong about which properties determine how we in practice classify things under the term. But the whole point of a political critique of classificatory practices as ideological is that the correspondence between our classificatory practices and unsavory properties is *anything but* transparent to us; if ideologically determined classificatory practices are to serve unsavory political functions our own conception of those practices must be a favorable one.

The upshot is that what a debunking anti-moralist critic requires is a conception of the referential semantics of moral terms according to which the real (but hidden) definitions of those terms is (in fact, but not by convention) provided by the critic's own theory of the nature of morality, rather than by the prevailing moral conception. She needs, in other words, a *realist* conception of the semantics of moral terms.

Thrasymachus and Marx were thus moral realists of a sort. Moral realism is *not* the view that moral discourse is about *objectively valuable* real features of the world. Moral realism is an epistemological, semantic, and metaphysical thesis not a normative one.

NOTES

1   I am indebted to Professor Nicholas Sturgeon for discussions on these points and especially for his emphasis on the point that moral relativism often has a materialist or naturalist motivation. For a discussion of related matters see Sturgeon forthcoming.

2   In Boyd (1992) I consider versions of neo-Kantian constructivism which are characterized by a *dialectically complex* conception of conventionality according to which principles may be approximately, rather than exactly, true by convention. I ignore this possibility here, speaking always of propositions true by convention rather than of propositions approximately true by convention. Nevertheless, the arguments I present here are designed to hold for the case of dialectically complex conventionality as well; see Boyd (1992) for more details.

REFERENCES

Boyd, Richard (1990a) "Realism, approximate truth, and philosophical method," in Wade Savage (ed.) *Scientific Theories*. Minnesota Studies in the Philosophy of Science, vol. 14. Minneapolis: University of Minnesota Press.
—— (1990b) "Realism, conventionality, and 'realism about'," in George Boolos (ed.) *Meaning and Method*. Cambridge: Cambridge University Press.
—— (1991) "Realism, anti-foundationalism, and the enthusiasm for natural kinds," *Philosophical Studies* 61, 127–48.
—— (1992) "Constructivism, realism, and philosophical method," in John

Earman (ed.) *Inference, Explanation and Other Philosophical Frustrations.* Berkeley: University of California Press.

Foot, Philippa (1958-9) "Moral beliefs," *Proceedings of the Aristotelian Society* 59.

Guyot, K. (1987) *What if anything is a higher taxon?*, unpublished Ph.D. dissertation. Ithaca: Cornell University.

Harman, Gilbert (1977) *The Nature of Morality*, New York: Oxford University Press.

Mackie, John L. (1977) *Ethics: Inventing Right and Wrong*, London: Penguin Books.

Putnam, Hilary (1970) "Is semantics possible?" in H. Kiefer and M. Munitz (eds) *Language, Belief, and Metaphysics.* Albany: SUNY Press.

—— (1975) "The meaning of 'meaning'," in H. Putnam, *Mind, Language and Reality.* Cambridge: Cambridge University Press.

Sturgeon, Nicholas (to appear) "Ethical naturalism," in Edward Craig (ed.) *Routledge Encyclopedia of Philosophy.* London: Routledge.

16 How to be an Ethical Antirealist

Simon Blackburn

Some philosophers like to call themselves realists, and some like to call themselves antirealists. An increasing number, I suspect, wish to turn their backs on the whole issue.[1] Their strengths include those of naturalism, here counseling us that there is none except a natural science of human beings. From this it follows that there is no "first philosophy" lying behind (for instance) physics, or anthropology, enabling the philosopher to know how much of the world is "our construction" (antirealism) or, on the contrary, "independent of us" (realism).

This naturalism bestows small bouquets and small admonishments to each of the previous parties. The antirealists were right to deny that there exists a proper philosophical (a priori) explanation of things like the success of physics, which some people were acute enough to discern, from their armchairs, while others did not. A scientist can say that there was a certain result because a neutrino or electron did this and that, but a philosopher has nothing to *add* to this. If she tries to say, "Not only did the result occur because of the neutrino, but also because neutrino theory depicts (corresponds with, matches, carves at the joints) the world," she adds nothing but only voices a vain, and vainglorious, attempt to underwrite the science. This attempt may have made sense in a Cartesian tradition, when the mind's contact with the world seemed so problematical, but its time has passed. On the other hand, antirealists, sensing the futility of this road, stress instead the dependence of the ordinary world on us, our minds and categories, and again the additions they offer are unacceptable.[2] Characteristically, if realism fails because it is vacuous, antirealism fails because it strays into mistakes – making things dependent on us when they obviously are not, for example.[3] Again, and perhaps even more clearly, it is plausible to see antirealism as attempting to theorize where no theory should be – in this case, making the unnatural, Cartesian mind into a source of worlds. These theories are naturally described as "transcendental," and the word reminds us that for all his hostility to rational psychology, Kant himself failed to escape this trap.

The transcendental aspect can be seen if we put the matter in terms of what I call "correspondence conditionals." We like to believe that if we exercise our sensory and cognitive faculties properly and end up believing that p, then p. What kind of theory might explain our right to any such confidence? If p is a thesis from basic physical theory, only the theory itself. To understand why, when we believe that neutrinos exist, having used such-

and-such information in such-and-such a way, then they probably do, is just to understand whatever credentials neutrino theory has. That is physics. Any attempt at a background, an underwriting of the conditional from outside the theory, is certain to be bogus.

When considering such global matters as the success of our science, the nature of our world, it seems that naturalism ought to win. But in local areas, it seems instead that battle can be joined. In this paper I would like to say in a little more detail why I think this is so. The main problem to which I turn is that of seepage, or the way in which antirealism, once comfortably in command of some particular area of our thought, is apt to cast imperialistic eyes on neighboring territory. The local antirealist faces the problem of drawing a line, which may prove difficult, or that of reneging on naturalism, and allowing that global antirealism must after all make sense. The second part of my paper is thus an exploration of this specific problem.

Why can battle be joined in local areas? What I said about physics might be retorted upon any area. To understand how, when we believe that twice two is four, we are probably right requires arithmetical understanding. To understand why, when we believe that wanton cruelty is wrong, we are also right requires ethical understanding. Where is the asymmetry?

Let us stay with the example of ethics. Here a "projective" theory can be developed to give a perfectly satisfying way of placing our propensities for values. According to me the surface phenomena of moral thought do not offer any obstacle to it. They can be explained as being just what we should expect, if the projective metaphysics is correct. (I call the doctrine that this is so "quasi-realism" – a topic I return to later.) I have also argued that this package contains various explanatory advantages over other rivals and alleged rivals. The projectivism is not, of course, new – the package is intended indeed to be a modern version of Hume's theory of the nature of ethics, but without any commitment to particular operations of passions such as sympathy. Emotivism and Hare's prescriptivism are also immediate ancestors. Anything new comes in the quasi-realism, whose point is to show that, since projectivism is consistent with, and indeed explains, the important surface phenomena of ethics, many of the arguments standardly used against it miss their mark. These arguments allege that projectivism is inadequate to one or another feature of the way we think ethically; the quasi-realism retorts that it is not, and goes on to explain the existence of the features. Such features include the propositional as opposed to emotive or prescriptive form, the interaction of ethical commitments with ordinary propositional attitude verbs, talk of truth, proof, knowledge, and so forth. I must urge the reader to look elsewhere for the details of the program; here, it is its relationship with naturalism that is to be determined.

I

The first link is this. I think that naturalism demands this view of ethics, but in any case it motivates it. It does so because in this package the fundamental state of mind of one who has an ethical commitment makes natural sense. This state of mind is not located as a belief (the belief in a duty, right, value). We may *end up* calling it a belief, but that is after the work has been done. In fact, we may end up saying that there really are values (such as the value of honesty) and facts (such as the fact that you have a duty to your children). For in this branch of philosophy, it is not what you finish by saying, but how you manage to say it that matters. How many people think they can just *announce* themselves to be realists or antirealists, as if all you have to do is put your hand on your heart and say, "I really believe it!" (or, "I really don't")? The way I treat the issue of realism denies that this kind of avowal helps the matter at all. The question is one of the best theory of this state of commitment, and reiterating it, even with a panoply of dignities – truth, fact, perception, and the rest – is not to the point.

The point is that the state of mind starts theoretical life as something else – a stance, or conative state or pressure on choice and action. Such pressures need to exist if human beings are to meet their competing needs in a social, cooperative setting. The stance may be called an attitude, although it would not matter if the word fitted only inexactly: its function is to mediate the move from features of a situation to a reaction, which in the appropriate circumstances will mean choice. Someone with a standing stance is set to react in some way when an occasion arises, just as someone with a standing belief is set to react to new information cognitively in one way or another. It matters to us that people have some attitudes and not others, and we educate them and put pressure on them in the hope that they will.

So far, two elements in this story are worth keeping in mind, for it will be important to see whether a projective plus quasi-realist story can do without them. These are: (1) the fundamental identification of the commitment in question as something other than a belief; (2) the existence of a neat natural account of why the state that it is should exist.

Obviously, the emergence of cooperative and altruistic stances is not a mere armchair speculation. It can be supplemented by both theoretical and empirical studies.[4] It is noteworthy that the account will insist upon the nonrepresentative, conative function for the stance. The evolutionary success that attends some stances and not others is a matter of the behavior to which they lead. In other words, it is the direct consequences of the pressure on action that matter. Evolutionary success may attend the animal that helps those that have helped it, but it would not attend an allegedly possible animal that thinks it ought to help but does not. In the competition for survival, it is what the animal *does* that matters. This is important, for it shows that only if values are intrinsically motivating, is a natural story of their emergence possible. Notice, too, the way the evolutionary success arises. Animals with standing dispositions to cooperate (say) do better in terms of other needs like freedom from fleas or ability to survive failed hunting expeditions by begging meals from others. No right, duty, or value plays any explanatory role in this history. It is not as if the creature with a standing disposition to help those who have helped it does well *because* that is a virtue. Its being a virtue is irrelevant to evolutionary biology. There is no such naturalistically respectable explanation.

The commitment may have psychological accretions consistently with this being its core or essence. The precise "feel" of an ethical stance may be a function of local culture, in its scope, or some of its interactions with other pressures and other beliefs. A pressure toward action can be associated variously with pride, shame, self-respect, and there is no reason to expect a simple phenomenology to emerge. The essence lies in the practical import, but the feelings that surround that can vary considerably. There is no reason for a stance to feel much like a desire, for example. Consider as a parallel the way in which a biological or evolutionary story would place attraction between the sexes, and the culturally specific and surprising ways in which that attraction can emerge – the varieties of lust and love (whose imperatives often do not feel much like desire either, and may equally be expressed by thinking that there are things one simply *must* do. I say more about this later.) So, if a theorist is attracted to the rich textures of ethical life, he need not, therefore, oppose projectivism. No "reduction" of an ethical stance to one of any other type is needed.

Now contrast the kind of evolution already sketched with any that might be offered for, say, our capacity to perceive spatial distance. Again, what matters here is action. But what we must be good at is acting according to the very feature perceived. A visual–motor mechanism enabling the frog's tongue to hit the fly needs to adapt the trajectory of the tongue to the place of the fly relative to the frog, and an animal using perceived distance to guide behavior will be successful only if it perceives distances as they are. It is because our visual mechanisms show us far-off things as far off and near things as near that we work well using them. That is what they are *for*. We can sum up this contrast by saying that although the teleology of spatial perception is spatial, the teleology of ethical commitment is not ethical. The good of spatial perception is to be representative, but the good of ethical stances is not.

The possibility of this kind of theory, then, provides the needed contrast between the general case of science, where an attempt to provide a further, background "theory" is transcendental, and the local particular case of ethics, where there are natural materials for such a story ready at hand. It also means that philosophers wanting a general realism versus antirealism issue cannot take comfort from the local case; the materials to generate theory there exist, as it were, by contrast with anything that can be provided in the general case.

These simple naturalistic points are not always respected. Consider, for example, the position associated with John McDowell and David Wiggins. This goes some way in the same direction as projectivism, at least in admitting that a person's ethical outlook is dependent on affective or conative aspects of his make-up. But it takes those aspects as things that enable the subject to do something else – to perceive value properties. It is only if one is moved or prone to be moved in a certain way that one sees the value of things, just as it is only if one is prone to be moved in some way that one perceives the sadness in a face.[5] This is supposed to do justice to the obvious point that sentiments have something to do with our capacity to make ethical judgment, yet to retain a "perceptual" and cognitive place for moral opinion.

Let us suppose that this is a substantial theory and different from projectivism (in the light of what is to come, neither supposition is beyond doubt). The view is substantial if it holds that changes in one's sensibilities enable one to do something else: *literally* to perceive ethical properties in things. Or if the "something else" is not literal perception, then at least its kinship with perception must be very close – so close that it cannot be explained as projection of a stance. For the view is no different from projectivism if this "something else" is nothing else at all, but merely a different label for reaching an ethical verdict because of one's sentiments. In other words, it is only different from projectivism if this literal talk of perceiving plays a theoretical role, and not just a relabeling of the phenomena. This is not at all obvious. Theoretically low-grade talk of perception is always available. Everyone can say that one can "see" what one must do or what needs to be done, just as one can see that 17 is prime. When I said that it is not what one finishes by saying, but the theory that gets one there, this is one of the crucial examples I had in mind.

Literal talk of perception runs into many problems. One is that the ethical very commonly, and given its function in guiding choice, even typically, concerns imagined or described situations, not perceived ones.[6] We reach ethical verdicts about the behavior of described agents or actions in the light of general standards. And it is stretching things to see these general standards as perceptually formed or maintained. Do I see that ingratitude is base only on occasions when I see an example of ingratitude? How can I be sure of the generalization to examples that I did not see (I could not do that for color, for instance. Absent pillar-boxes may be a different color from present ones; only an inductive step allows us to guess at whether they are). Or, do I see the timeless connection – but how? Do I have an antenna for detecting timeless property-to-value connections? Is such a thing that much like color vision? Perhaps these questions can be brushed aside. But in connection with naturalism, the question to ask of the view is why nature should have bothered. Having, as it were, forced us into good conative shape, why not sit back? Why should this be merely the curtain raiser for a perceptual system? It seems only to engender dangerous possibilities. It ought to make us slower to act, for we must process the new information perceived. Worse, it might be that someone moved, say, by gratitude comes to see the goodness of gratitude and then has, quite generally, some other (negative) reaction to what is seen. Perhaps typically, the conative pressure opens our eyes to these properties, about which we then have a different, conflicting feeling. Or is it somehow given that what comes back is what went in – that the property perceived impinges on us with the same emotional impact required for perceiving it? How convenient! But how clumsy of nature to go in for such a loop! And why did we not evolve to short-circuit it, as projectivism claims? In other words, we have here the typical symptoms of realism, which not only has to take us *to* the new properties but also has to take us back *from* them, showing how perception of them contrives to have exactly the effects it does.

This extravagance came from taking literally the talk of perception made possible by changes of sensibility. But the theory seems to be meant literally.

Wiggins, for example, thinks that although projectivism can be dismissed (values "put into [or onto like varnish] the factual world"), the right view is that there are value properties and sensibilities for perceiving them "made for each other" as "equal and reciprocal partners."[7]

Can this be understood? Projectivism, from which the theory is supposed to be so different, can easily embrace one half of the doctrine – that the properties are made for the sensibility. The embrace ought to be a bit tepid, because we shall see better ways of putting the view that value predicates figure in thought and talk as reflections or projections of the attitudes that matter. But it is the other half, that the sensibilities are "made for" the properties, that really startles. Who or what makes them like that? (God? As we have seen, no natural story explains how the ethical sensibilities of human beings were made for the ethical properties of things, so perhaps it is a supernatural story.)

Wiggins, I think, would reply that nothing extraordinary or unfamiliar is called for here. Refinement or civilization makes both sensibility and property. It is the process of education or moral refinement that makes sensibilities end up in good harmony with values. "When this point is reached, a system of anthropocentric properties and human responses has surely taken on a life of its own. Civilization has begun." The implicit plea that we get our responses to life into civilized shape is admirable, but is it enough to locate a view of the nature of ethics, or is there a danger of confusing uplift with theory? Certainly, it is true that when we have gone through some process of ethical improvement, we can turn back and say that now we have got something *right* – now we appreciate the value of things as they are, whereas before we did not. This Whiggish judgment is often in place, but it is, of course, a moral judgment. It is not pertinent to explaining *how* sensibilities are "made for" values. Is it a good theoretical description or explanation of the fact that we value friendship that, first, it is good and, second, civilization has "made" our sensibilities "for" the property of goodness? It seems overripe, since it goes with no apparent theory of error (what if our sensibilities are unluckily not made for the properties?), no teleology, and no evolutionary background. Its loss of control becomes clear if we think how easy it is to generate parallels. Perhaps something similar made our arithmetical powers for the numbers, or our tastes for the niceness of things. Or, perhaps, on the contrary, the talk of our sensibilities being made for the properties is theoretically useless and the more economical remainder is all that is really wanted.

Might there still be room for a view that the properties are "made for" the sensibility, which avoids projectivism? The analogy with colors, for all its many defects, might be held to open such a possibility. But color at this point is a dangerous example. If we ask seriously what color vision is made for, an answer can be found – but it will not cite colors. Color vision is probably made for enhancing our capacities for quickly identifying and keeping track of objects and surfaces, and this asymmetry with, for instance, spatial perception remains the most important point of the primary–secondary property distinction.

Any analogy with color vision is bound to run into the problem of dependency. If we had a theory whereby ethical properties are literally made by or for sensibilities, ethical truth would be constituted by and dependent on the way we think. This might not repel Wiggins. It agrees with the analogy with colors, and in the course of discussing Russell's worry ("I find myself incapable of believing that all that is wrong with wanton cruelty is that I don't like it"), Wiggins freely asserts that "what is wrong with cruelty is not, even for Bertrand Russell, just that Bertrand Russell does not like it, but that it is not such as to call forth liking given our *actual* responses."[8] But is it? I should have said not. It is because of our responses that we *say* that cruelty is wrong, but it is not because of them that it is so. It is true that insertion of the "actual" into the sentence makes it wrong to test the alleged dependence by the usual device of imagining our responses otherwise and asking if that makes cruelty any better.[9] But our actual responses are inappropriate for the wrongness of cruelty to depend upon. What makes cruelty abhorrent is not that it offends us, but all those hideous things that make it do so.

The projectivist can say this vital thing: that it is not because of our responses, scrutinized and collective or otherwise, that cruelty is wrong. The explanation flows from the way in which quasi-realism has us deal with oblique contexts. It issues an "internal" reading of the statement of dependence, according to which it amounts to an offensive ethical view, about (of course) what it is that makes cruelty wrong. Critics of this explanation allow the internal reading, but complain that the quasi-realist is being wilfully deaf to an intended "external" reading, according to which the dependency is a philosophical thesis, and one to which the projectivist, it is said, must assent.[10] The crucial question, therefore, is whether the projectivist wilfully refuses to hear the external reading. According to me, there is only one proper way to take the question "On what does the wrongness of wanton cruelty depend?": as a moral question, with an answer in which no mention of our actual responses properly figures. There *would* be an external reading if realism were true. For in that case there would be a fact, a state of affairs (the wrongness of cruelty) whose rise and fall and dependency on others could be charted. But antirealism acknowledges no such state of affairs, and no such issue of dependency. Its freedom from any such ontological headache is not the least of its pleasures. A realist might take this opportunity for dissent. He might say, "I can just *see* that the wrongness of cruelty is a fact (perhaps an eternal one) that needs an ontological theory to support it – no theory that avoids providing such support is credible." In that case I gladly part company, and he is welcome to his quest – for what kind of ontology is going to help? The Euthyphro dilemma bars all roads there.[11]

It is tempting to think: on this metaphysics the world contains nothing but us and our responses, so that fact that cruelty is bad *must* be created by our responses. What else is there for it to be dependent upon? The prejudice is to treat the moral fact as a natural one, capable of being constituted, made or unmade, by sensibilities. The wrongness of wanton cruelty does indeed depend on things – features of it which remind us how awful it is. But locating these is giving moral verdicts. Talk of dependency is moral talk or nothing. This is not, of course, to deny that "external" questions make sense – the projectivist plus quasi-realist package is an external philosophical theory about the nature of morality. But external questions must be conducted in a different key once this package is brought in. We may notice, too, how this undermines a common way of drawing up the realist versus antirealist issue, according to which antirealism asserts that truth in some or all areas is "mind dependent" and realism denies this. For here is the projection, as antirealist a theory of morality as could be wished, denying that moral truth is mind dependent in the only sense possible.

The point can be made as follows. As soon as one *uses* a sentence whose simple assertion expresses an attitude, one is in the business of discussing or voicing ethical opinion. Such sentences include "The fact that *cruelty is wrong* depends on . . ." or "Our refined consensus makes it true that *cruelty is wrong*," and so on. If one generalizes and says things like "moral facts depend on us," the generalization will be true only if instances are true or, in other words, if one can find examples of truths like those. Since these ethical opinions are unattractive, they must be judged incorrect, as must generalizations of them. If one attempts to discuss external questions, one must use a different approach – in my case, a naturalism that places the activities of ethics in the realm of adjusting, improving, weighing, and rejecting different sentiments or attitudes. The projectivist, then, has a perfect right to confine external questions of dependency to domains where real states of affairs, with their causal relations, are in questions. The only things in this world are the attitudes of people, and those, of course, are trivially and harmlessly mind-dependent. But the projectivist can hear no literal sense in saying that moral properties are made for or by sensibilities. They are not in a world where things are made or unmade – not in this world at all, and it is only because of this that naturalism remains true.

The charge that projectivism refuses to hear an explanatory demand as it is intended can be returned with, I suggest, much more effect. I was severe earlier with Wiggins's theoretical description of us as indulging in a kind of coordination of responses and properties as we become civilized. But it is telling that the Whiggish appeal to a value ("civilization") is introduced at that point. For the introduction of values into explanatory investigations is echoed in other writings in this tradition, notably in those of John McDowell.[12] The strategy is that in a context purportedly comparing explanations of a practice – the practice of ethical judgment – we allow ourselves to invoke the very commitments of that practice. Why are we afraid of the dark? Because it is fearful. Why do we value friendship? Because it is good and we are civilized. Why do I dislike sentimentality? Because it merits it. And so on.

The refusal to stand outside ethics in order to place it is supposed to tie in with one strand in Wittgenstein. This is the thought that there is characteristically neither a reduction nor an explanation of the members of any major family of concepts in terms of those of another. Ethical notions require ethical sensibilities to comprehend them. Similarly, why should it not require an ethical sensibility to comprehend an explanation of the views we hold? Only those who perceive friendship as good will understand why we do so, and to them it can be explained why we do so by reminding them that it is good, or making them feel that it is so. The rest – aliens, outsiders, Martians – cannot be given the explanation, but this is as it must be. What I said about the explanation of our spatial capacities will make it apparent that the circularity exists there in exactly the same way. Only those who appreciate distance can understand the distance-centered explanation of visual perception.

This returns us to a theme that has been touched at many points in this essay. The insistence on hearing explanatory demands only in a way in which one can invoke values in answering them had a respectable origin. We agreed earlier that the parallel would be true of thinking about the correspondence conditionals in the case of physics. But I hope I have said enough to show that nature and our theory of nature surround our ethical commitments in a way that gives us a *place* from which to theorize about them. Nothing and no theory surrounds our physics. In other words, the difference in the ethical case comes in the theses I labeled (1) and (2) – the brute fact that an external explanatory story is possible. We already know that in even more local cases, where what is at question is not "the ethical" in a lump, but particular attitudes and their etiologies. Social anthropology is not confined to explaining the rise of puritanism to puritans or the evolution of polygamy to polygamists. Similarly, nothing in Wittgenstein offers any principled obstacle to explaining the general shape and nature of ethical attitudes and their expressions in projective terms.

Indeed much in Wittgenstein is sympathetic to doing so. Not only is Wittgenstein himself an antirealist about ethics. He is in general quite free in admitting propositions or quasi-propositions whose function is not to describe anything – the rules of logic and arithmetic, for instance. It is clear that what he wants to do is to place mathematical practice, not as a representation of the mathematical realm, but as "a different kind of instrument," commitment to which is not like central cases of belief, but much more like other kinds of stance. It is also interesting that some of the apparently irritating or evasive answers he gives when faced with the charge of anthropocentricity are exactly those which a projectivist can give if quasi-realism has done its work, and that according to me, no other philosophy of these matters can give. For example, when Wittgenstein approaches the question whether on his anthropocentric view of mathematical activity, mathematical truth is yet independent of human beings, he says exactly what I would have him say:

> "But mathematical truth is independent of whether human beings know it or not!" – Certainly, the propositions "Human beings believe that twice two is four" and "twice two is four" do not mean the same. The latter is a mathematical proposition; the other, if it makes sense at all, may perhaps mean: human beings have *arrived* at the mathematical proposition. The two propositions have entirely different *uses.*[13]

The proposition expresses a norm that arises in the course of human activities, but it does not describe those activities, and it has no use in which the correctness of the norm (the truth of the proposition) depends upon the existence or form of those activities. *That* question simply cannot be posed; it treats what is not a dependent state of affairs belonging to the natural world at all, as if it were.

I have tried to show that naturalism, which turns away from realism and antirealism alike in the global case turns toward projective theories in the ethical case. This theory is visibly antirealist, for the explanations offered make no irreducible or essential appeal to the existence of moral "properties" or "facts"; they demand no "ontology" of morals. They explain the activity from the inside out – from the naturally explicable attitudes to the forms of speech that communicate them, challenge them, refine them, and abandon them, and which so mislead the unwary.

So far I have talked of the issue of mind dependency in fairly abstract terms, and relied upon a relatively subtle move in the philosophy of language to defend my view. I now want to discuss these points in practical terms. It is evident that a more fundamental mistake underlies some discomfort with projectivism. The mistake is visible in Wiggins's critique of "non-cognitive theories" in his British Academy Lecture.[14] It results in the charge that projectivism cannot be true to the "inside of lived experience." Other writers (I would cite Nagel, Williams, and Foot) seem to illustrate similar unease. The thought is something like this: it is important that there should be some kind of accord in our thinking about ethical stances from the perspective of the theorist, and from that of the participant. Our story about ethical commitment is to explain it, not to explain it away. But projectivism threatens to do the latter (many people who should know better think of Hume as a skeptic about ethics, and, of course, John Mackie saw himself as one). It threatens to do so because it shows us that our commitments are not external demands, claiming us regardless of our wills or in direct opposition to our passions. It makes our commitments facets of our own sentimental natures; this softens them, destroying the hardness of the moral must.

From the inside, the objects of our passions are their *immediate* objects: it is the death, the loved one, the sunset, that matters to us. It is not our own state of satisfaction or pleasure. Must projectivism struggle with this fact, or disown it? Is it that we projectivists, at the crucial moment when we are about to save the child, throw ourselves on the grenade, walk out into the snow, will think, "Oh, it's only me and my desires or other conative pressures – forget it"?

It ought to be sufficient refutation of this doubt to mention other cases. Does the lover escape his passion by thinking, "Oh it's only my passion, forget it"? When the world affords occasion for grief, does it brighten when we realize that it is we who grieve? (The worst thing to think is that if we are "rational," it should, as if rationality had anything to tell us about it.)

There is an important mistake in the philosophy of action that, I think, must explain the temptation to share Wiggins's doubt. The mistake is that of supposing that when we deliberate in the light of various features of a situation we are *at the same time* or "really" deliberating – or that our reasoning can be "modeled" by representing us as deliberating – about our own conative functioning. Representing practical reasoning as if it consisted of contemplating a syllogism, one of whose premises describes what we want, encourages this mistake. But just as the eye is not part of the visual scene it presents, the sensibility responsible for the emotional impact of things is not part of the scene it takes for material. Nor is our sense of humor the main thing we find funny. This does not mean that our sensibility is hidden from us, and when we reflect on ourselves we can recognize aspects of it, just as we can know when we are in love or grieving. But it does mean that its own shape is no part of the input, when we react to the perceived features of things. Furthermore, even when we reflect on our sensibility, we will be using it if we issue a verdict: when we find our own sense of humor funny, we are not escaping use of it as we do so.

This misconstruction leads people to suppose that on a projective theory all obligations must be "hypothetical," because properly represented as dependent upon the existence of desires. But the lover who hears that she is there and feels he has to go, or the person who receiving bad news feels he must grieve, has no thoughts of the form "if I desire her / feel sad then I must go / grieve." Nothing corresponds to this. The news comes in and the emotion comes out; nothing in human life could be or feel more categorical. In ordinary emotional cases, of course, a third party may judge that it is only *if* he desires her that he must go; this is not so in ethical cases. One ought to look after one's young children, whether one wants to or not. But that is because we insist on some responses from others, and it is sometimes part of good moralizing to do so.

Once these mistakes are averted, is there any substance left to the worry about failure of harmony of the theoretical and deliberative points of view? I think not. Sometimes theory can help to change attitudes. One might become less attached to some virtue, or less eager in pursuing some vice, after thinking about its etiology or its functioning. One might qualify it a little (we see an example in what follows). But sometimes one might become more attached to the virtue, and sometimes everything stays the same. Does the story threaten to undermine the promise that the stances cited in this theory of ethics make good natural sense (does it take something divine to make the claims of obligation so pregnant with authority)? Not at all – I have already mentioned the "musts" of love and grief, and those of habit and obsession are just as common.

There is one last charge of the would-be realist. This claims that projectivism must lead to relativism. "Truth" must be relative to whatever set of attitudes is grounding our ethical stances; since these may vary from place to place and time to time, truth must be relative. The very analogies with other conative states press this result: what to one person is an occasion for love or grief or humor is not to another. Consider a young person gripped by the imperatives of fashion. The judgment that people must wear some style, that another is impossible, has its (naturally explicable and perfectly intelligible) function; it appears quite categorical, for the subject will think that it is not just for him or her that the style is mandatory or impossible (it was so in the parents' time as well, only they did not realize it). Yet, surely this is a mistake. The verdict is "relative," having no truth outside the local system of preferences that causes it. The image is plain: a projectivist may inhabit a particular ethical boat, but he must know of the actual or potential existence of others; where, then, is the absolute truth?

The answer is that it is not anywhere that can be visible from this sideways, theoretical perspective. It is not that this perspective is illegitimate, but that it is not the one adapted for finding ethical truth. It would be if such truth were natural truth, or consisted of the existence of states of affairs in the real world. That is the world seen from the viewpoint that sees different and conflicting moral systems – but inevitably sees no truth in just one of them. To "see" the truth that wanton cruelty is wrong demands moralizing, stepping back into the boat, or putting back the lens of a sensibility. But once that is done, there is nothing relativistic left to say. The existence of the verdict, of course, depends on the existence of those capable of making it; the existence of the truth depends on nothing (externally), and on those features that make it wrong (internally). For the same reasons that operated when I discussed mind dependency, there is no doctrine to express relating the truth of the verdict to the existence of us, of our sentiments, or of rival sentiments.

What, then, of the parallel with the other emotions, or with the fashion example? The emotions of grief and love are naturally personal; if the subject feels they make a claim on others, so that those unstricken somehow *ought* to be, then, she is nonrelativistically, absolutely wrong. Similarly with fashion: the underlying story includes the need to a self-presentation that is admirable to the peer group, and if what is admirable changes rapidly as generations need to distance themselves from their immediate pre-decessors, then the teenager who thinks that her parents were wrong to like whatever clothes they did is mistaken in the same way as the subject of an emotion who imputes a mistake to those who cannot feel the same. But the strongest ethical judgments do not issue from stances that are properly variable. They may sometimes be absent, from natural causes, as if a hard life destroys a capacity for pity. But this is a cause for regret; it would be better if it were not so. In the variations of emotion, and still more of fashion, there is no cause for regret. In saying these things I am, of course, voicing some elements of my own ethical stances, but as I promised, it is only by doing this that ethical truth is found.

II

If projective theories have everything going for them in ethics, how much can they jettison and still have *something* going for them? The two ingredients I highlighted are: the possibility of identifying the commitment in a way that contrasts it usefully with belief, and a "neat, natural account" of why the state that it is should exist. In the case of ethics we have conative stances, and a visible place for them in our functioning. But what in other cases?

Color commitments might attract attention, because not everybody will be happy that the agreed story about what color vision is and why we have it leaves realism as a natural doctrine about colors. Here the second ingredient is present. There is a neat, natural story of our capacity for color discrimination, and in its explanatory side, both physically and evolutionarily, it makes no explanatory use of the *existence* of colors. But there is no way that I can see usefully to contrast color commitments with *beliefs*. Their functional roles do not differ. So, there will be no theory of a parallel kind to develop, explaining why we have propositional attitudes of various kinds toward color talk, or why we speak of knowledge, doubt, proof, and so forth in connection with them. If anything can be drawn from a realism versus antirealism debate over color (which I rather doubt), it would have to be found by different means.

Modal commitments are much more promising. Our penchant for necessities and possibilities, either in concepts or in nature, is not easy to square with a view that we are representing anything, be it a distribution of possible worlds, or (in the case of natural necessity) a timeless nomic connection between universals.[15]

First, consider the case of logical necessity. A theory insisting on a non-representative function for modal commitment is clearly attractive. Here, however, although I think the first desideratum is met – we can do something to place the stance as something other than belief in the first instance – the second is not so easy. The kind of stance involved in insistence upon a norm, an embargo on a trespass. Saying that $2 + 2$ is anything other than 4 offends against the embargo, and the embargo in turn makes shared practices, shared communication possible. So far so good, but what of a "neat, natural theory" of the emergence of the embargo? That shared practices should exist is good – but do they so clearly depend upon such policing? If they do, it appears to be because of something else: because we can make no sense of a way of thinking that flouts the embargo. It introduces apparent possibilities of which we can make nothing. This imaginative limitation is, in turn, something of which no natural theory appears possible, even in outline. For when we *can* make sense of the imaginative limitation, we do find it apt to explain away or undermine the original commitment to a necessity. If it seems only because of (say) confinement to a world in which relative velocities are always slow compared to that of light, that we find a relativistic view of simultaneity hard to comprehend, then that already shows how we would be wrong to deem the theory impossible. If it is only because of the range of our color vision that we cannot imagine a new primary color, then we would be unwise to rule out the possibility that some natural operation might result in our admitting one. Natural explanation is here the enemy of the hard logical must.

It is not obviously so in the case of natural necessity. Once more the paradigm is Hume – not the Hume of commentators, but the real Hume, who knew that talk of necessity was irreducible, but gave a projective theory of it. The explanation here has us responsive to natural regularity, and forming dispositions of expectation (we might add, of observing boundaries in our counterfactual reasoning), which in turn stand us in good stead as the regularities prove reliable. Here, once we accept the Humean metaphysics, the naturalism seems quite in place. The upshot – talk of causation – is not undermined but is explained by this interpretation. This accords exactly with the case of ethics. There is a difference, however. I do not think metaphysical obstacles stand in the way of the conception of nature that does the explanatory work in the example of ethics. But many writers have difficulty with the conception of nature that is supposed to do it in Hume's metaphysics of causation. Regularities – but between what? Events – but how are these to be conceived, stripped of the causal "bit" (to use the computer metaphor)? Events thought of as changes in ordinary objects will scarcely do, for as many writers have insisted, ordinary objects are permeated with causal powers. Nothing corresponds to the easy, sideways, naturalistic perspective that strips the world of values.

What is the option? All sides carry on talk of causation in whichever mode they find best. The new realists like to produce apparent ontologies – universals, timeless connections, and the rest. The Humean does not mind, so long as the explanatory pretensions of these retranslations are kept firmly in their place (outside understanding). Is there scope for a debate here? It is a place where the ghosts are hard to lay, and I for one do not like being there alone in the gloom.

NOTES

1   For example, see Arthur Fine, "Unnatural attitudes: realist and instrumentalist attachments to science," in *Mind*, 1986.
2   On Putnam in this connection, see Ruth Garrett Millikan, "Metaphysical anti-realism," in *Mind*, 1986.
3   My favorite example is Putnam, *Reason, Truth and History*, 52.
4   R. Axelrod, *The Evolution of Cooperation* (New York, 1984).
5   John McDowell, "Non-cognitivism and rule following," in *Wittgenstein: To Follow a Rule*, edited by S. Holtzman and C. Leich (London, 1981). Also, Sabina Lovibond, *Realism and Imagination in Ethics* (Oxford, 1984). Other writers influenced by the analogy include Mark Platts, *The Ways of Meaning*, and Anthony Price, "Doubts about projectivism," in *Philosophy*, 1986.
6   John Locke, *An Essay Concerning Human Understanding*, IV, ch. IV, 6–7.
7   D. Wiggins, *Truth, Invention and the Meaning of Life* (British Academy Lecture, 1976), 348.
8   "A sensible subjectivism," *Needs, Values, Truth* (Oxford, 1987), 210.
9   The use of "actual" to make rigid the reference to our present attitudes, and thereby fend off some natural objections to dispositional subjective analyses, is exploited in this connection by Michael Smith.
10   Cassim Quassam, "Necessity and externality," in *Mind*, 1986.
11   I enlarge upon this in "Morals and modals," in *Truth, Fact and Value*, edited by Graham MacDonald and Crispin Wright (Oxford, 1986).
12   For instance in his "Values and secondary properties," in *Value and Objectivity: Essays in Honour of J. L. Mackie*, edited by T. Honderich (Oxford, 1985).
13   Ludwig Wittgenstein, *Philosophical Investigations* (Oxford, 1953), 226.
14   Ibid. (note 6) section 4.
15   David Armstrong, *What Is a Law of Nature?* (Cambridge, 1983), Chapter 6.

Bibliography on Contemporary Materialism

MATERIALISM AND NATURALISM

Armstrong, D. M. (1968) *A Materialist Theory of Mind*, London: Routledge & Kegan Paul.
—— (1973) *Belief, Truth and Knowledge*, Cambridge: Cambridge University Press.
—— (1983) *What is a Law of Nature?*, Cambridge: Cambridge University Press.
Bigelow, J. and Pargetter, R. (1990) *Science and Necessity*, Cambridge: Cambridge University Press.
Boyd, R. (1980) "Materialism without reductionism: what physicalism does not entail," in Ned Block (ed.) *Readings in Philosophy of Psychology*, vol. 1, 67–106. Cambridge, Mass.: Harvard University Press.
—— (1981) "Scientific realism and naturalistic epistemology," in P. Asquith and R. Giere (eds) *PSA 1980*, vol. 2. East Lansing, MI: Philosophy of Science Association.
Charles, D. and Lennon, K. (eds) (1992) *Reduction, Explanation, and Realism*, Oxford: Clarendon Press.
Globus, G., Maxwell, G. and Savodnik, I. (eds) (1976) *Consciousness and the Brain*, New York: Plenum.
Hooker, C. (1981) "Towards a general theory of reduction, parts I–III," *Dialogue* 20, 38–60, 201–35, 496–529.
Horgan, T. (1981) "Token physicalism, supervenience, and the generality of physics", *Synthese* 49, 395–413.
—— (1982) "Supervenience and microphysics," *Pacific Philosophical Quarterly* 63, 29–43.
Kim, J. (1978) "Supervenience and nomological incommensurables," *American Philosophical Quarterly* 15, 149–56.
MacDonald, G. (1987) "The possibility of the disunity of science," in G. MacDonald and C. Wright (eds) *Fact, Science, and Morality*. Oxford: Blackwell.
Moser, P.K. (1994) "Naturalism and psychological explanation," *Philosophical Psychology* 7, 63–84.
Robinson, H. (ed.) (1993) *Objections to Physicalism*, Oxford: Clarendon Press.
Snowdon, P. F. (1989) "On formulating materialism and dualism," in J. Heil (ed.) *Cause, Mind, and Reality: Essays Honoring C. B. Martin*, Dordrecht: Kluwer.
Teller, P. (1984) "A poor man's guide to supervenience and determination," *The Southern Journal of Philosophy* 22, 137–62 (supplement).
Wimsatt, W. (1976) "Reductionism, levels of organization, and the mind–body problem," in G. Globus, G. Maxwell, and I. Savodnik (eds) *Consciousness and the Brain*. New York: Plenum.

MATERIALISM AND MIND

Antony, L. (1989) "Anomolous monism and the problems of explanatory force," *The Philosophical Review* 98, 153–88.

Baker, L. R. (1987) *Saving Belief: A Critique of Physicalism,* Princeton: Princeton University Press.

Block, N. (1978) "Troubles with functionalism," in N. Block (ed.) (1980) *Readings in Philosophy of Psychology,* vol. 1. Cambridge, Mass.: Harvard University Press.

—— (1980) "Introduction: what is functionalism?" in N. Block (ed.) *Readings in Philosophy of Psychology,* vol. 1. Cambridge, Mass.: Harvard University Press.

—— (1986) "Advertisement for a semantics for psychology," in P. French, T. Uehling, and H. Wettstein (eds) *Midwest Studies in Philosophy, Vol. 10: Studies in the Philosophy of Mind.* Minneapolis: University of Minnesota Press.

Brand, M. and Harnish, R. (eds) (1986) *The Representation of Knowledge and Belief,* Tucson: University of Arizona Press.

Burge, T. (1979) "Individualism and the mental," in P. French, T. Uehling, and H. Wettstein (eds) *Midwest Studies in Philosophy, Vol. 4: Studies in Metaphysics.* Minneapolis: University of Minnesota Press.

—— (1986) "Individualism and psychology," *The Philosophical Review* 95, 3–45.

—— (1989) "Individuation and causation in psychology," *Pacific Philosophical Quarterly* 70, 303–22.

Churchland, P. M. (1979) *Scientific Realism and the Plasticity of Mind,* Cambridge: Cambridge University Press.

—— (1981) "Eliminative materialism and the propositional attitudes," *Journal of Philosophy* 78, 67–90. Reprinted in this volume.

—— (1985) "Reduction, qualia, and the direct introspection of brain states," *Journal of Philosophy* 82, 8–28.

—— (1989) *A Neurocomputational Perspective,* Cambridge, Mass.: MIT Press.

Churchland, P. M. and Churchland, P. S. (1983) "Stalking the wild epistemic engine," *Nous* 17, 5–18.

Churchland, P. S. (1980a) "A perspective on mind–brain research," *Journal of Philosophy* 77, 185– 207.

—— (1980b) "Language, thought, and information processing," *Nous* 14, 147–70.

—— (1982) "Mind–brain reduction: new light from the philosophy of science," *Neuroscience* 7, 1,041–47.

—— (1986) *Neurophilosophy,* Cambridge, Mass.: MIT Press.

Crane, T. (1991) "All the difference in the world," *Philosophical Quarterly* 41, 1–25.

Davidson, D. (1980) *Essays on Actions and Events,* Oxford: Clarendon Press.

—— (1984) *Inquiries into Truth and Interpretation,* Oxford: Clarendon Press.

Dennett, D. (1971) "Intentional systems," *Journal of Philosophy* 68, 87–106.

—— (1978) *Brainstorms,* Montgomery, VT: Bradford Books.

—— (1981a) "Three kinds of intentional psychology," in R. Healey (ed.) *Reduction, Time and Reality.* Cambridge: Cambridge University Press.

—— (1981b) "True believers: the intentional strategy and why it works," in A. Heath (ed.) *Scientific Explanation.* Oxford: Oxford University Press.

Dretske, F. (1988) *Explaining Behavior,* Cambridge: Mass.: MIT Press.

Enc, B. (1982) "Intentional states of mechanical devices," *Mind* 91, 161–82.

—— (1983) "In defense of the identity theory," *Journal of Philosophy* 80, 279–98.

Fodor, J. A. (1975) *The Language of Thought,* Cambridge, Mass: Crowell.

—— (1981) *Representations,* Cambridge, Mass.: MIT Press/Bradford Books.

—— (1987) *Psychosemantics,* Cambridge, Mass.: Bradford Books/MIT Press.

—— (1990) *A Theory of Content and Other Essays,* Cambridge, Mass.: Bradford Books/MIT Press.

Heil, J. (1992) *The Nature of True Minds*, Cambridge: Cambridge University Press.

Heil, J. and Mele, A. (eds) (1993) *Mental Causation*, Oxford: Clarendon Press.

Hill, C. S. (1991) *Sensations: A Defense of Type Materialism*, Cambridge: Cambridge University Press.

Kim, J. (1993) *Mind and Supervenience*, Cambridge: Cambridge University Press.

Lewis, D. (1972) "Psychophysical and theoretical identifications," *Australasian Journal of Philosophy* 50, 249–58.

Loar, B. (1981) *Mind and Meaning*, Cambridge: Cambridge University Press.

—— (1988) "Social content and psychological content," in D. Merrill and R. Grimm (eds) *Content of Thought*, Tucson: University of Arizona Press.

Lycan, W. G. (1987) *Consciousness*, Cambridge, Mass.: MIT Press.

Millikan, R. G. (1984) *Language, Thought, and Other Biological Categories*, Cambridge, Mass.: MIT Press.

Moser, P. K. and Trout, J. D. (1995) "Physicalism, supervenience, and dependence," in Ü. D. Yalçin and E. E. Savellos (eds) *Supervenience: New Essays*. Cambridge: Cambridge University Press.

Peacocke, C. (1983) *Sense and Content*, Oxford: Clarendon Press.

Searle, J. (1984) *Minds, Brains, and Science*, Cambridge, Mass.: Harvard University Press.

—— (1992) *The Rediscovery of the Mind*, Cambridge, Mass.: MIT Press.

Segal, G. (1989a) "Seeing what is not there," *The Philosophical Review* 98, 189–214.

—— (1989b) "The return of the individual," *Mind* 98, 39–57.

—— (1991) "Defence of a reasonable individualism," *Mind* 100, 485–94.

Sterelny, K. (1990) *The Representational Theory of Mind*, Oxford: Blackwell.

Stich, S. (1978a) "Autonomous psychology and the belief–desire thesis," *The Monist* 61, 573–91.

—— (1978b) "Beliefs and subdoxastic states," *Philosophy of Science* 45, 499–518.

—— (1983) *From Folk Psychology to Cognitive Science*, Cambridge, Mass.: MIT Press.

Trout, J. D. (1991) "Belief attribution in science: folk psychology under theoretical stress," *Synthese* 87, 379–400.

Tye, M. (1992) "Naturalism and the mental," *Mind* 101, 42–41.

Yablo, S. (1992) "Mental Causation," *The Philosophical Review* 101, 245–80.

MATERIALISM AND MEANING

Bach, K. (1987) *Thought and Reference*, Oxford: Clarendon Press.

Blackburn, S. (1984) *Spreading the Word*, Oxford: Clarendon Press.

Boolos, G. (ed.) (1990) *Meaning and Method: Essays in Honour of Hilary Putnam*, Cambridge: Cambridge University Press.

Boyd, R. (1979) "Metaphor and theory change," in A. Ortony (ed.) *Metaphor and Thought*. Cambridge: Cambridge University Press.

Dennett, Daniel (1982) "Beyond belief," in A. Woodfield (ed.) *Thought and Object*, Oxford: Clarendon Press.

Devitt, M. (1981) *Designation*, New York: Columbia University Press.

—— (1991) *Realism and Truth*, 2nd edn, Oxford: Blackwell.

Devitt, M. and Sterelny, K. (1987) *Language and Reality*, Cambridge, Mass.: MIT Press.

Dretske, F. (1981) *Knowledge and the Flow of Information*, Cambridge, Mass.: MIT Press.

Evans, G. (1982) *Varieties of Reference*, Oxford: Clarendon Press.

Field, H. (1972) "Tarski's theory of truth," *Journal of Philosophy* 69, 347–75.

—— (1973) "Theory change and the indeterminacy of reference," *Journal of Philosophy* 70, 462–81.

Field, H. (1974) "Quine and the correspondence theory," *The Philosophical Review* 83, 200–28.

—— (1992) "Physicalism," in J. Earman (ed.) *Inference, Explanation, and Other Frustrations*, Berkeley: University of California Press.

Fodor, J. A. (1984) "Semantics, Wisconsin style," *Synthese* 59, 231–50.

Grice, H. P. (1957) "Meaning," *The Philosophical Review* 66, 377–88.

—— (1975) "Logic and conversation," in P. Cole and J. Morgan (eds) *Syntax and Semantics, volume 3: Speech Acts*. Orlando, FL: Academic Press.

Putnam, H. (1975) "The meaning of 'meaning'," in H. Putnam, *Mind, Language and Reality*. Cambridge: Cambridge University Press.

Quine, W. (1960) *Word and Object*, Cambridge, Mass.: MIT Press.

Soames, S. and Salmon, N. (eds) (1988) *Propositions and Attitudes*, Oxford: Oxford University Press.

Stalnaker, R. (1976) "Propositions," in A. MacKay and D. Merrill (eds) *Issues in the Philosophy of Language*. New Haven, Conn.: Yale University Press.

—— (1984) *Inquiry*, Cambridge, Mass.: MIT Press.

—— (1989) "On what's in the head," in J. Tomberlin (ed.) *Philosophical Perspectives, Volume 3: Philosophy of Mind and Action Theory*. Atascadero, CA: Ridgeview Publishing Company.

Stampe, D. (1977) "Toward a causal theory of linguistic representation," in P. French, T. Uehling, and H. Wettstein (eds) *Midwest Studies in Philosophy*, vol. 2. Minneapolis: University of Minnesota Press.

—— (1986) "Verification and a causal account of meaning," *Synthese* 69, 107–37.

Yourgrau, P. (ed.) (1992) *Demonstratives*, Oxford: Oxford University Press.

MATERIALISM AND VALUE

Brink, D. (1989) *Moral Realism and the Foundations of Ethics*, Cambridge: Cambridge University Press.

Dennett, D. (1984) *Elbow Room*, Cambridge, Mass.: MIT Press.

Platts, M. (1981) "Moral reality and the end of desire," in M. Platts (ed.) *Reference, Truth and Meaning*. London: Routledge & Kegan Paul.

Post, J. (1987) *The Faces of Existence: An Essay in Nonreductive Metaphysics*, Ithaca, NY: Cornell University Press.

Sayre-McCord, G. (ed.) (1988) *Essays on Moral Realism*, Ithaca, NY: Cornell University Press.

Unger, P. (1990) *Identity, Consciousness and Value*, New York: Oxford University Press.

Index